North Mississippi Homeplace

LIBRARY

LIBRARY OF CONGRESS

FOREWORD BY CARLA D. HAYDEN, LIBRARIAN OF CONGRESS

THE UNIVERSITY OF GEORGIA PRESS ATHENS

PUBLISHED IN ASSOCIATION WITH THE LIBRARY OF CONGRESS

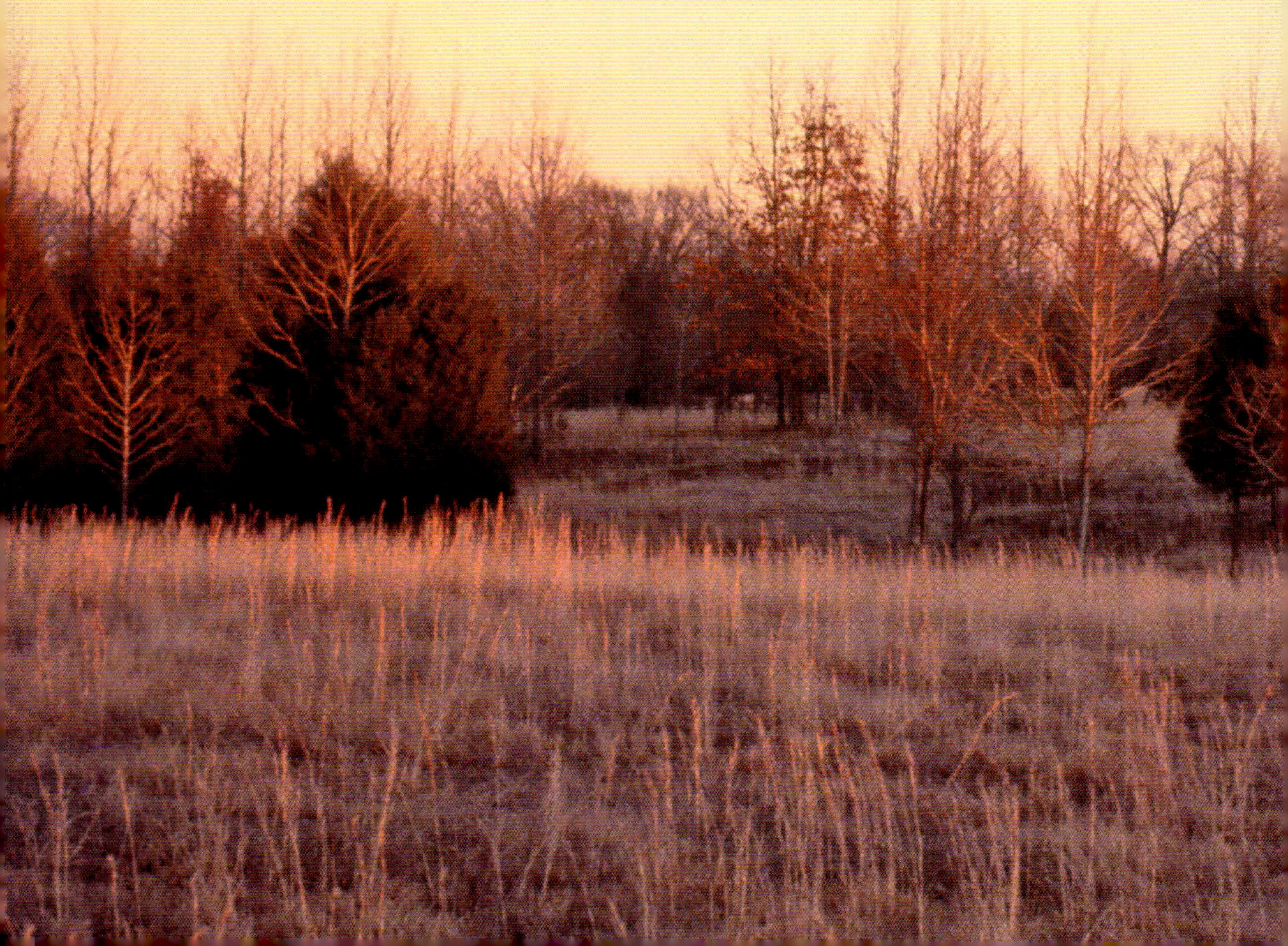

North Mississippi Homeplace

Photographs & Folklife

Michael Ford

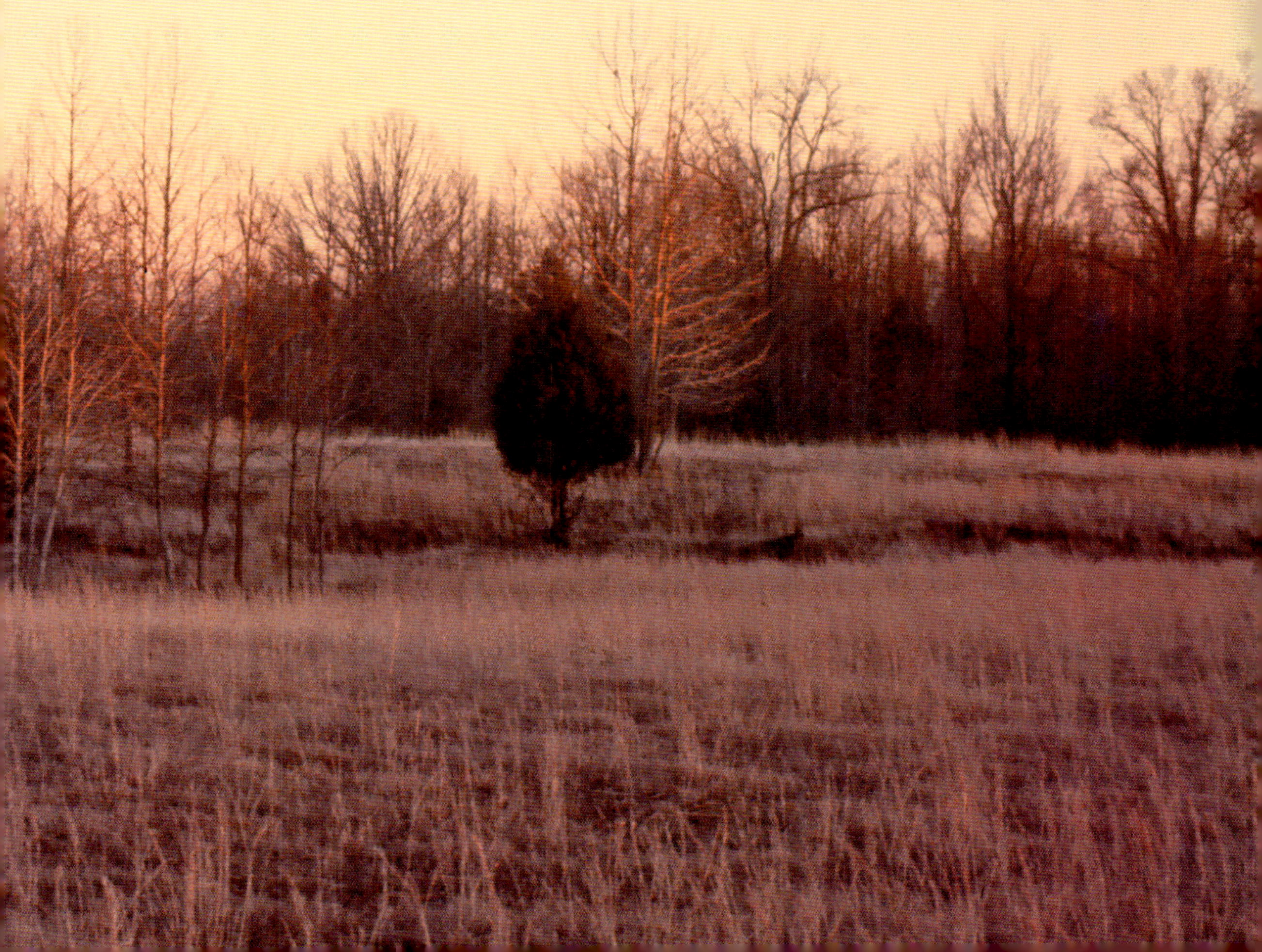

A Sarah Mills Hodge Fund Publication

This publication is made possible, in part, through a grant from the Hodge Foundation in memory of its founder, Sarah Mills Hodge, who devoted her life to the relief and education of African Americans in Savannah, Georgia.

Published by the University of Georgia Press
Athens, Georgia 30602
www.ugapress.org
in association with the Library of Congress

www.loc.gov

Designed by Erin Kirk New
Set in Miller Text with Jubilat display
Printed and bound by Four Colour Print Group
The paper in this book meets the guidelines for permanence and durability of the Committee on Production Guidelines for Book Longevity of the Council on Library Resources.

Most University of Georgia Press titles are available from popular e-book vendors.

Printed in China
23 22 21 20 19 C 5 4 3 2 1

Library of Congress Cataloging-in-Publication Data
Names: Ford, Michael, 1943– author. | Hayden, Carla Diane, 1952– writer of foreword.
Title: A North Mississippi Homeplace : Photographs and Folklife / by Michael Ford ; Foreword by Carla D. Hayden, Librarian of Congress.
Description: Athens : The University of Georgia Press, [2019]
Identifiers: LCCN 2018036506 | ISBN 9780820354408 (hardcover : alk. paper)
Subjects: LCSH: Mississippi—Social life and customs—20th century. | Mississippi—Pictorial works.
Classification: LCC F345 .F67 2019 | DDC 976.2/9063—dc23
LC record available at https://lccn.loc.gov/2018036506

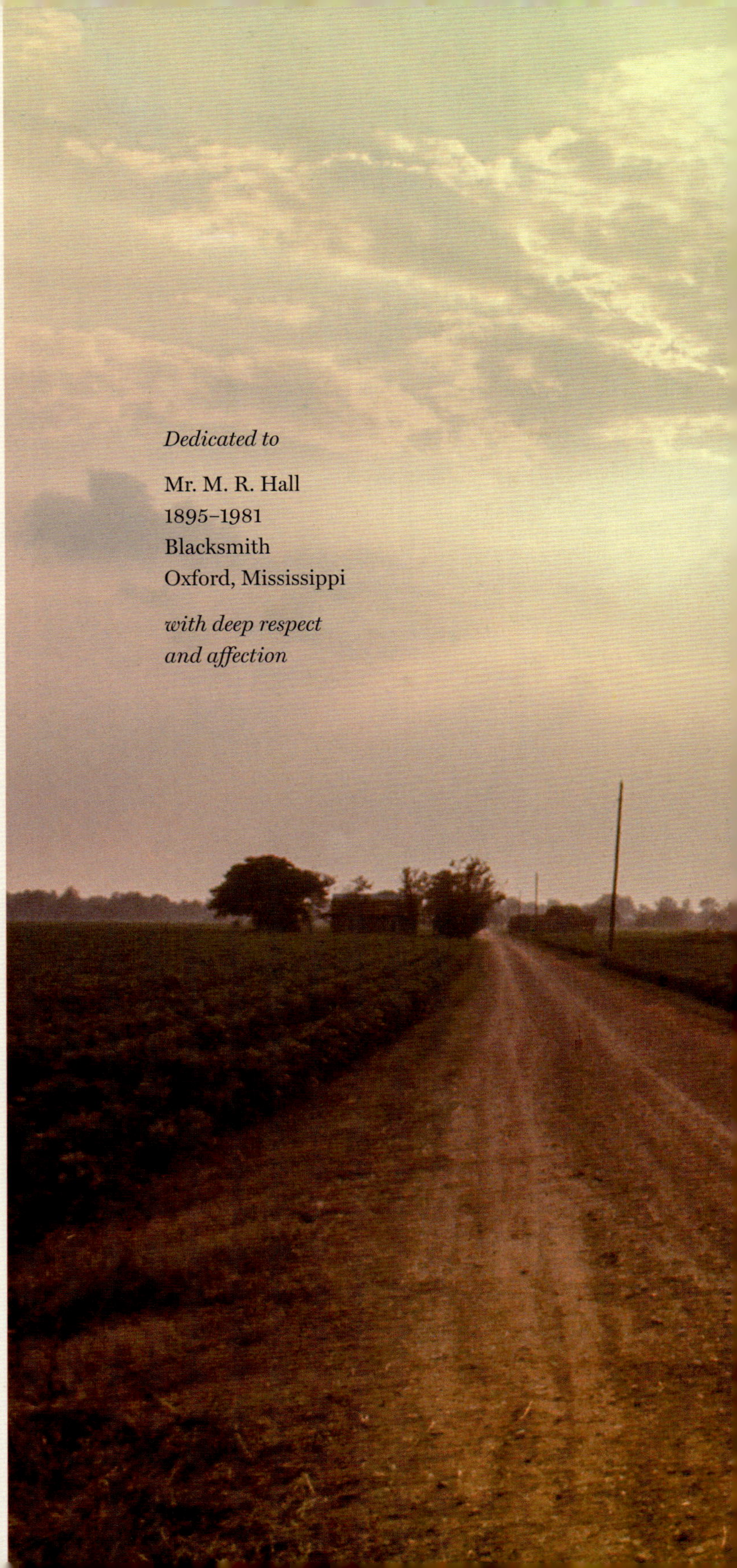

Dedicated to

Mr. M. R. Hall
1895–1981
Blacksmith
Oxford, Mississippi

with deep respect and affection

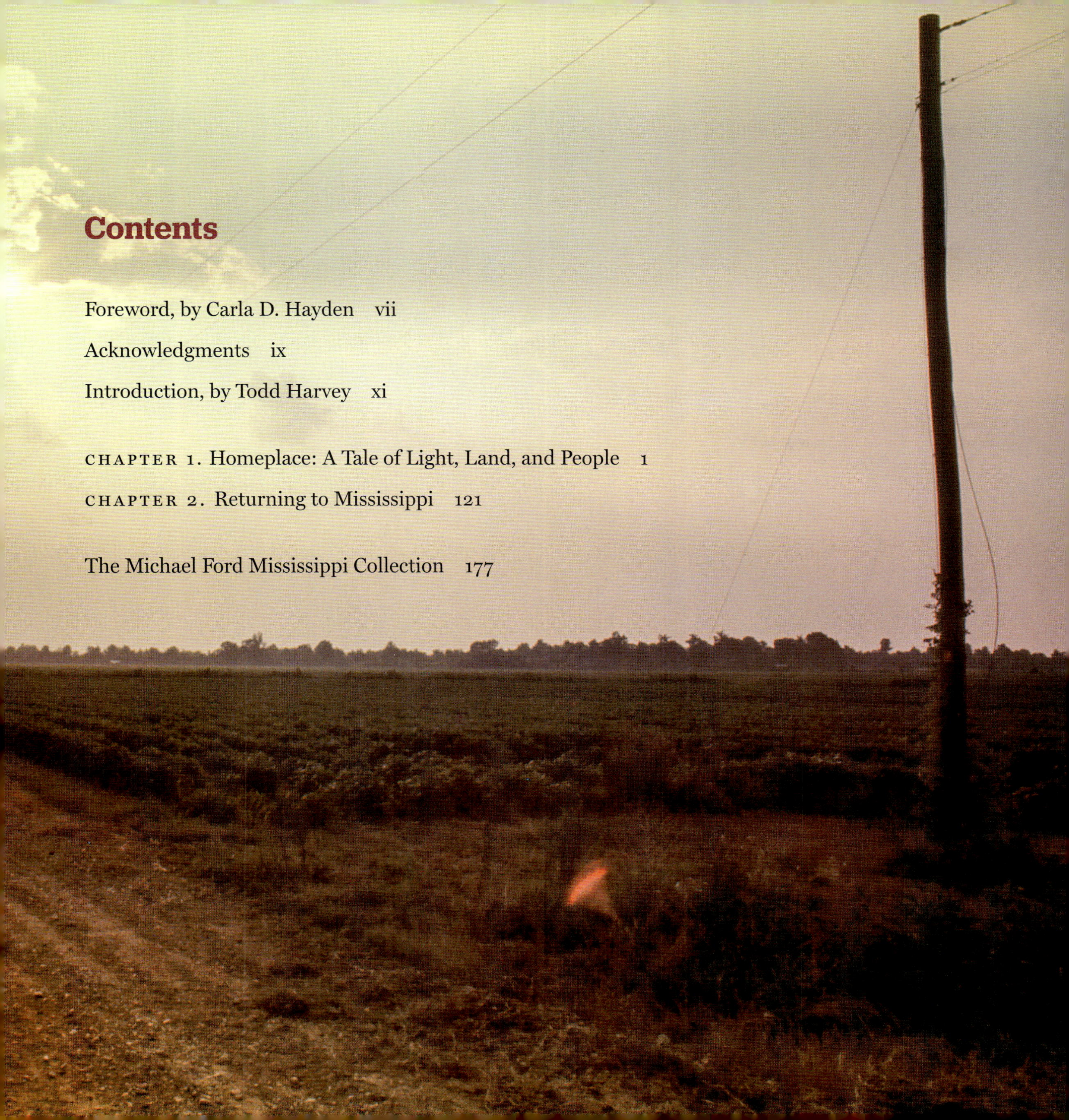

Contents

Foreword

Mississippi became a state in 1817, and in January 1818 the state legislature passed a resolution for the purchase of books and maps, which led to the organization of the Mississippi state library. A similar story describes the origin of the Library of Congress, which was created shortly after the United States became an independent nation, based on the idea that legislators need to refer to books, maps, and similar resources on a wide variety of topics to adequately perform their duties.

Mississippi brims with a rich literary tradition. It is the home state of a wide variety of writers, such as the playwright Tennessee Williams and the poet Natasha Trethewey. Eudora Welty drew inspiration from the Magnolia State's flavors and feelings, and she always came back to Jackson to write.

Mississippi similarly inspired Michael Ford when he lived there as a young man in the early 1970s. A few hundred miles north of Welty's Jackson, Ford found a place closer to the imaginings of another Mississippi writer—William Faulkner. Faulkner set most of his novels and stories in the fictional Yoknapatawpha County, which he based on Lafayette County and its county seat of Oxford. Like that of Faulkner, Ford's inspiration as a photographer and filmmaker came as much from the people who made their lives in the area surrounding Oxford as it did from the beautiful land, and he dedicated himself to capturing both with his camera. The results are the stunning photographs in this book, which bring back to life the unforgettable people and landscapes of the Mississippi hill country from a time now passed.

As I look at these photographs, I am reminded of the legions of photographers whose work enriches our understanding of unique places at particular times. The Library of Congress collections, now numbering more than 167 million items, include 14 million photographs. The Library's dedicated staff works hard to collect, conserve, and preserve these materials. Even more important is the Library's great responsibility to share its collections with the public. Onsite, the Library does this through its reading rooms, programs, and events. For those unable to visit in person, especially those in rural America, the Library is constantly expanding its offerings through digitization and virtual tours, live streams of onsite programs, traveling exhibits, mobile apps, and print publications. The Library of Congress is the nation's library, YOUR library, our library. I invite you to explore our treasures—in this book and through our website at www.loc.gov.

Dr. Carla D. Hayden
Librarian of Congress

Acknowledgments

I would like to thank the people who aided and supported me in the forging of *Homeplace* both then and now. There isn't enough room here to thank them adequately.

First and foremost.

Mr. Marion Randolph Hall, Blacksmith, teacher, friend and advisor. He made all the difference. Virgil to my Yankee Dante.

"There's always something to keep a man awake."

1971–1976	Ruth and Bill Eaton	AG Newson
	James Forward	Janice Stirling
	Columbus "Doc" James	Napoleon Strickland
	Billy Lester	Othar Turner
	Claude P Locke III	Hal Waldrip
	Dr. Ed Meek	
2013–2017	Deirdre Ford Aikin	Eric Kruize
	Scott Barretta	Billy Lester
	Chellius Carter	Albert Liesegang
	William Dunlap	Lou Linden
	Ralph Eubanks	Mark "Muleman" Massey
	Mary Flannery	Sharon McConnell-Dickerson
	Norman French	Dr. Ed Meek
	Katie Gates	Alice Pierotti
	Hillary Houston	Janice Stirling
	Jo Ann James	Andy Waller

Introduction

The Library founded its Archive of American Folk-Song (now the American Folklife Center) in 1928 as part of an impulse to include the wisdom of ordinary American people among its trove of national treasures. Within the rich cultural patchwork documented during subsequent decades, certain regions have seemed to overflow with human creativity. The Library's archival collections from these regions offer to the world a glimpse of the American genius. The North Mississippi hill country is one such place.

As a curator at the American Folklife Center, I've worked closely with the rich and varied collections from this region. So in 2012 when Michael Ford, a filmmaker who lives and works on Capitol Hill just a few blocks from the Library of Congress, invited me to screen film footage he had made in Mississippi during the 1970s, I eagerly accepted. This is how our relationships with donors often begin, but they don't always lead to acquisition of a life's work. Such acquisitions often resonate strongly with other Library of Congress collections and are also, by themselves, exemplars of the Library's role in American culture, which is to provide access to knowledge and to spark imagination and creativity.

Ford moved from the northeastern United States to North Mississippi at a liminal time in his life and lived in Oxford from 1971 to 1975. As a photographer he was drawn to the landscape, and the culture was something enticingly outside his previous experience. He apprenticed with an agricultural blacksmith, an encounter that provided a point of entry to the region's farming communities. Ford writes that his time evolved into patterns of blacksmithing and exploration, photographing the land, the light, and the people in northern Mississippi. Ford describes the light as luminescent, and this term gives evidence of his near reverence for what he has come to call his "homeplace."

The fraction-of-a-second opening of a camera lens enters the photographer into a conversation between the camera and the eye that can sometimes last decades. In a 2017 conversation Michael noted that a part of his current exploration is to scan analog negatives and alter the hue and saturation using digital editing software "to get it closer to what I actually saw at the moment."

In purely archival terms, the Michael Ford Collection of Documentary Materials for the Film, Homeplace (AFC 2013/004) comprises 725 pages of logs and transcripts, 90 audio recordings, 670 photographic images, and 63 film elements. The Library's cataloging describes the content as an examination of four individuals "who speak of their work and the vanishing lifestyle they lead in rural Mississippi." This is well-trodden ground at the Library of Congress.

A corpus of folklife collections came into being during the 1930s and early 1940s when the federal government sent documentarians to communities across the nation. This activity reflected a broad desire to understand current social conditions with an eye toward reform and was manifested in the Resettlement Administration and related programs. The Farm Security Administration (FSA) photographs that captured the poverty endured by many Americans also provided direction for social programs during the following decades and came to symbolize an endemic challenge faced by twentieth-century America—a bowed yet undaunted country, restless and vibrant.

To the FSA collection of photographs, the Federal Writers Project and the Library of Congress added sound recordings. Images of environmental refugees headed to the western United States made by Dorothea Lange and Gordon Parks correlate roughly with Library of Congress sound recordings made by Charles Todd and Robert Sonkin at a California migrant camp. Todd and Sonkin also made recordings at the African American community in Gees Bend, Alabama, that give voice to communities photographed by Arthur Rothstein. Similarly, photographer John Vachon and folklorist Sidney Robertson both documented communities in northern Minnesota. All of these materials are part of Library of Congress collections, and they are contextualized in print through Library of Congress publications such as *Documenting America, 1935–1943*.

Conditions in Mississippi during the Great Depression in particular commanded the attention of this documentary impulse. Federal fieldworkers made thousands of images, transcripts, films, and sound recordings, many of which related to the state's yawning social inequity. Some travelled to the North Mississippi hill country that includes Tate, Panola, and Marshall Counties.

The Library of Congress encountered the vibrant music culture of the hill country first through Herbert Halpert's 1939 recordings in Byhalia and Holly Springs and then through the historic sessions Alan Lomax made in 1942 with Sid Hemphill and his band. Lomax revisited the region in 1959 and made recordings that Atlantic Records released. Then, in the early 1970s, David and Cheryl Evans made recordings that the Library released as *Afro-American Folk Music from Tate and Panola Counties, Mississippi*. In 1978 Lomax returned again to film part of his PBS *American Patchwork* series. By benefit of these activities musicians such as Sid Hemphill, Lucius Smith, Annie McDowell, Ed and Lonnie Young, Napoleon Strickland, Othar Turner, Rosalie Hill, and Fred McDowell have all come to national attention.

Michael Ford drove his aging Volkswagen bus into this context. The photo essay that follows elucidates characteristics that complement those of earlier documentarians, yet some aspects are unique to the time and the filmmaker. The FSA images lack hill country blacksmiths. Ford gives us a protagonist who served as a social compass in Oxford blacksmith Marion Randolph Hall. Alan Lomax made no interviews or film footage with molasses makers. Ford introduces us to AG Newson and his mules. Ford filmed Othar Turner's fife-and-drum band working the crowd at a picnic, an event also filmed by Lomax and a tradition that is still today very much alive. But Ford also added the Reverend Leon Pinson and quilter Riller Smith and others to that cast of extraordinarily creative souls that informs our understanding of the Mississippi hill country.

Collections of primary source materials tend to convey an insular view of a particular topic. The breadth of Library of Congress holdings has particular importance, then, because in many instances a researcher can examine a topic through multiple lenses. Michael Ford's Oxford, Mississippi, is not the Oxford described in the Library's National Association for the Advancement of Colored People (NAACP) papers or in the Library's Civil Rights History Project. A mere decade later, his is not the Oxford experienced by James Meredith in 1962.

Indeed, the Depression-era federal documentation of Mississippi focuses strongly on social and economic injustice. Lomax made most of his Mississippi audio recordings, for example, in prisons and of largely African American populations. The Mississippi State Penitentiary at Parchman is just ninety minutes by car from Oxford. Michael Ford's idyll is perfect in its isolation—Mr. Hall and Ford repaired farm equipment for both black and white farmers—but the larger context shows a truly complicated situation of race and status.

Ford never posits himself as an insider. Indeed, his entire narrative is about being an outsider in a remarkable and unique place, and such an outsider has permission to cross social and racial lines. His father-in-law was a professor at the University of Mississippi, and one imagines that Ford could have existed within the "gown" bubble of academic segregation. Instead, he created "Homeplace."

Once the enterprise of making a film was begun, Ford set about augmenting his equipment beyond a Nikon still camera and a Beaulieu 16mm moving image camera. He needed to scout locations and make contacts, to process and edit the results. This is a markedly different enterprise than the one undertaken by Herbert Halpert in 1939, who drove through the South in a government truck outfitted with a state-of-the-art disc recorder. Whereas Halpert moved quickly from town to town, Ford committed to becoming, at least temporarily, a part of the community.

Donation of his collection to the Library of Congress reawakened Ford's interest in Mississippi. Documentary films such as *Skipjacks* (1982), *Tubabs in Africa* (2002), *Return to Belaye* (2002), and *The Gambia, Gateway to West Africa* (2004) intervened, but in 2013 he began an ongoing series of returns to northern Mississippi, now with digital cameras and a more seasoned eye.

About his return trips, Ford wistfully describes changes to the hill country during the intervening four decades—the modern amenities, the absence of certain obsolete practices—but quickly regains focus on the land, the light, and the people. Culture is immutable, no matter its form or shape. From the Library's perspective the new documentation tells the continuing story of this bedrock American cultural region. Michael Ford's photo essay in the following pages, then, provides for readers a Mississippi at turns far removed from the 1930s or from the 1970s and at times wholly reminiscent of both.

Todd Harvey
Curator, American Folklife Center, Library of Congress

North Mississippi Homeplace

"That's the reason they put the president on the dollar . . . His name will never die. You see, every time you get a dollar bill you got George Washington. Five-dollar bill is Abraham Lincoln. I don't know how many years he's been dead but still they're glad to call his name . . . He's there forever . . . His name coming see, and when we be dead and gone . . . Well, somebody see us by these pictures."

—**AG NEWSON,** Molasses Maker, Chulahoma, Mississippi, October 1972

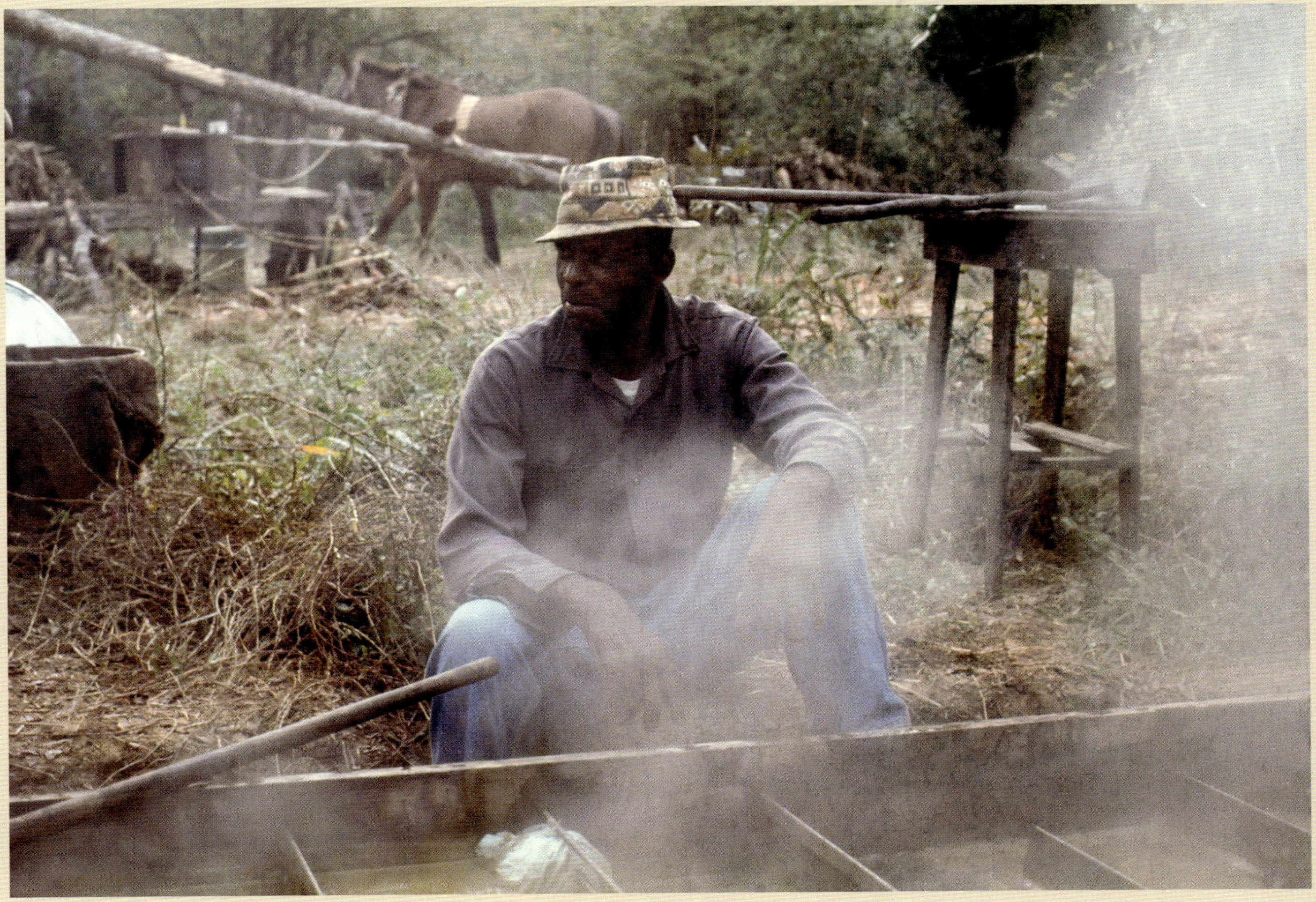

Chapter 1 Homeplace *A Tale of Light, Land, and People*

Some stories impose themselves on the storyteller. Griots in West Africa must sing witness to the past. The Celtic Seanachaí's burden is to carry the "old lore." If you're really lucky, a good story has a way of finding you and making you tell it. It happened to me.

For many southerners, their homeplace—a family home or farm handed down through generations—holds lasting significance. My homeplace was not handed down. I found it by accident, but it holds as much significance for me as if I inherited it. I found my homeplace in the North Mississippi hill country in December 1971 on a trip to visit in-laws. That trip changed my life to its very core. Everything I've done since has its roots in that experience.

From Mississippi came my first documentary film, *Homeplace*. *Homeplace* begat my film production company, Yellow Cat Productions, and Yellow Cat has been my life for forty-plus years—a life full of experiences with a lot of variety and satisfaction. I've gotten to see a lot of this world with a camera in hand.

In 1971 I was a graduate student in film at Boston University (BU). Previously I had graduated from Rochester Institute of Technology (RIT) with a BFA in photography. After that, I shot film for a local news station for a couple of years before leaving to get a master's degree at BU, thinking maybe I'd teach. I'd tried a lot of different things. I had been in the navy with three overseas deployments, hitchhiked in Europe, traveled through the Mediterranean and the Caribbean, and worked in a morgue. Who could know the most exotic place I'd find was right here in the USA: Mississippi.

As a kid in Bethlehem, Pennsylvania, I'd seen the woods and fields where I played disappear under streets, houses, and strip malls. In Rochester, while studying at RIT, I'd often go out past the growing suburbs to the rather

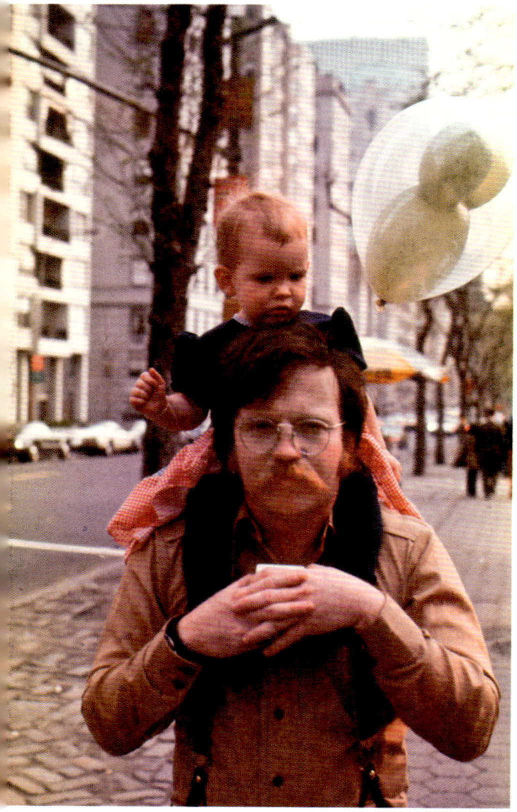

My daughter Deirdre and I in New York City, 1972. Photo by Janice Sterling.

desolate countryside of upstate New York to photograph long-abandoned farms. Sad homes—each one unique and filled with the remnants of those who'd lived within. They were the opposite of the relatively homogenized places of my youth.

When I got to BU, I was thinking about some kind of thesis film about rural America, maybe to be shot in Vermont or New Hampshire. Friends from Rochester had returned to old homes in New Hampshire for a simpler existence. I'd visited them and their cows. It seemed there might be a story about loss and change to be told.

Meanwhile, the family of my wife, Janice, had recently moved from Rochester to Oxford, Mississippi, where her father, Dr. John Fox, was the new chair of the Department of Mechanical Engineering at the University of Mississippi. For Christmas 1971 we drove south in our red VW bus with New York plates and a peace sign. As we plunged south at fifty-five miles per hour, straining over the hills of Tennessee, I began to wonder whether this was the smartest thing I'd ever done. Up to that point my only frame of reference for the South was the film *Easy Rider*. Only a few years previous, James Meredith, Medgar Evers, and three bodies in a dam had created a dreadful phantasm of Mississippi, a place to be shunned.

Finally we arrived in Oxford. The sound of people's voices had changed. It was a lot warmer.

During our visit, the number-three intake valve of the VW busted, giving literal meaning to the term "gone south." A friend of the Foxes, Bill Eaton, worked as a mechanic at the VW dealer and moonlighted at rebuilding my engine. So I'd sit around all day and work with Bill at night. It was a very limited existence, and I was getting a tad stir crazy.

My old friend James Forward had followed the Foxes (or, more accurately, one Fox: my wife's sister) down to Oxford from Rochester. He lived near them while attending Ole Miss. One day he asked if I wanted to see some North Mississippi hill country. Of course I did. I needed to get out.

We borrowed Dr. Fox's pickup truck and drove north of Oxford and west along the north shore of Sardis reservoir. The first frost had just occurred overnight. Next to country shacks, large iron kettles were simmering over open fires. First frost is hog-killing time. "Singletrees," short wooden bars

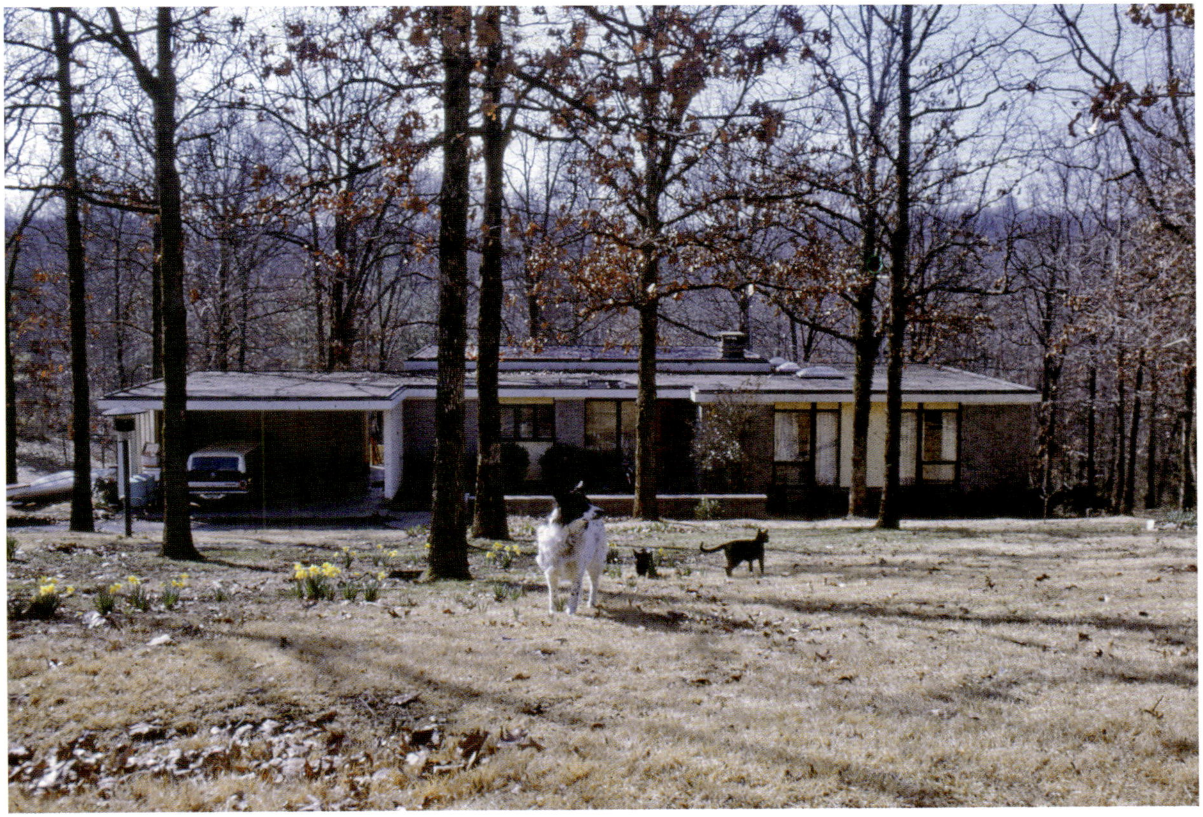

My in-laws' house, Oxford, 1972. We stayed at the so-called Fox Den with Mama and Papa Fox; Janice's two brothers and sister; plus Dino, a border collie; and a pack of cats. Everyone was glad to see us.

used to separate harness traces, were hoisted into the branches of large trees. They held wide the hogs' rear legs so that they could be gutted and quartered. I had no camera.

The next four days we continued our travels north of Sardis. I was gobsmacked, awestruck, and dazed. I didn't know anything looked like this in America in 1972. The area north of the reservoir was as remote as it could get in both time and space.

At RIT I had had the good fortune to study the history of photography with Beaumont Newhall, the renowned photo historian who served as curator and director of the George Eastman House. In his classes we looked at the way photographers such as T. H. O'Sullivan, Edward Weston, Ansel Adams,

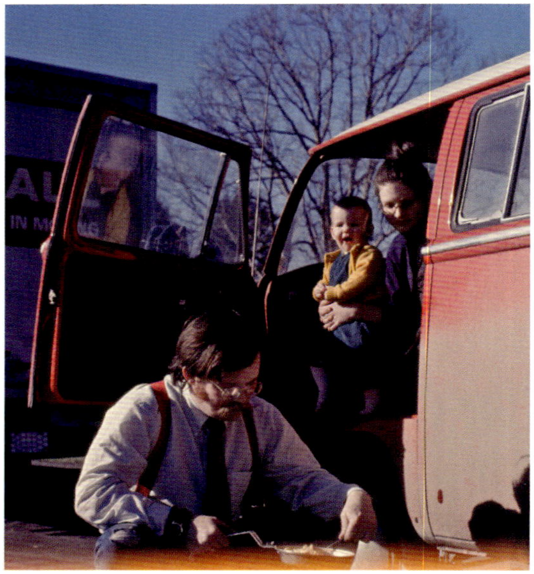

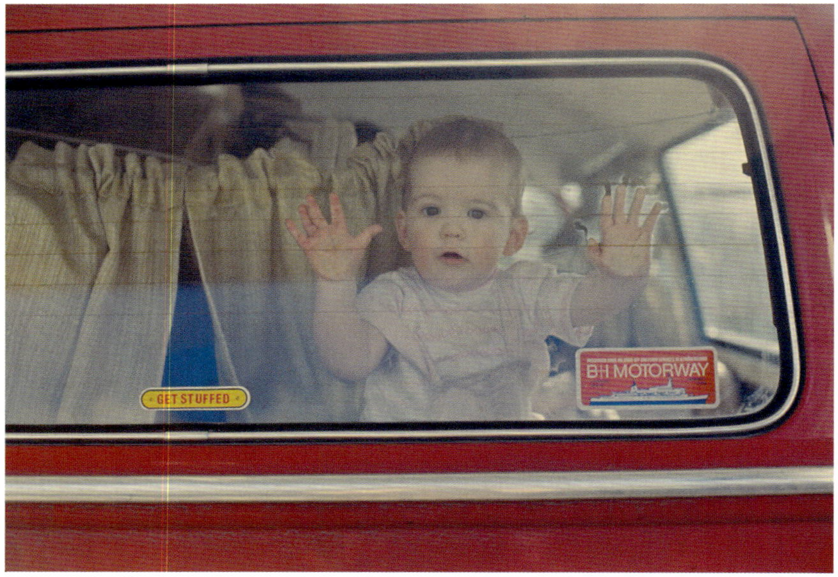

Janice, Deirdre, and I at a roadside dinner somewhere in Tennessee, New Year's Day, 1972. Photo by James Forward.

Deirdre in the VW, 1972. The VW was also the red bus mobile playpen. This was well before seatbelts were mandatory, much less car seats.

Robert Capa, Henri Cartier Bresson, and Lucien Aigner looked at, and engaged with, their worlds. We talked of the disciplines they worked within. Among the treasures he showed us were the works of the FSA photographers: Walker Evans, Dorothea Lange, Gordon Parks, Arthur Rothstein, Russell Lee, and Eudora Welty. I loved their work.

Suddenly a world of FSA scenes I hadn't known existed was there before me, live and in color. I had no reference. As far as I knew, I was the only photographer to ever see these communities. What was I to do with what was in front of me? Drive away? Go back north and research? Try to pitch a concept to someone, somewhere? Make a movie? Now that was a scary thought. But it stuck.

It was one of those times you realize you can't turn down what's been handed to you. With no thought, but rather a trust in instinct, I made the snap decision to move to Mississippi.

Friends thought me insane.

With wife and child in tow, I abandoned a new teaching job at Emerson College I had worked very hard to get. We left Boston in our second U-Haul in four months. We camped along the way in state parks. All the way down, rolling in a battered convoy of Dr. Fox's pickup truck, a U-Haul, and a VW bus crammed full, I worried. I had no contacts in Mississippi. More than once I wondered, "What in God's name have I done?"

We moved into a large, old farm-style house with a part-tin roof two blocks from the courthouse on Jackson Avenue in Oxford. Rent was $125 a month. My GI bill gave us $250 a month. That left half for everything else, but I figured I'd find something to do that might turn a few dollars.

It was a great old place, nice and open and light compared with our Boston basement. There was a huge yard shaded by six big pecan trees. The house was built up on blocks, and under the southwest corner was an L-shaped trench in the earth. "That's your tornado shelter," our landlord told us. "When you hear the sound of that freight train you want to be down in there." We learned to read the sky.

Next door lived the Dooleys, a retired couple. Across the street was Mrs. Kimmons, a "widow lady" who was the reigning Queen of Jackson Avenue.

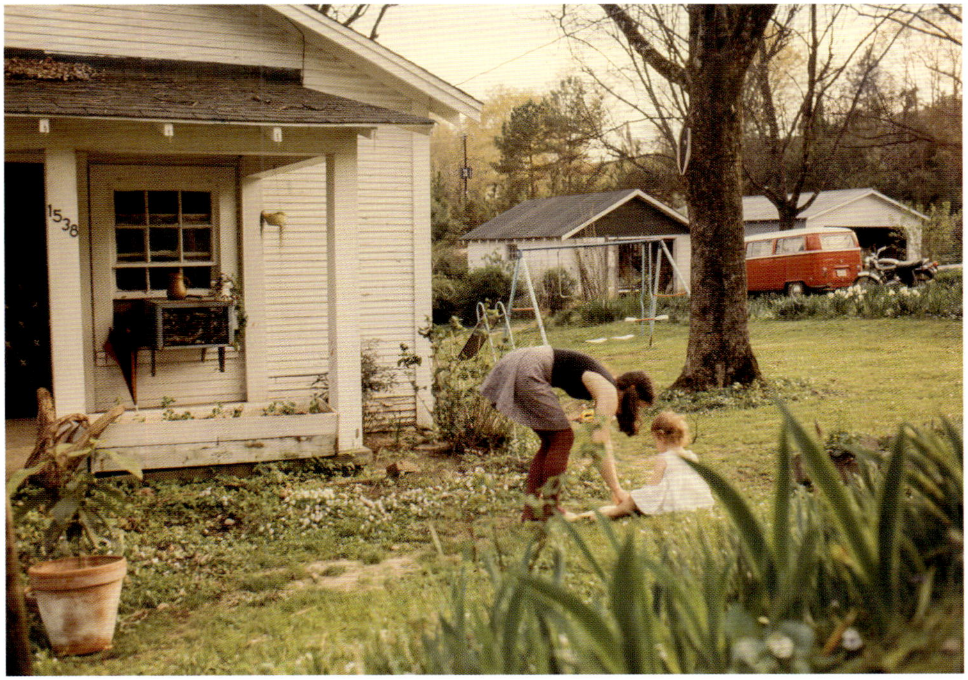

Our home in Oxford, 1973.

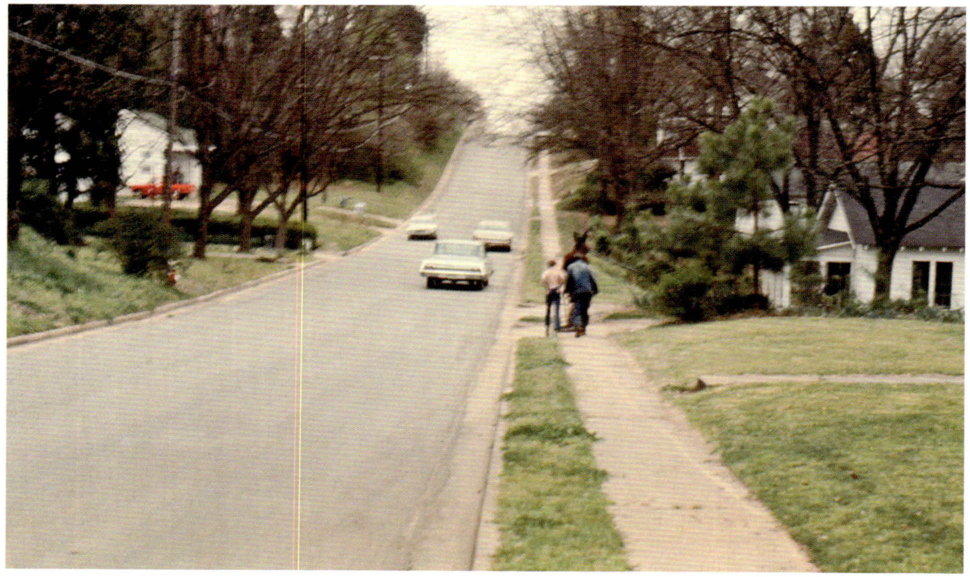

Mr. Washington and his mule, Oxford, 1972–75. A chicken coop and a big garden had lain fallow in the back of our house for many years. Soon after we moved in, an old man knocked on our door. "Plow your garden for three dollars?" Mr. Washington's mule waited patiently by the curb on Jackson Avenue.

She instantly became "Granny Kimmons" to us, a guide and mentor to southern small-town living.

Oxford seemed welcoming, though we had to make some adjustments. Oxford, then, was still Faulkner's fictional town of Jefferson. It was a dry town. No booze, no beer. There were no franchise restaurants. All the fast-food joints were local mom-and-pop ventures. At the Jitney Jungle supermarket just off the square you could get all the basics, but there were no pretzels to be had, much less liverwurst, salami, or bagels. Stacks of blank bank checks sat at the checkout. Find one with your bank's name, no ID or account number needed. Just fill it out, name and address. No worries. Why would you lock your door? Why would you lock your car?

This was a time long before the crack cocaine and methamphetamine epidemics hit the countryside and changed things forever. There didn't seem to be any major crime or theft. Once in Oxford I left my Nikon on the dashboard of the bus out on the street for three days with the window open. Any passerby could have reached in and had it, but it didn't happen. In the early morning I would see shipments sitting in the open, waiting for the owners of the unopened stores on the square. To a northern city boy it was unbelievable, but down here it was the way people expected to live their lives. And it seemed to work okay.

I'd always lived in cities or suburbs. This was a new experience. You could walk to most anything you needed, yet you were worlds away from a lot you might want. The courthouse was the center of town and activity. Around it, on the town's square, were stores for hardware, dry goods, and drugs. Some jewelers, lawyers, and bankers could be found too, as well as the post office. In summer, the square was lined with faded old men in faded overalls selling produce from the back of sun-faded pickup trucks. Off to one side Neilson's department store stood in quiet elegance. Although most of the customers were from the university, you'd also see folks from all over North Mississippi seeking their local version of Lord & Taylor or Saks.

The Square, Oxford, 1972–75.

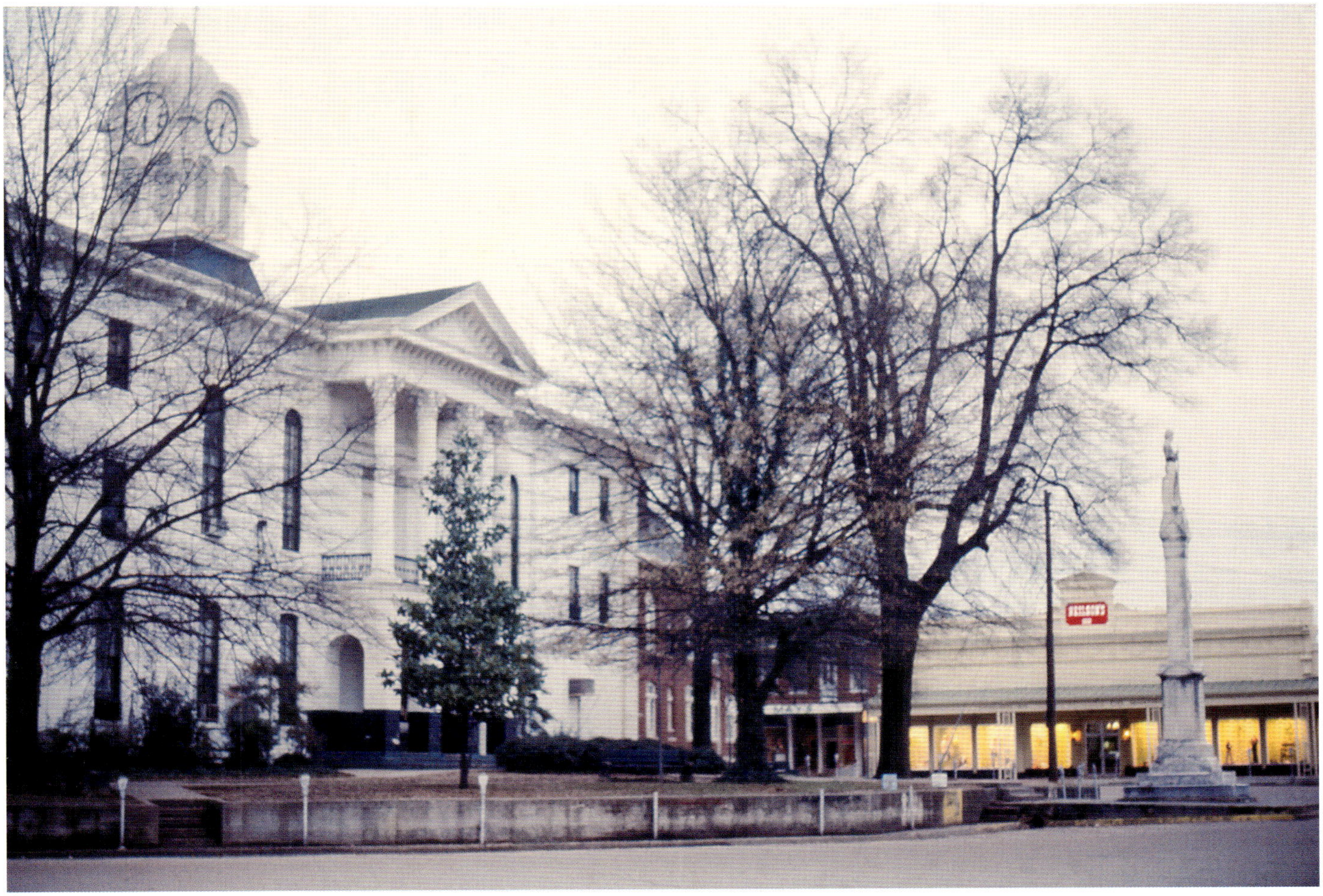

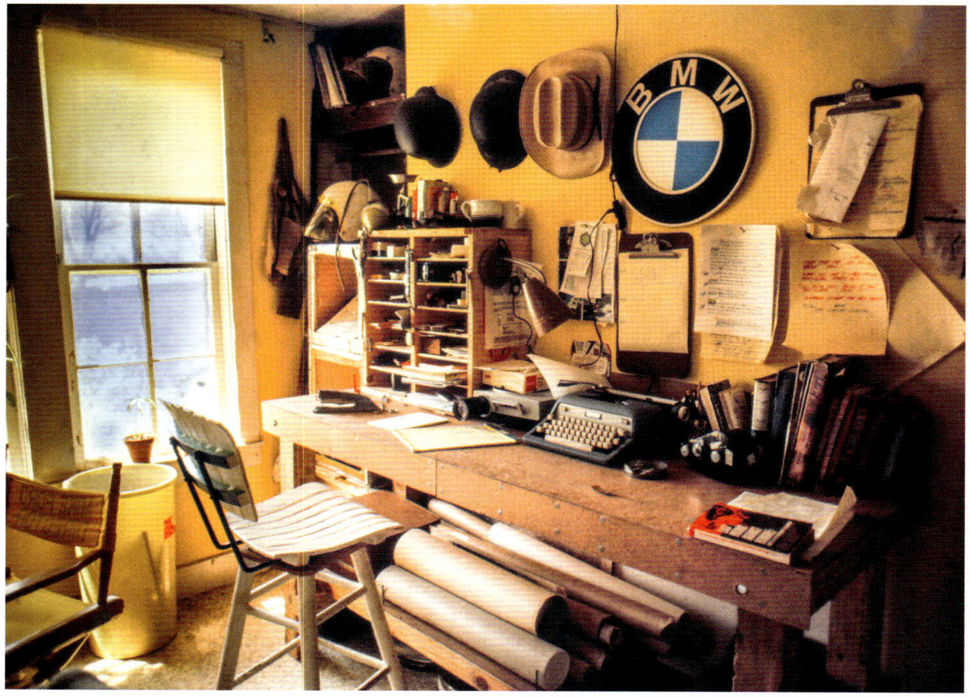

My home office, Oxford, 1972–75.

There was a quiet about things. Clocks seemed less important. We had no television. The sound of the rain on a tin roof became a soporific lullaby. I read Faulkner for the first time and started riding out to the country on my motorcycle.

In the back of the house I set up an office that looked out at the garden and the old pecan trees. I built a worktable and put my projector and typewriter on it, spread out my maps and a rotating stack of books: folktales, histories, biographies, works of Mississippi writers, god knows what else. *The Whole Earth Catalog*, a counterculture handbook for independent creative living, steered me to the topographic maps I used; the topo sheets covered all of North Mississippi.

I began to assemble materials, gather information, and prepare for the task ahead. I already owned a Nikon FTn, a few lenses, and a Beaulieu R16 film camera with three prime lenses. I started searching for the various bits I'd need to make the movie. First came the changing bag, tanks, and agitators, then film clips and thermometers, cardboard slide mounts, slide mount press, slide cases, light boxes, magnifiers, and lint free cotton gloves. I found Motion

Picture Laboratories (MPL), a film lab that would rent me sync sound gear and could process 16mm film in Memphis, eighty miles away, but there was no local processing for the 35mm stills shot during scouting. I'd have to do it myself. Processing took place late at night in my kitchen during the summer. I'd wait—sometimes until two in the morning—for the air outside to cool to the proper ambient temperature of 85 degrees Fahrenheit (plus or minus half a degree) for processing. These exposure tests were necessary because 16mm film was too expensive to explore with, so stills had to suffice. Bearing in mind the "operate from within a discipline" concept I had learned at RIT, I only shot with the Nikon and only a 35mm lens. If you want a different frame, you've got to move your body. Full frame, no cropping (like film).

The poor old VW bus got transformed. My snow tires became mud grips. James and I built a platform with lockers underneath, boat style. We learned to carry a full mechanic's tool kit, a first aid kit, water, spare gas, flashlights, a tire pump, and a shovel. We discovered that a high lift jack and two lengths of chain made your whole day better when you got mudded up to your axles in some obscure bottomland of the Tallahatchie River miles from a real road.

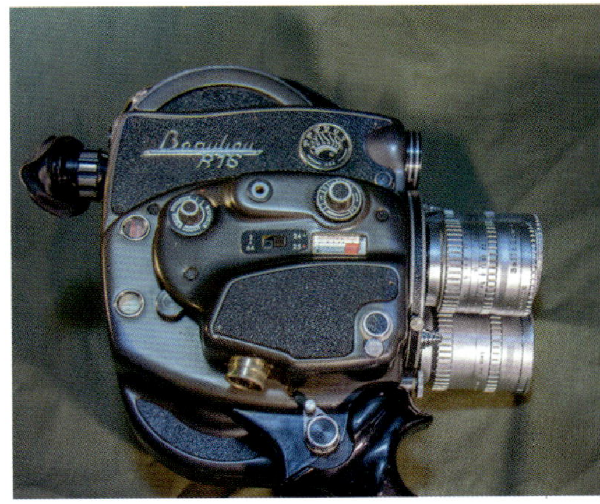

My Beaulieu R16, the film camera I used to make a lot of *Homeplace*.

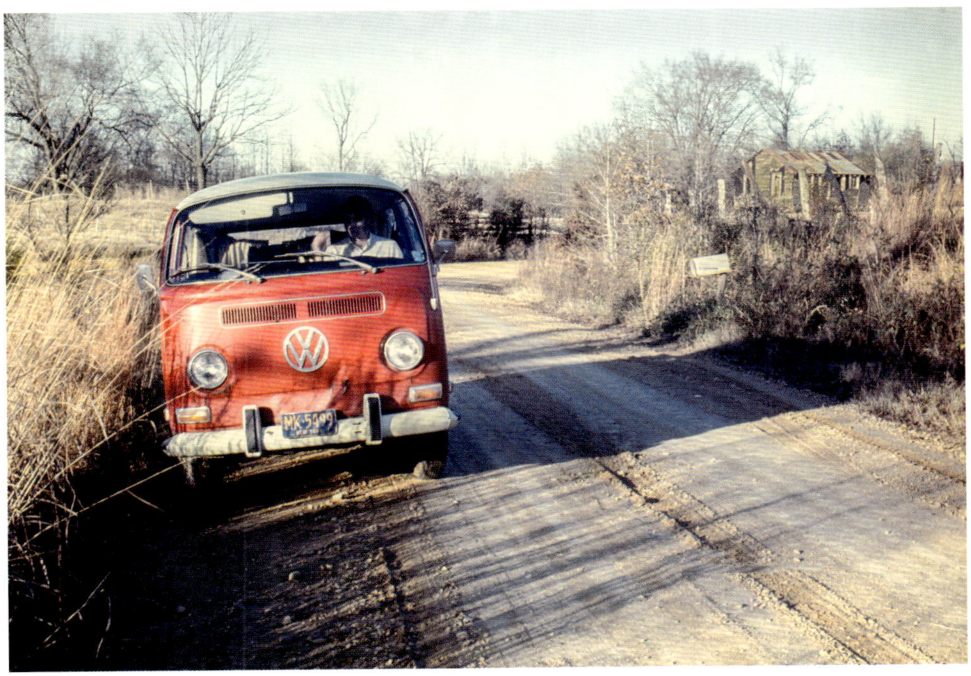

The VW bus, 1972–75.

At first we meandered about aimlessly, just trying to get a sense of the place and the people who lived here. This was the America of the FSA. This was the world of Walker Evans, Gordon Parks, and Dorothea Lange. In front of me was a visual treasure, but how to access it? How was I to make sense of it?

I was far out of my depth. I knew nothing of the South, or rural America for that matter, or of cultural anthropology, ethnography, or folklife. Years later someone would tell me that I was "a participant-observer in a material folk process," but I didn't know that at the time. I just knew that what I was seeing was so fragile and evanescent that it had to be captured before it disappeared. I learned, and was given the luck, or grace perhaps, to find two oases where the past was alive and well and welcoming.

Number one was Mr. Marion Randolph Hall's blacksmith shop. Someone told me that there was an "old timey" blacksmith in Oxford just off the square by Avent's Cotton Gin. Mr. Hall had opened his shop in 1910 and was still open six days a week sixty-two years later. I was captured immediately by his forge and the rich, spiced, dusky smell of the coal burning, the roaring of air as it fanned the fire to almost white heat and the sweet glow of hot iron. In no time I joined the long procession of strikers, or apprentices, to Mr. Hall.

The forge was the best classroom and resource I could ask for. Decades later when I joined the Blacksmiths' Guild of the Potomac in Virginia, I realized what a specialist Mr. Hall had been. Most of the smiths in the guild are artisans and artists who create beautiful things from bright yellow hot steel: ironbound chests, pot racks, cutlery of all sorts, carving tools—good utilitarian articles as well as objets d'art. Mr. Hall, by contrast, was a blacksmith plain and simple, one of the last agricultural smiths. He knew plows, wagons, wheels, tools, and tack. He had worked on every type of mule or horse-drawn implement or conveyance there was. He could make the right tool for any job. We fixed, repaired, and sharpened saws, shovels, axes, and hoes. We put new handles on every type of item that ever bore a handle. Only rarely would he make a knife or a set of firedogs (a pair of metal stands used to hold logs over a fire). Usually those things were commissions from customers. For four years I worked with Mr. Hall, slowly absorbing culture, cadence, and courtesy. A long time later I realized how lucky I was to be there, right where I needed to be. Still later I wondered if maybe it was happy fate rather than dumb luck.

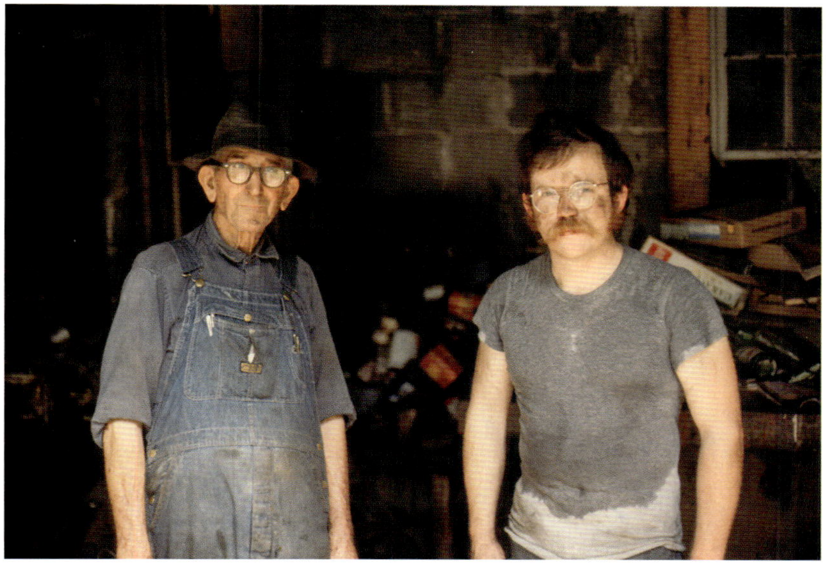

Mr. Hall and I, 1972–75. Photo by Janice Sterling.

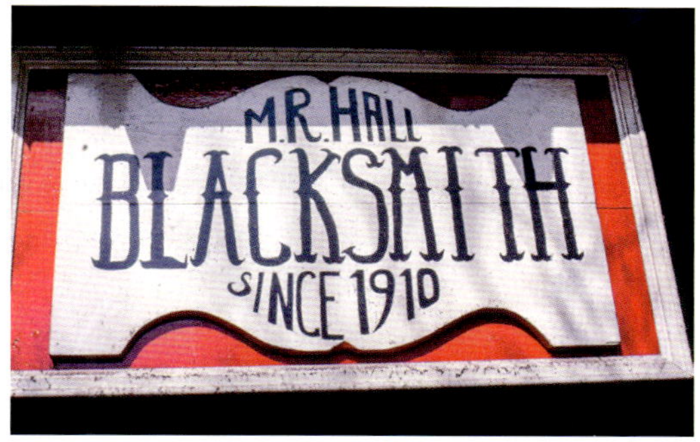

The sign at Mr. Hall's forge, 1972–75.

Under Mr. Hall's tutelage I learned about late nineteenth- and early twentieth-century technology and everything it entailed. You couldn't sharpen a froe (a tool for cleaving wood) if you didn't know how it was used. I helped repair mule-drawn plows and wagons and learned how they worked in the bargain. We fixed other folks' tools and unbent the twisted. As long as Mr. Hall was there to fix things, the farmers using mules could keep going the way they had for centuries. Where else could you get your middle-buster (a type of plow) repaired? No one else could fix a singletree or doubletree (used to hitch a team up to a wagon). Plow handles and plowshares must be set up right to keep the plow in the earth. Most of this now is lost knowledge.

Mr. Hall was a man of infinite patience and kindness. He had a way of quietly teaching what you needed to know. For example, I'd be holding something up to the grinder, and he'd say, "Well, Mykall"—that's the way he said my name—'Well, Mykall, I used to know a feller that did it thata way."

Over time I learned my proper response: "And what happened to him, Mr. Hall?"

"Well, he put out his eye."

That was my cue to ask, "How *should* I be doing this, Mr. Hall?"

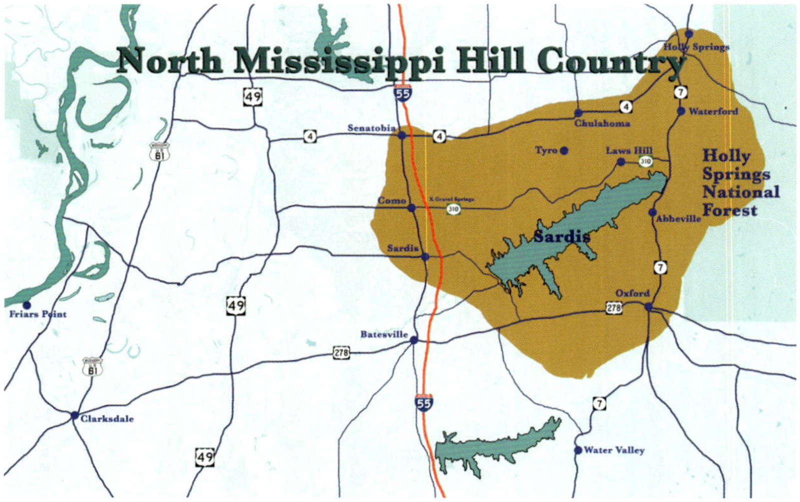

“Shadow of Sardis,” the area where we spent most of our time.

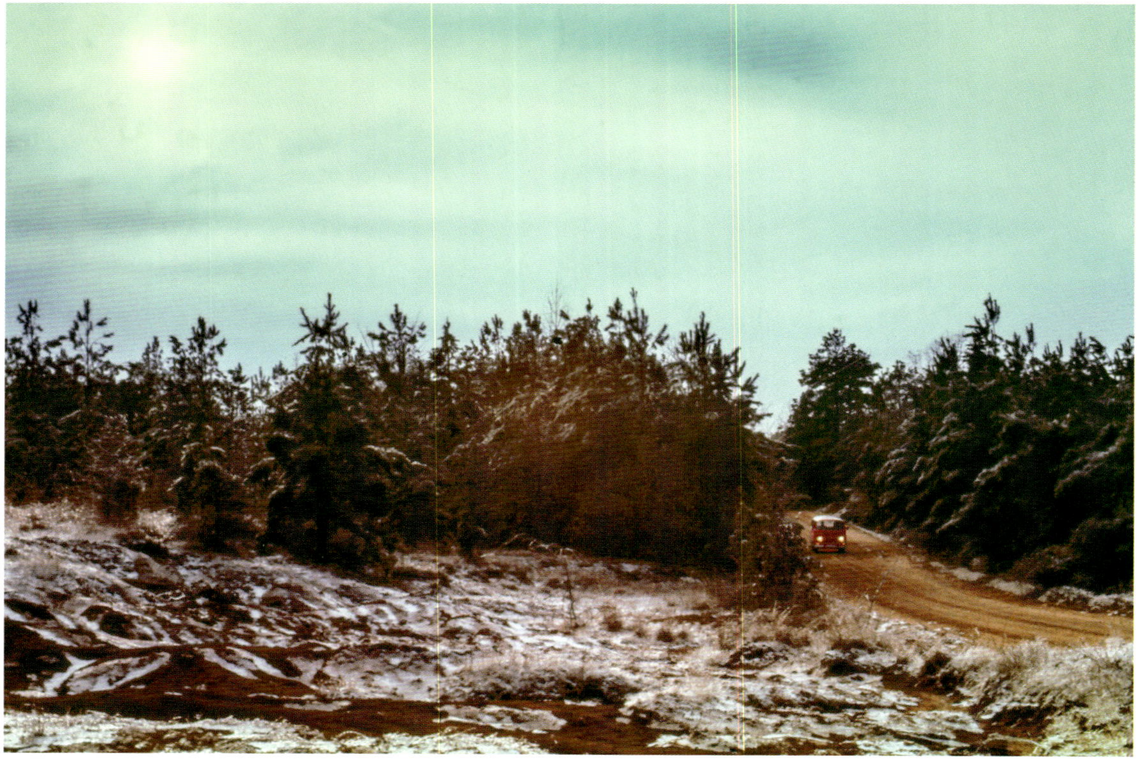

Winter, north of Sardis, 1972.

I listened, learned, respected, and photographed. At the same time, I learned lessons in hot metal, the proper treatment of people, resolute endurance, handiness, honesty, resourcefulness, ingenuity, and fortitude. My speech pattern slowed down a good bit. For forty years since then, almost every day, I've used something I learned in that shop. I still forge steel, still compulsively fix stuff, and still glean lessons from the seemingly smaller aspects of life.

The second oasis was that remote area north of Sardis Lake that had first beckoned me to the South. The lake forms a barrier some twenty miles long between Oxford and Memphis. You have to go around it to get anywhere. Along the southern shore were a few fishing camps, a summer place or two, and a catfish restaurant called Hurricane Landing. But the land north of the lake felt like it had been forgotten. It was in a penumbra we called the Shadow of Sardis. There was no reason to be there unless you lived there.

When things were slow at the forge, James and I would head north of Sardis in the vw bus. For months we roamed the North Mississippi hills trying to get a sense of the place, to find out what was there. Navigating with our topographic maps and a compass, we drove all the roads there were. First we fanned out in all directions, from Senatobia east to Holly Springs, down to Waterford, Oxford, Abbeville, Water Valley, Potts Camp, or Taylor, or out further east to Pontotoc.

Our travels had the flavor of exploration in far more exotic climes. We made some forays from the hill country to the flat Delta. The people there seemed to live in a more modern world yet somehow in poorer straits than the hill folks. It seemed harder in the Delta. Sometimes we went far to the east, toward Tupelo, the birthplace of Elvis. We didn't know what we were searching for, but we knew we'd know if we found it.

A few places we returned to more often: Holly Springs, Harmontown, Laws Hill, Blackwater, Liberty Hill, Galena, Como, Chulahoma. To this day I can't tell you why those places felt different. Something drew me to center in on this tiny area. Eventually, we wound up back where we started: north of Sardis.

I found myself weaving three threads in the photographs: the land, the light, and the people. I started off photographing the land. The land was soft, easy on the eye. North of Sardis the land was dominated by a big, ofttimes dramatic sky over slow rolling hills. The colors were amazing. There's no Grand Canyon

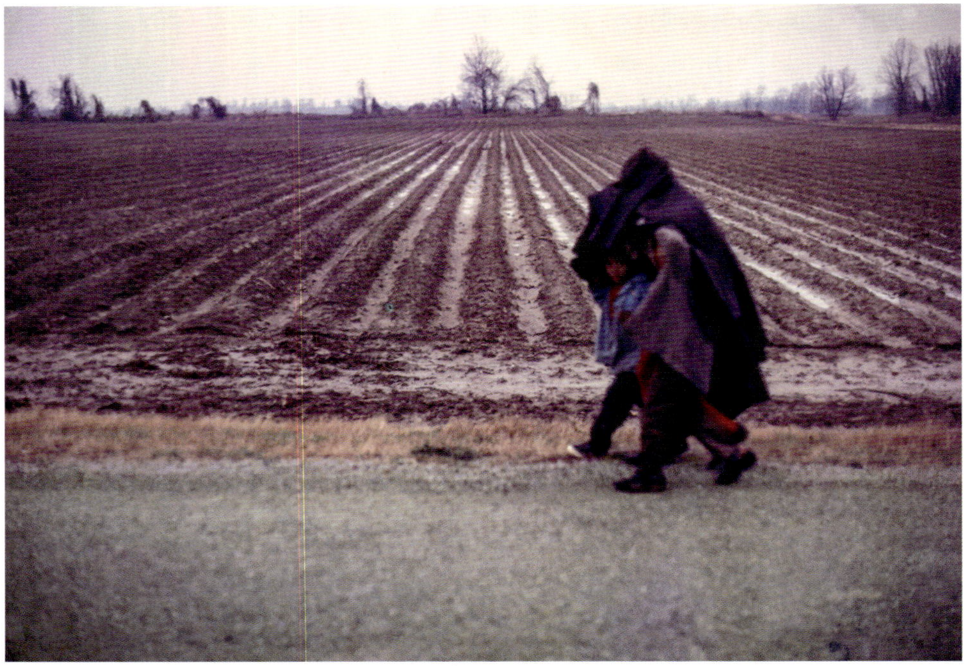

The Delta, outside Clarksdale, winter of 1973.

here. No giant Redwoods or rocky coasts. No awe. Instead the gentle landscape invites you to have a long, slow look at it. Mississippi amasses its details subtly into a lovely whole. Soft hills loop their way north to the Appalachians. It can be stark and somber in winter, but as much beauty is to be found then as at other times of the year. For years I wondered whether it was the stark contrast to the Northeast that so caught my eye. I'm still moved by the look of that land.

The light had a clarity I had only seen at sea. The light in North Mississippi has a unique quality that suffuses the land in the same way that "Dutch Light" bathes paintings of Holland. In most parts of our country people will speak of the "Golden Hour," that warm light that a clear evening brings. In Mississippi there is also a winter light that I can only describe as a luminescent "Pearl Hour." Perhaps it was the clarity of the air, but the light just seemed to give character to everything. The winter colors and light captured me as I tried to capture them. I'm still trying to get it right.

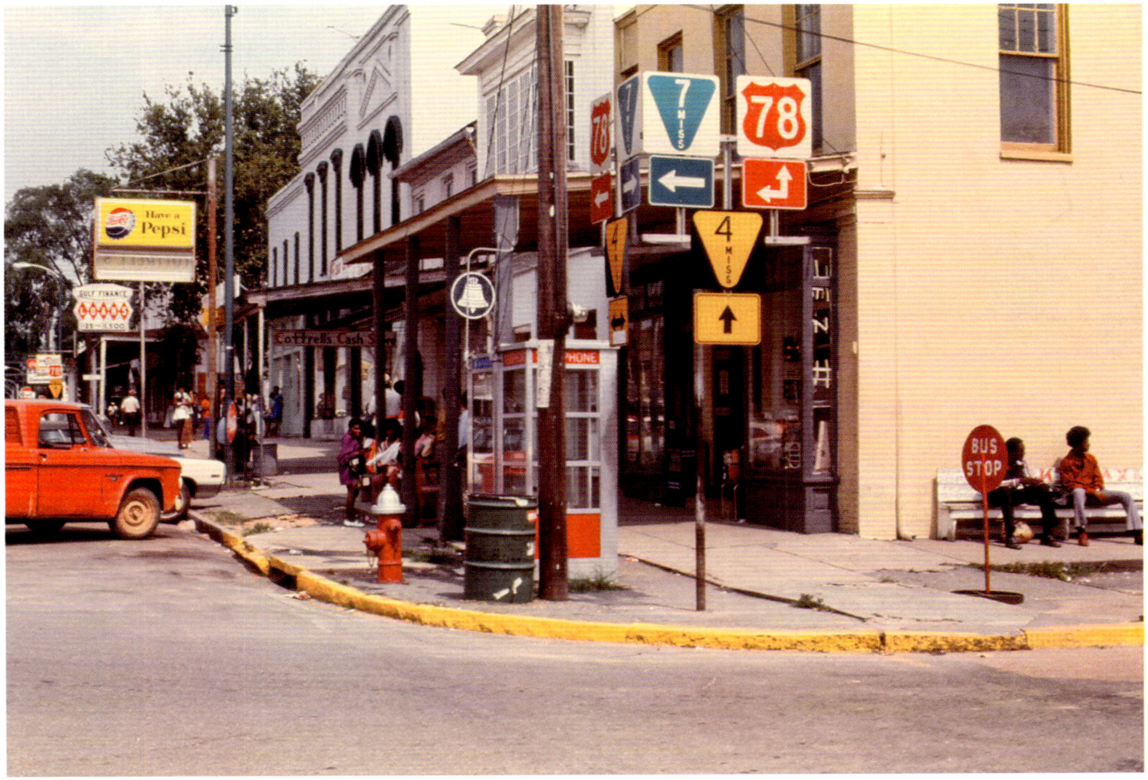

Holly Springs, 1972–75.

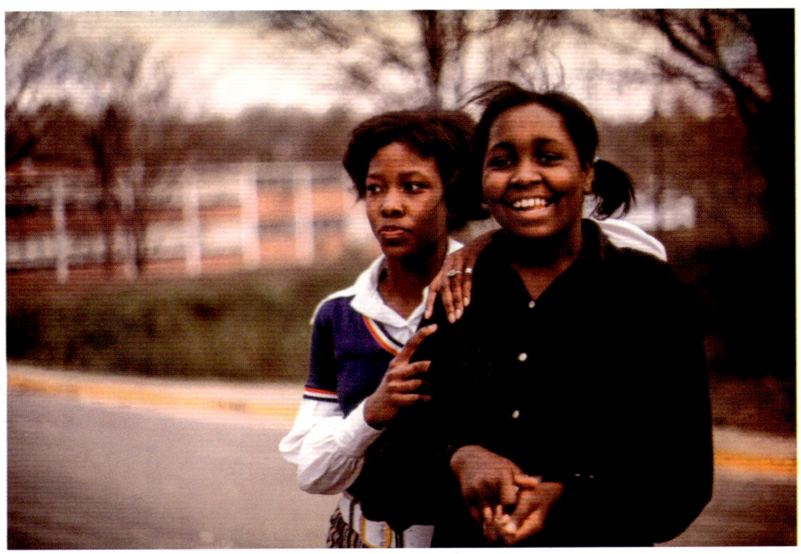

High school students, Oxford, 1972–75.

Slowly, as I grew more comfortable, I started photographing the people I met. Most people, both black and white, were hospitable and seemed glad to meet and talk with strangers. James and I would drive slowly along unpaved country roads looking for a reason to stop. Somebody would wave or I'd see a gesture that meant, "Pull over." Or we'd stop at a store, buy gas, ask directions, and see who wanted to talk. Most everybody did. It was a natural part of life to drop by and sit for a moment with a glass of sweet tea or well water. Almost invariably we'd be invited to "set a spell and have something to eat."

By the nature of our effort we encountered lots of folks and centered on those who were welcoming. They seemed to like us and wanted us to photograph and record what we saw; many times there was an amused tolerance of my efforts to take my pictures. People seemed eager to show and tell the Yankee boys what was going on, and we were often passed on to other people. "You ought to go talk to so-and-so" was a common refrain. I met a lot of people who liked to tell stories and to have new faces to tell them to. Oftentimes we enjoyed each other's company and became friends.

Folks wanted to know who we were, who our people were, and how we fit in. Often, I found that saying I worked for Mr. Hall and lived across the street from Mrs. Kimmons was all I needed to establish acceptance. With such credentials, I had a good chance for an easy give-and-take.

The stills I took served both as a way to absorb the places around me and as a bridge to the people I photographed. We'd poke our noses in here and there, and where we were welcome I'd ask to photograph. Then we'd come back with the photos. It helped us to earn trust.

One day heading west from Holly Springs on Route 4, we stopped for a cold drink at a crossroad halfway to Senatobia, where blues musician Junior Kimbrough's juke joint would be twenty years later. We had a long chat with the owner of the store, who seemed to mean it when he said, "Y'all come back to see us, hear." We did, and so became regulars at Waldrip's General Store in Chulahoma.

Hal Waldrip knew he was running his store on borrowed time, but it helped keep his town alive as a community. The store served as post office, grocery, feed store, clothing shop, community center, informal bank, telephone center, and snack bar. It was a place to meet on a Friday or Saturday night and catch up with friends. It was a place to hear stories.

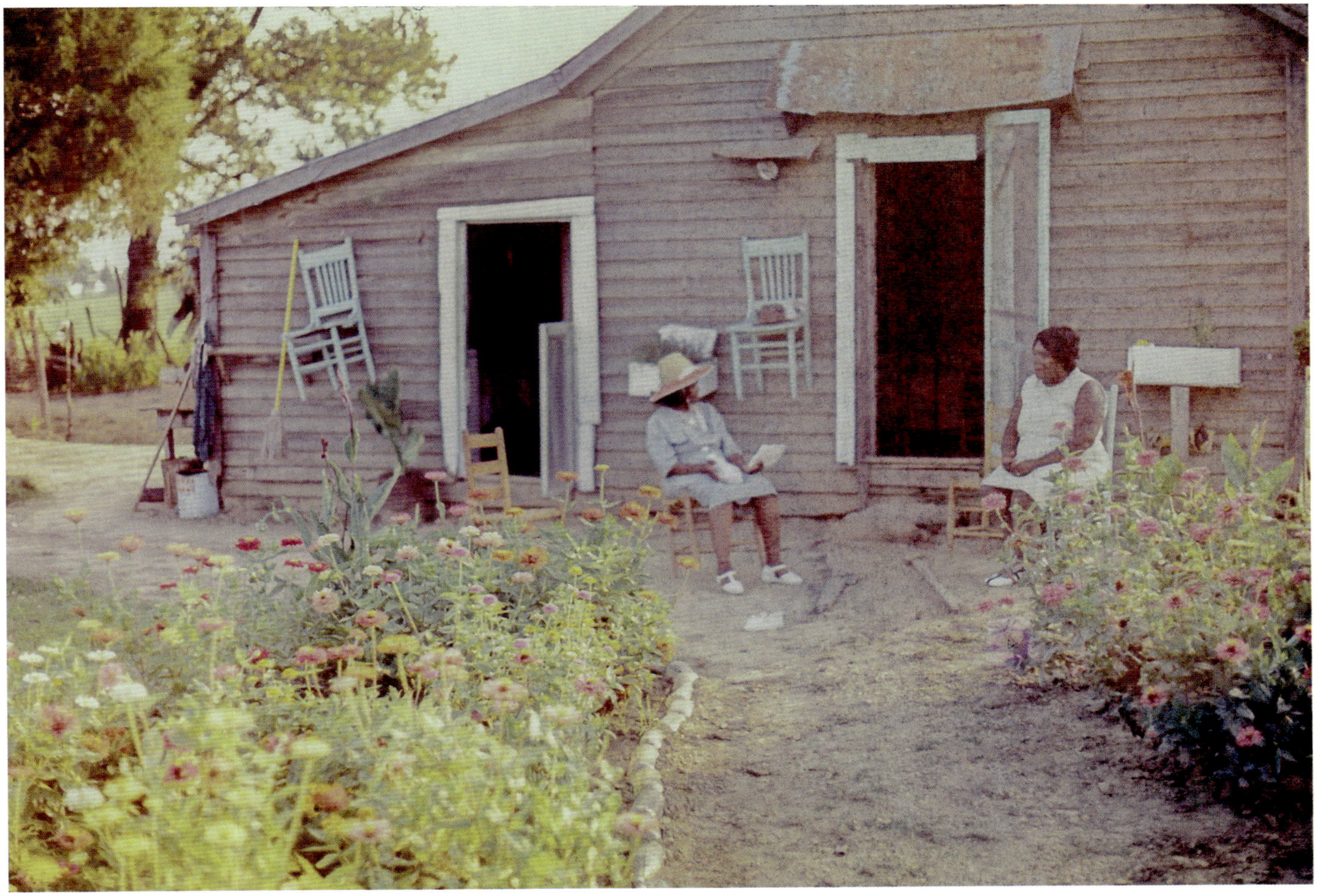

Aubrey Jefferies's homeplace, Chulahoma, 1972–75.

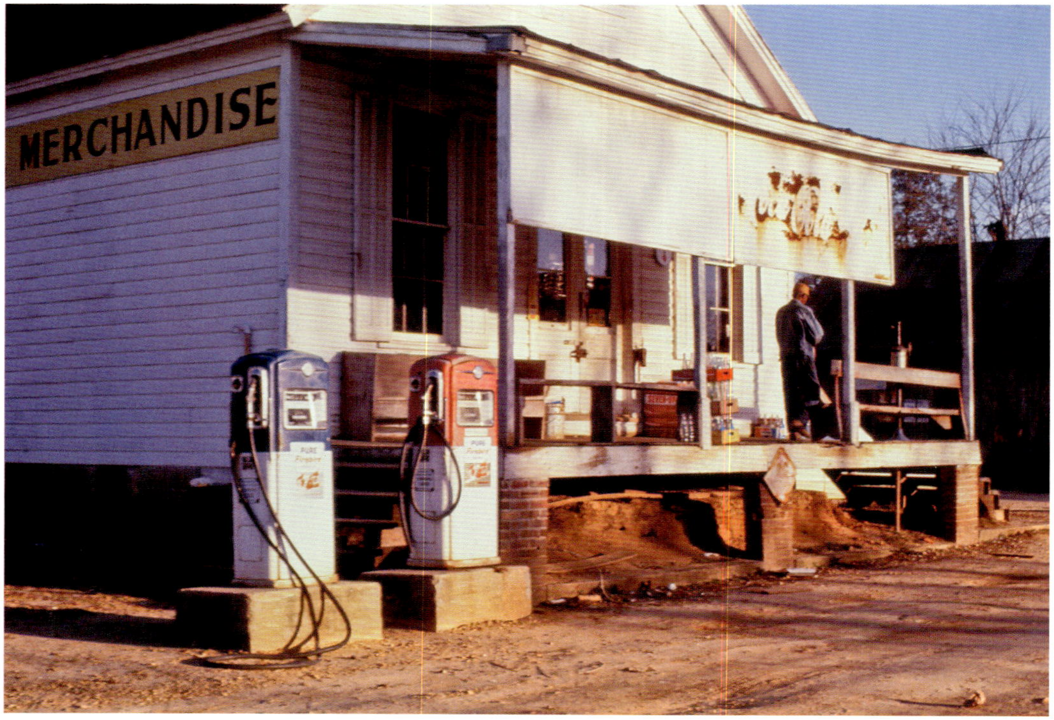

Waldrip's General Store,
Chulahoma, 1972–75.

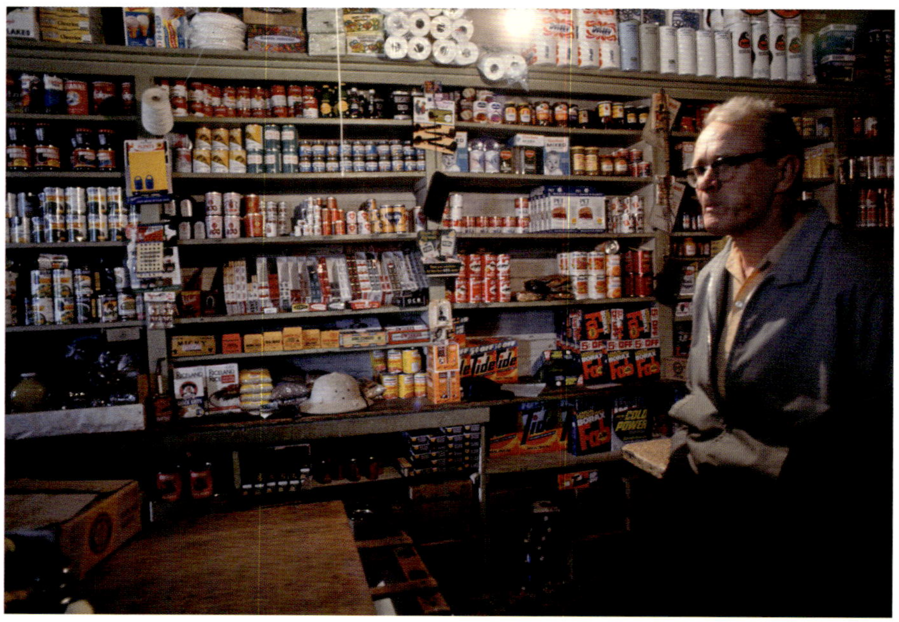

Hal Waldrip, proprietor of
Waldrip's General Store,
Chulahoma, 1972–75.

Hal was an outgoing, thoughtful man. He took me out on an old mare along the ridges at dusk a couple of times to watch night come on. And we talked and talked. I think he was lonely for a certain kind of conversation. One evening he told me that, given the times, he felt he needed to rethink everything he thought he knew. And he did think about things, as I found out some years later.

It took some time to make the connections between people and places. The stills were a form of research. I ran some film tests with the Beaulieu, but shooting sync sound would require renting another camera. I had to hold off until I felt I was seeing the complete story.

A number of things set the hill country apart from the rest of Mississippi. First is the land itself: the red soil is far less fertile than the dark, alluvial earth of the Delta. Cotton was far less important here. The Delta was settled by people migrating west from Georgia and the Carolinas. They brought along their cultures, which included large plantations, grand houses, an "aristocracy," and a lot of slaves. The hill country, by contrast, was settled by Scots-Irish folks coming south out of Kentucky and Tennessee. They tended to be small freeholders who farmed their own land. The old word is yeoman. Slavery was not as widespread in the hills.

When I arrived in the early 1970s, the "furnishing time" was over. That was when a general store or commissary would furnish one's needs for a year against the value of a crop. Tenant farming and sharecropping were other names for that hard life. But it was still part of living memory. People would speak of those times and shake their heads at the recollection. Hal Waldrip told me, "People at that time, when the furnishing time was, they'd sell all their corn in the wintertime 'cause they had to have something to eat. And when spring come, they'd go to buying it back in meal . . . Now talking about poverty . . . that was poverty then. We had it then."

By the early 1970s, abandoned farms and homes were numerous enough that it looked like half the inhabitants had left. The Great Migration of African Americans from the 1910s to the 1970s had drained the population away; a lot of people had left for jobs in the land to the north stretching from Memphis to

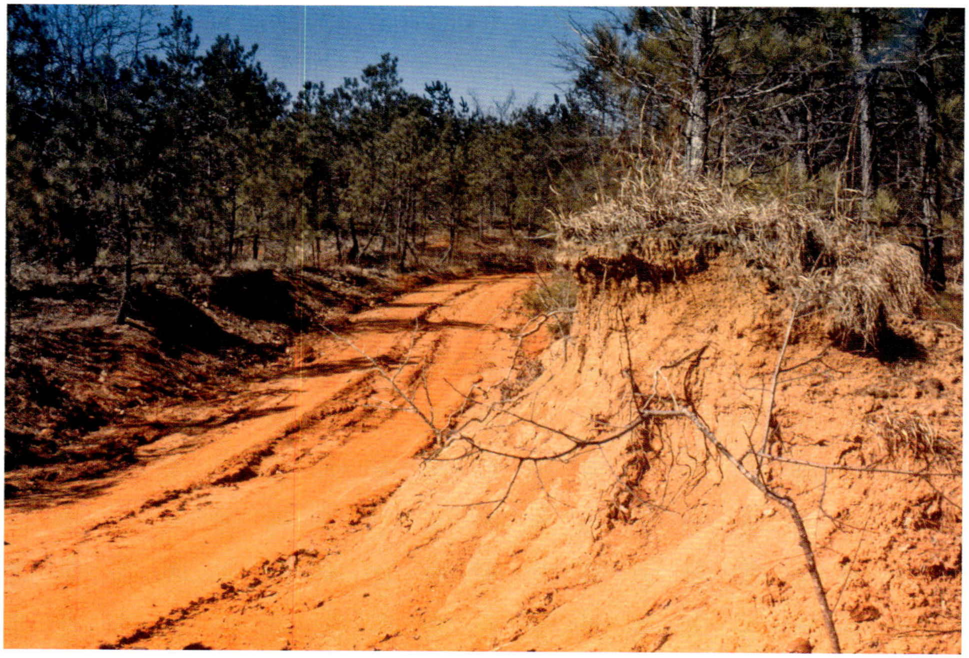

Near Tyro, 1972–73. To me Mississippi means the red clay of the hill country.

Chicago. More than a few grandparents were raising children on small farms while the parents sent home money. Young folks had fled for urban charms and industrial security. What was left seemed to have been dipped in amber—not the type of amber that freezes life but the amber that preserves the past. The older abandoned homes were taken over by kudzu and slowly falling down. Some of the deserted homes seemed like the owner had just stepped away for a moment.

Although few houses were painted, each homeplace had its own character and set of colors. Many times a glance at a dogtrot or shotgun house would tell you a lot about the people it contained. While old and weathered, there was often a neatness and order to the home, a solidity that bespoke volumes of the inhabitants.

Never before had I met people with such deep attachment to the earth they stood on. People often lived in what would now be called compounds. Many times an older log building would sit behind an old frame building or two that

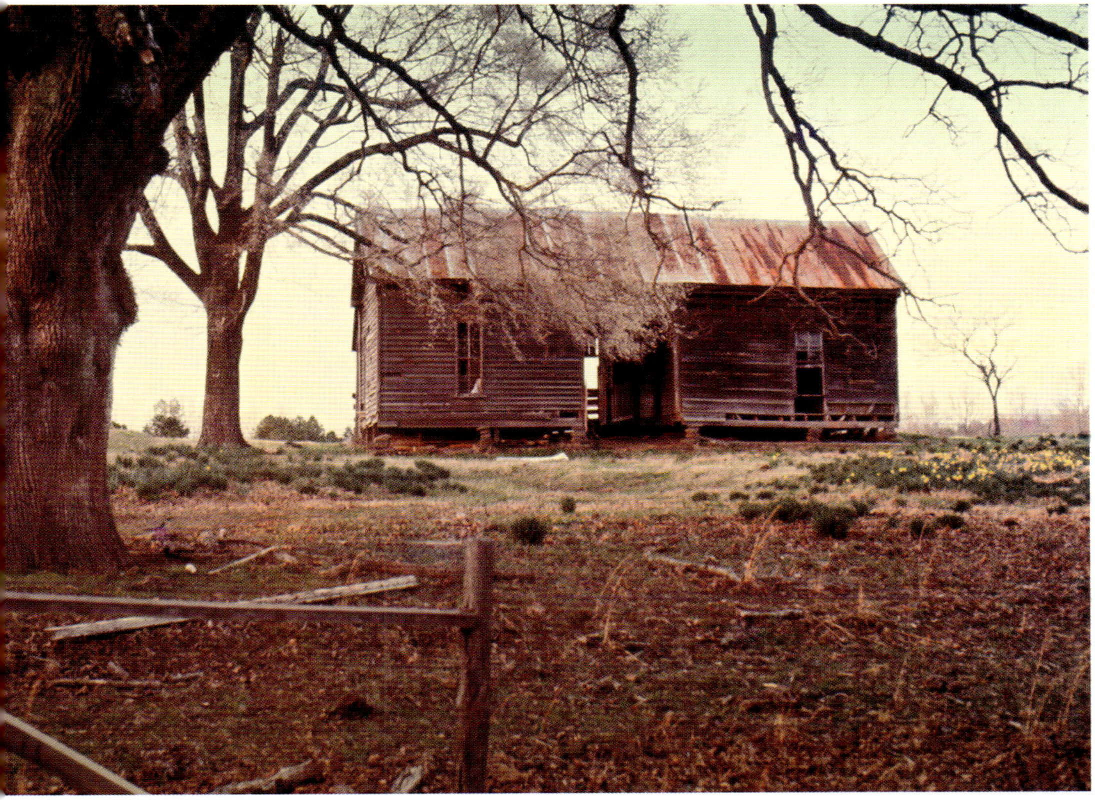

Old dogtrot home,
Lafayette County,
1972–75.

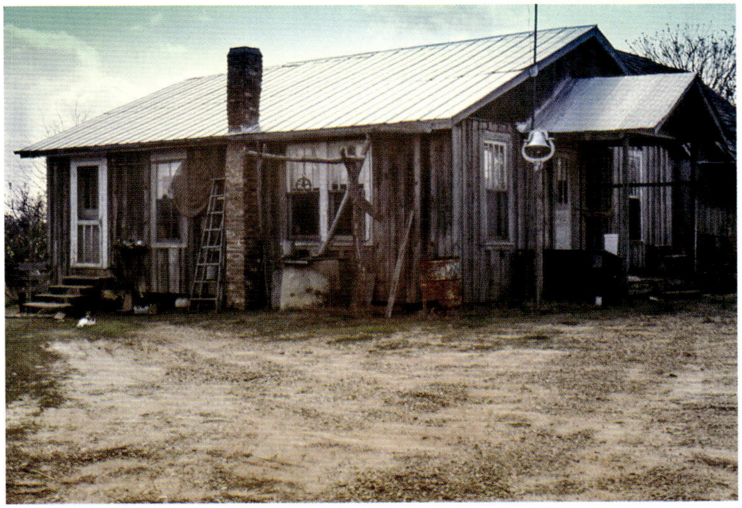

Someone's homeplace,
Marshall County, 1972–75.

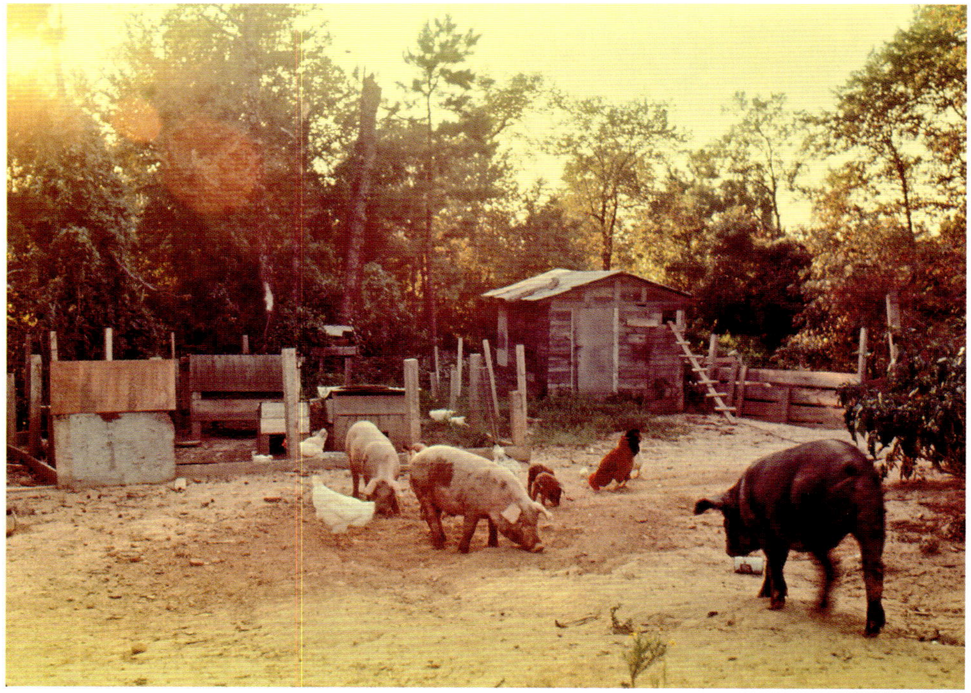

Othar Turner's place, Como, 1972–75.

would in turn stand behind a newer double-wide trailer. Four generations could be living in various homes on the same piece of land.

Almost every home had outbuildings: barns, stables, outhouses, wells, chicken coops, doghouses, and corn cribs. And livestock: chickens, hogs, cows, horses, and a team of mules. For many people, life essentially consisted of "raising a living." They planted and harvested, raised and slaughtered most of what they consumed. Vegetables were "put up" for winter dinners. Any surplus was turned into cash for things like clothing, flour, gasoline, shoes, maybe some candy or soda for the kids. Almost everyone I knew had a small patch of ground, plus a huge garden, chickens for eggs and meat, a pig or two. I learned to respect the small farmer and the amazing skills it took to make a crop. If you weren't any good, your family went hungry.

Fixing things was an integral part of rural life. Tools were everywhere and used often. Repairs were sometimes quite inventive. Fences, roofs, farm equipment, and trucks were all maintained one way or another. Only after trying and failing would things be taken to someone like Mr. Hall for repair. The houses were usually old and always made of wood—sometimes of hand-hewn logs, more often of frame construction. That didn't mean the houses were wrecks. A lot of good lumber, with which one could make repairs or build additions, was to be had from abandoned buildings. The tools and skills were close at hand. No cash needed.

Most places had a well for water, which might operate with a three- or four-foot-high pump using a big handle or a crank. Sometimes, though rarely, a smaller hand pump was installed in the kitchen. Most water was obtained with a bucket and a rope. Electric pumps and water tanks for indoor plumbing were

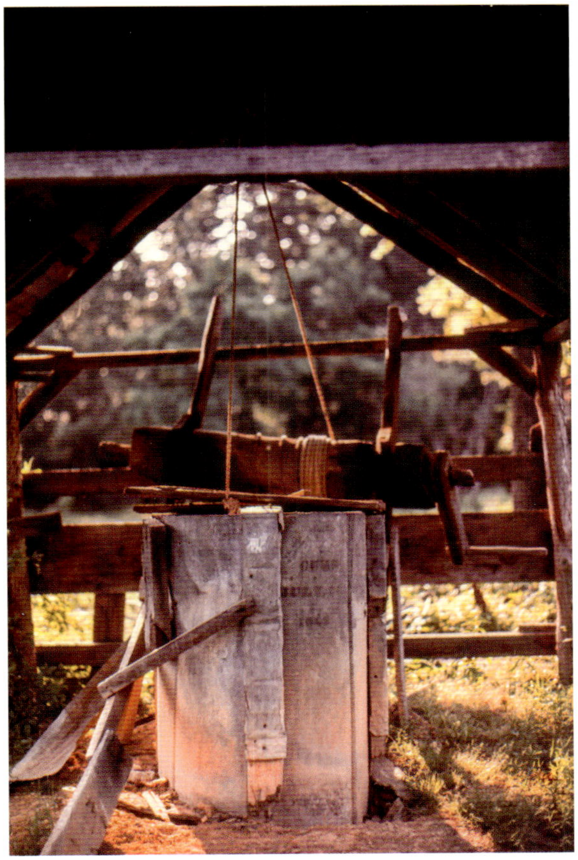

A typical well, Marshall County, 1972–75.

just becoming available. Generally there was an outhouse, and in summer the kitchen stove and its heat were carried outdoors.

Almost all places were hooked up with electricity, and there was sure to be a radio and a black-and-white TV. The larger world came into these homes. A lot of porches had a wringer washer and/or refrigerator sitting on them, next to a row of chairs facing a dirt road.

In Mississippi—indeed, in rural America—you learn how deeply connected everyone is to everyone else. There are few long-term strangers. After a while I learned to see some of the connections. Hal Waldrip had the general store in Chulahoma. Doc James traded at Hal's store. It was where he sold his sweet sorghum molasses. Doc hired AG Newson to cook his sorghum crop into that molasses. AG Newson was one of the few cooks left in the area, and he brought his evaporating pan to Mr. Hall to be patched up. I helped Mr. Hall solder the pinholes in it and overhaul the frame. So when AG picked up the pan to make the crop, he knew me. He invited me along to his molasses cook not because I was a filmmaker but because he knew that if I worked for Mr. Hall, I had to be all right.

The cook was on a fine October day in 1972 in a bottom near Tyro. There were six men, a couple of kids, two dogs, and Doc's mules, Frank and Jake.

The one chair was reserved for AG since he was the crew boss and his job was the toughest. He set up the operation. He found the right place for the pan and mill, then dug a trench in the earth and set the pan over it. Wood was gathered and the chimney erected in place.

The process seemed simple: cut the cane, crush it for the juice, and boil it down to molasses in an evaporating pan. Add the heat of the day and the humidity of the rich bottomland, however, and the task was a whole lot rougher. The mill needed constant feeding. The pan needed juice. The heat of the fire was staggering, and it had to be constantly stoked. The mules knew what to do. Their human coworkers cleared the "pommens," as the crushed cane is called, and moved sloshing tin tubs to a holding barrel. The juice was filtered through cloth before being ladled into AG's pan.

The pan was a labyrinth of channels containing the juice in its transmutation to a rich brown syrup. The flow was controlled by bundles of cloth

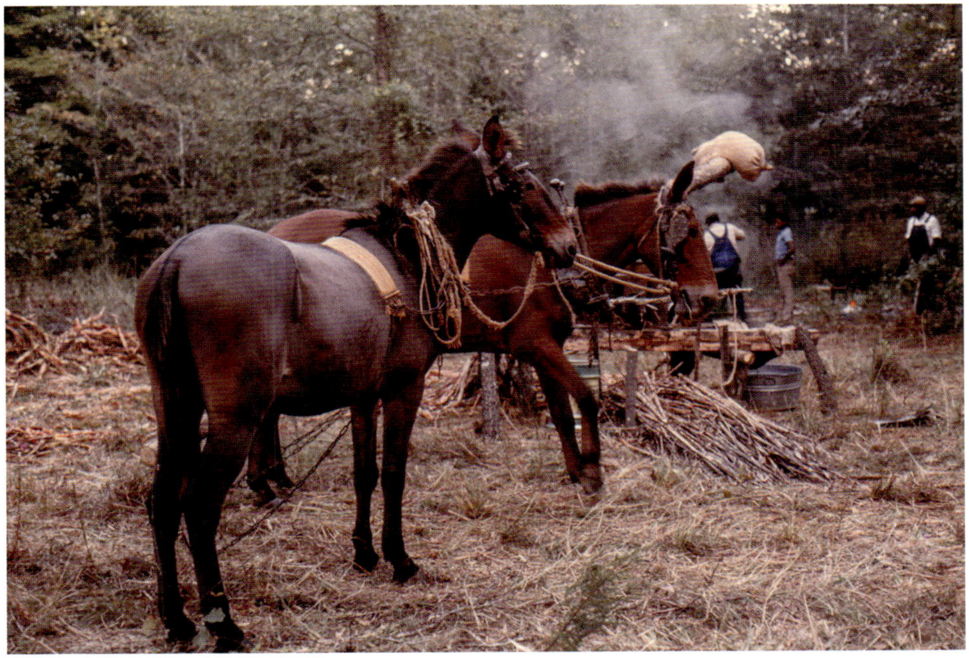

Frank and Jake making Doc James's molasses crop, Chulahoma, October 1972.

acting as valves. Finally the syrup was filtered through a box of washed river stones into an iron kettle dug into the earth. AG set the pace and controlled the rhythm. If a backup occurred, a simple command from Doc to Frank and Jake stopped things real quick.

Although the air was thick with delirious bees, no one was stung, neither mule nor man. The mill beam groaned slightly as the mules pulled it around. The crushed cane was spread to keep the mules from wearing a rut in the earth, and the air was filled with the smell of the ground and the cane, wood smoke and mule sweat. Among the sounds was the jangle of the mules' harness, the trickle of the juice falling into the tub, the songs of the mockingbirds, the crackle of the fire, and the gentle banter of old friends.

Lunch came, carried by Mae Liza, Doc's wife, in big tin basins covered with cloth. Mounds of perfect fried chicken, homemade potato salad, greens, and biscuits. Cold water, sweet tea, and sodas were the libations.

AG stoked the fire and kept it burning evenly, while he skimmed bits of cane.

Each of us worked at our trades—AG and his crew crushing cane, toting juice, and boiling it down to molasses; I moving from still to film camera and back a dozen times. Finally the shadows lengthened, and it was time to be done. We all packed up our tools. Doc James left with about two hundred gallons of molasses. I left with memories I could share with someone else.

I knew there was another face to Mississippi that I didn't ever see, maybe because I wasn't looking. I knew the racial history. Part of me was on guard for a good while, but that faded. There must have been hard faces, but we never grew to know them. Of course, those faces can be anywhere you go.

What I did see was a set of mediums older than money. Family, church, friendship, working the land, and seasons made community a living thing.

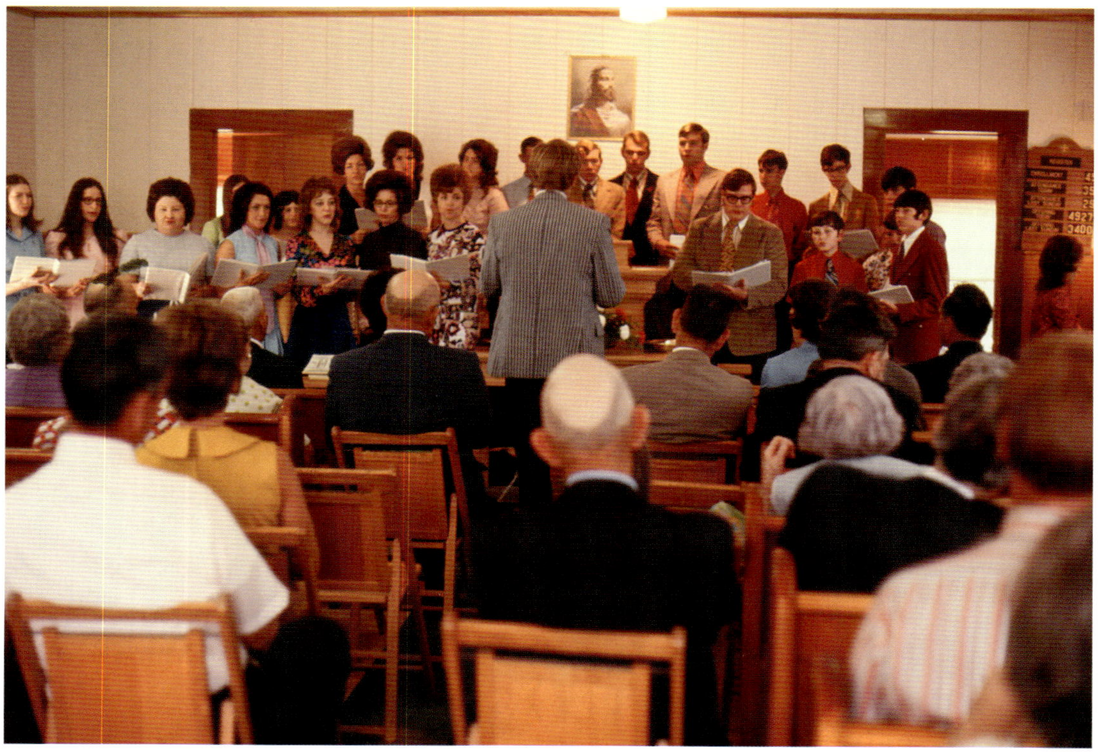

Cambridge Methodist Church, Oxford, 1972–75.

It was a very tough, and often unfair, life. But there was a self-reliant confidence and a dignity that you don't see as much of anymore. People could, and did, take care of themselves. That included taking care of friends and neighbors when needed. People could, and did, count on each other. Old-fashioned, real hospitality. Folks died in their own beds.

Who were these people? I can use a bunch of words like honest, friendly, self-sufficient, solid, dignified, and on and on. But it was how they carried themselves that made me respect them. That's what I tried to capture.

Music is a deep tradition around Como. This is the birthplace of the bottleneck blues. Mississippi Fred McDowell, Sid and Jessie Mae Hemphill, Napoleon Strickland, and Othar Turner all came from this dot in the North Mississippi hills. In 1942 Alan Lomax made the first recordings of fife-and-drum bands here. This music's roots reach back centuries to musicians playing in state militia units during the Revolutionary War. African Americans and Native Americans were recruited as band members to free up white men who could carry a rifle. These sounds became the work-gang field marches of the nineteenth century.

If you lived in rural America in the twentieth century, you existed within the community of your neighbors. All communities had their way of strengthening bonds: churches, revivals, county fairs, planting and harvest fests, funerals. In Como, it was the picnic, and it wasn't a picnic without drums. As Othar Turner explained, "You ain't got no drums, you ain't got no picnic."

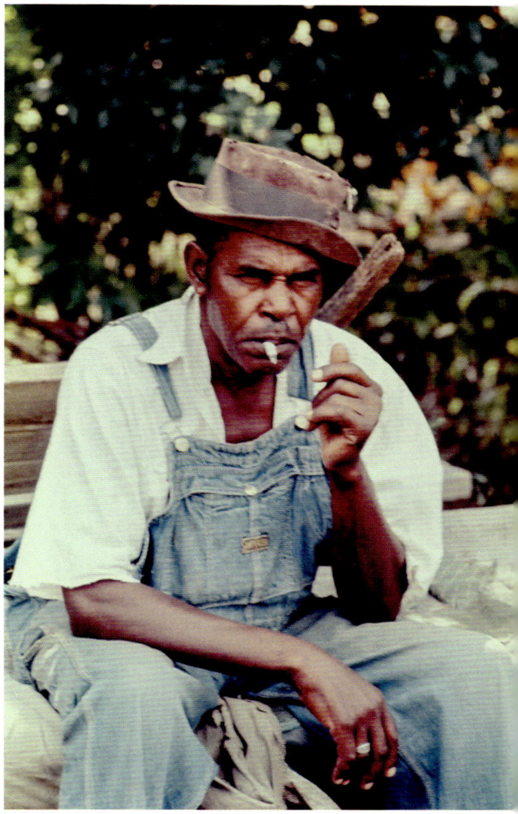

Othar Turner, Como, 1972–75.

I met Othar in Gravel Springs, which is near Como, through Napoleon Strickland, his friend and fellow musician. Othar was a fife player, impresario, and raconteur. But first and foremost he was a farmer. He made sure to balance his hard work with a good time among friends.

The picnic season ran from Memorial Day through early September. Othar's multiple-day events were the best. Friday night was the barbeque, when the meat was cooked for Saturday's picnic. Saturday was the big event. Tradition called for the festivities to end at midnight sharp with a spiritual before the Sabbath arrived.

In the militias the drums would signal strict marching maneuvers and tempos. At Othar's picnic they beat a shifting polyrhythm, as marchers dipped and swayed. As night fell, the fife wailed in the shadows. People who lived a very hard and strenuous life found a short moment to be lost within.

After about six months of traveling, talking, and photographing, time came for the motion picture cameras. I could shoot only silent film in the Beaulieu and had to spend sparse money to rent a sound camera. MPL was kind enough to rent me an Éclair ACL sound camera and a Nagra sync tape recorder from noon on Friday to be returned by noon on Monday for a one-day rental fee. I was able to do that five times.

The locations to shoot were obvious by then. The dark recesses of Mr. Hall's forge, of course. The general store in Chulahoma and its cast of characters lead by the store's owner, Hal Waldrip. The bottomland on a warm autumn day with molasses cooking in a pan I'd helped repair. The farm Othar Turner worked, where we would catch an a cappella moment as he plowed his crop. A picnic on the ridge behind his house, shot in the fading light of evening. I had so few opportunities to shoot sync sound that I'd be worrying, watching the weather, checking the bus, loading camera spools days and days before we'd actually do something. I remember thinking that someday someone was going to pay me to do this stuff. It turned out I was right.

Over the course of the next three years I spent as much free time and money as I could to finish the picture edit and sound mix. The process was to make some money at an odd job, then rent the gear and facilities needed to work on the film. It took a lot of time. Finally I cut the A-B rolls and sent off everything for my first answer print.

On Christmas Eve 1975 I grabbed a projector, a sheet, an extension cord, and my brand-new first answer print of *Homeplace* and headed to Waldrip's General Store.

I got up to the store in the early afternoon and announced the film's evening showing. By seven the place was packed. We strung the sheet across the aisle midway down the building, so half the people had to watch it backward. No one cared. Lights went down. Music came up. It was showtime. There was a lot of excitement—laughs and comments. The buzz increased as Chulahoma came on the screen. On the big white sheet a local named Roman came into view.

Sometimes there's a story inside a story you don't even know is there when you're telling it. In those days, when we shot 16mm film, the sound of a whirring camera was the sound of dollars flying away. We had to set up scenes to shoot we hoped were true to life. Wireless mics were yet to be invented; we used a shotgun mic and hoped for the best. We set up a scene with Hal and Roman Jones, a cordial man with a sense of fun. I liked him, and he wanted a role in the movie. I explained what we'd do. Roman would enter the store and buy something. OK. Buy what? Anything. Improv.

So Roman walked into the scene . . .

HAL WALDRIP: "Hi there, Roman."
ROMAN: "Pretty good. How are you doing?"
HAL: "Roman, what I do for you?"
ROMAN: "[I] guess I want a piece of bologna, I guess."
HAL (cuts a slab): "And what do you want to drink?"
ROMAN: "I think I want to drink a Pepsi drink."
HAL (walks to cooler): "Where you been all week? I ain't seen you much."
ROMAN: "Well, I've been up on the lake."

An old step stool is in the way, and Roman moves it behind him while Hal goes for the Pepsi. Walking back, Hal is turned away from the mic and says something softly. It's garbled.

HAL: "[Garbled] . . . I hope you enjoy that."
ROMAN (reaches back, pulls the step stool up, and sits down): "I hope so myself."

The place went nuts at this point. I didn't know why.

Later I found out that Hal's garbled words were "sit down," and that was the first time a black man had sat at the counter to eat. When Hal thought about his store being recorded for posterity, he decided it was going to be a place where a person was welcome to sit down. He had rethought.

Homeplace won awards at a few film festivals, and some prints were sold. It was broadcast as far away as Sweden. Mississippi ETV aired it. I went on to make a career in filmmaking, eventually landing in Washington, D.C. Throughout my career, the process has remained much the same as in

Mississippi: go off to shoot something not knowing exactly what it will be till you're done. You've really got to trust your instincts and have a good serendipity generator. When it works, it is very satisfying.

One of the things I feel about the Mississippi photos is that they are simple. They're about the land—and about the people living their lives as best they can in the circumstances they are in. I was there in a rural America that was at its end.

In the four short years I lived there, I could see the changes coming to Oxford. In late 1972 Oxford went from dry to wet. (For warm beer, that is. Cold beer wouldn't be sold openly for another four decades.) Repealing local prohibition laws seemed a major advance into the modern world. Meanwhile, the first "foreign" restaurant started when a Chinese grad student brought his mother from Hong Kong to cook in their instantly successful closet-sized operation.

Kroger, a chain supermarket, in Oxford's first shopping mall encroached on the Jitney Jungle, introducing liverwurst, pretzels, and bagels, albeit of the frozen variety. Mechanization of agriculture pushed people off the land. There was a wave of immigrants from the North fleeing winter and rust.

The year 1972 feels so, so long ago. In one sense it's a mere four decades, and in another it's a world away, almost as if it never existed. But even though all the homeplaces and people are gone, we can still call their names.

Photographs, 1972–1975

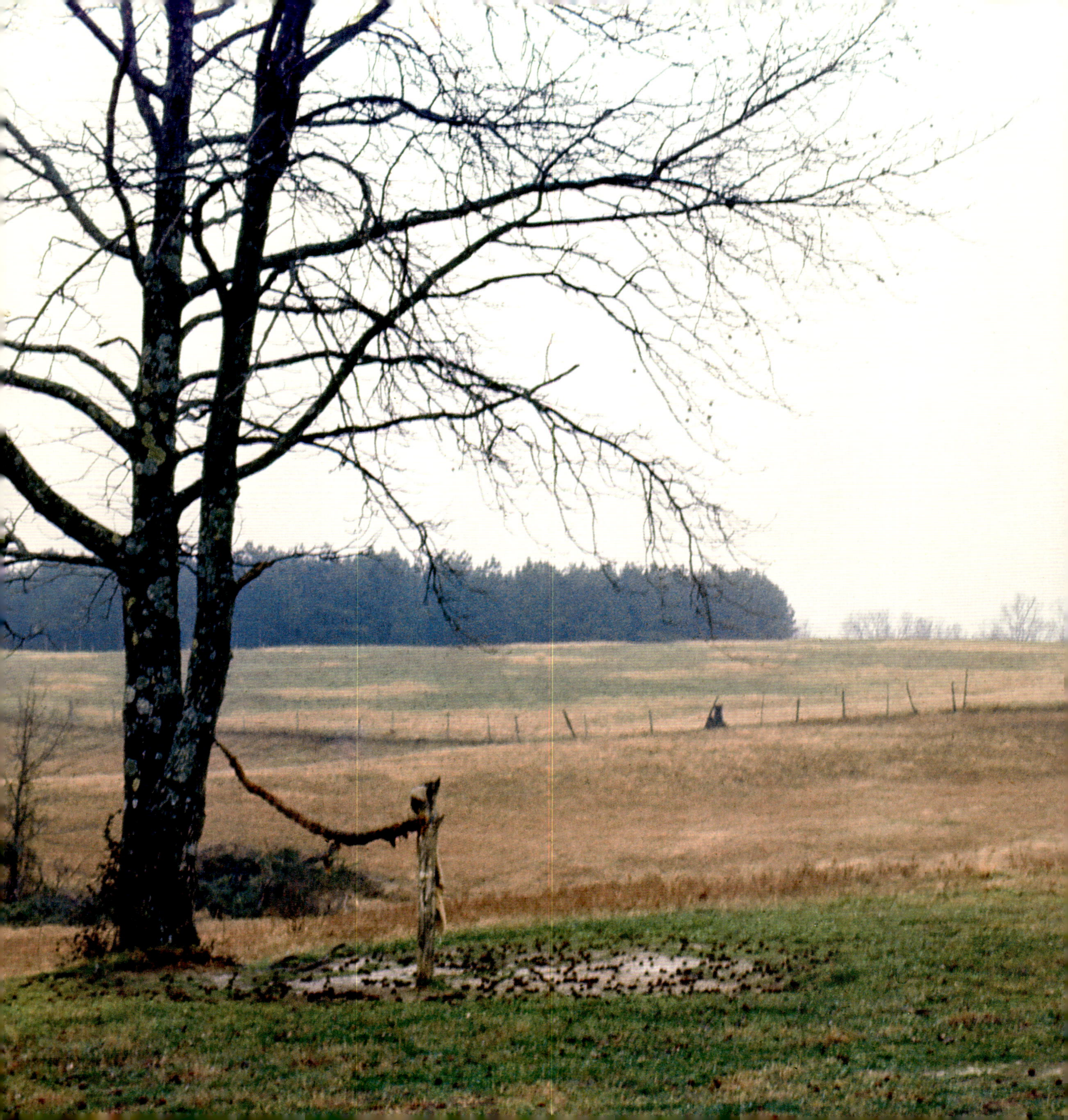

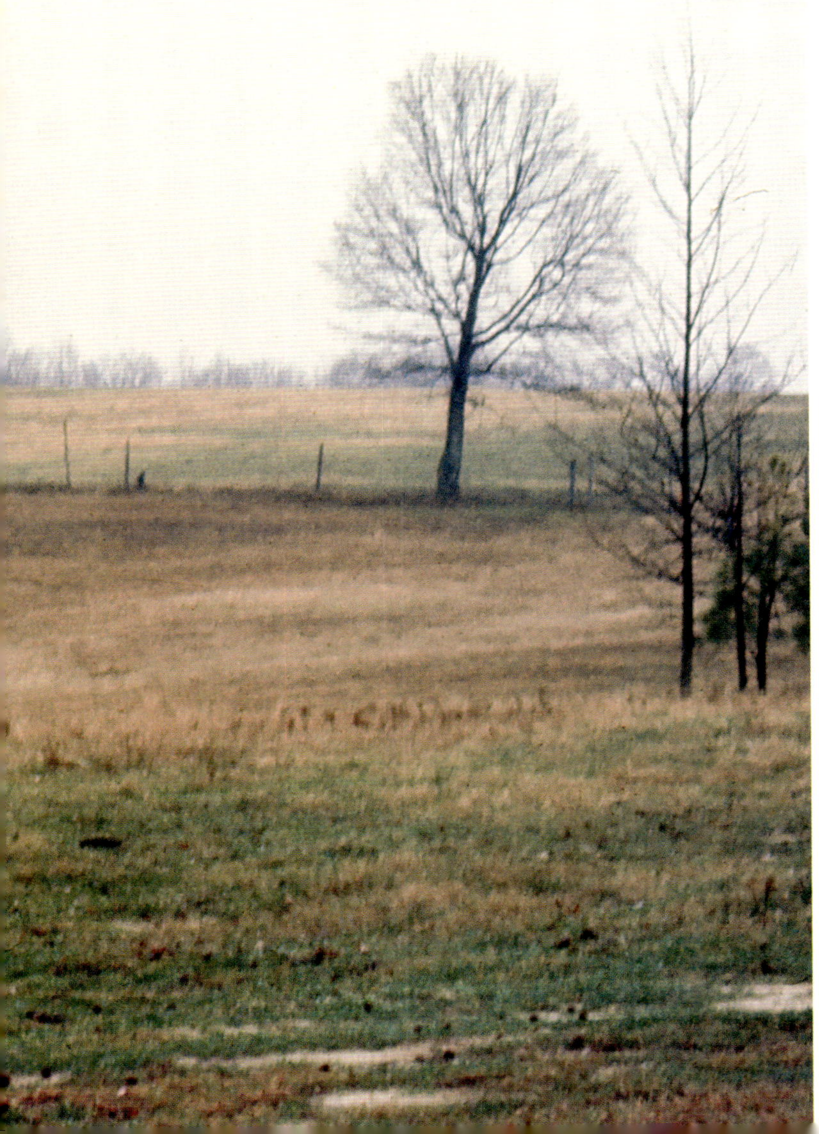

Winter landscape with cattle oiler, Lafayette County, 1972–75. I was attracted to these winter colors and the soft curves of the hill country, so easy on the eye. The cattle oiler hooked to the tree provided a topical treatment for parasites and a well-worn place for cows to gossip.

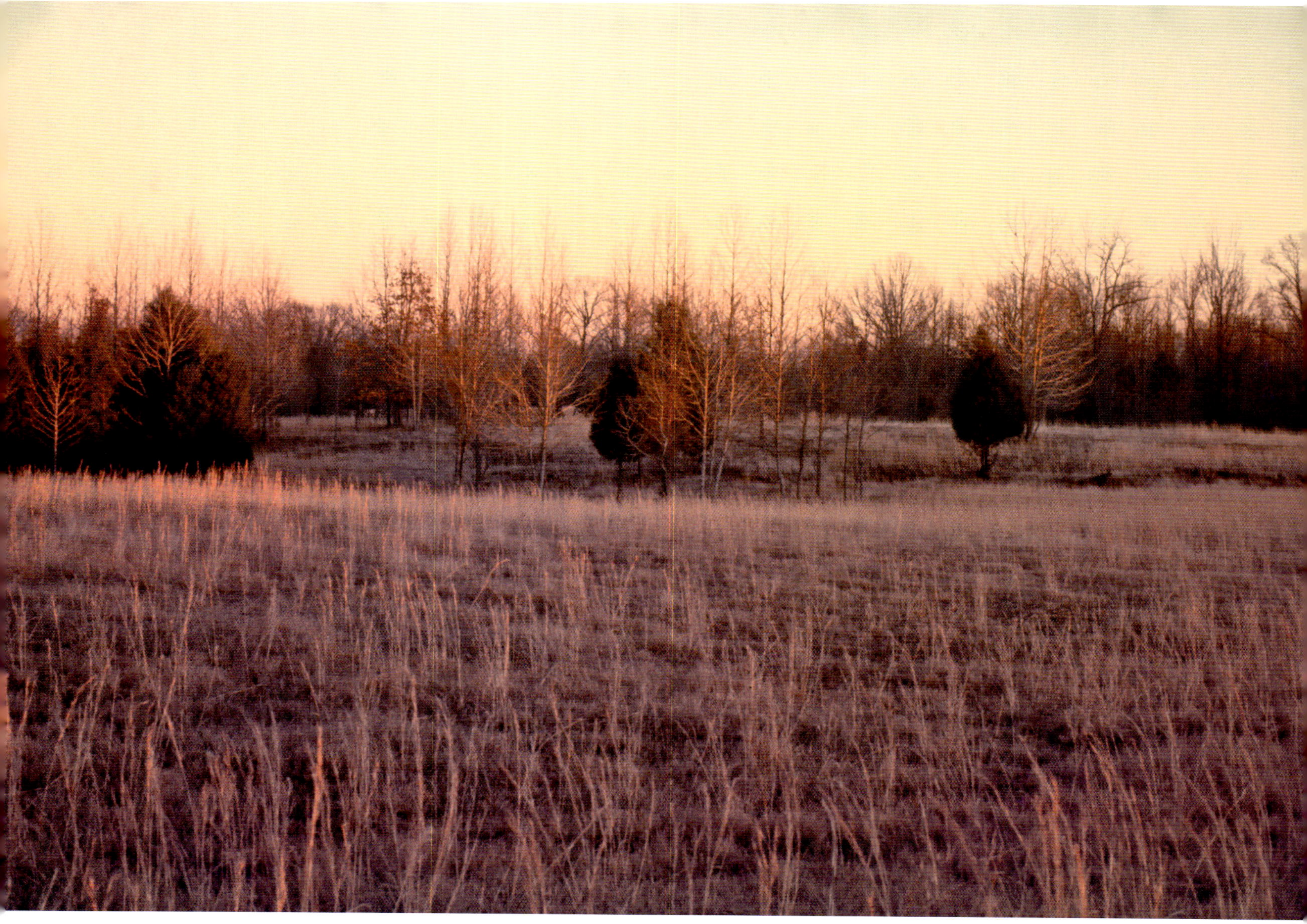

Winter pearl hour, Lafayette County, 1972–75. The quality of the light, the soft colors, and the gentle contours of the land still enthrall me.

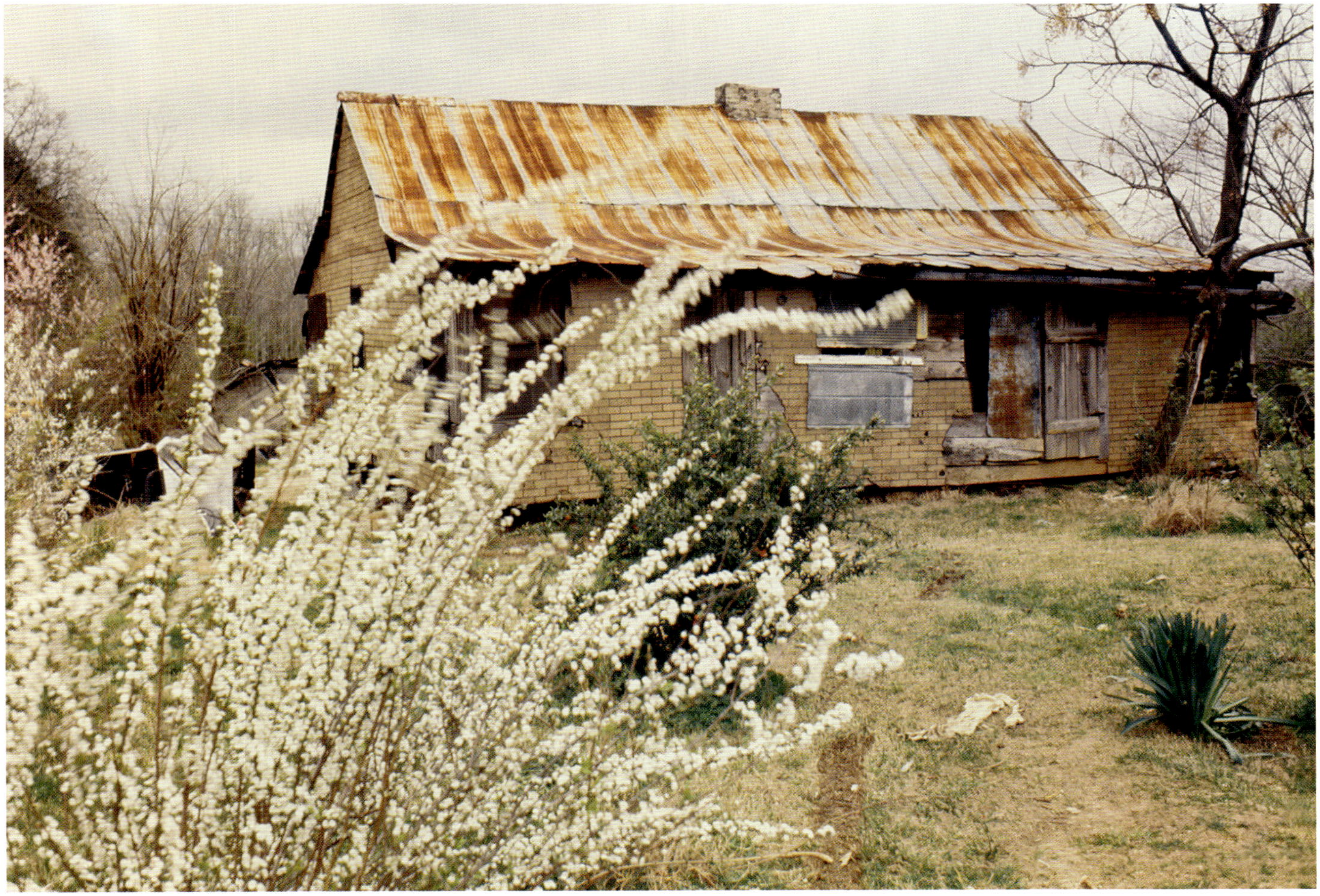

Spring in Holly Springs National Forest, Holly Springs, 1972–75.

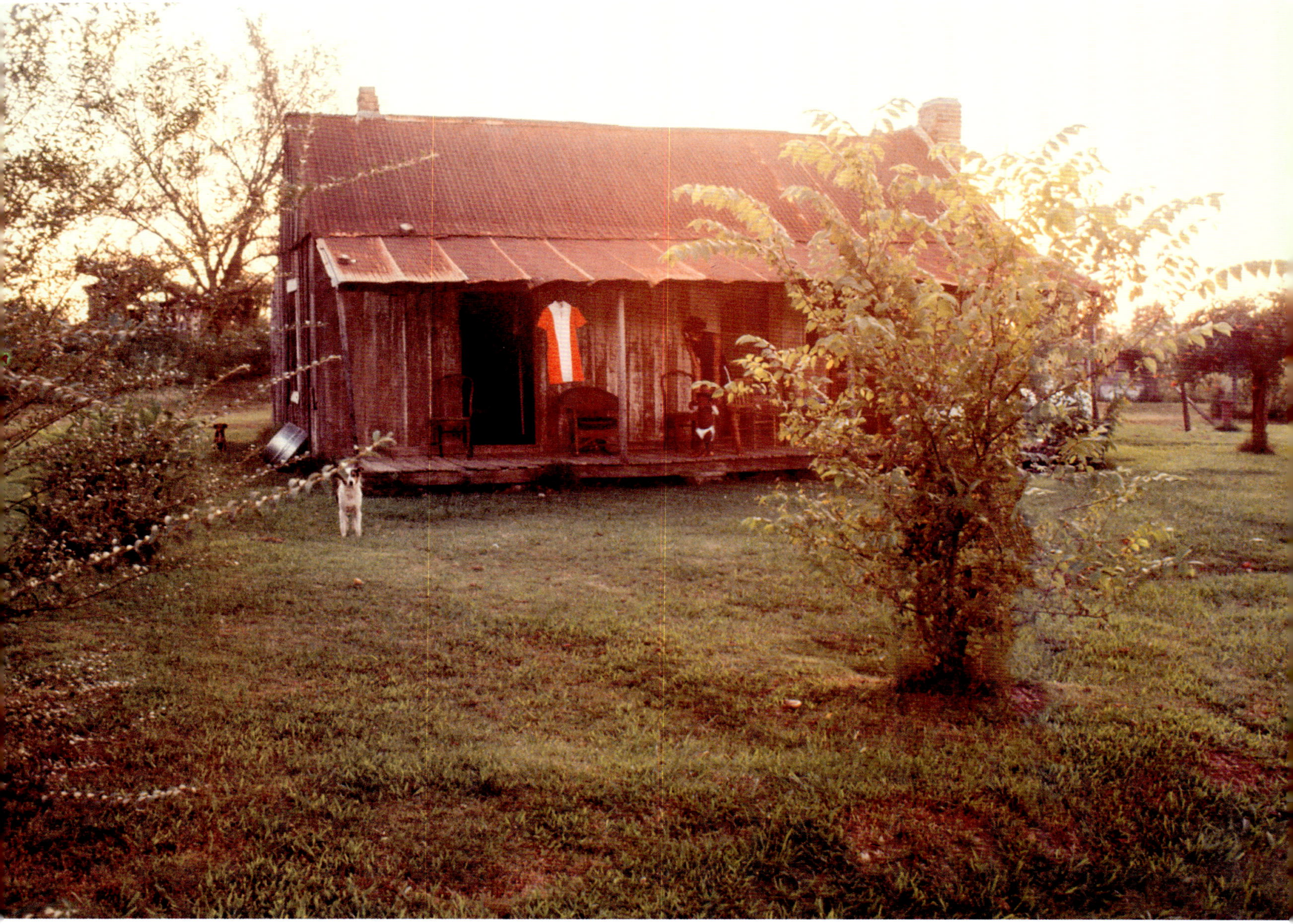

Red dress home, out on Route 310, north of Sardis, 1972–75.
The flash of the red dress hanging on the front porch first caught my eye. When I approached the house, the dogs came out and barked a welcome. A baby toddled out on the porch. I pressed the shutter.

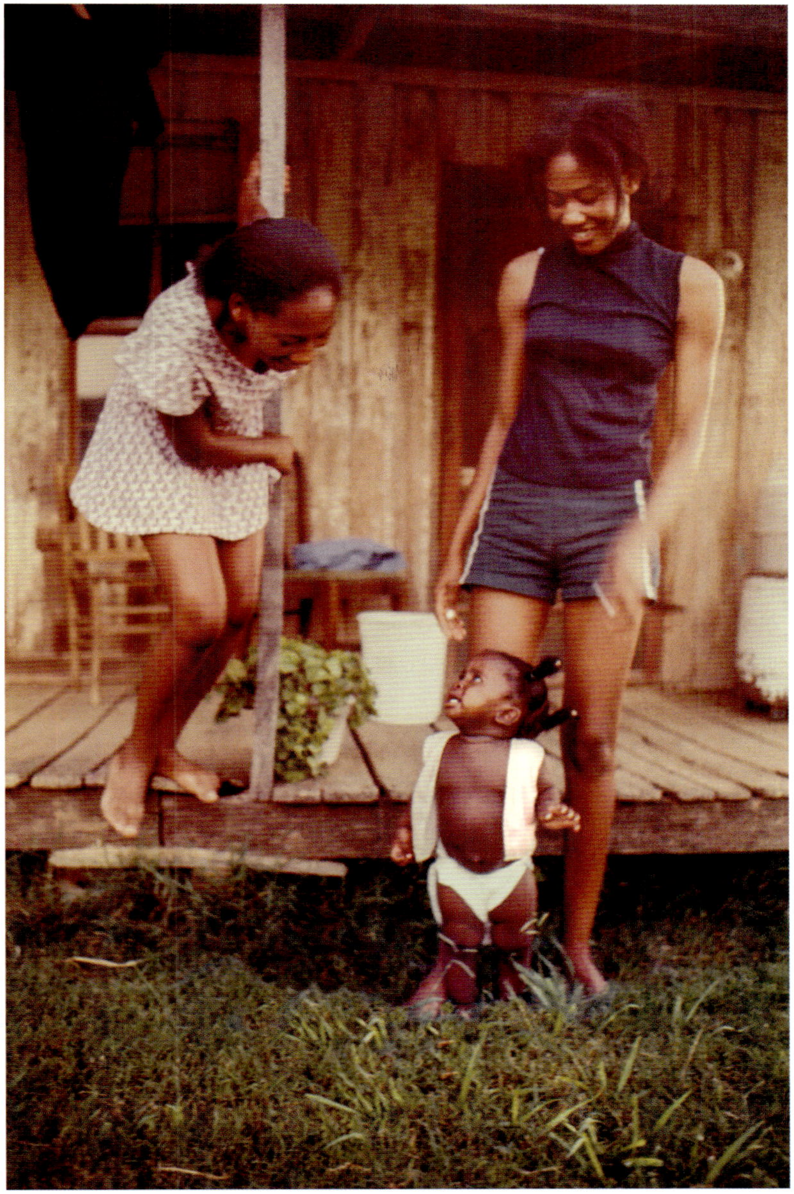

Porch of the red dress home, two ladies and a baby, out on Route 310, north of Sardis, 1972–1975.

Bottle and roots, texture and shape,
Holly Springs National Forest, Holly Springs, 1972–75. The view below the ground fascinated me.

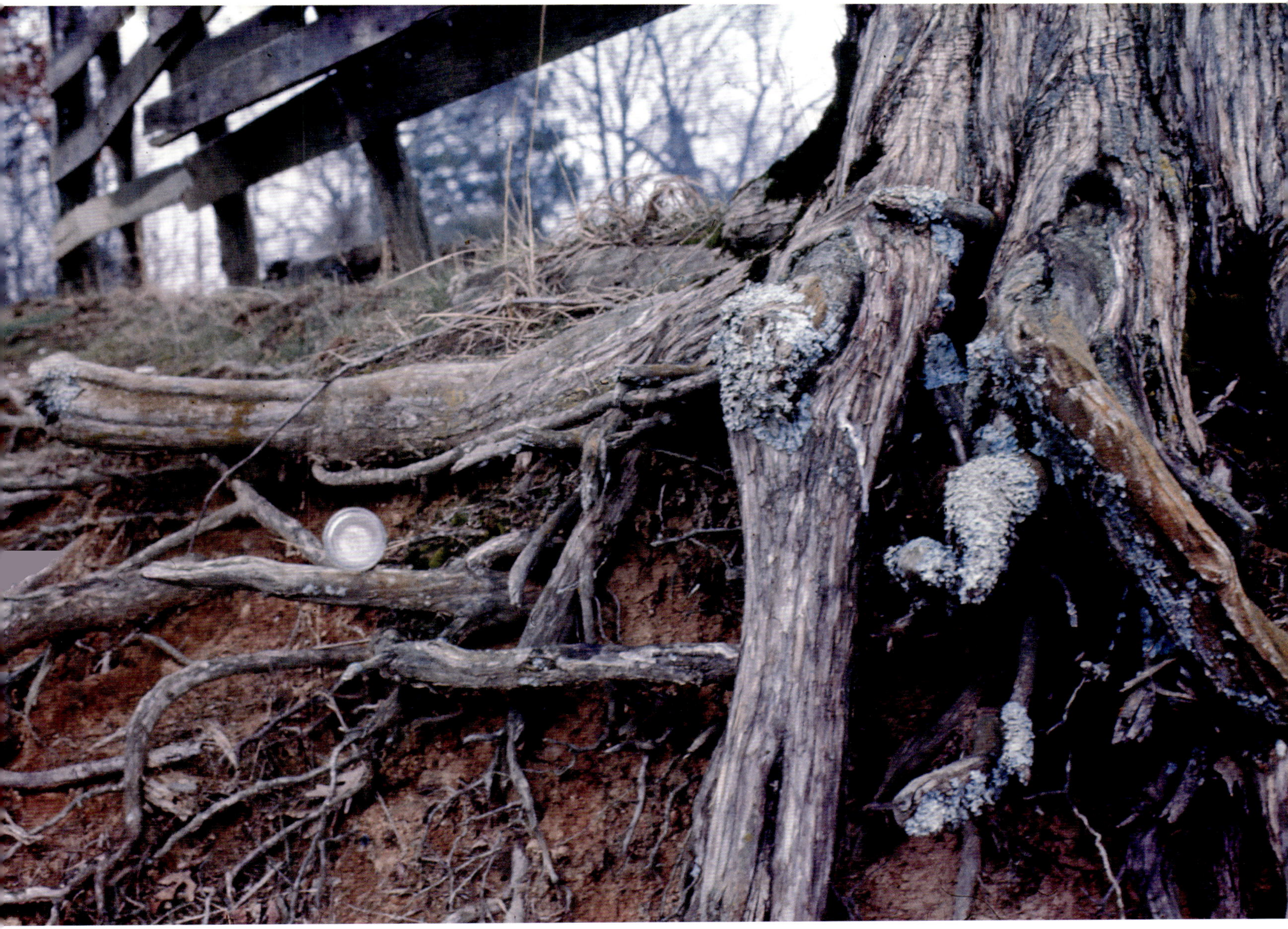

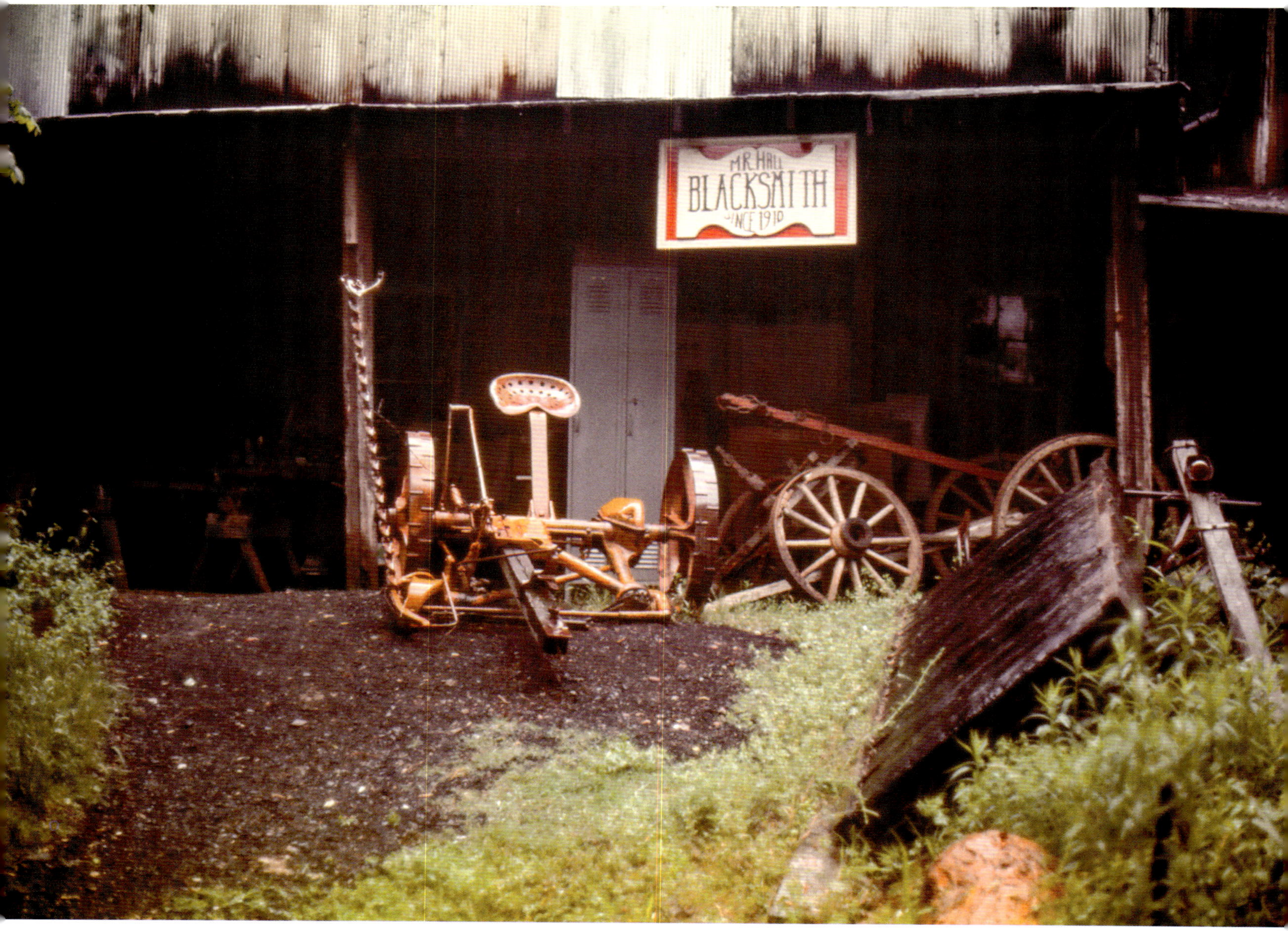

Exterior of Mr. Hall's shop, Oxford, 1972. AG Newson's molasses pan is lying on the right, waiting to be repaired.

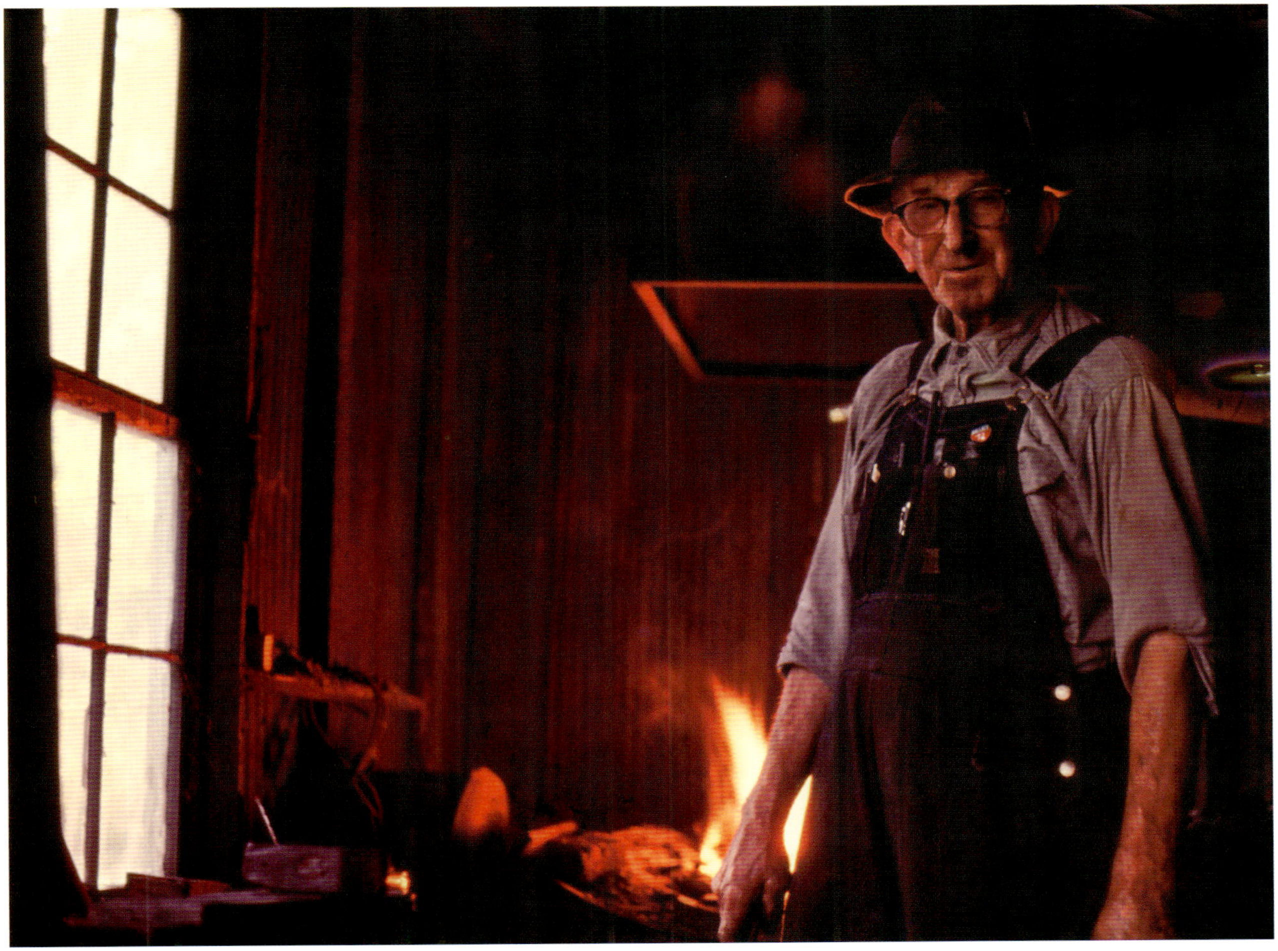

Mr. Hall at his forge, Oxford, 1972–75. Mr. Hall, age eighty-four, told me, “Well I never wanted to do a thing but blacksmith. That’s all I wanted to do. Daddy had a little blacksmith shop . . . I was a little old bitty thing . . . and he’d go up and leave me and I couldn’t stay away from the shop . . . I wanted out there, hammering on something . . . making a little something like that, you know . . . always wanting to make something.”

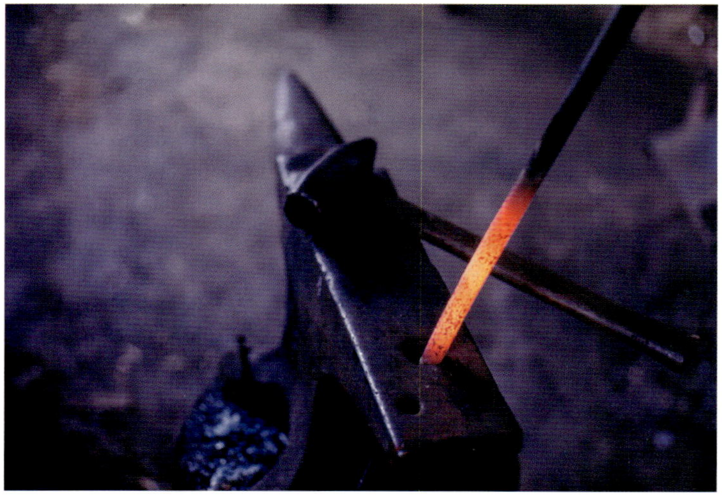

Ready for bending, Oxford, 1972–75. The color of hot steel tells you its temperature. The orange in the center of the bar is about 1800°F (982°C) and cools through cherry red to blood red, then ruby red to black. Yellow and bright orange is what you hammer. Black steel can still be 800°F (426°C).

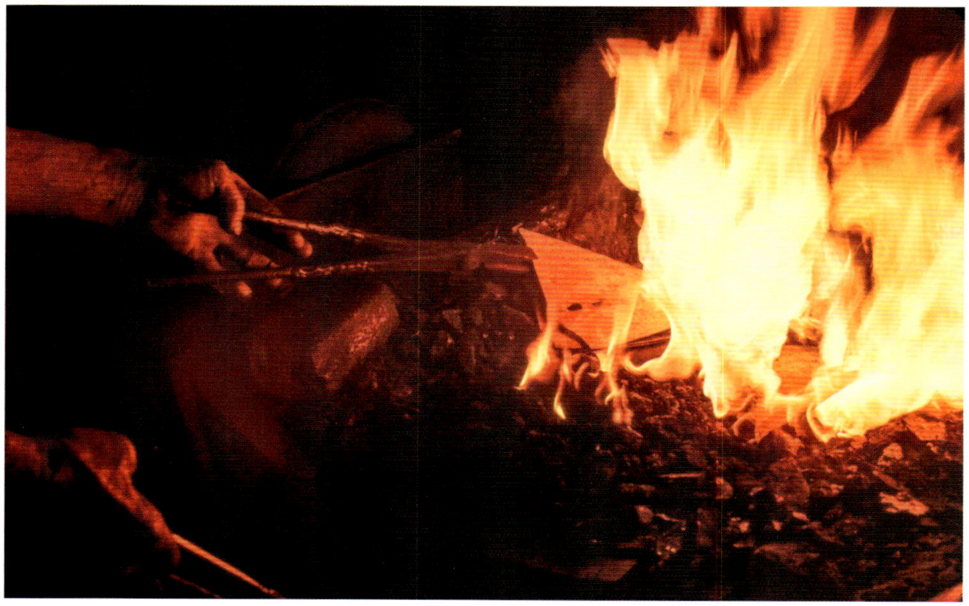

Heating a cultivator blade, Mr. Hall's forge, Oxford, 1972–75. Forty years later, in May 2013, I was given these tongs by Andy Waller, another apprentice of Mr. Hall's, and now use them all the time.

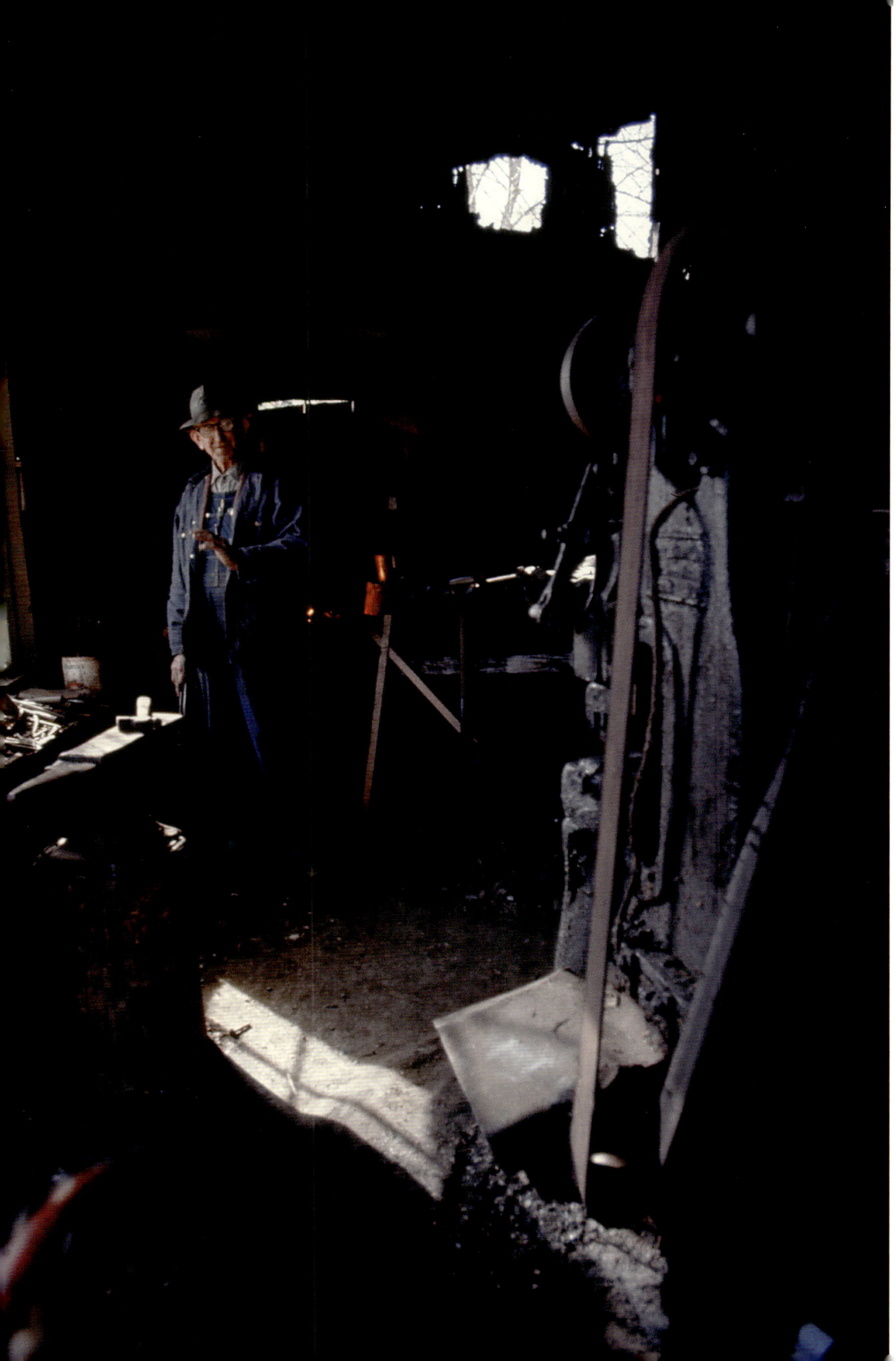

Mr. Hall's forge with Vermeer lighting, Oxford, 1972–75. It was light enough to see, yet dark enough to tell the color of the metal.

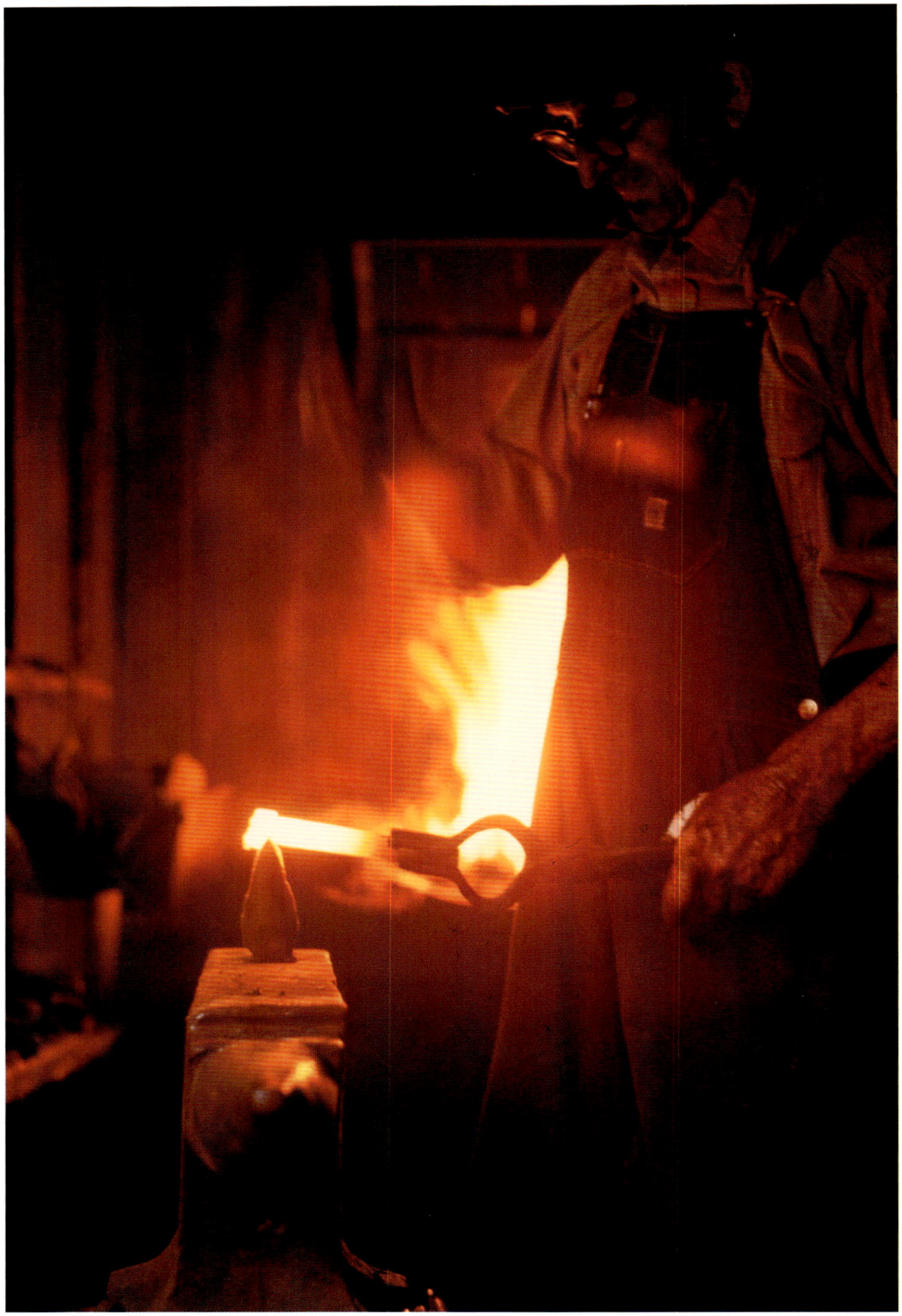

Hot cutting on a hardy,
Oxford, 1972–75.

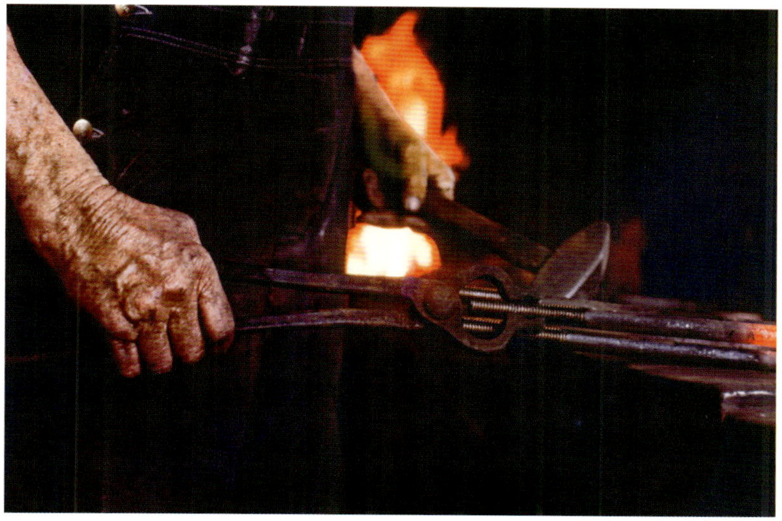

Mr. Hall's history is written on his hands, Oxford, 1973.

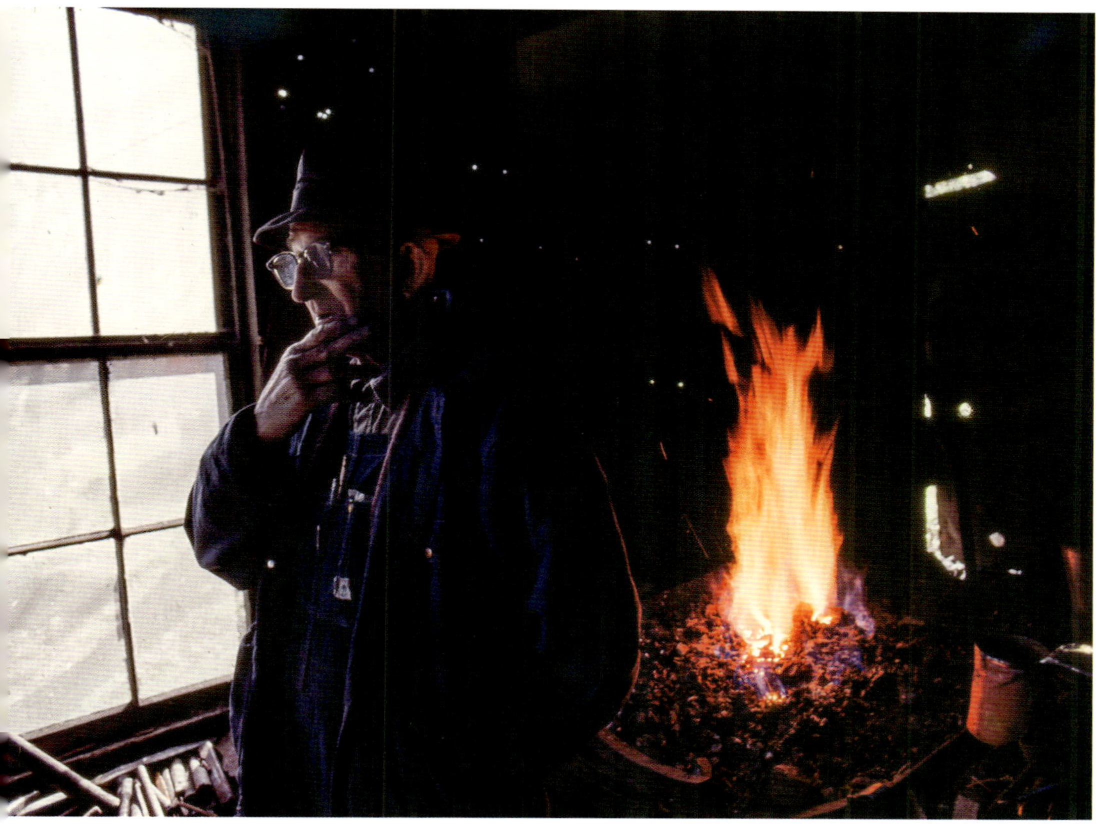

Mr. Hall, Oxford, winter, 1972–75. The blue flames are from green coal turning into coke. Coke is what you want to forge with.

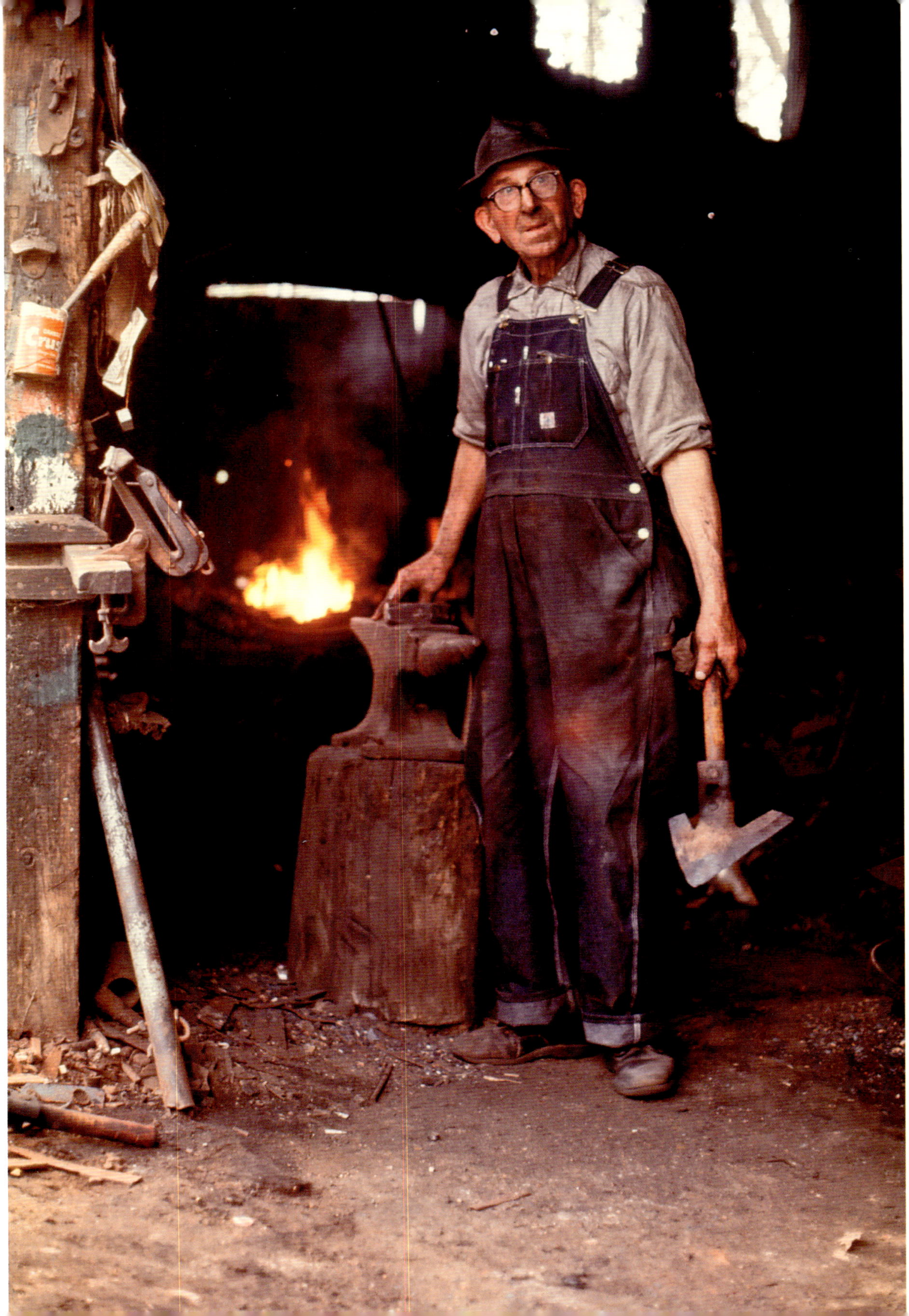

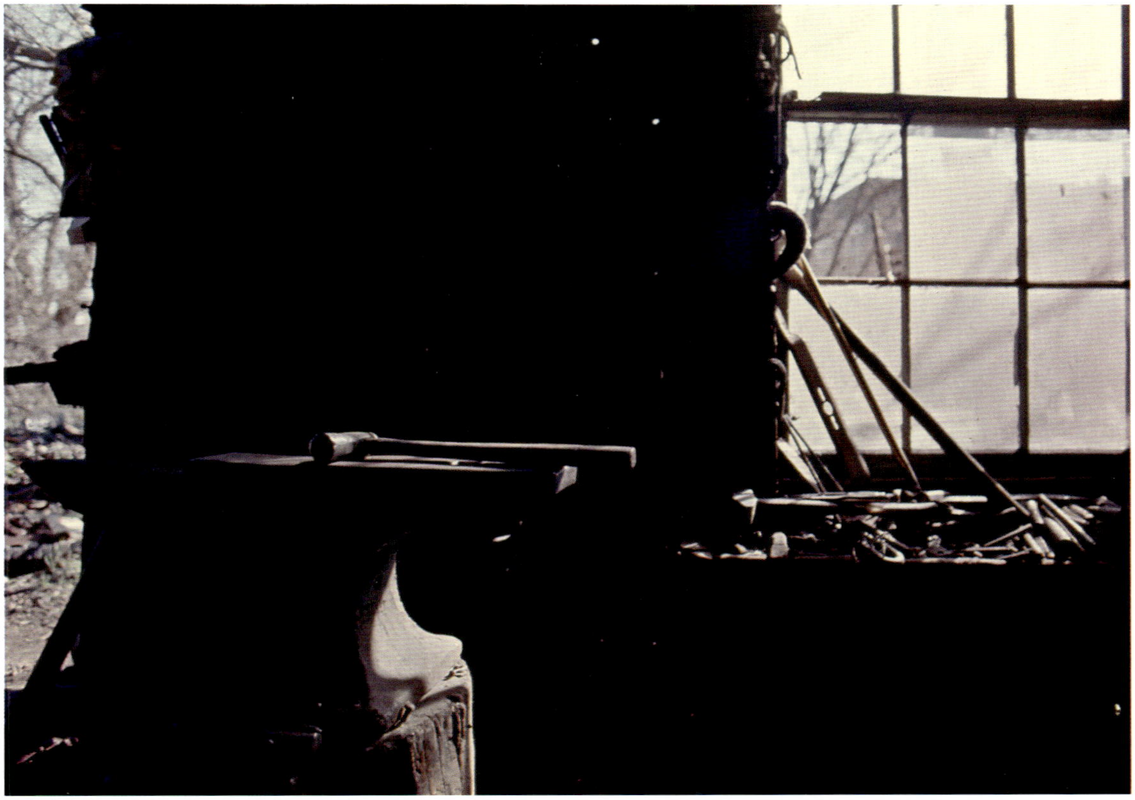

Mr. Hall's anvil, Oxford, 1972–75. An awful lot can be said about an anvil and its many uses. Every inch has meaning; every part has a name and function. They have beautiful shapes evolved over centuries. The edges of the face vary from sharp to gently curved. Mr. Hall's anvil was made by the Hay Budden Foundry in Brooklyn, New York, about 1905. Hay Budden made about three hundred thousand anvils between 1892 and 1925. Beneath the window a shelf is piled with drifts, punches, fullers, sweges, and bits of steel ready to become tools.

Sharpening a cultivator blade, Oxford, 1972–75. Notice that Mr. Hall's sleeves are rolled inside so that there's no cuff for a spark to catch in.

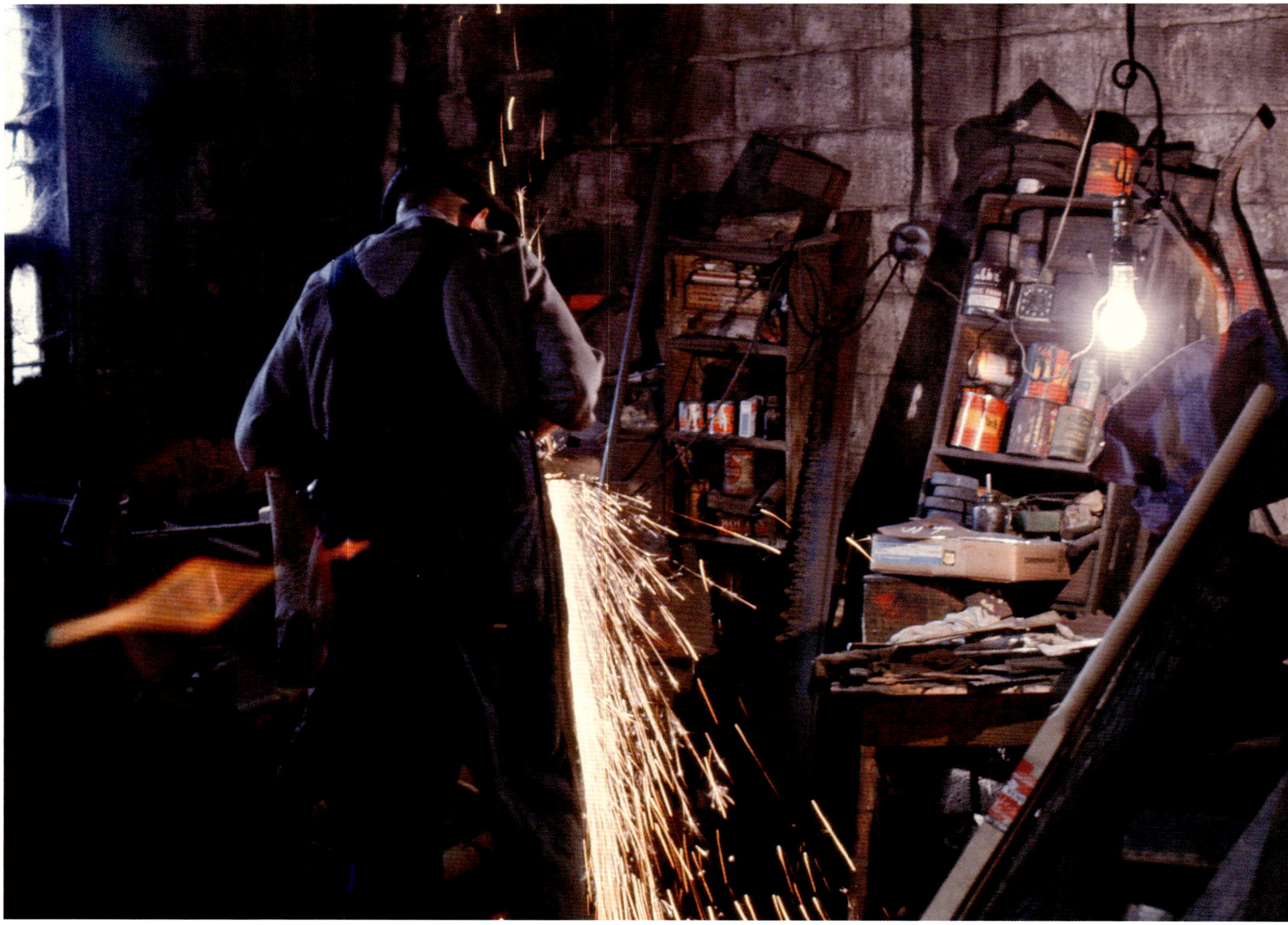

Mr. Hall at the grinder, Oxford, 1972–75.

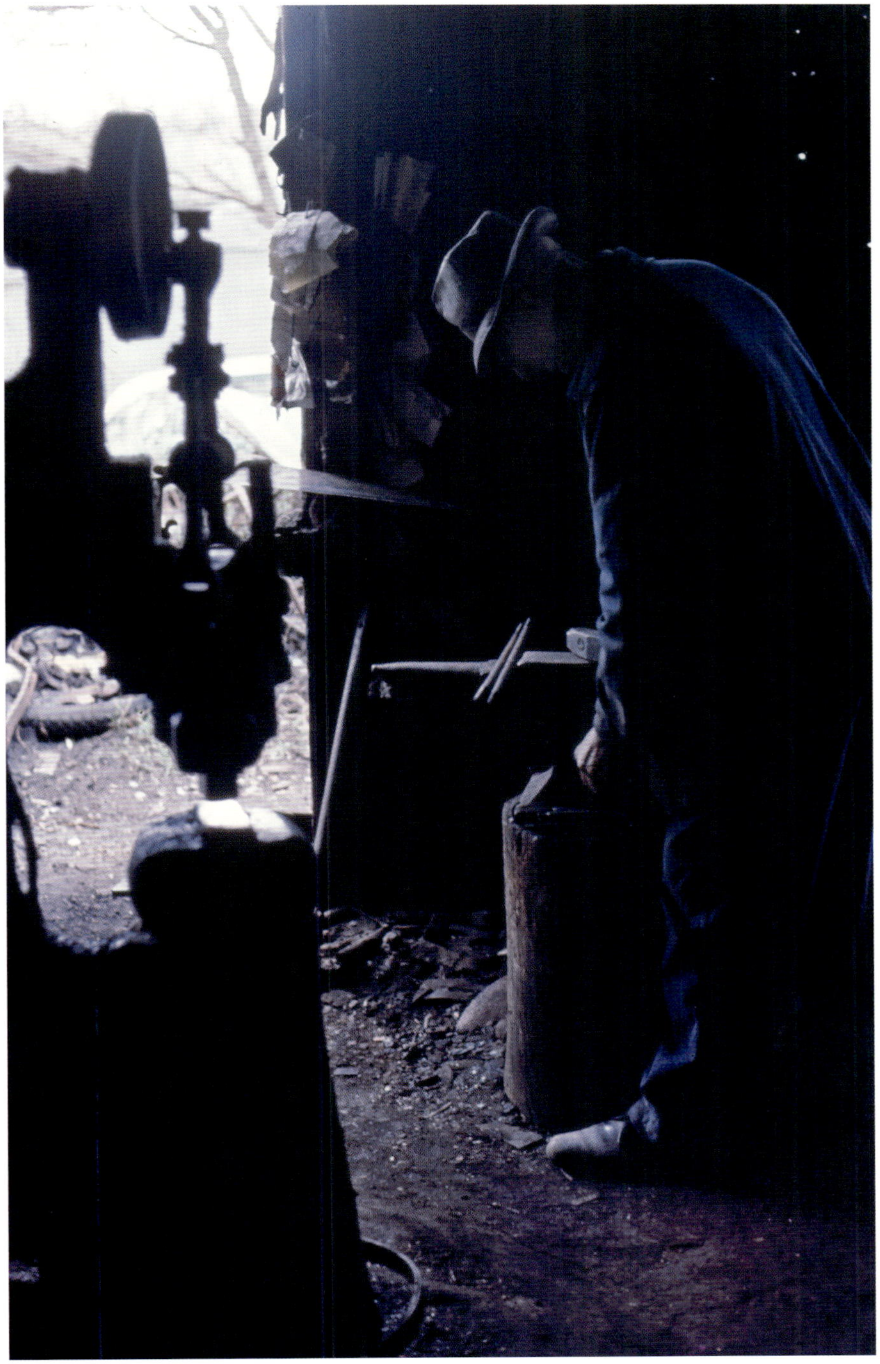

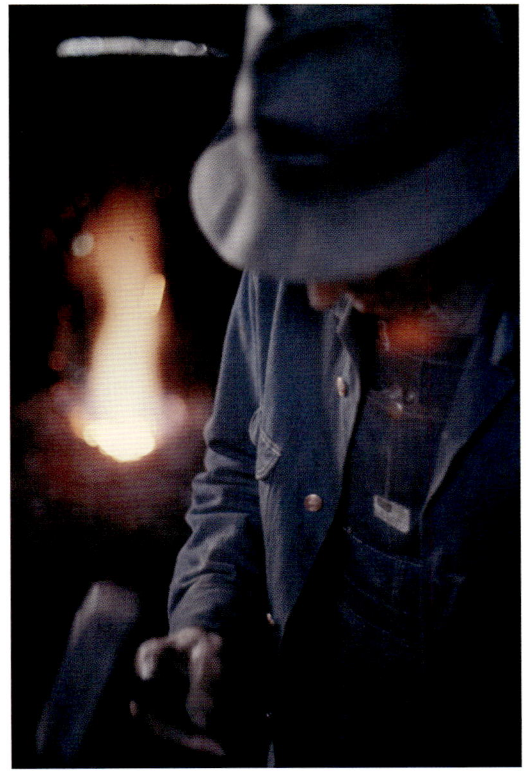

Winter forge 2, Oxford, 1972–75. Mr. Hall said to me once, "Remember, Michael, it ain't what's in a man that defines him. It's what he lets out." I hope the photographs capture something of who Mr. Hall was. Perhaps you can see his gentle strength.

A study in blue, winter at the forge, Oxford, 1972–75.

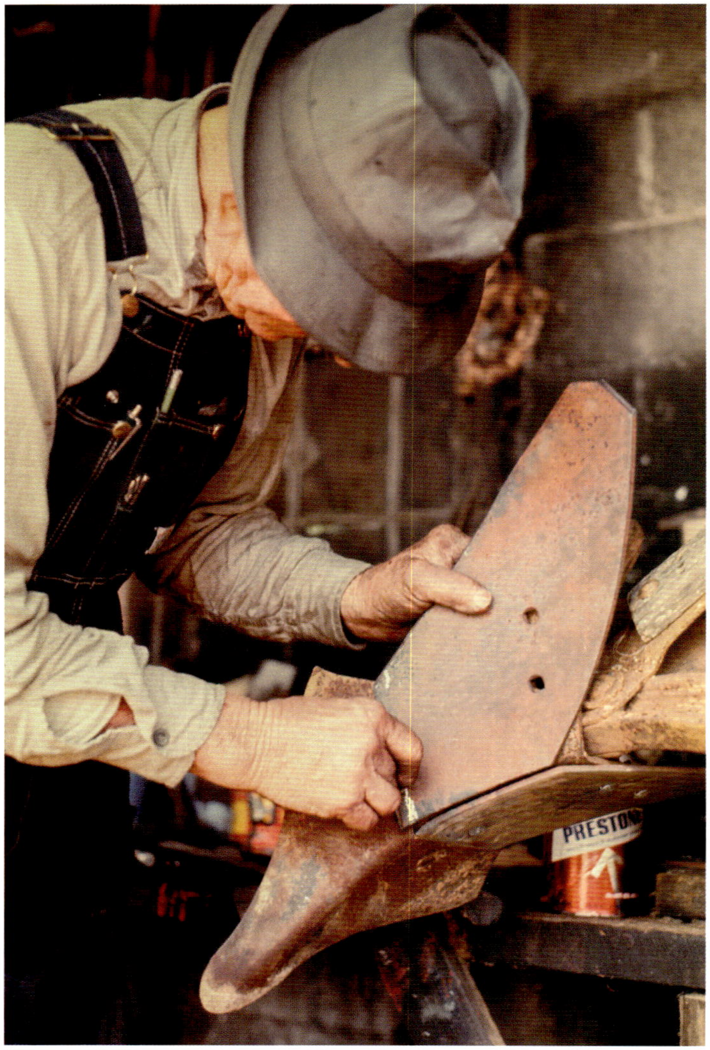

Fitting a moldboard on a middle buster, Oxford, 1972–75.

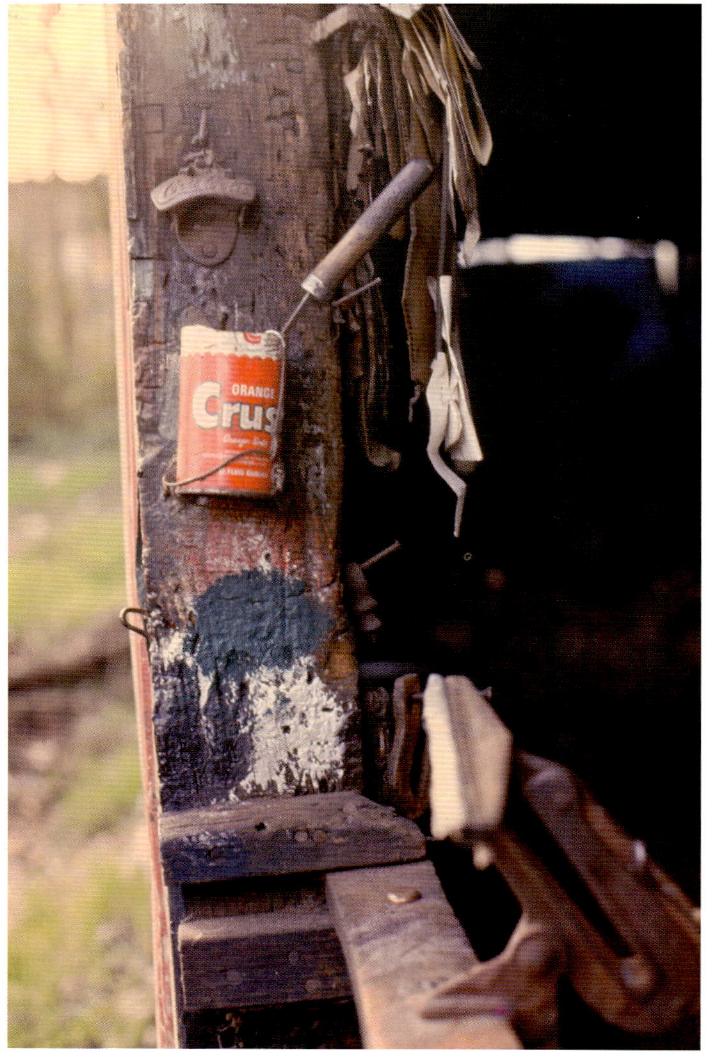

Saw sharpening vise, Oxford, 1972–75. The Orange Crush can caught bottle caps and held the saw-sharpening file.

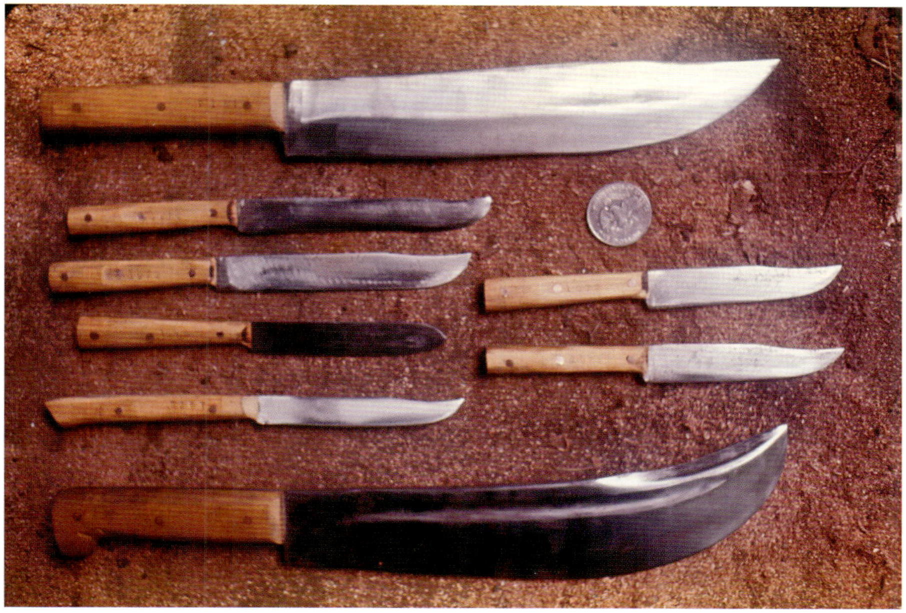

Mr. Hall's knives, Oxford, 1972–75. When things were slow after harvest or during winter, Mr. Hall would make knives. The blades were forged from old car springs, saw blades, or any good carbon steel. The handles were walnut and hickory. But the best wood was bo'doc, osage orange, or bois d'arc, as it never rots.

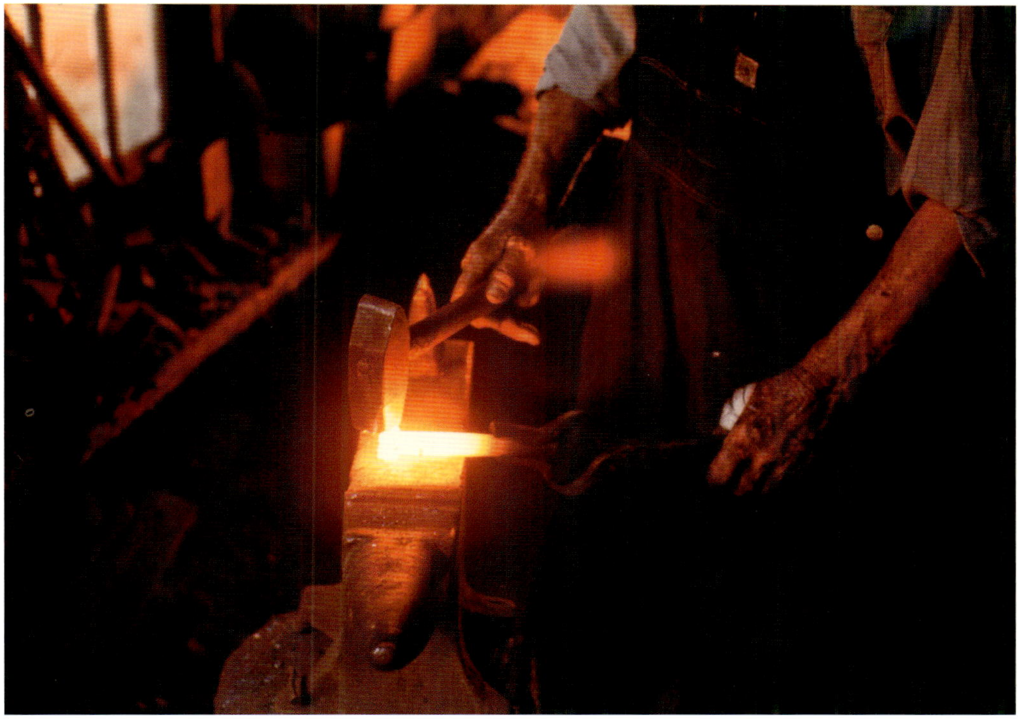

Bright yellow, forging heat, Oxford, 1972–75. Mr. Hall trues up a piece with a hammer and a set of bolt tongs. There's a kind of Zen to hammering hot metal. "Where do I strike?" I would ask Mr. Hall. "Where it is needed," he'd say.

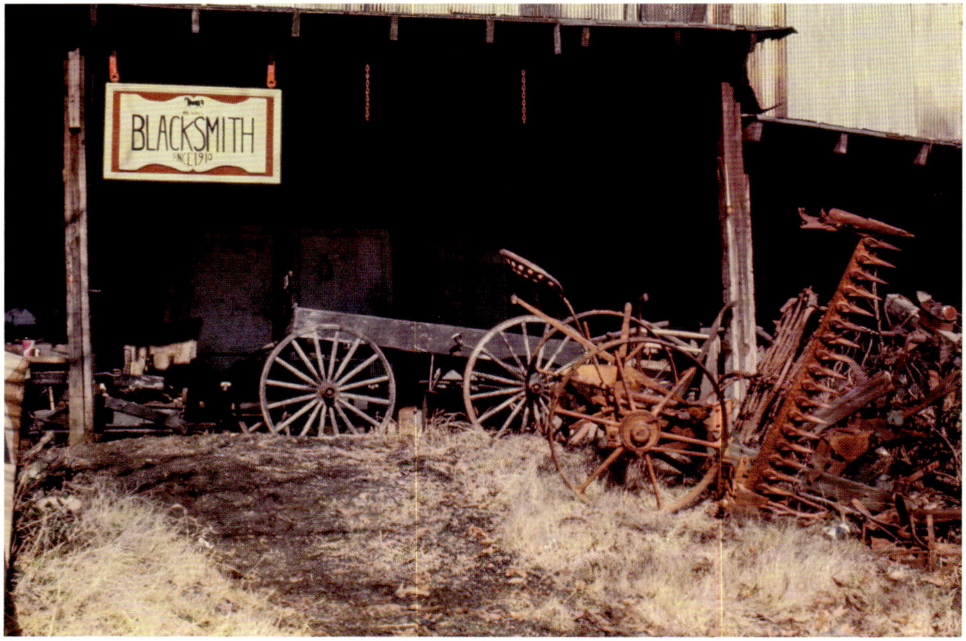

Stolen sign chains, Oxford, 1972–75. Billy Lester, another apprentice, made the original shop sign, which hung from the chains on the right. About a year later the sign was stolen. Billy made a new sign immediately and hung it from steel straps. Several years later, Billy received a call from the police; the sign had been found in a student's apartment. Billy recovered that one and still has it; the one pictured here is gone.

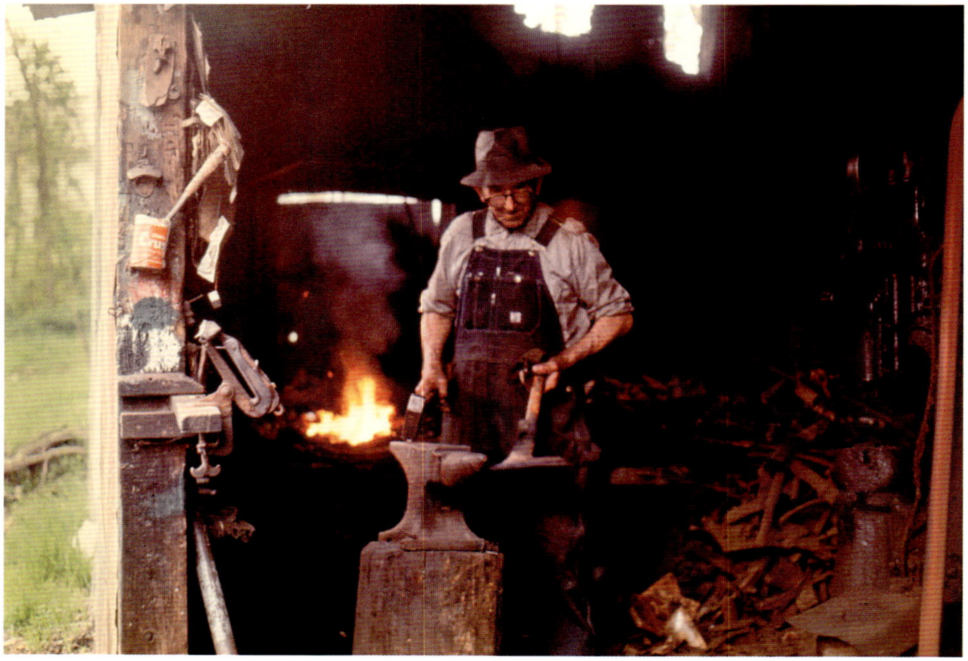

Straightening a cultivator blade, Oxford, 1972–75. A small portion of the scrap pile lies behind.

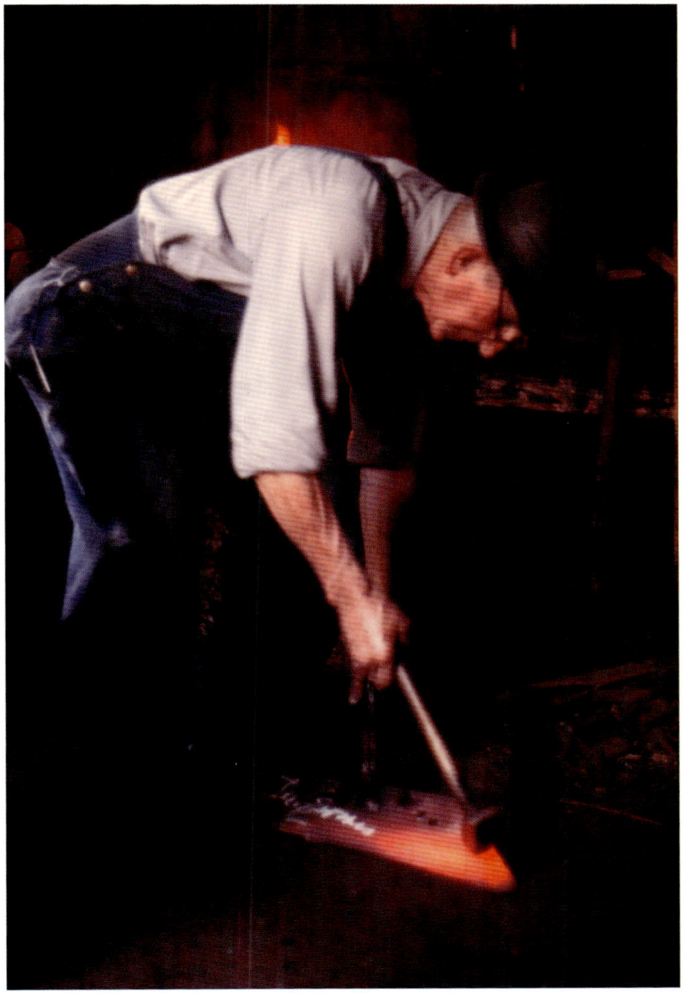

Beating a plowshare into a plowshare, Oxford, 1972–75. The edge is drawn out and straightened. It's cooled slowly, then put on the grinding wheel. Reheat, quench. Mr. Hall would charge $1.50, maybe $2.00.

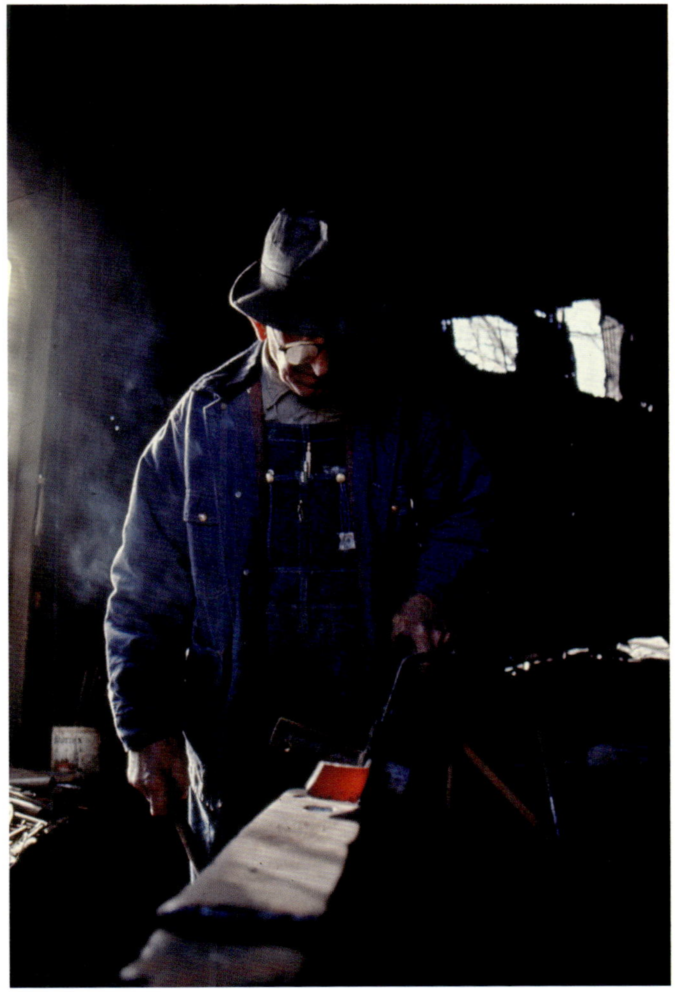

Preparing for spring, Oxford, 1972–75. Drawing out a rototiller blade.

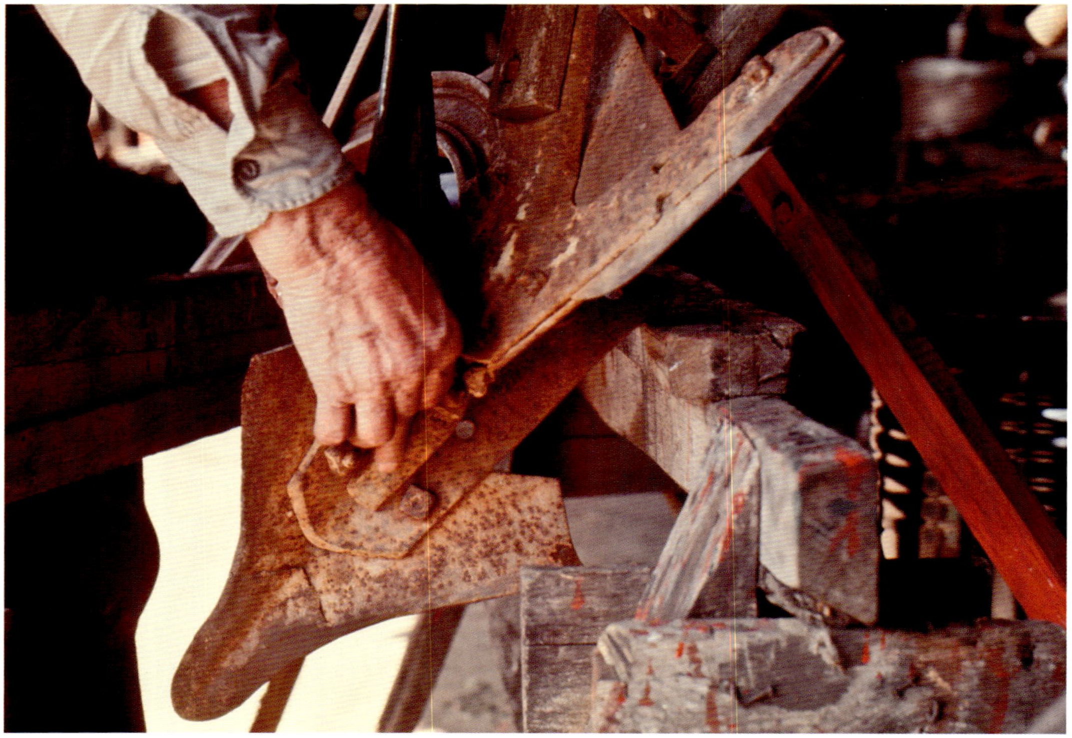

Middle buster plow, Oxford, 1972–75.
The point cups down—that keeps the plow in the earth.

A special order, Oxford, 1972–75.
Quail-topped firedogs accompany this fireplace tools set.

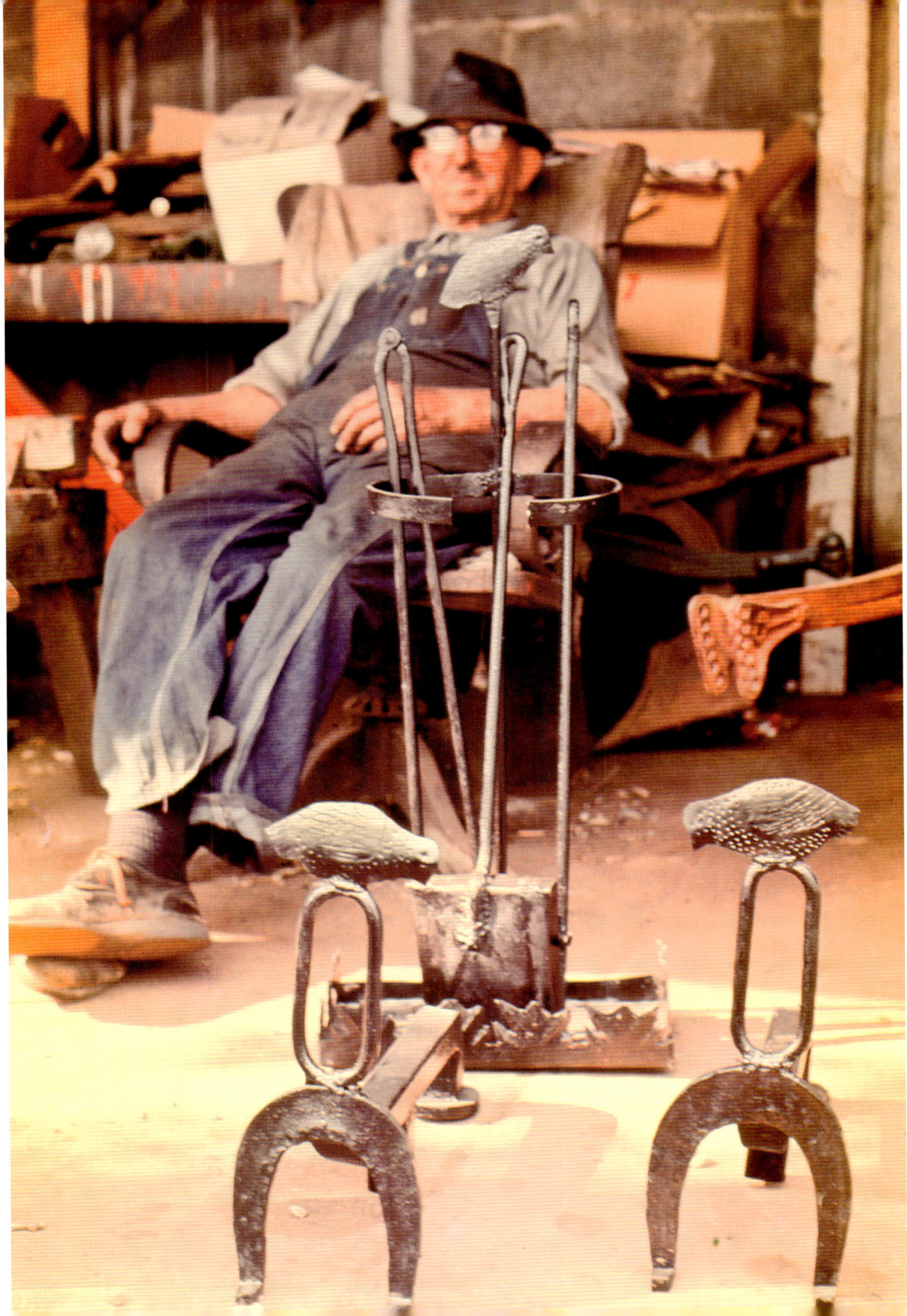

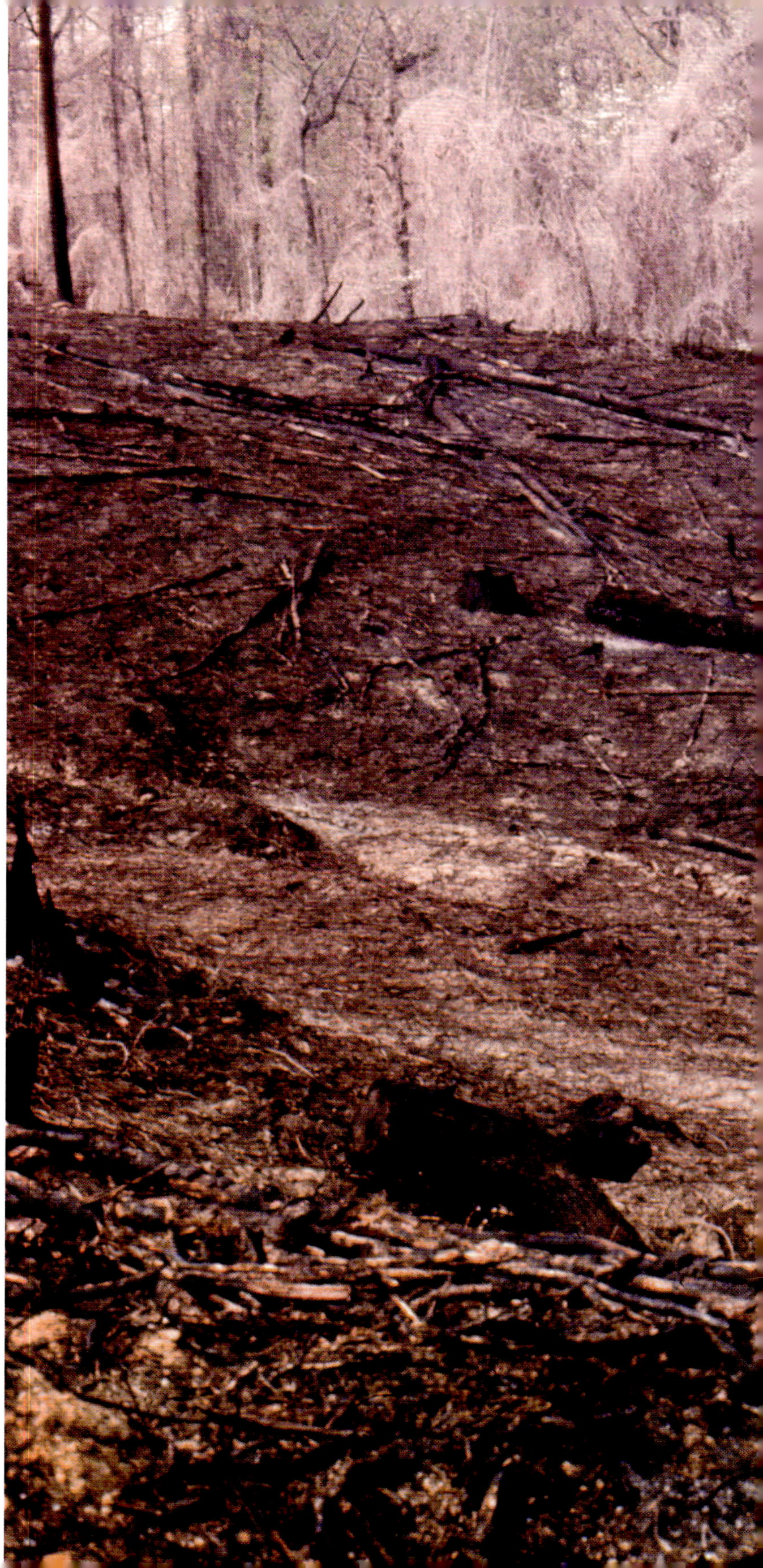

Burnt Kudzu, Highway 7,
Lafayette County, 1972–75.

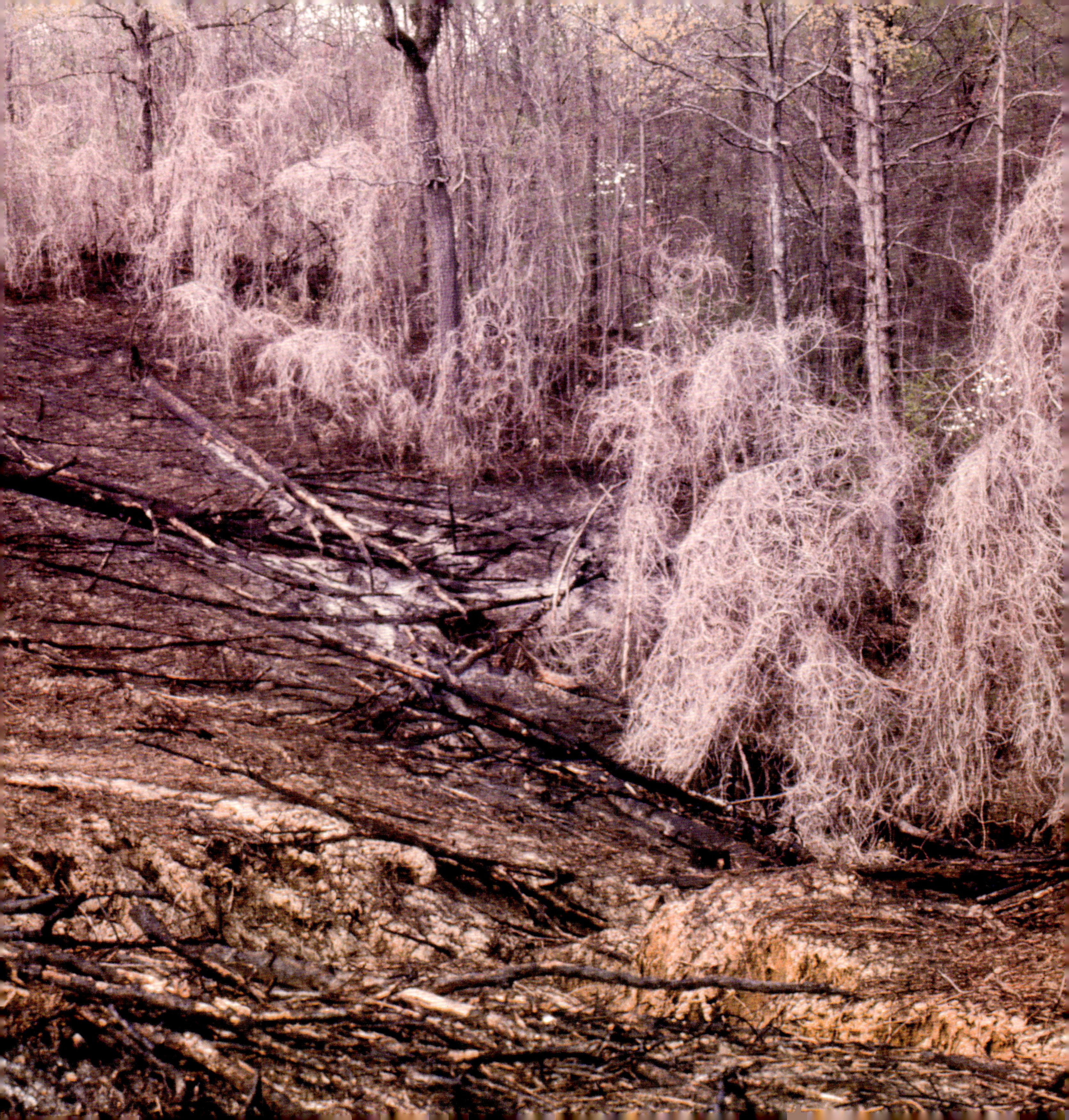

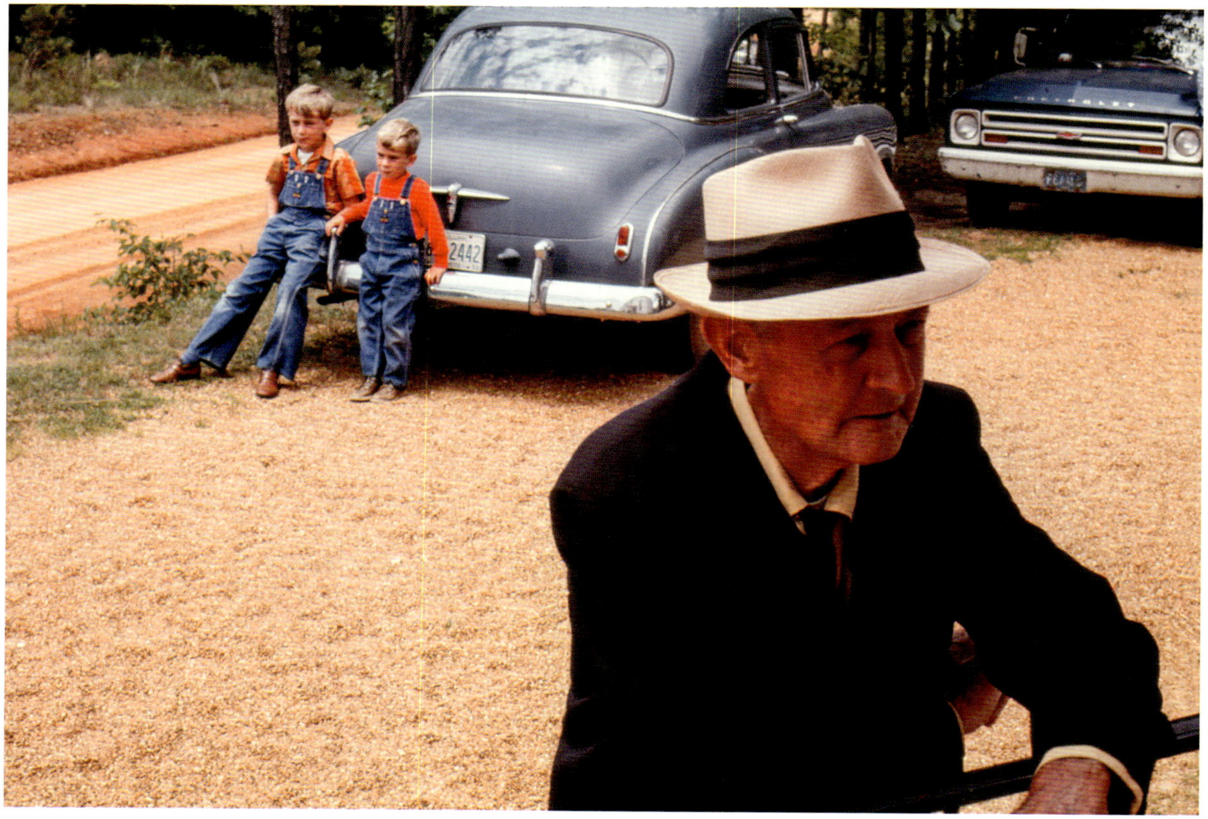

Sunday, Cambridge Baptist Church,
Oxford, 1972–75.

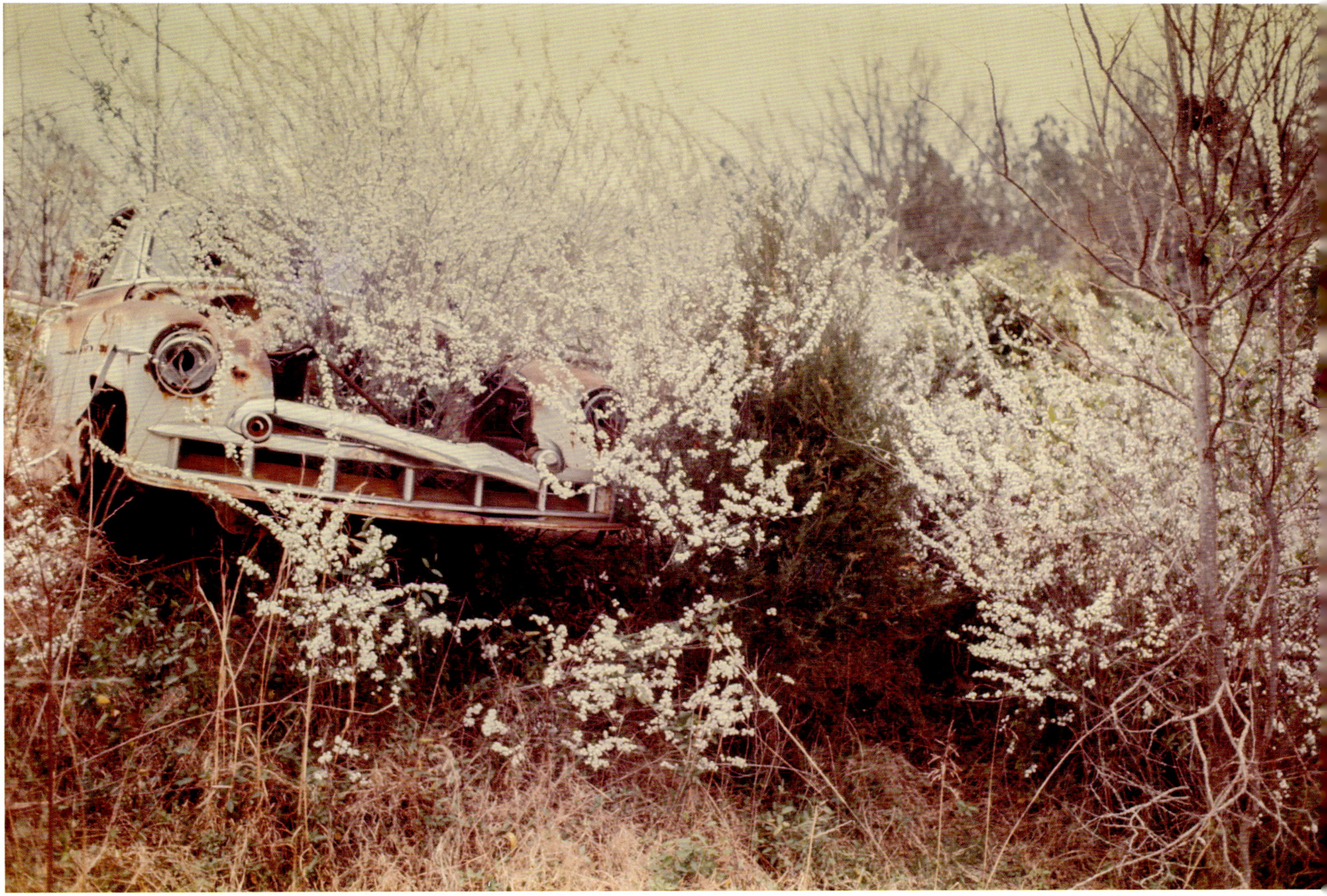

Spring, Holly Springs National Forest,
Holly Springs, 1972–75.

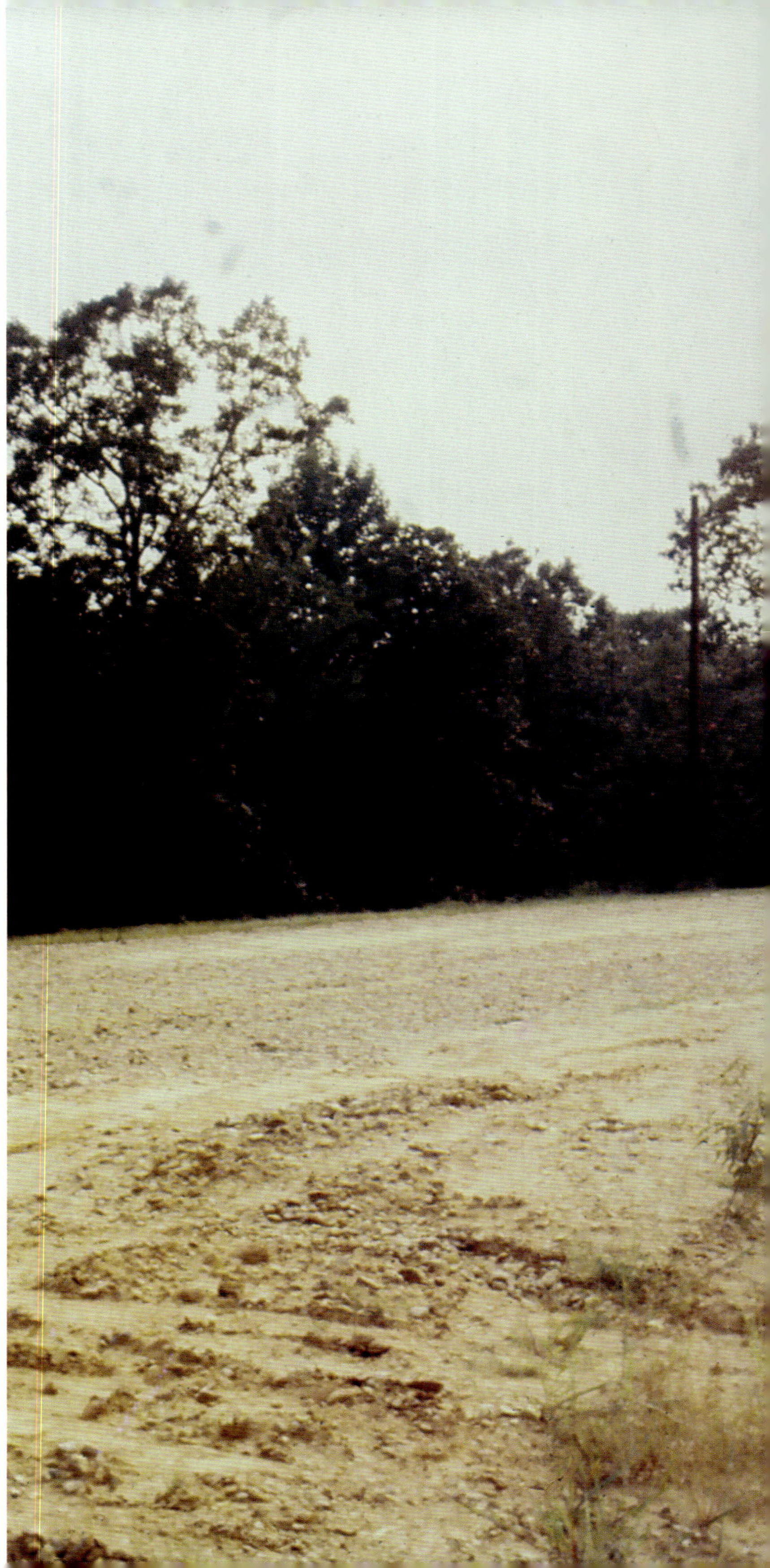

Mt. Hope Missionary Baptist Church,
Taylor, 1972–75.

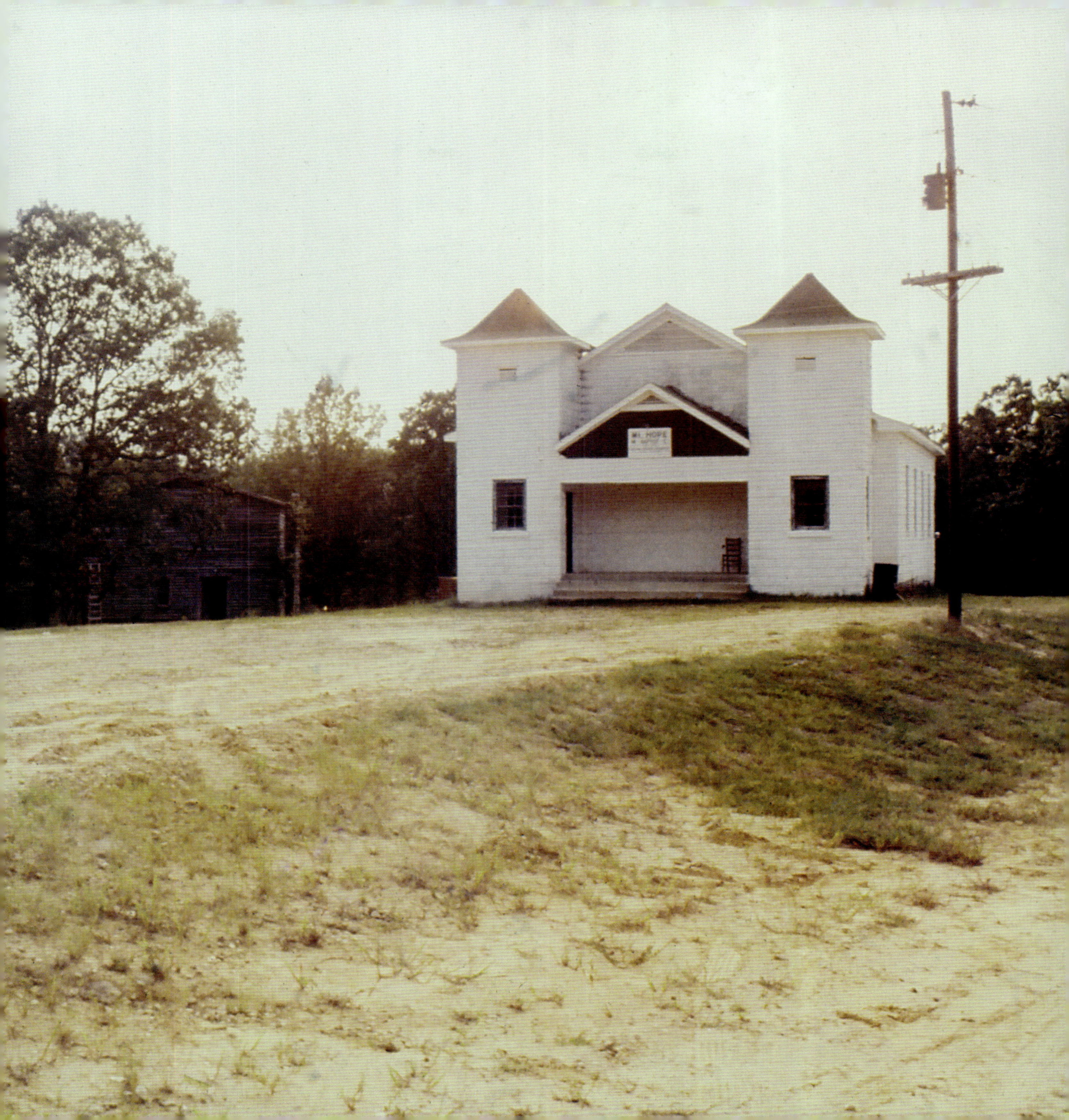

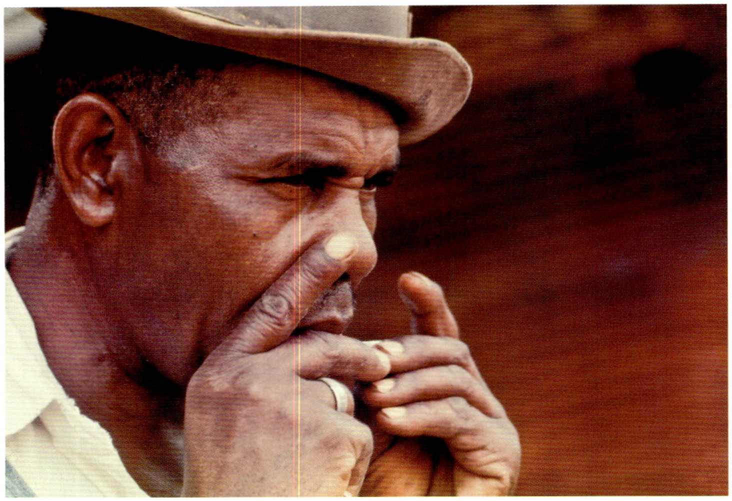

Othar rolling his own, Gravel Springs community, Como, 1972–75. You could go buy a single, ready-made cigarette for five cents at the store, but this was cheaper still.

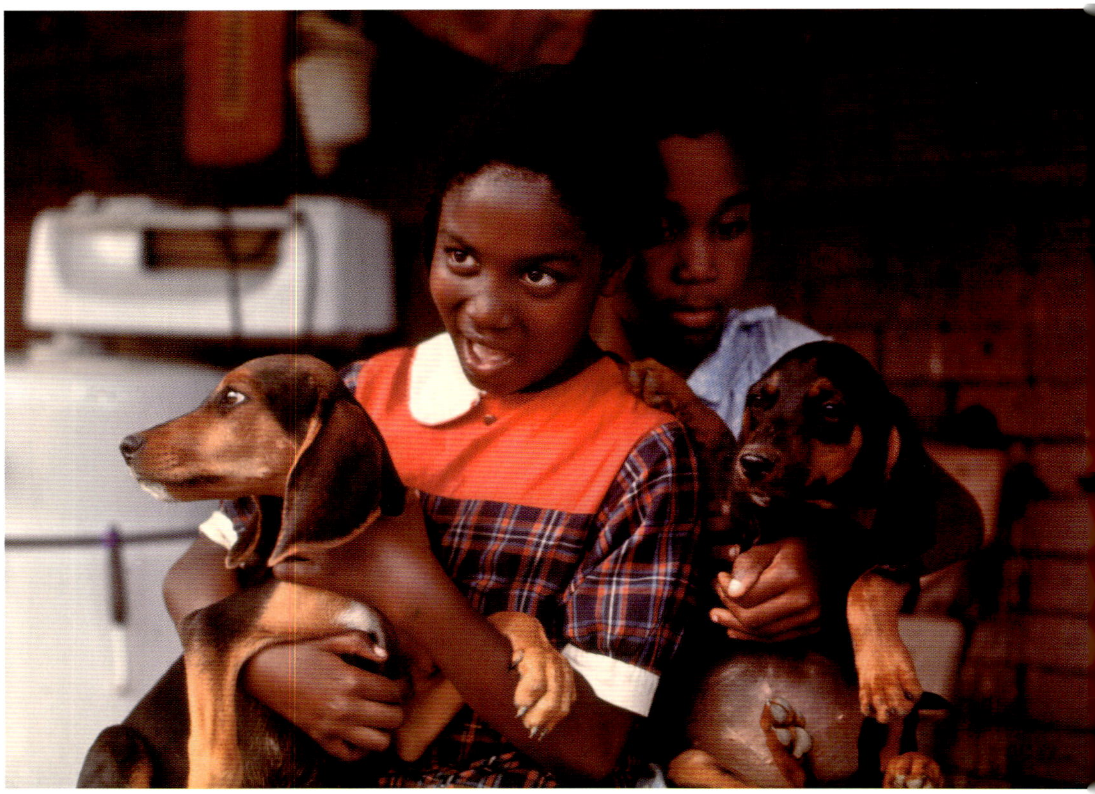

Kids and hounds, Como, summer, 1972–75. Alameda and Nettie Turner linger on the porch of the Turner homeplace.

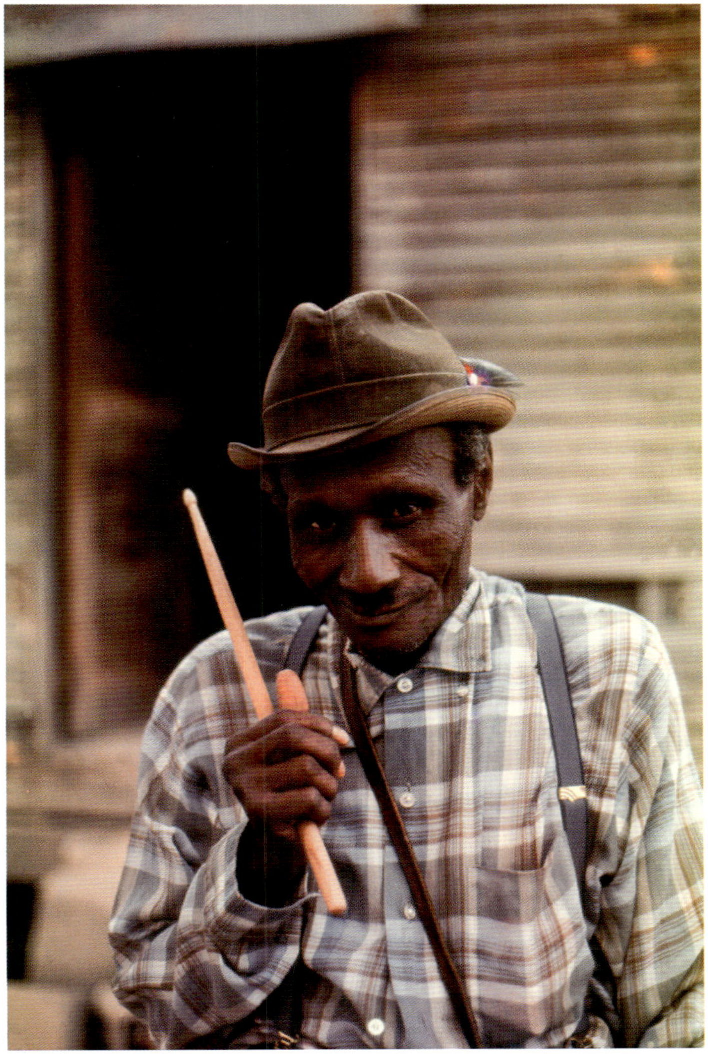

G. D. Young, drummer with the Gravel Springs Fife and Drum Band, Como, August 12, 1972. G. D. had a wiry energy that let him move and drum and dance for hours.

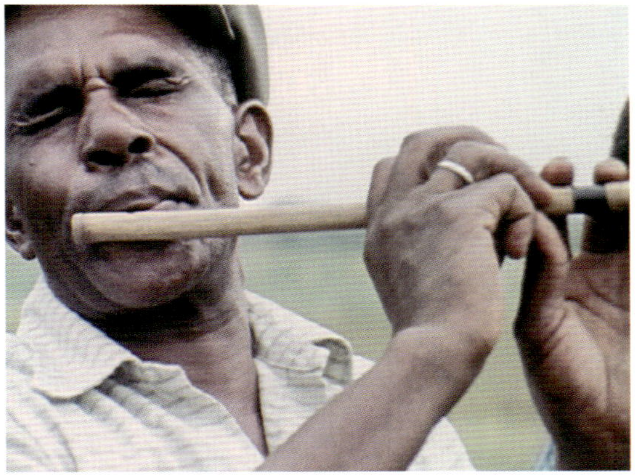

Othar playing the cane, as fifes were called, Como, 1972–75.

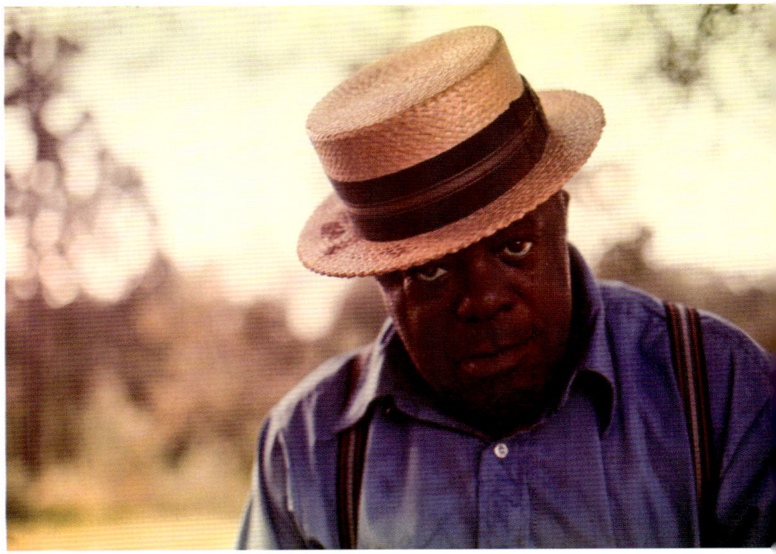

"Uncle Paul" at Othar's picnic, Como, August 12, 1972.

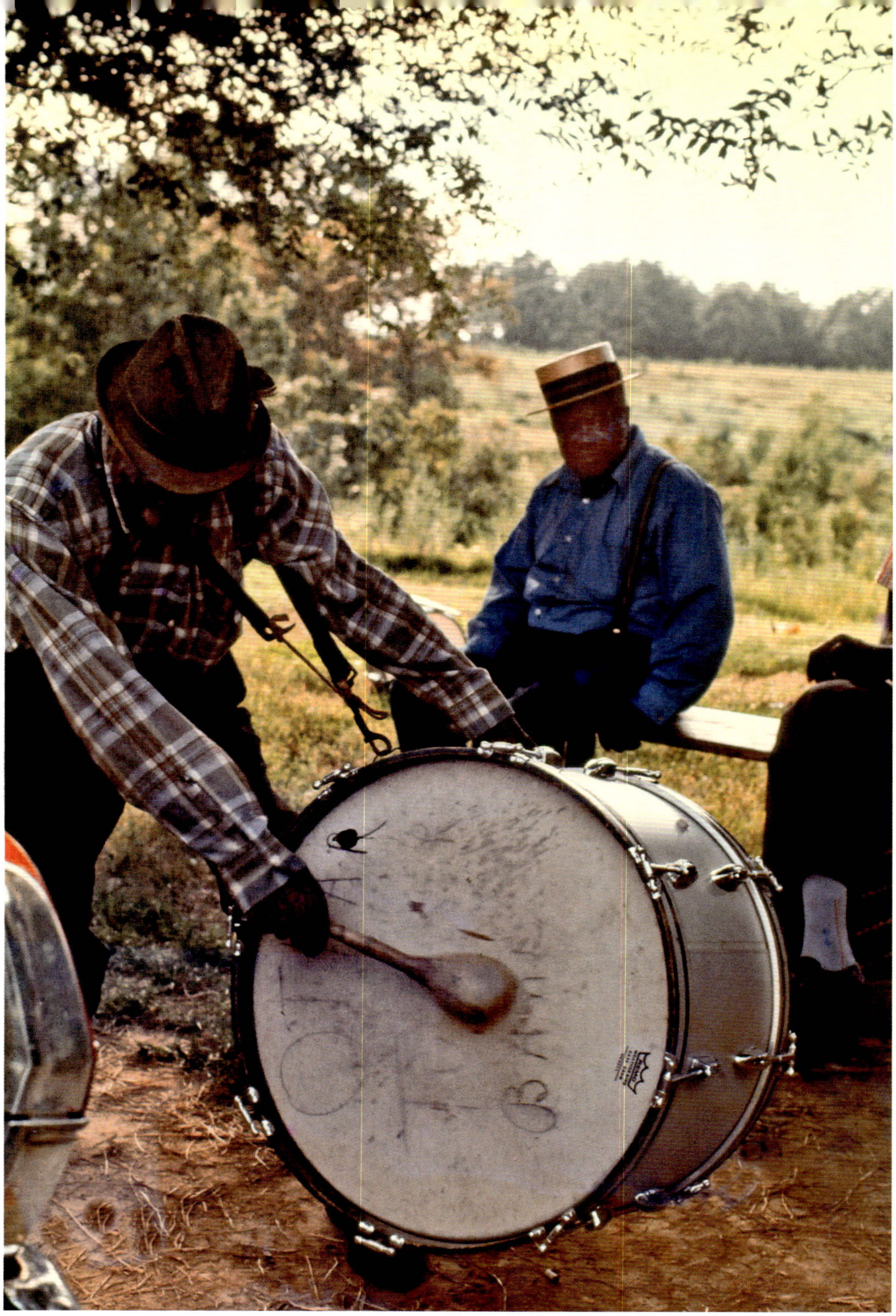

G. D. Young, Como, August 12, 1972.
G. D. Young plays the bass at Othar Turner's picnic.

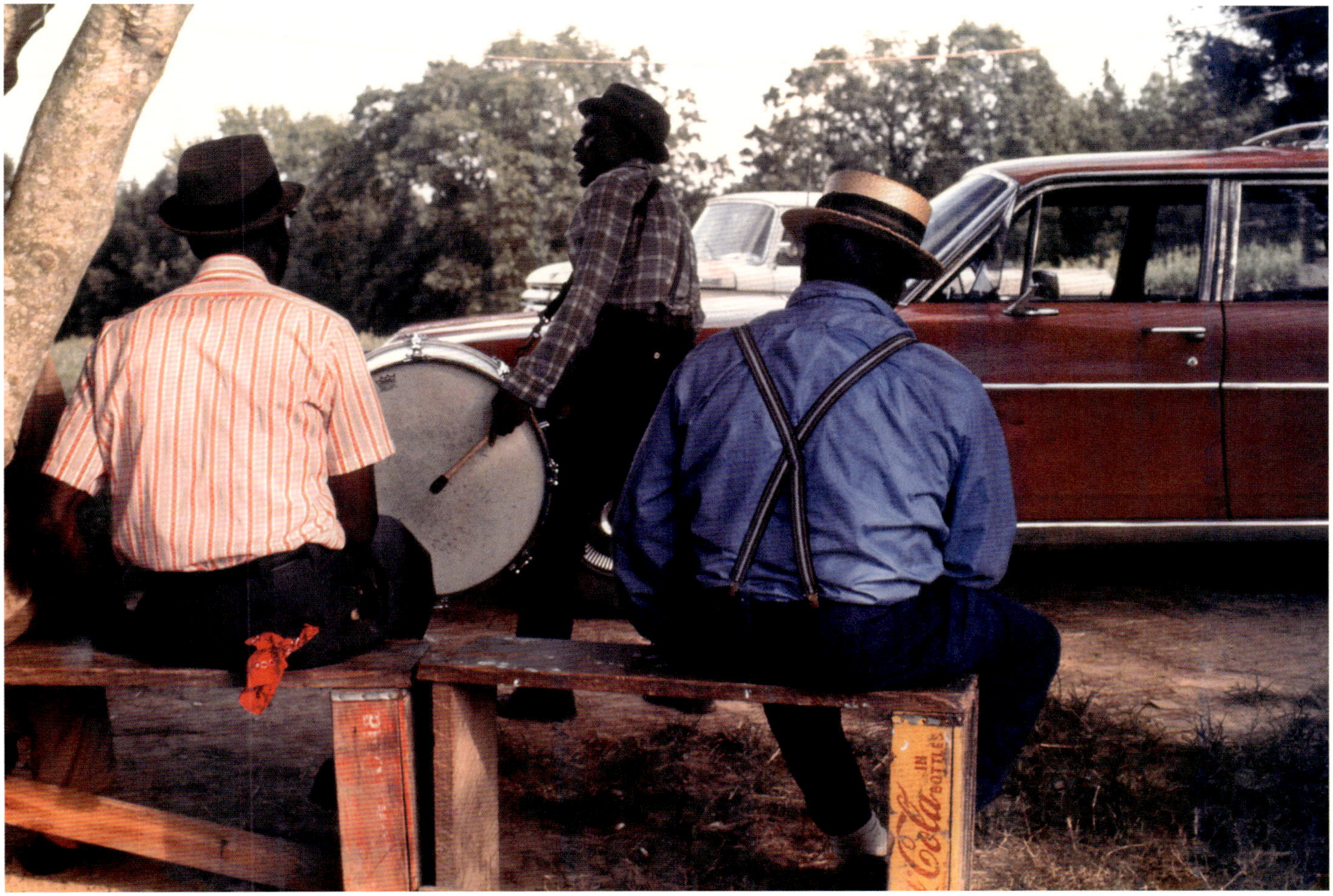

Calling, Como, August 12, 1972. G. D. Young calls people to Othar Turner's picnic. Othar explained, "For the people to hear the drums . . . that's the sound . . . that's the echo . . . When you get on a hill to play you can hear them drums . . . six and seven and eight and nine, ten, fifteen mile. See the echo spreads . . . Well I do that to call the people, to let them know . . . My picnic is out and I'm supposed to give it and I told them I was gonna give a picnic. This part of the picnic now . . . I'm giving a party, I've got something to sell. Fresh meat . . ."

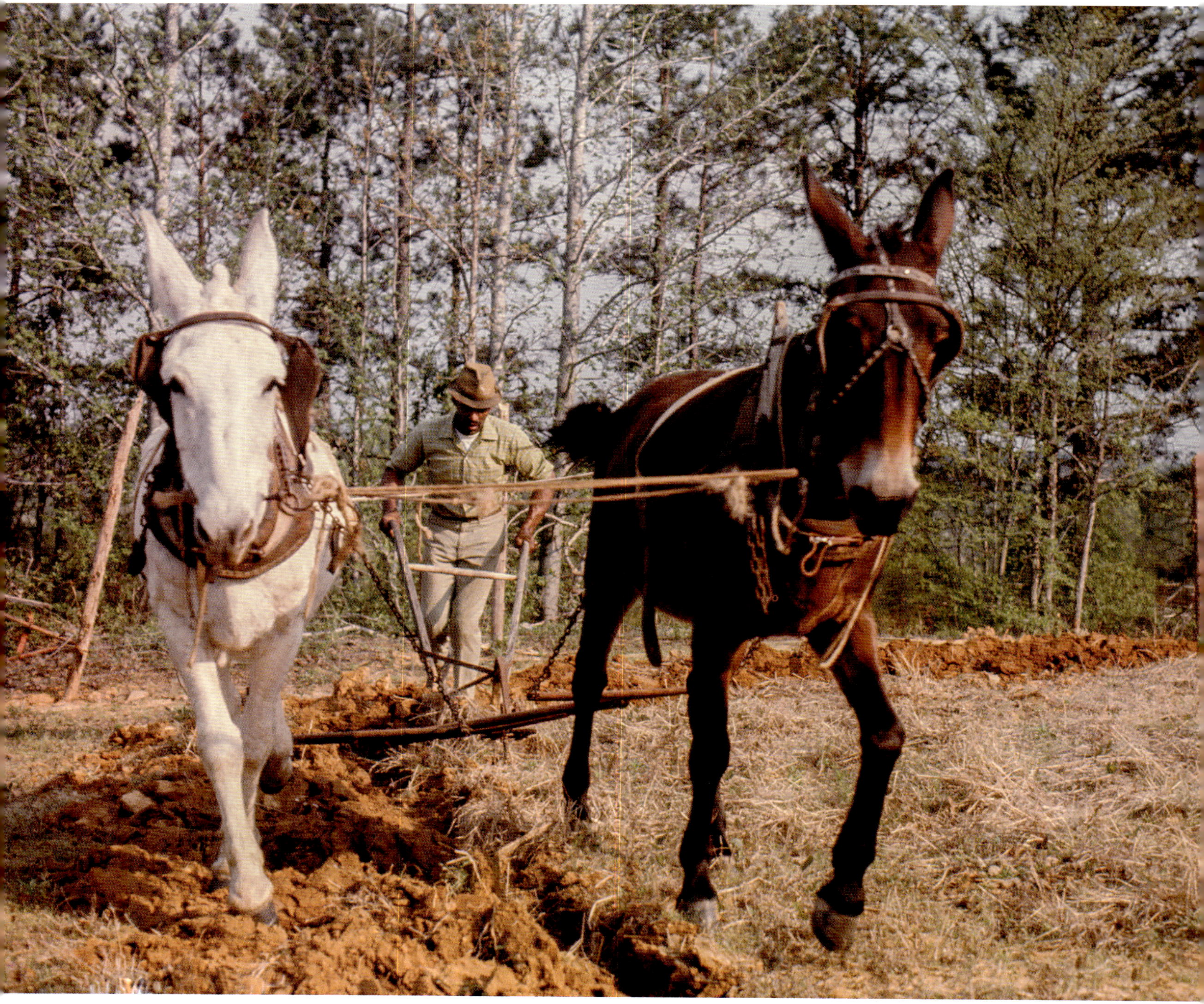

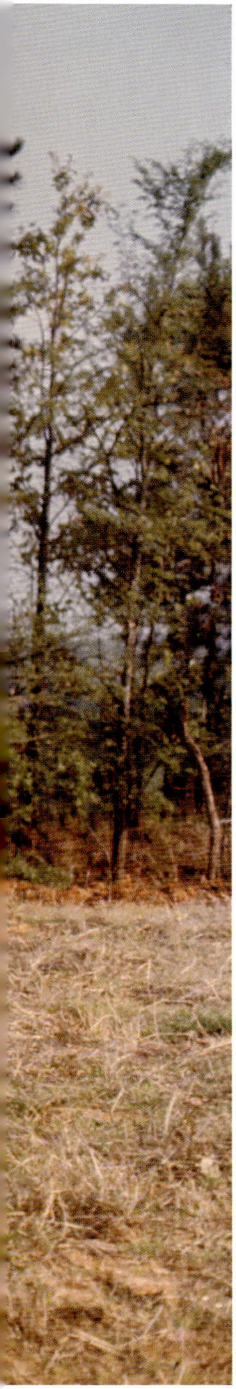

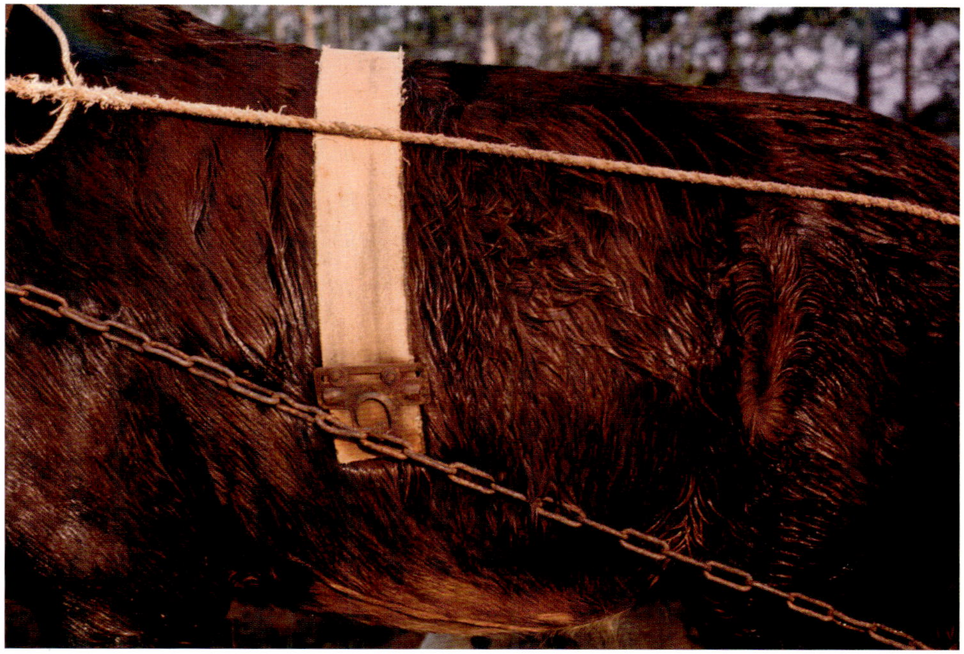

Mule Power, College Hill, 1974.

Plowing a team of mules, College Hill, 1974.

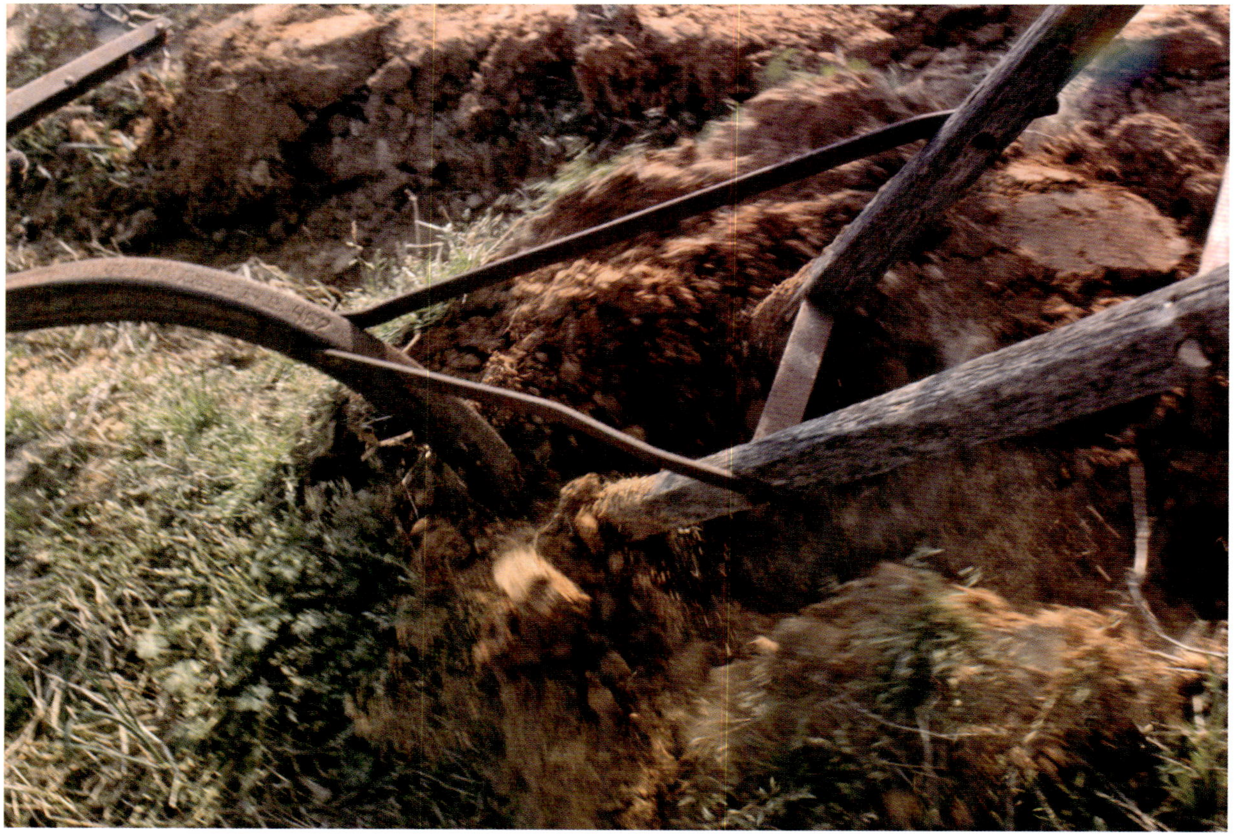

Opening a furrow, College Hill, 1974.

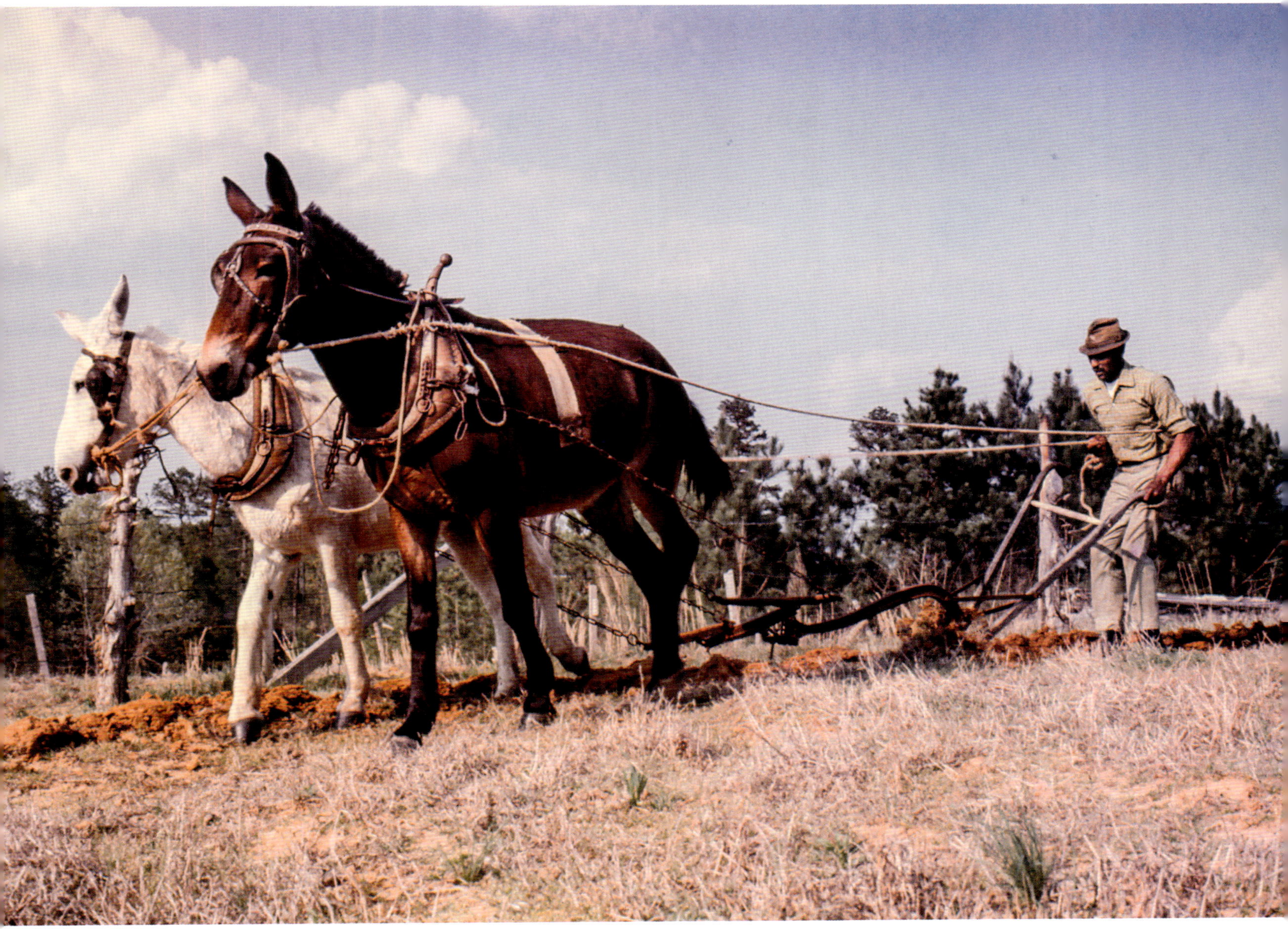

Plowing a team, College Hill, 1972. A good team was three beings who kept each other fed. After thousands of years, mule labor has disappeared entirely in the last forty.

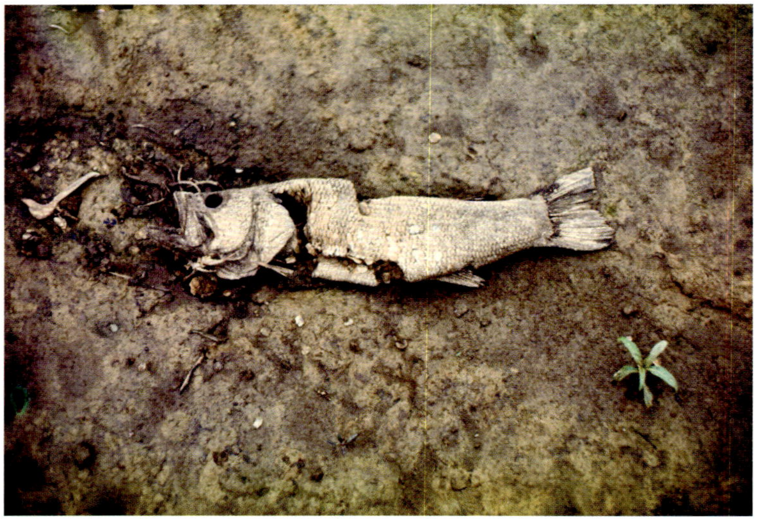

Dry Sardis in winter, Marshall County, 1972–75. Sardis Lake is part of the Tallahatchie watershed and serves as a buffer in flood control, emptying and filling according to the wetness of the seasons.

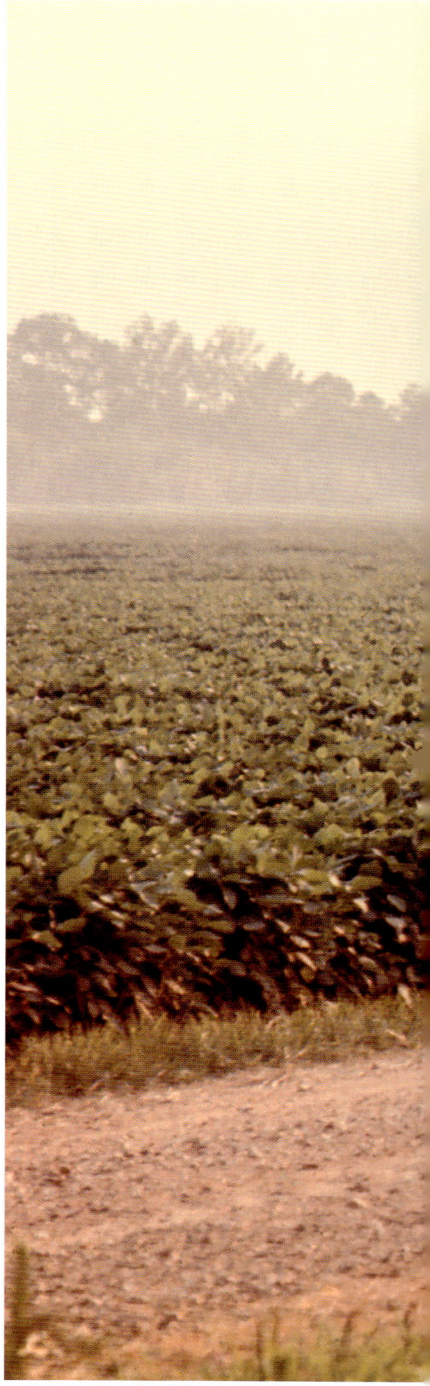

Delta Summer, near Clarksdale, 1972–75.

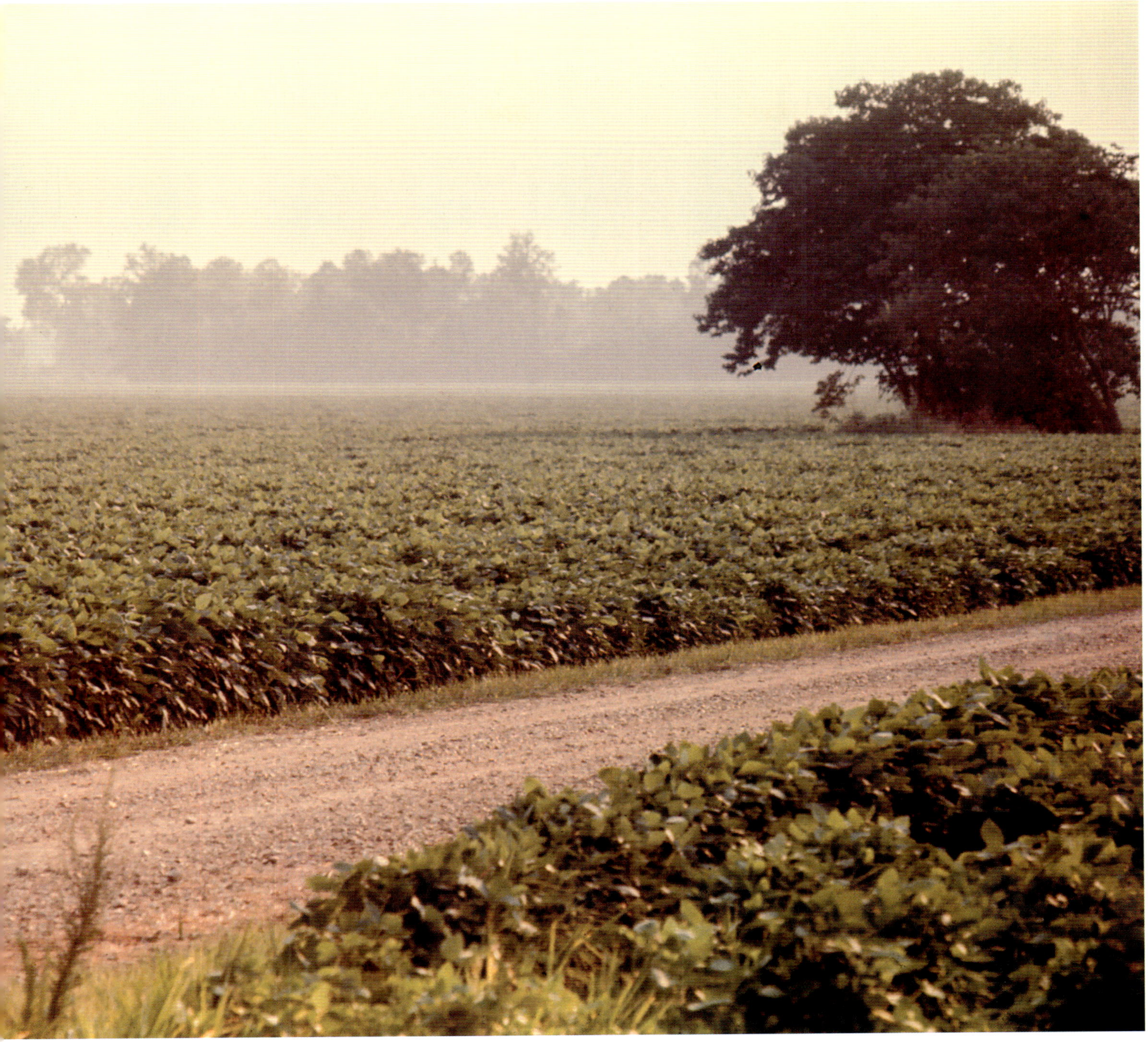

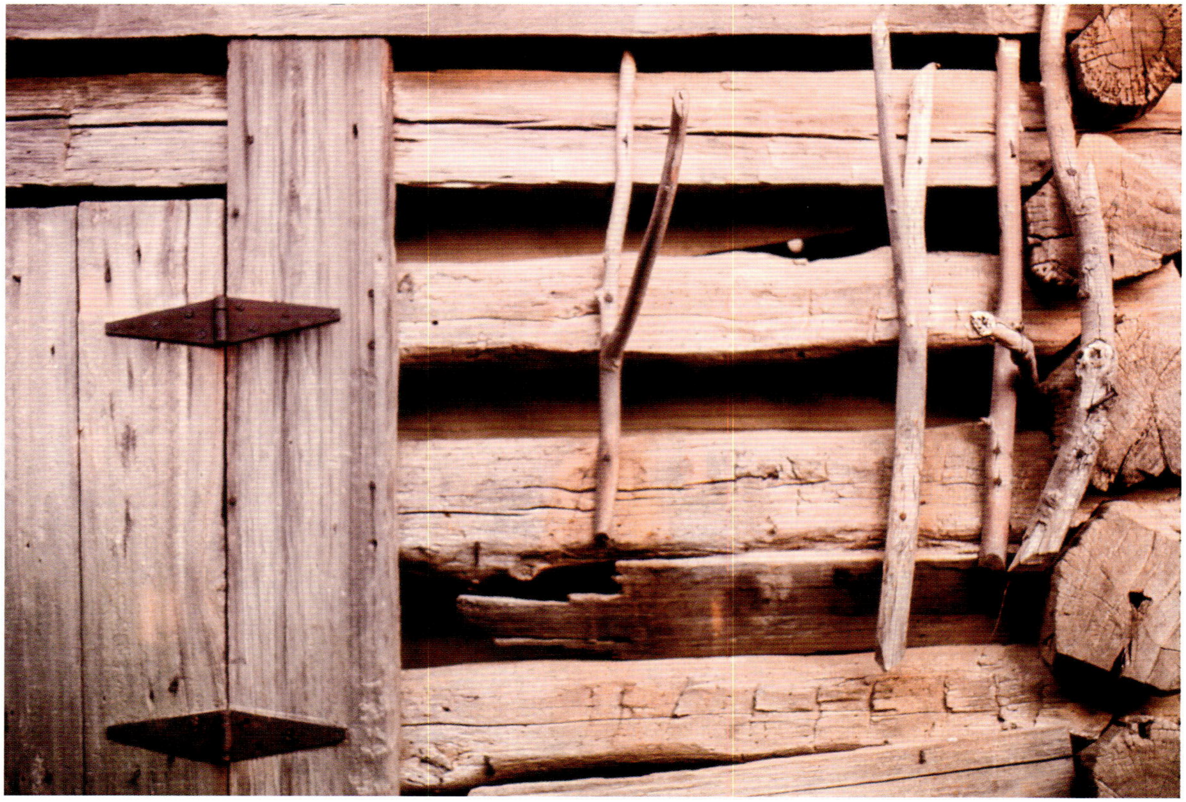

Hand-hewn harness racks, Marshall County, 1972–75.

"Squeaky," Oxford, 1972–75. Robert Lee Gordon, killed by a shotgun blast during an argument in 1980, stands along Molly Barr Road, which is now paved and four lanes wide.

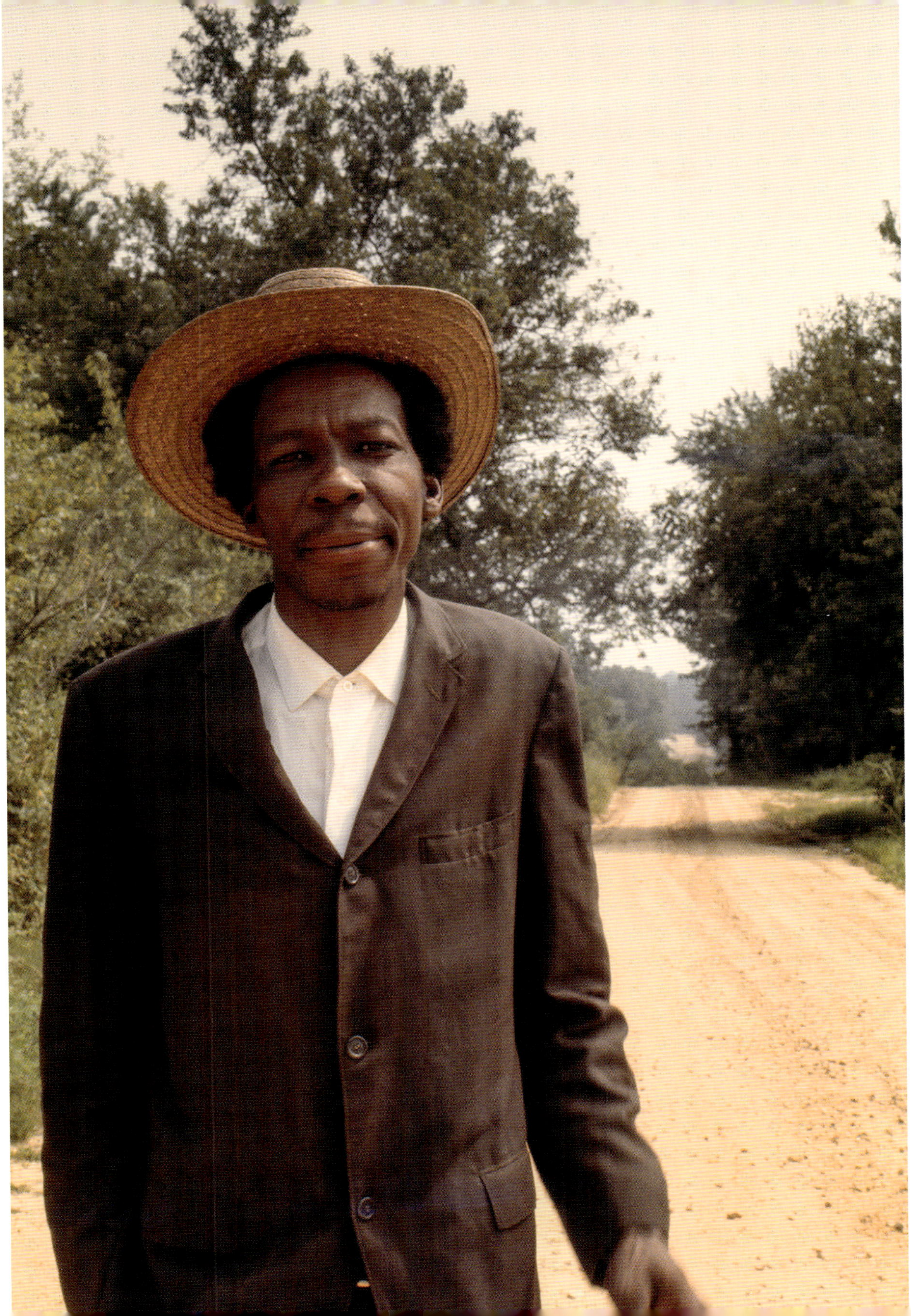

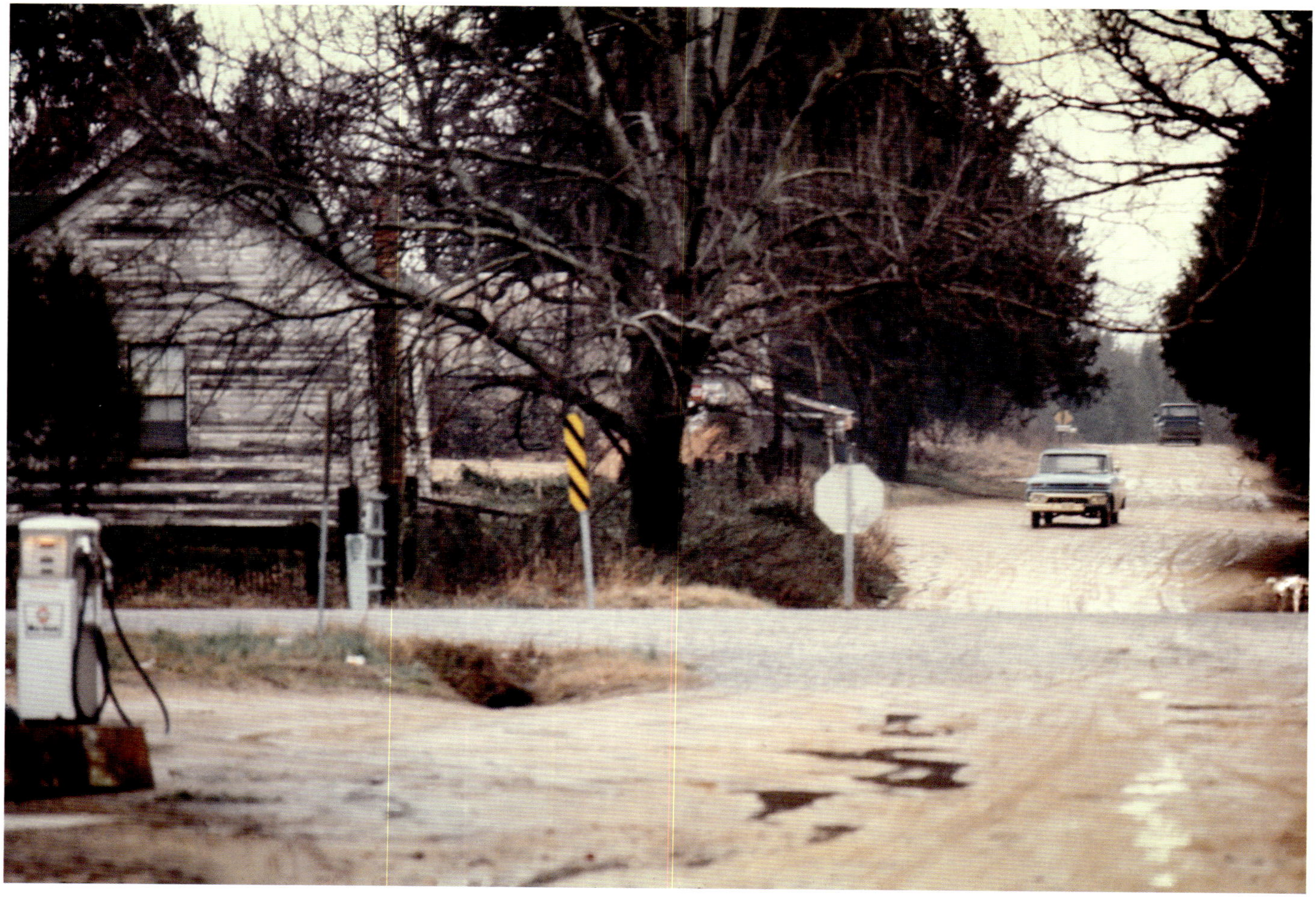

Crossroads, Chulahoma, 1972–75.

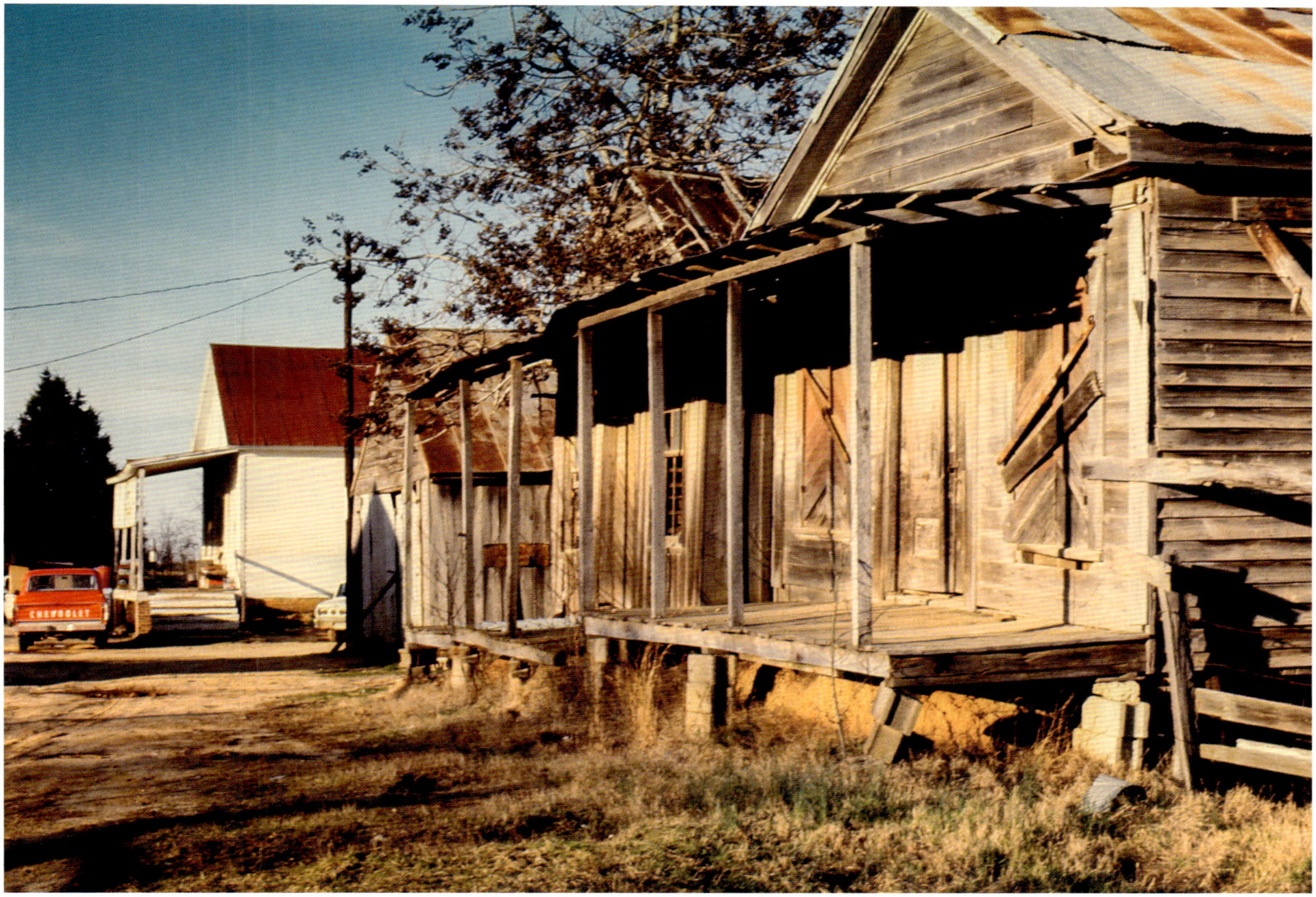

Main Street, abandoned, Chulahoma, 1972–75. Before the Civil War, Chulahoma was a large, prosperous community and an important stop on the road from Jackson to Memphis. There were many churches, more than thirty stores, a post office, a tailor shop, a funeral home, cotton gins, grist mills, a Masonic lodge, a Baptist Female Seminary, and the Chulahoma College for Girls. It was burned during the Civil War and by the early 1970s, not much was left. There were several blocks of abandoned wooden stores linked by a crumbling boardwalk.

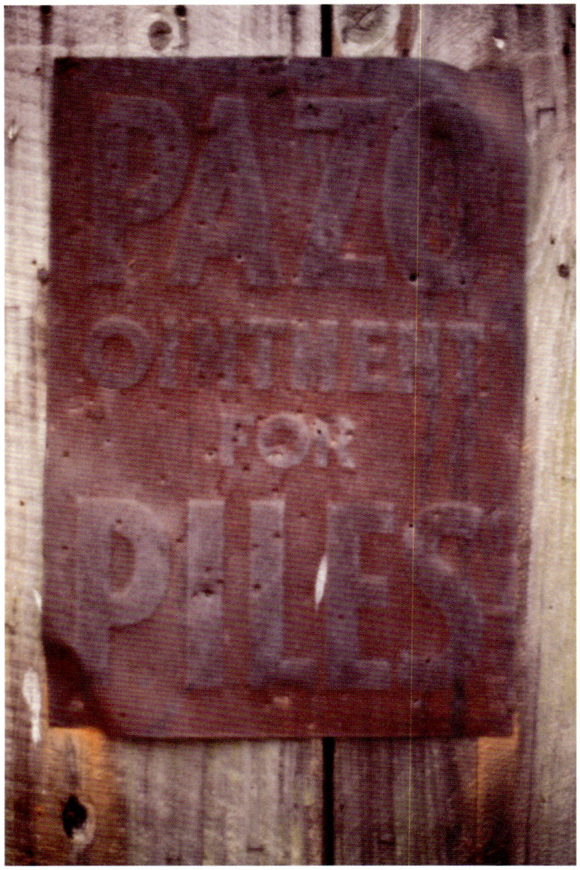

Pazo for Piles with birdshot, Chulahoma, 1972–75.

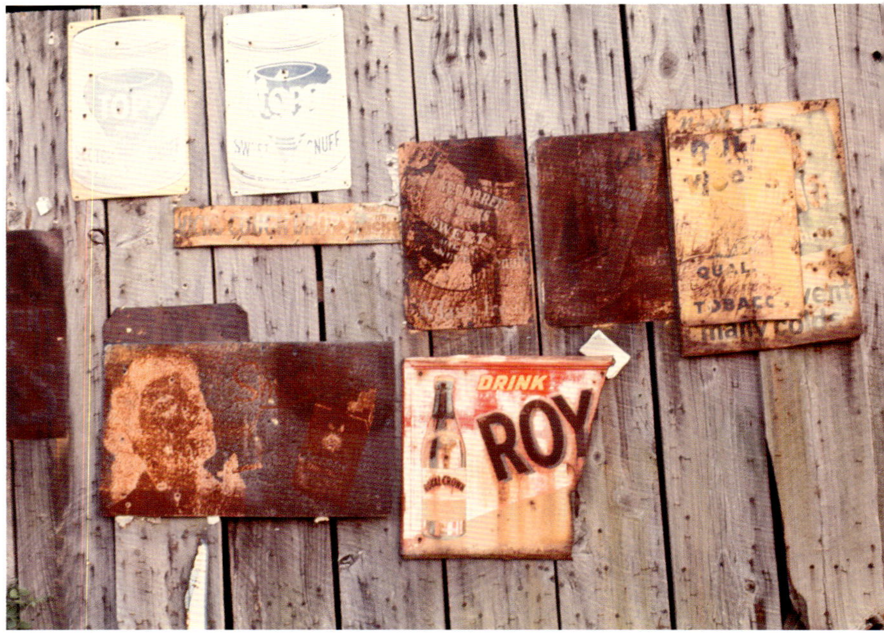

Tin graffiti, Chulahoma, 1972–75.

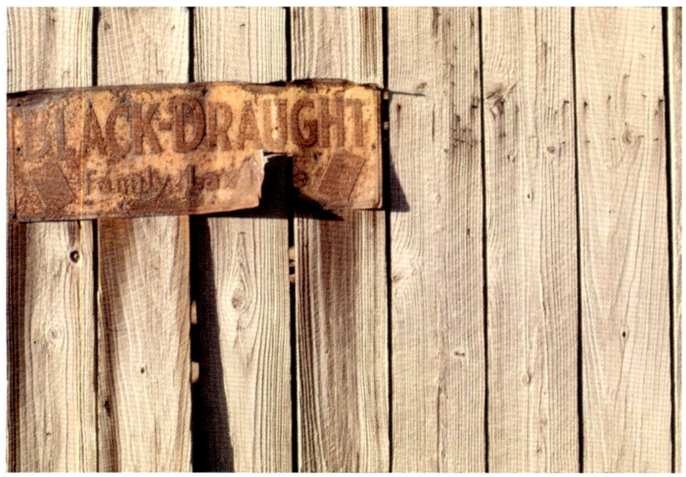

Black Draught tin sign, Chulahoma, 1972–75. The abandoned buildings of Chulahoma were held together by the tin signs on them.

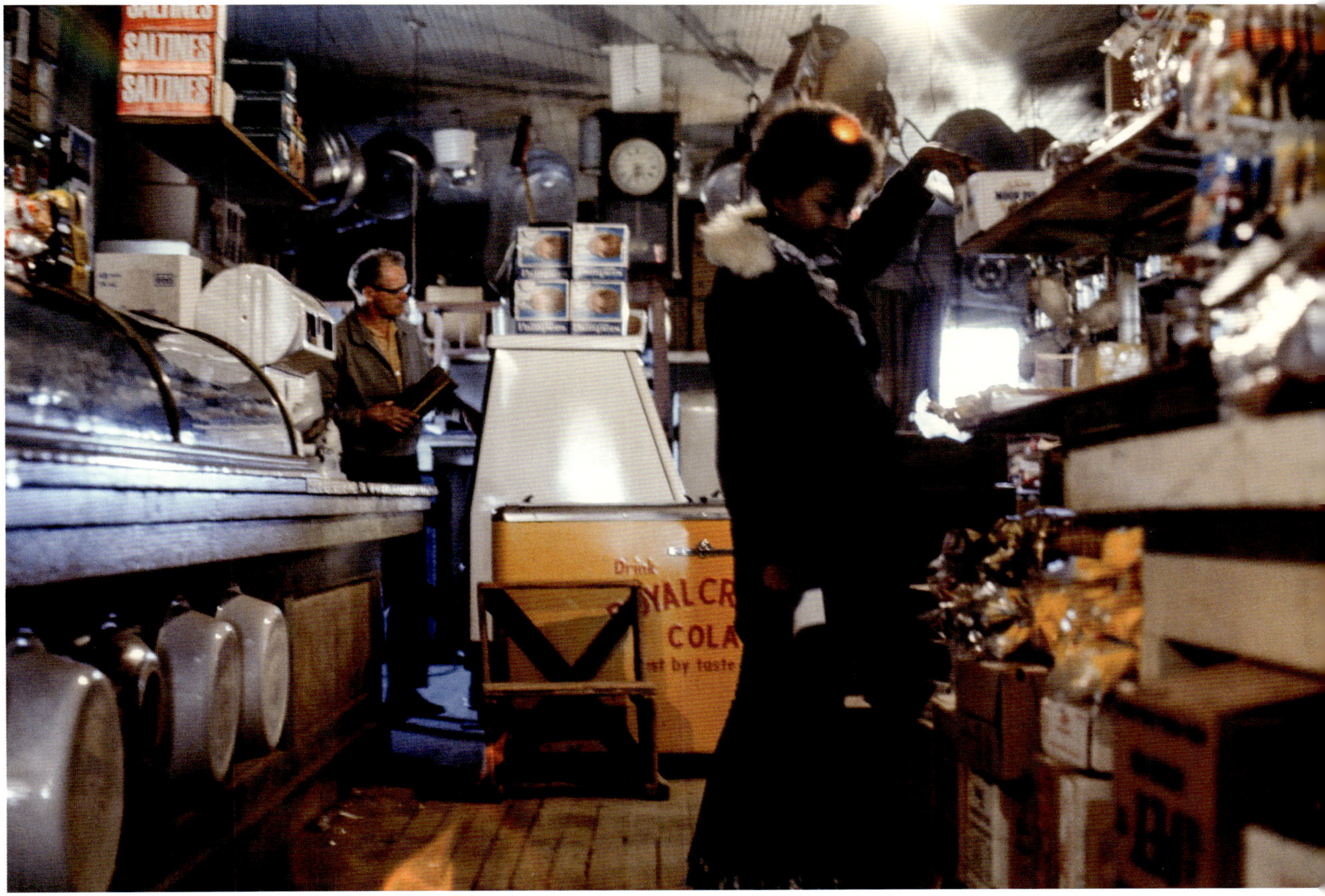

Inside Waldrip's General Store, Chulahoma, 1972–75. Hal Waldrip knew he was running his store on borrowed time, but it helped keep Chulahoma alive as a community. It served as post office, grocery, feed store, clothing shop, community center, informal bank, telephone center, and snack bar.

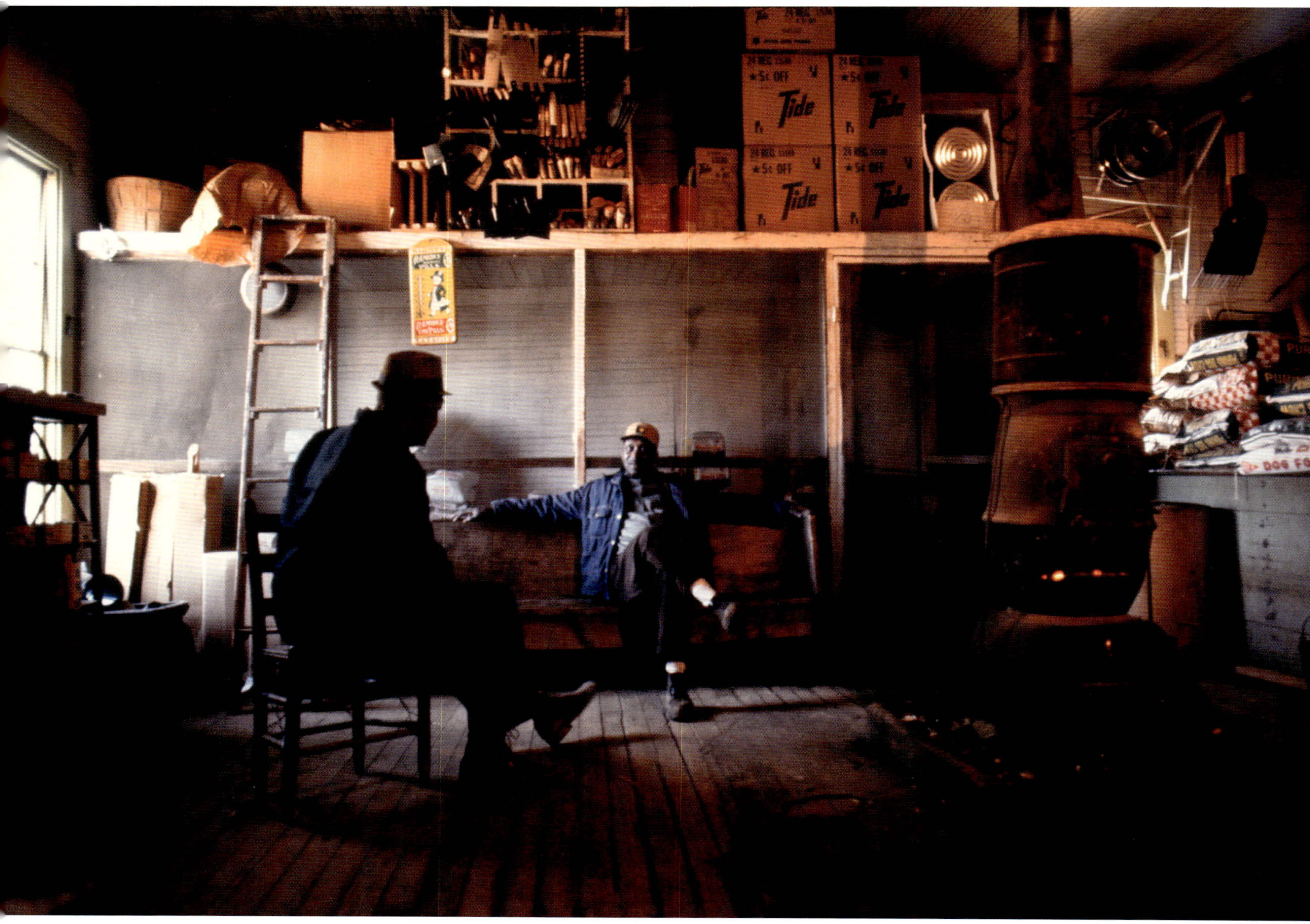

Winter, Chulahoma, 1972–1975. Morris Shaw and Elvan Clark around the stove in Waldrip's General Store. Hal said, "People still want a place to hang out. In wintertime, when hunting season comes up, sometimes you'll have twenty, thirty in here eating dinner . . . Cut 'em off a piece of bologna, give them a nickel's worth of crackers . . . or cut 'em a can of sardines, or whatever they might want."

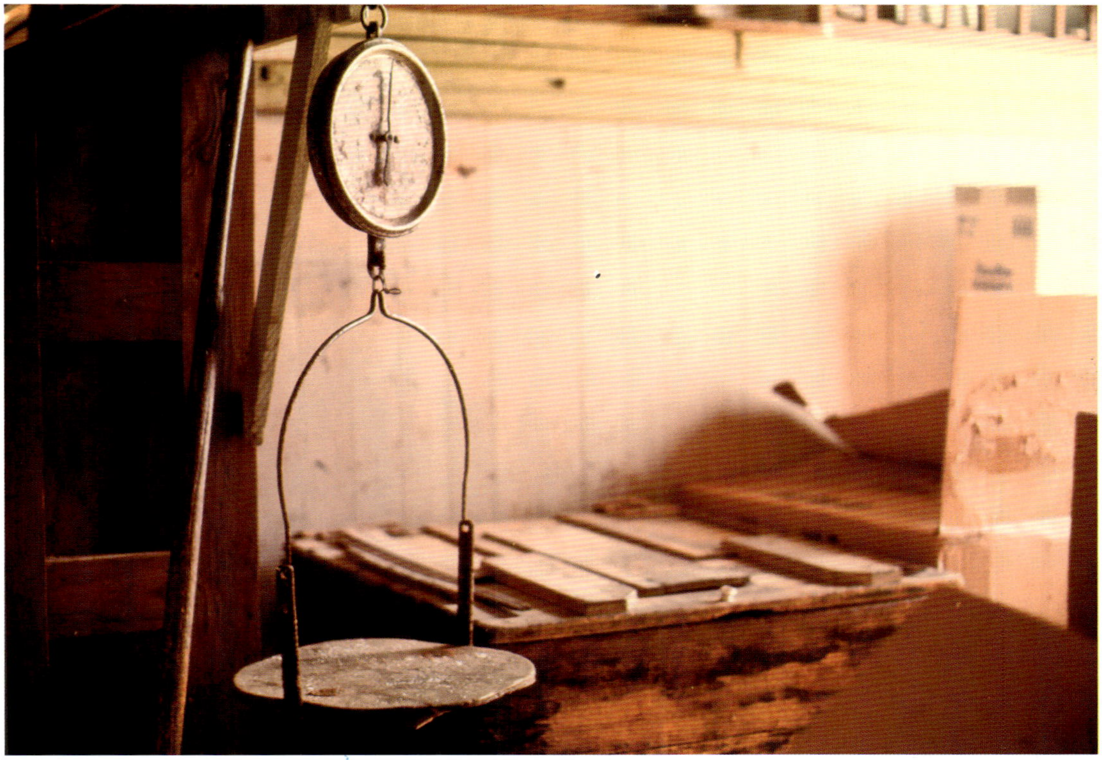

Scales for sacks of feed in the back of Waldrip's store,
Chulahoma, 1972–75.

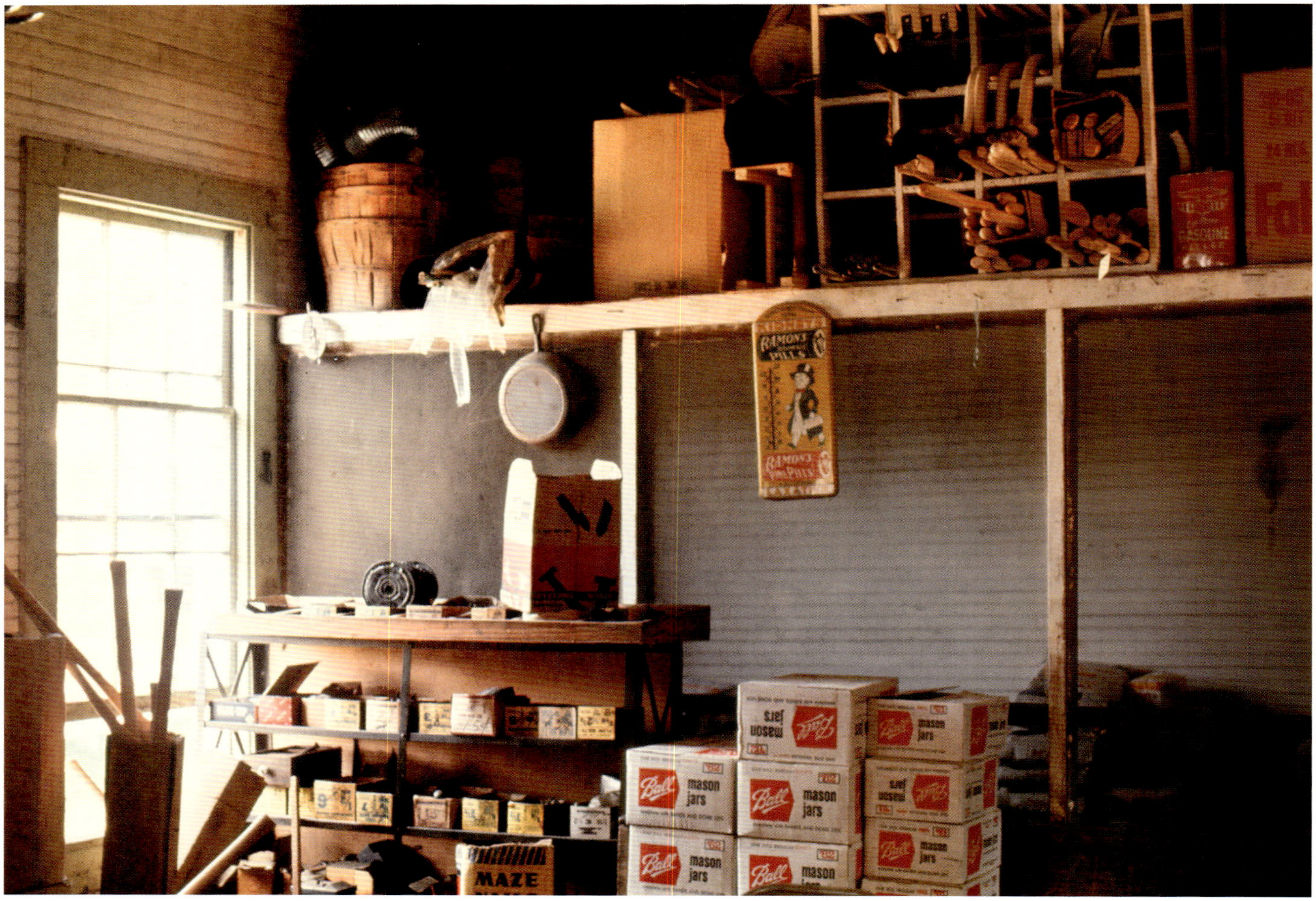

The back of Waldrip's store, Chulahoma, 1972–75.

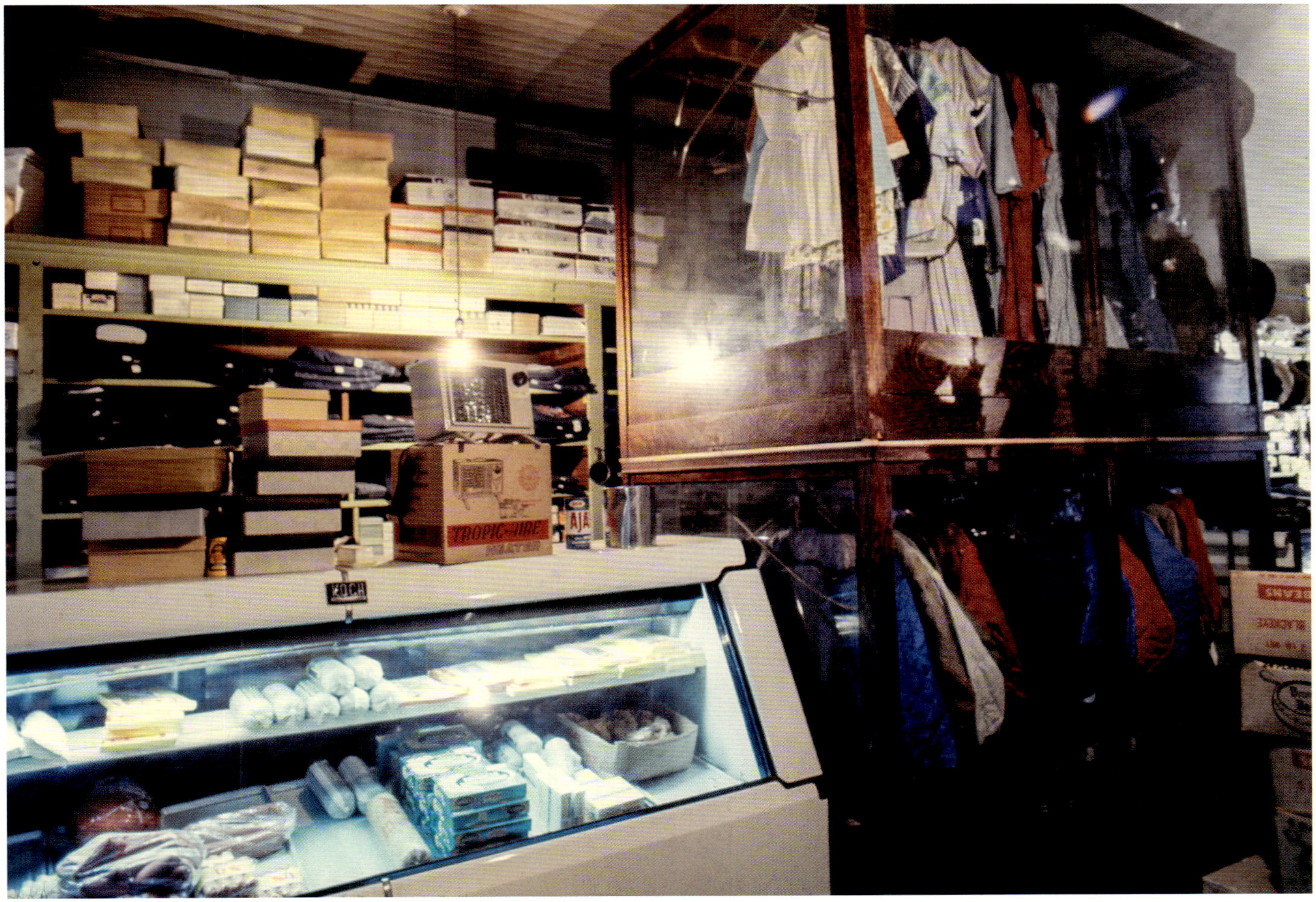

You could buy most anything you needed but not everything you might want,
Waldrip's store, Chulahoma, 1972–75.

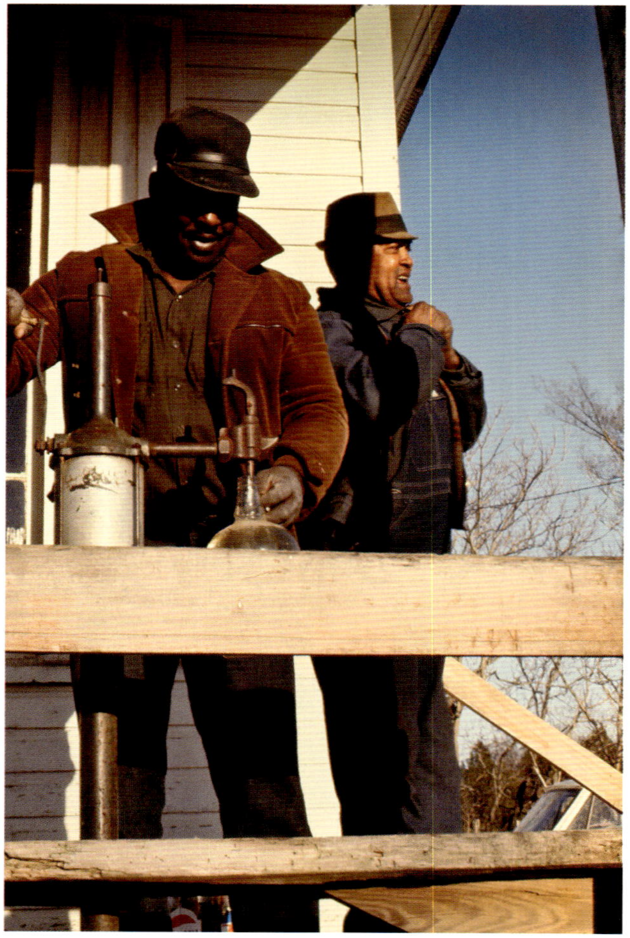

Winter, Waldrip's store, Chulahoma, 1972–75. As one customer draws kerosene, Morris Shaw passes by.

Waldrip's store, Chulahoma, 1972–75. Sling blades were $3.00. Hal said, "There's a handle for every tool you'd ever need to have."

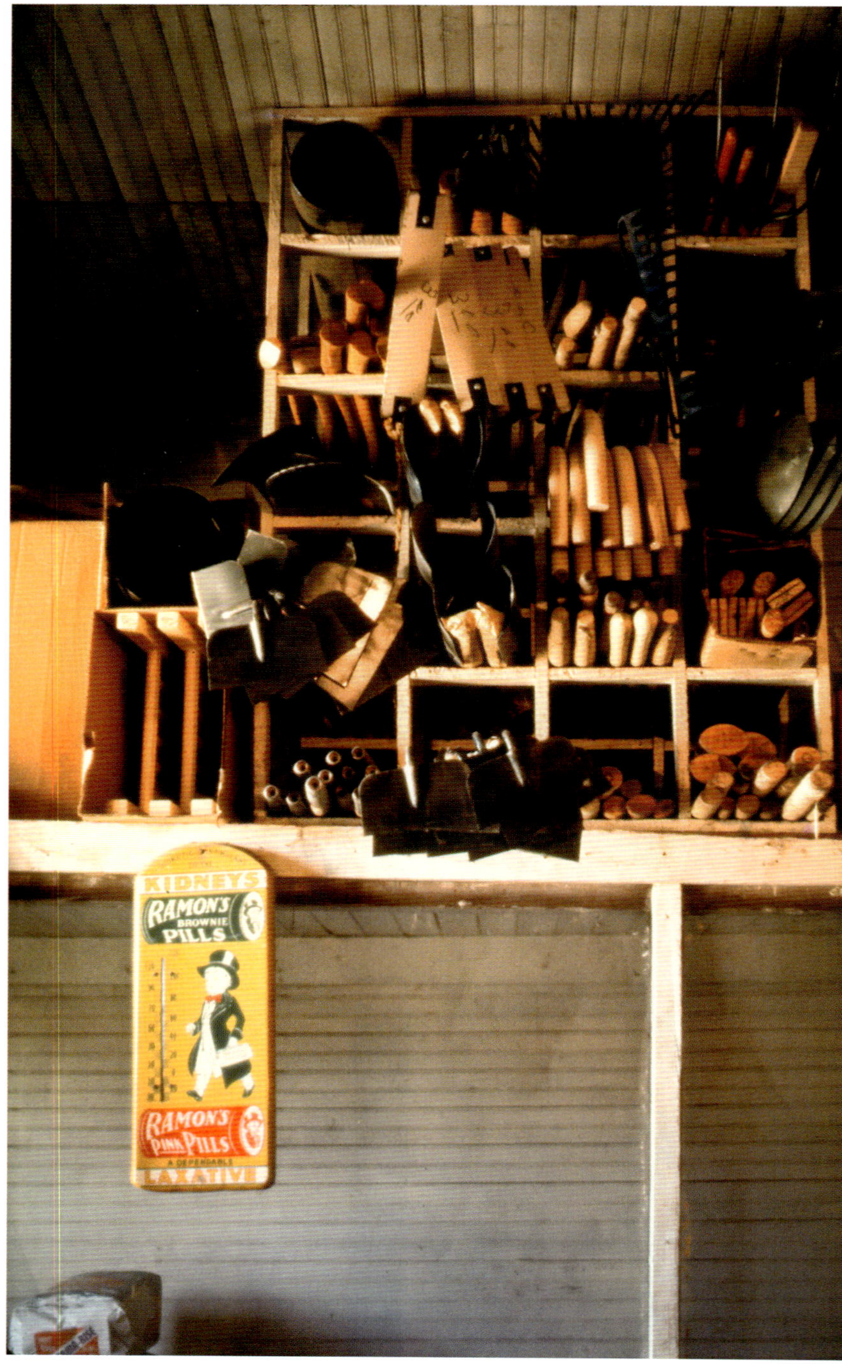

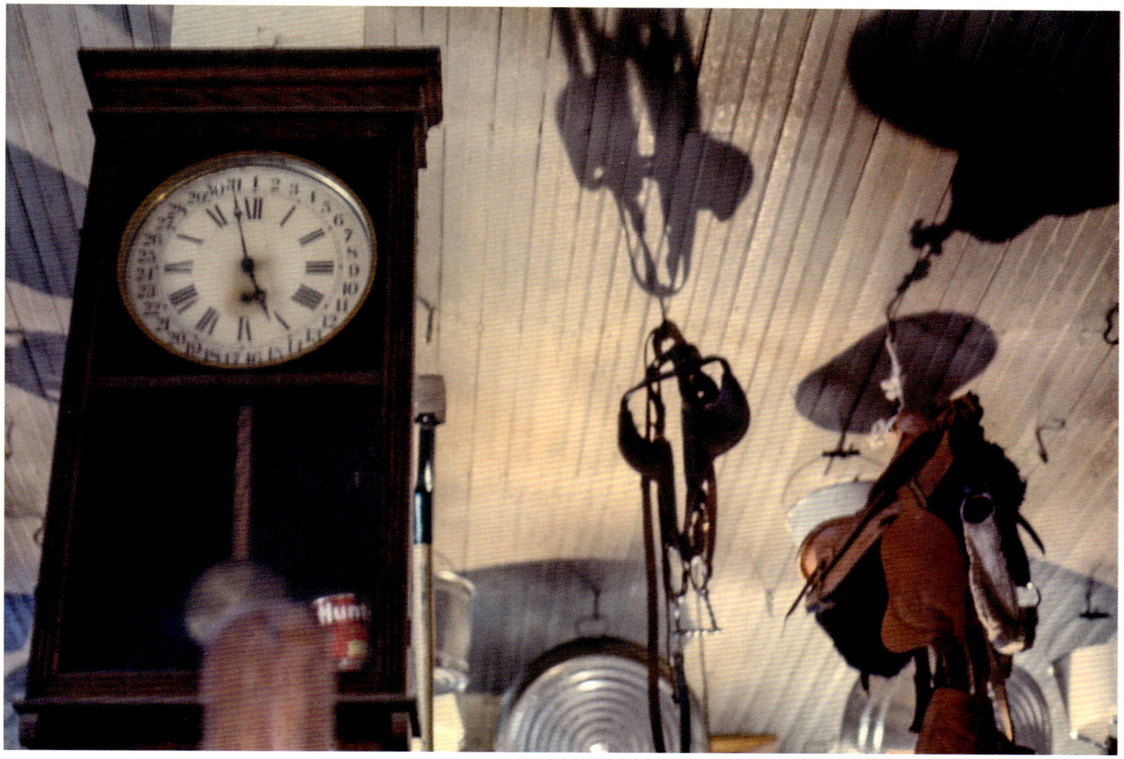

Stopped clock, Waldrip's Store, Chulahoma, 1972–75. This timepiece could be a visual metaphor for the store itself. Hal considered modernizing his store: "I think I could do more business with a different type [of] store, and I know I could do it easier. If I had it heated, air-conditioned where it wouldn't get so dusty and dirty . . . then I could put it all out on a table and let them wait on themselves and be up in the front, see . . . I wouldn't have to do all the walking . . . let them do the walking . . . I think we'd lose some of the old-timey atmosphere, I reckon you'd call it . . . But I don't think we'd lose any . . . any money . . . I don't know, I just don't do it . . . I don't know if I ever will or not. Probably won't."

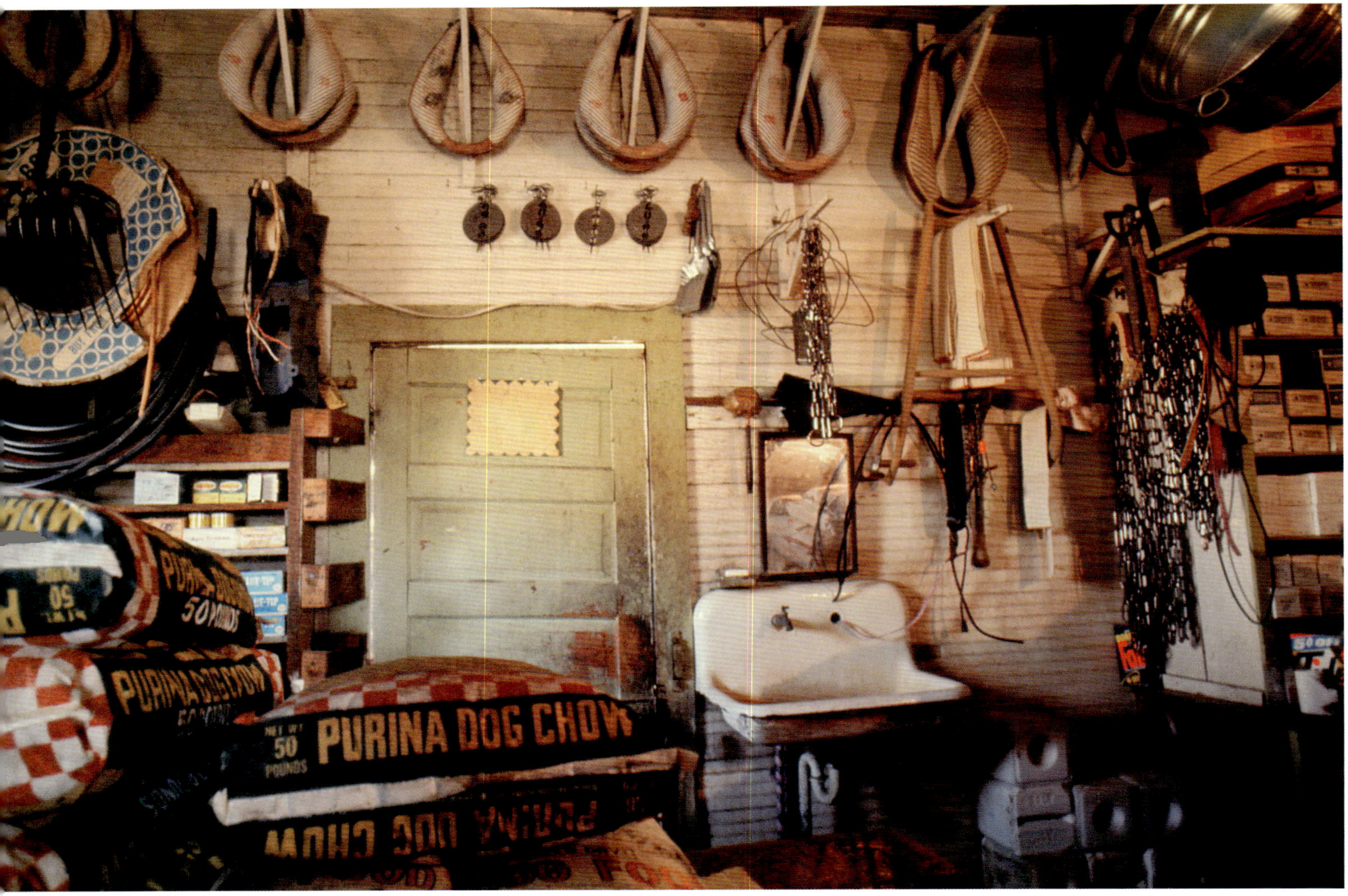

Feed and mule collars back of Waldrip's store,
Chulahoma, 1972–75.

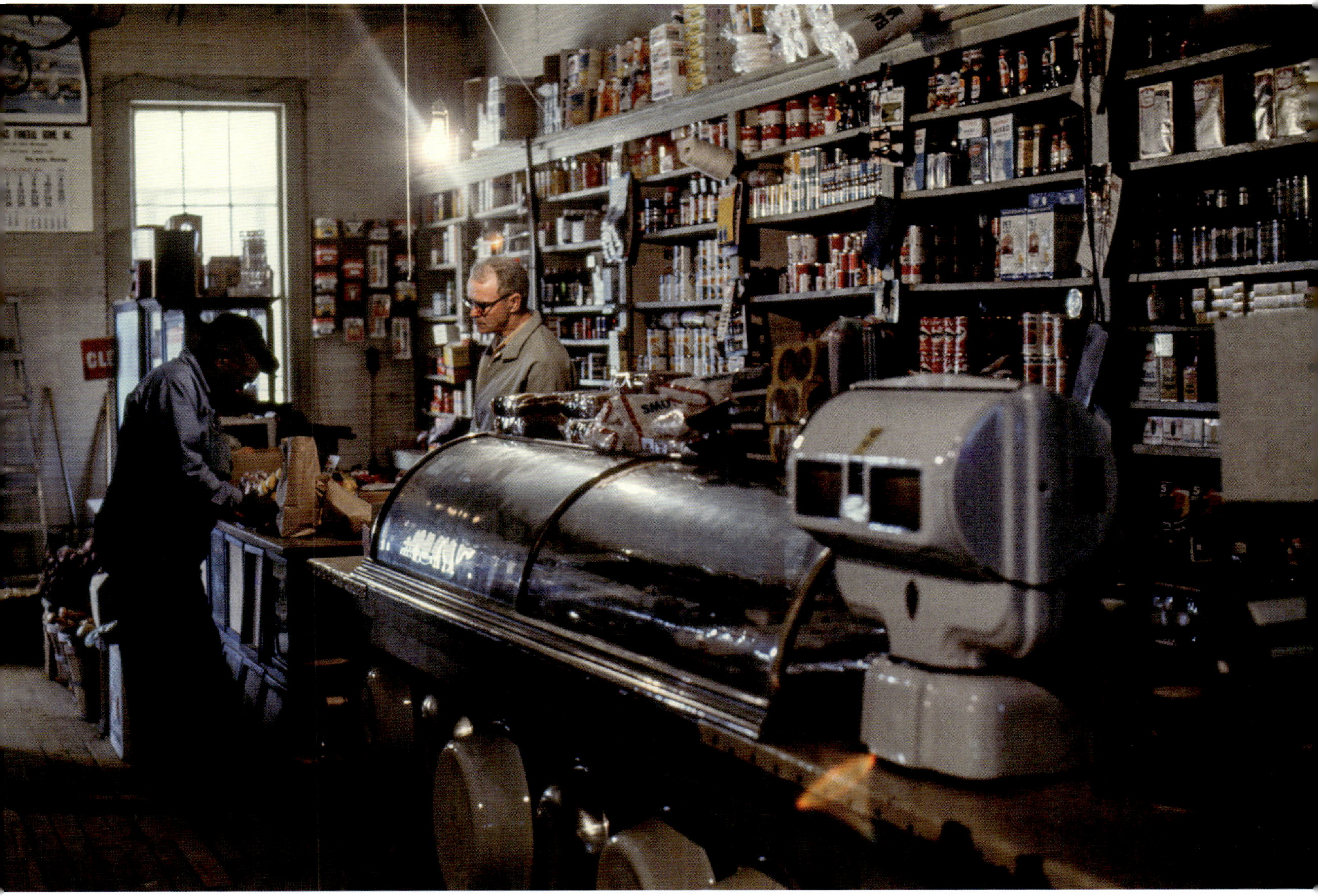

Doc James and Hal at the counter in Waldrip's General Store, Chulahoma, 1972–75.

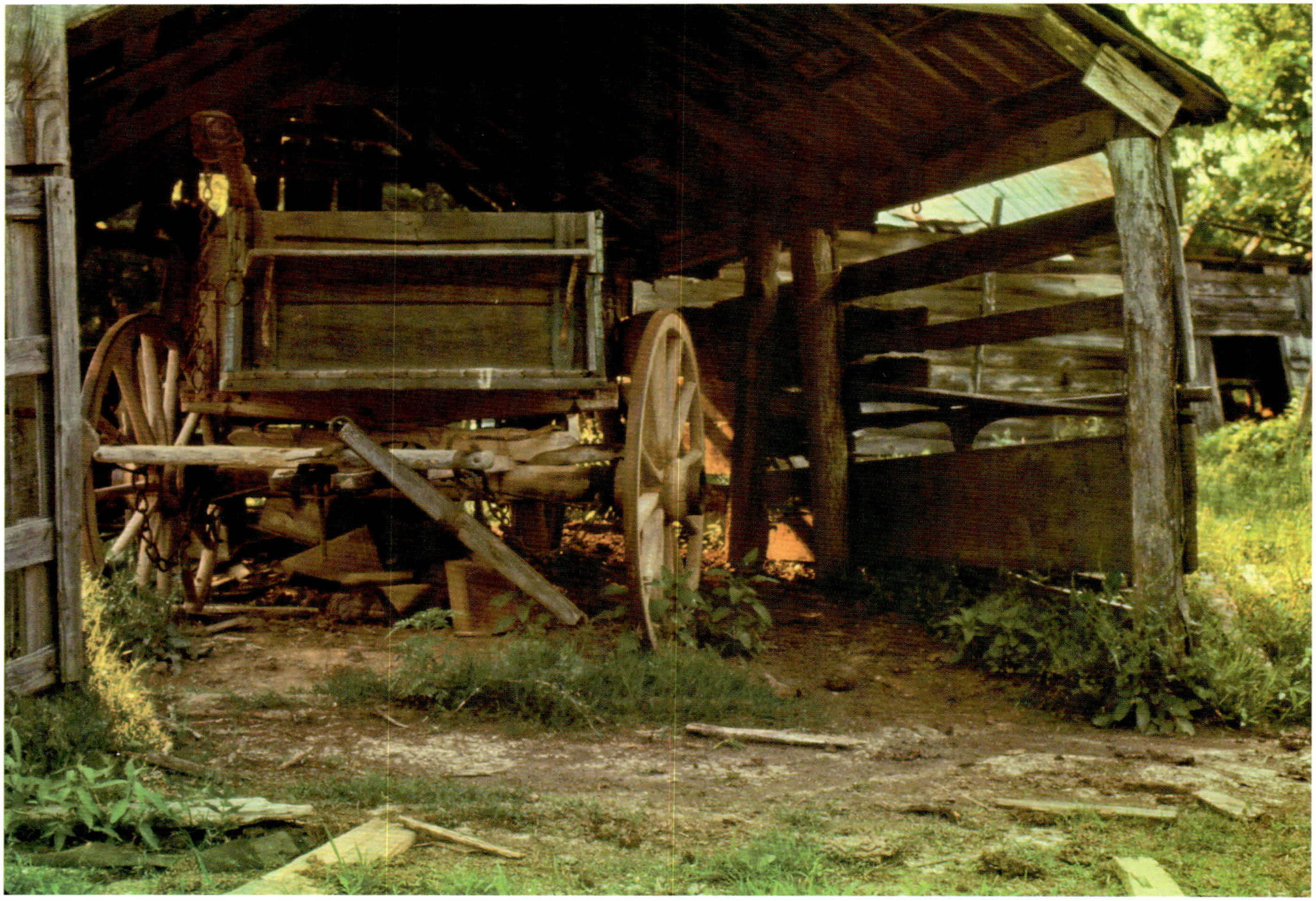

Old wagon with singletree, Panola County, 1972–75.

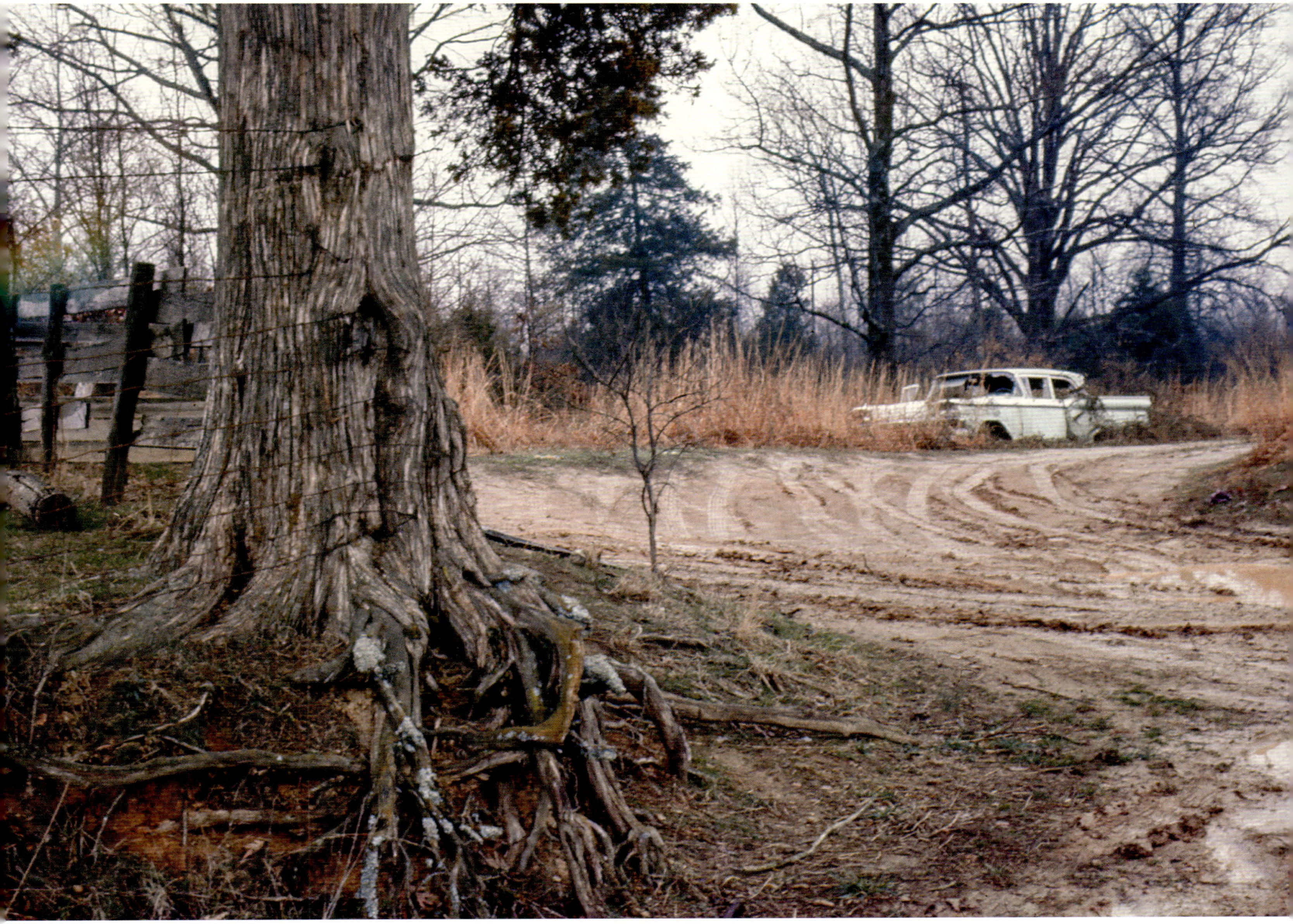

Old Ford and cedar, winter colors, near Waterford, 1972–75.

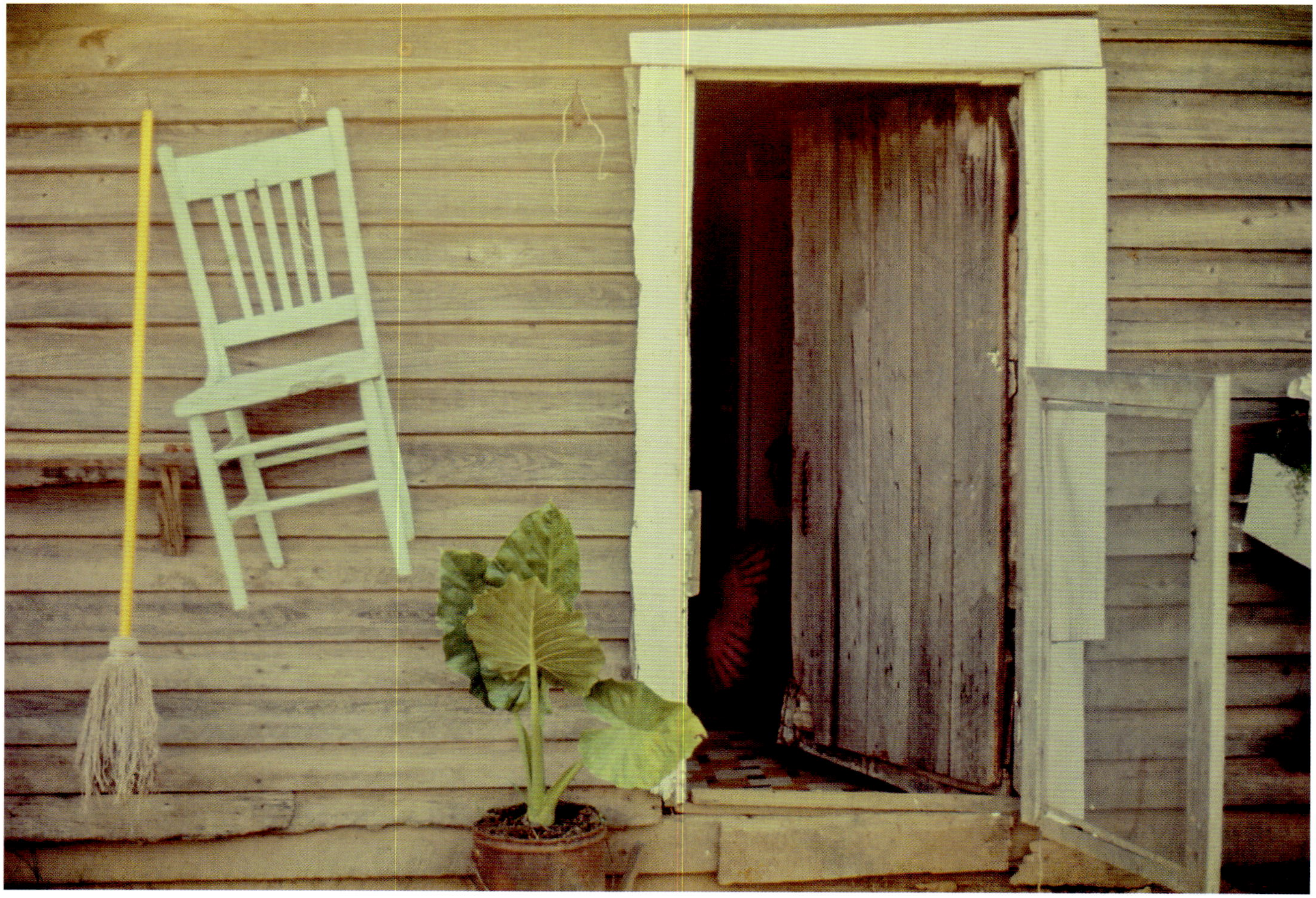

Wall storage, Aubrey Jefferies's homeplace, Chulahoma, 1972–75. Aubrey Jefferies really cared for his place. Everything was orderly and in good repair. Large gardens of flowers added color.

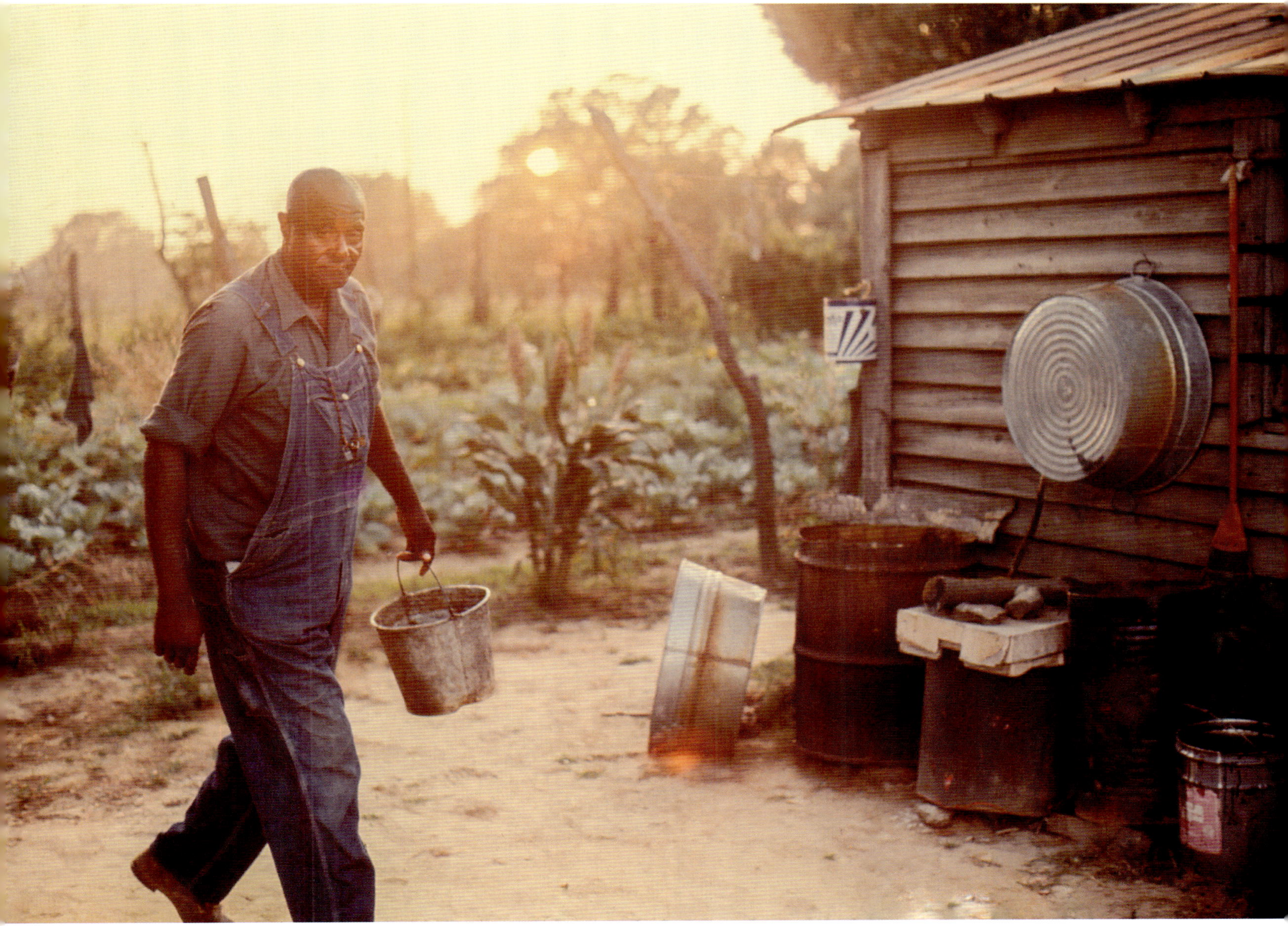

Aubrey Jefferies at his homeplace, Chulahoma, 1972–75. We called Jefferies's home Circle Stacks because of the way he piled his firewood into round beehive-looking stacks.

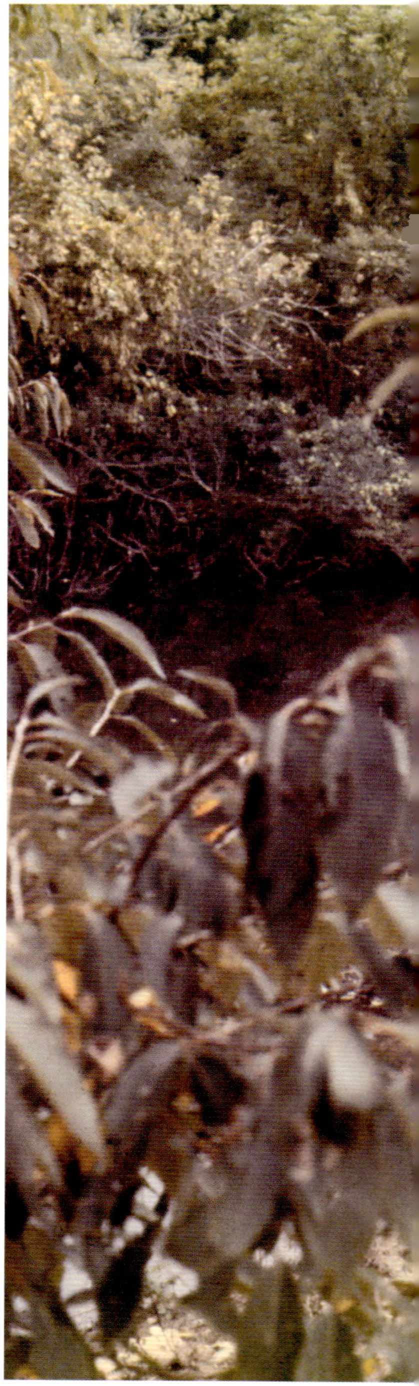

Fishing on the Tallahatchie River,
Lafayette County, 1972–75.

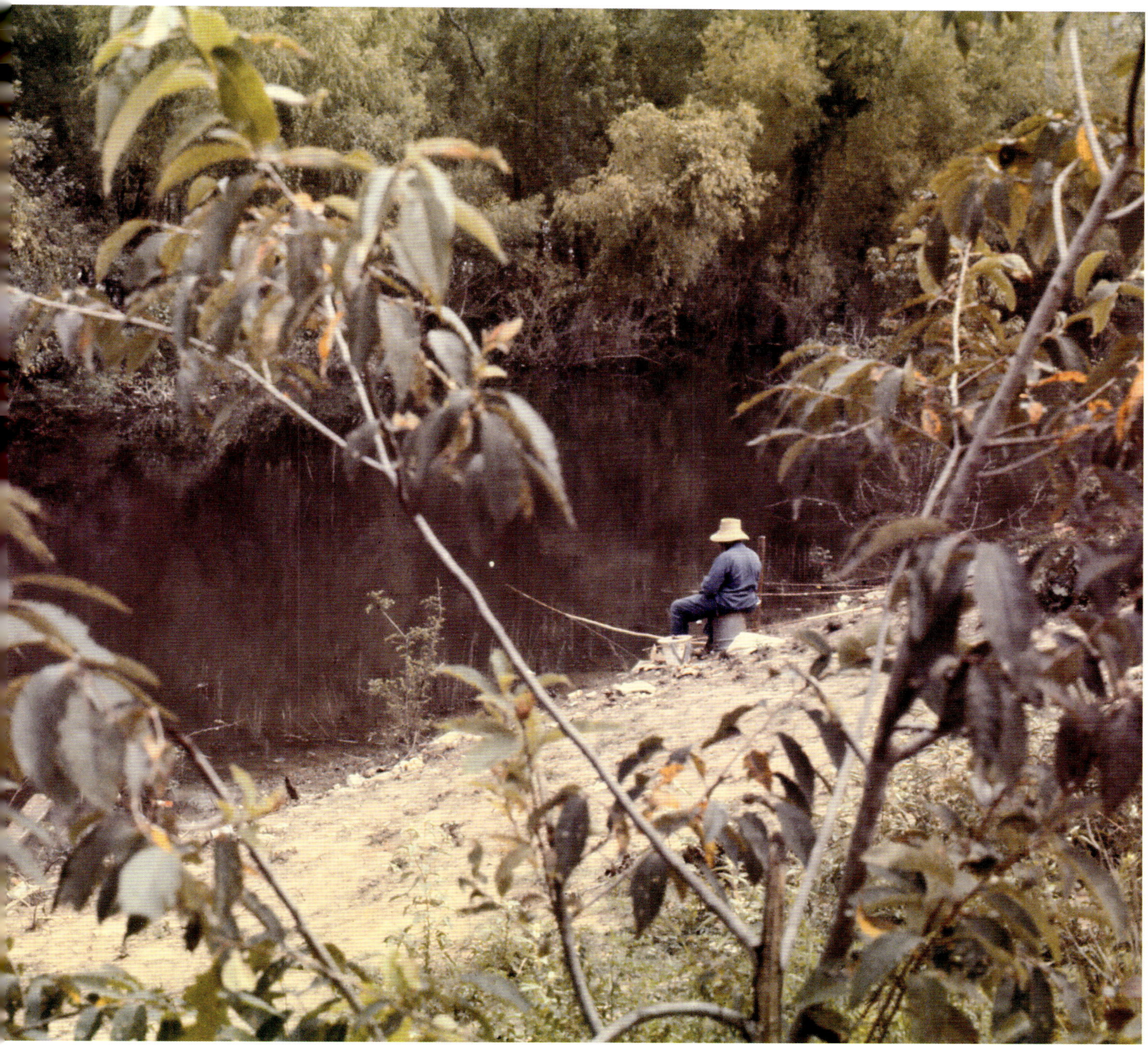

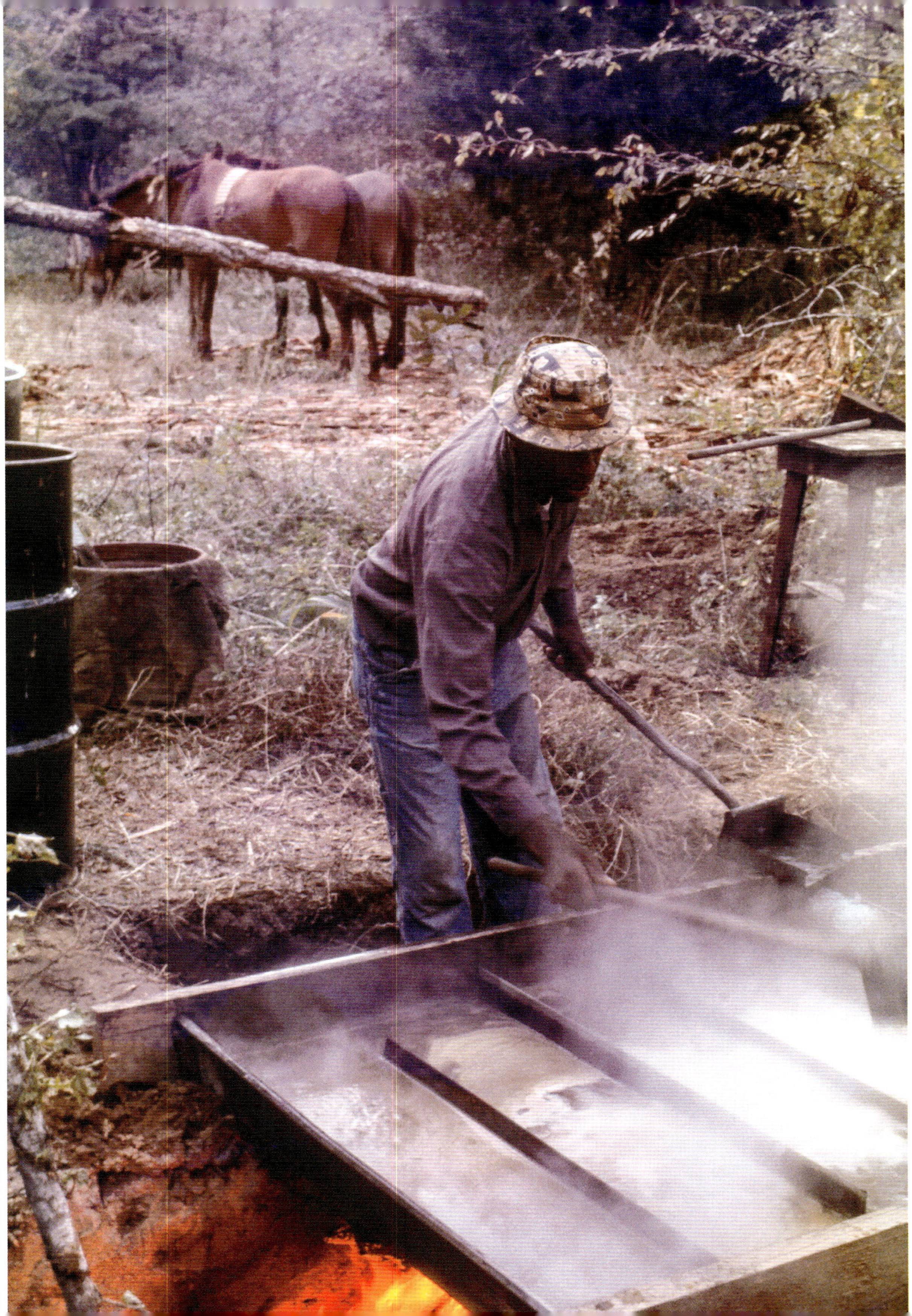

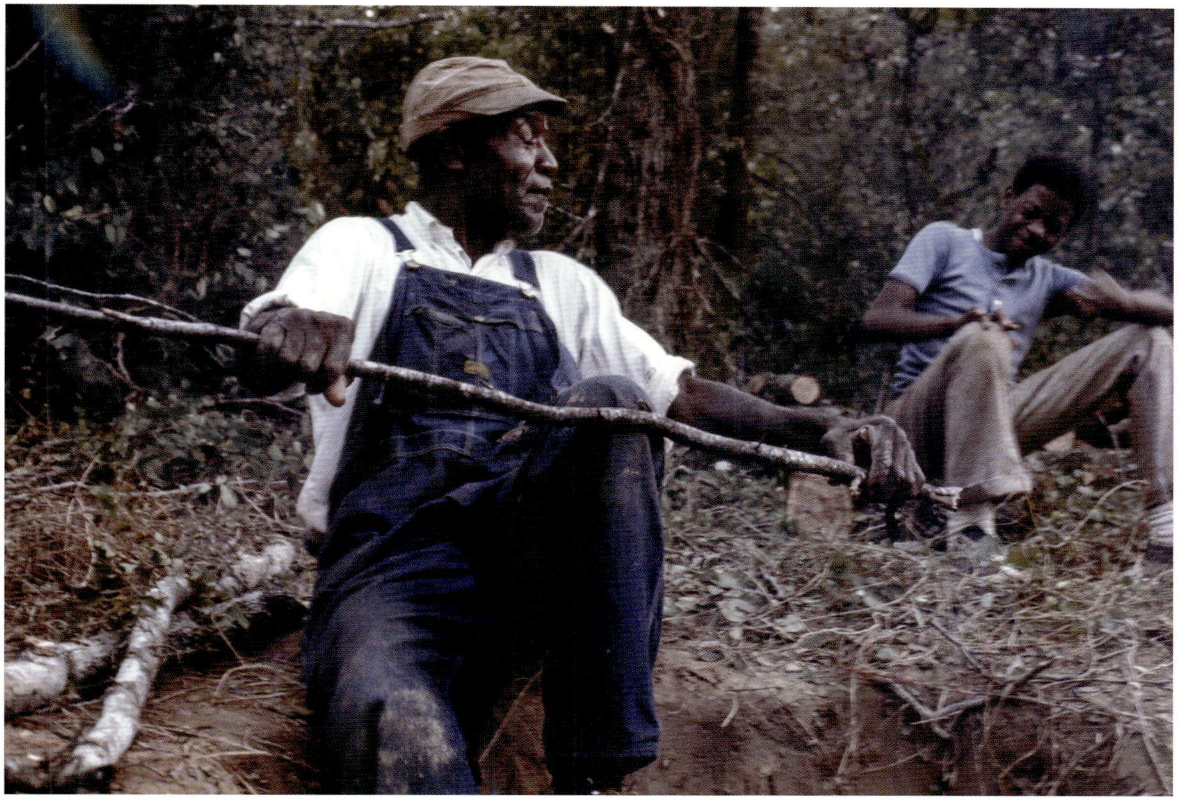

Judge Dean keeping the fire burning,
near Chulahoma, October 1972.

AG Newson cooking down molasses,
near Chulahoma, October 1972.

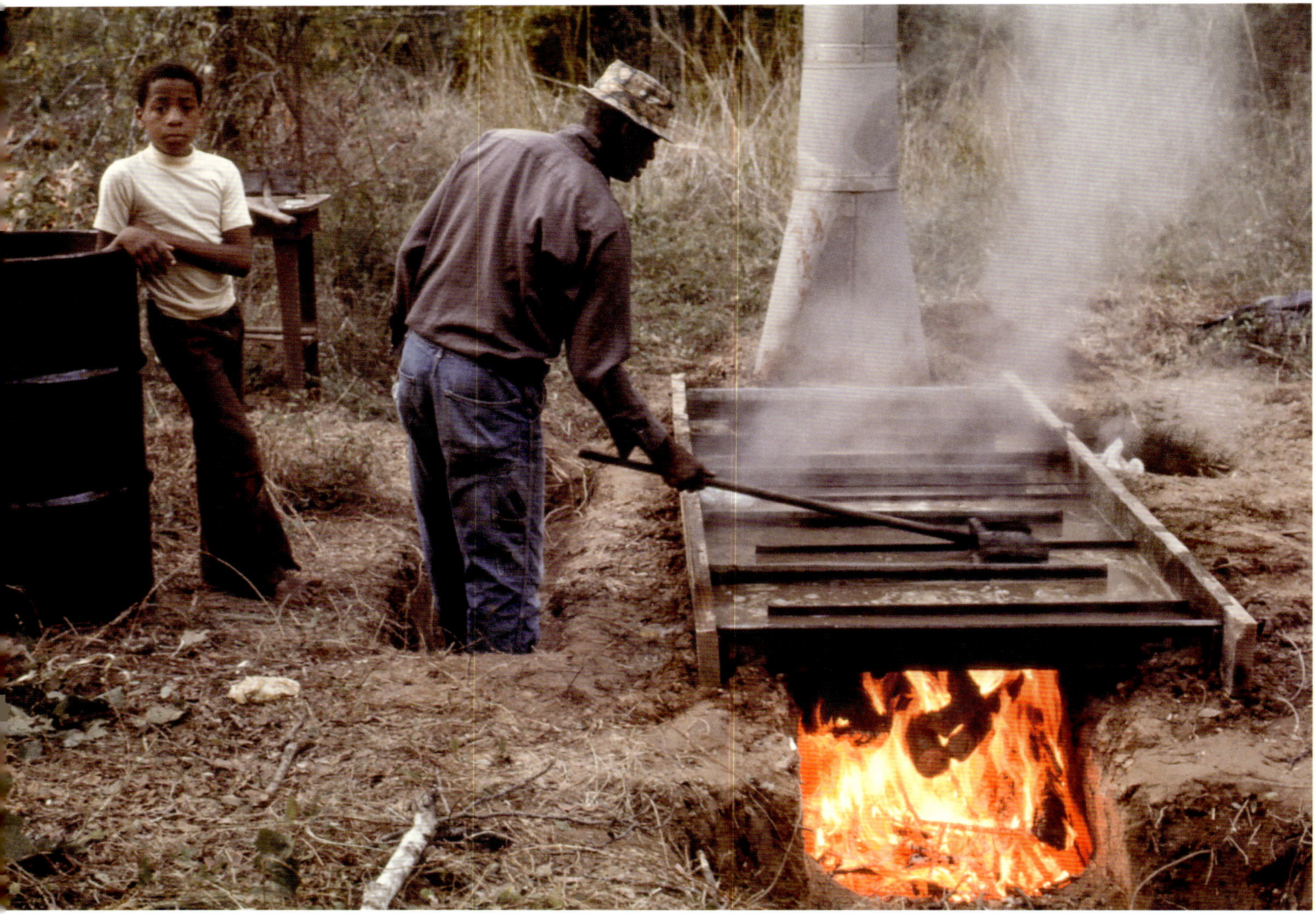

AG Newson and Doc James's grandson Calvin, near Chulahoma, October 1972. AG Newson: "It made me boil before it did though . . . putting that wood in it. You gotta look up in there and see where to put it. That's what's rough. It's hot. It ain't too much work. It's just hot standing over it. I'll tell you what you got to go up against. Ten gallons of juice make one gallon of molasses . . . that's how much you've got to boil it. If your fire don't burn good, it's liable to take a long time . . . and that barrel there holds sixty gallons. You know it takes a whole lot to boil it."

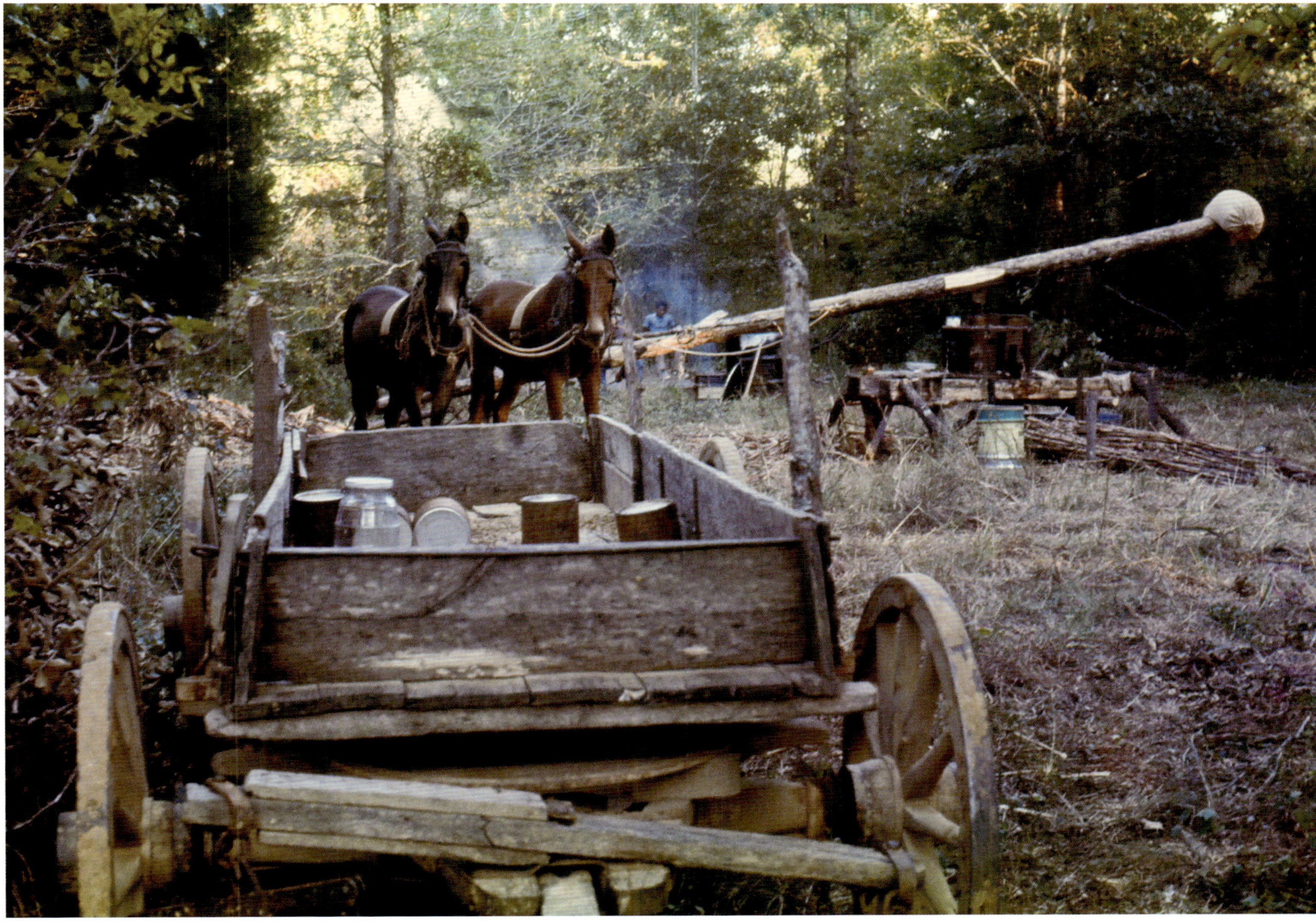

Frank and Jake, near Chulahoma, October 1972. Doc James said, "Old Jake and Frank. That's the only thing I had to make it. We made . . . we made two hundred gallons of 'lasses 'bout three years ago. And we ground every bit of it with them two mules. Just take them out at dawn time and water 'em . . . and give 'em some food. Hook 'em right back up."

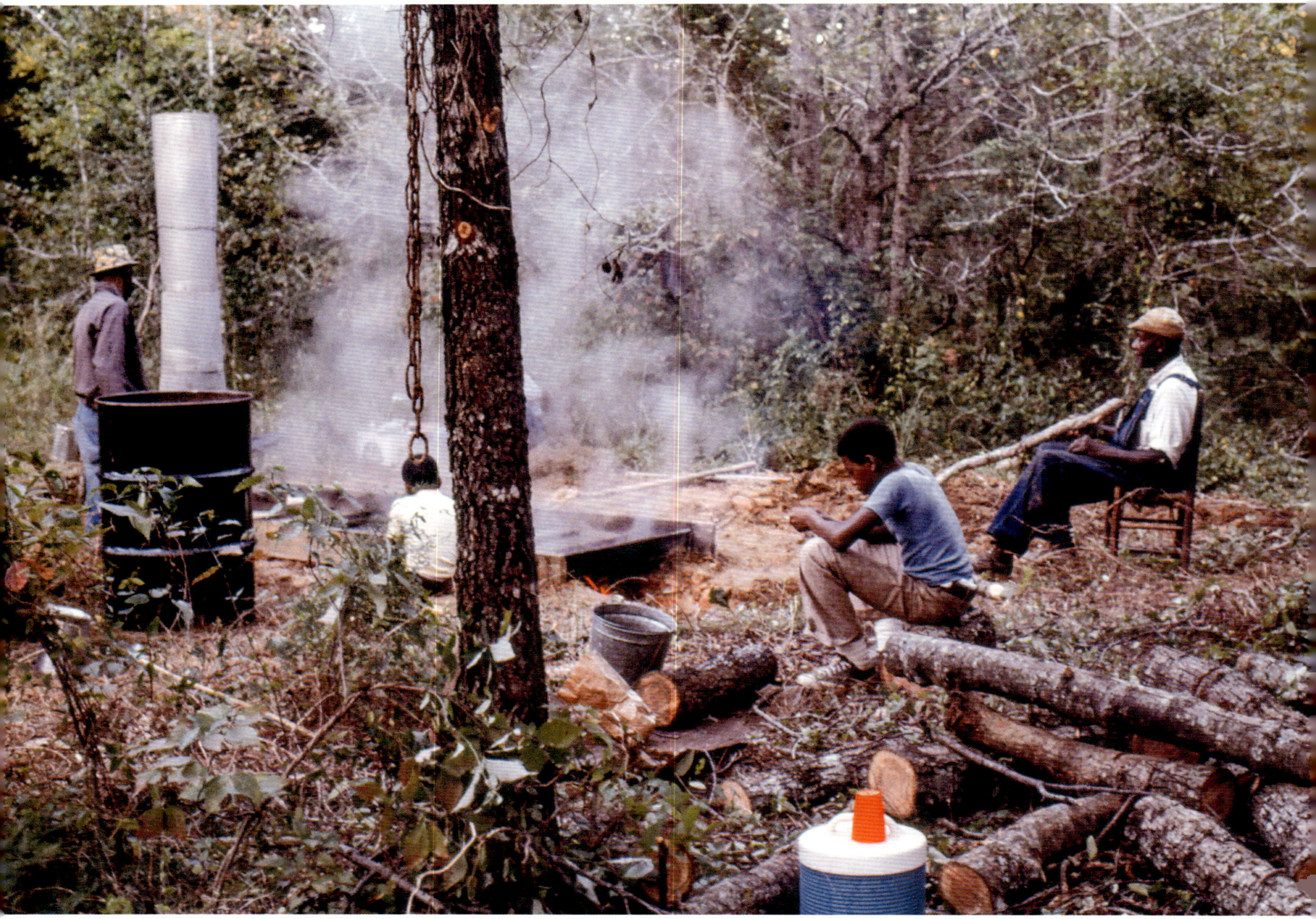

A small clearing in some bottomland, near Chulahoma, October 1972. The air was a medley of opposing scents. Raw earth, wood smoke, steaming molasses, and the tang of sweating mules. Somehow bended into a perfume that was well suited and help define the time and place. I wish I could let you smell it. Never forgotten.

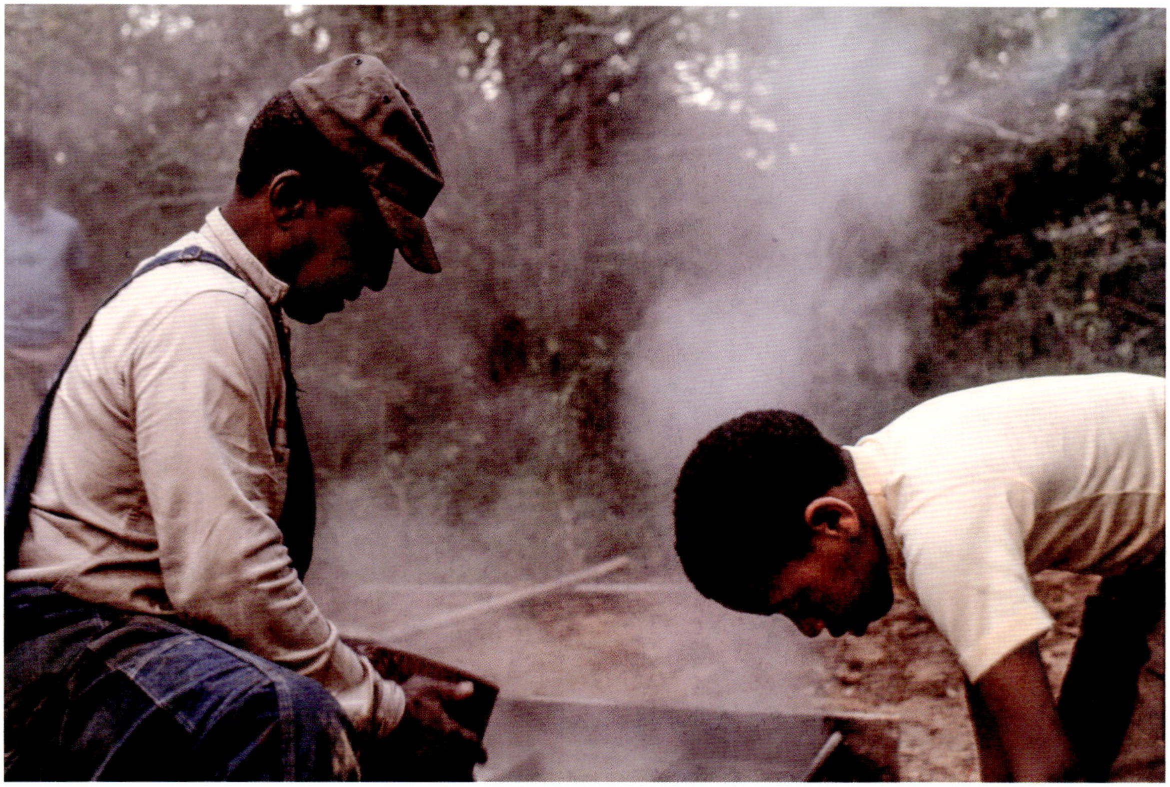

Doc James and his grandson Calvin James,
near Chulahoma, October 1972. Calvin later became a first sergeant of the 101st Airborne and an alderman in Holly Springs.

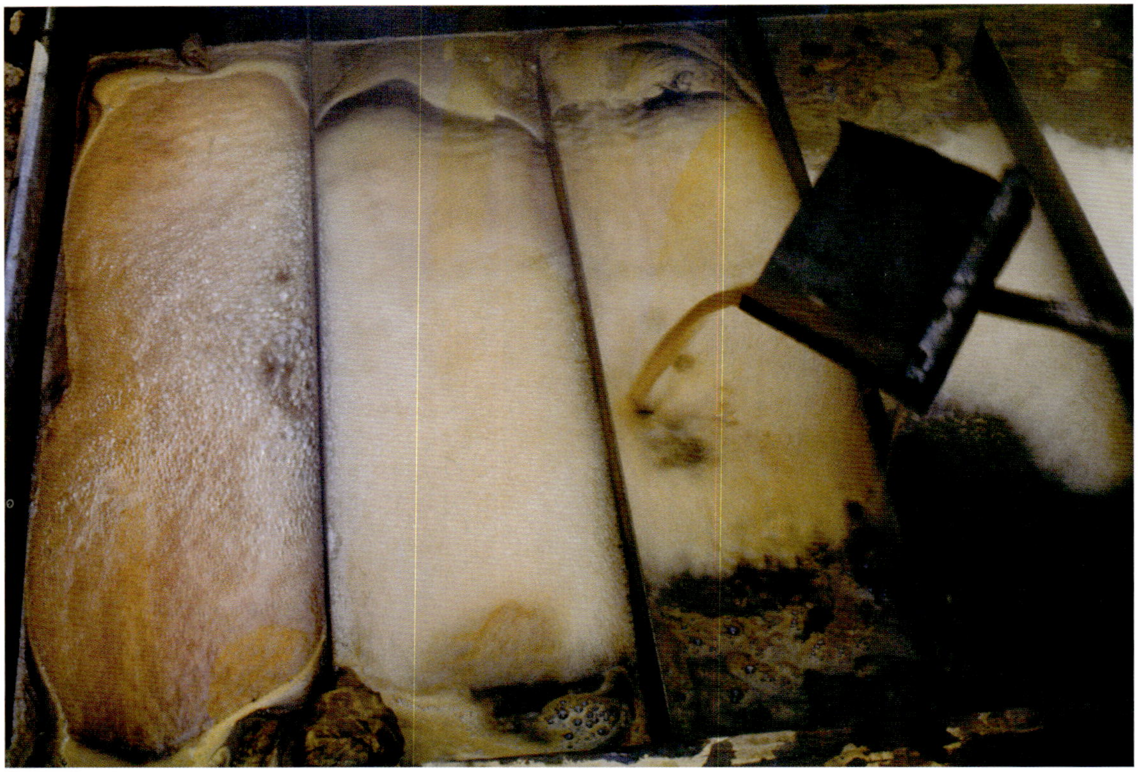

Skimming the pan, near Chulahoma, October 1972. AG described the boil: "See you got to boil it . . . Ten gallons of juice make[s] one gallon of molasses . . . and that's how much you've got to boil it."

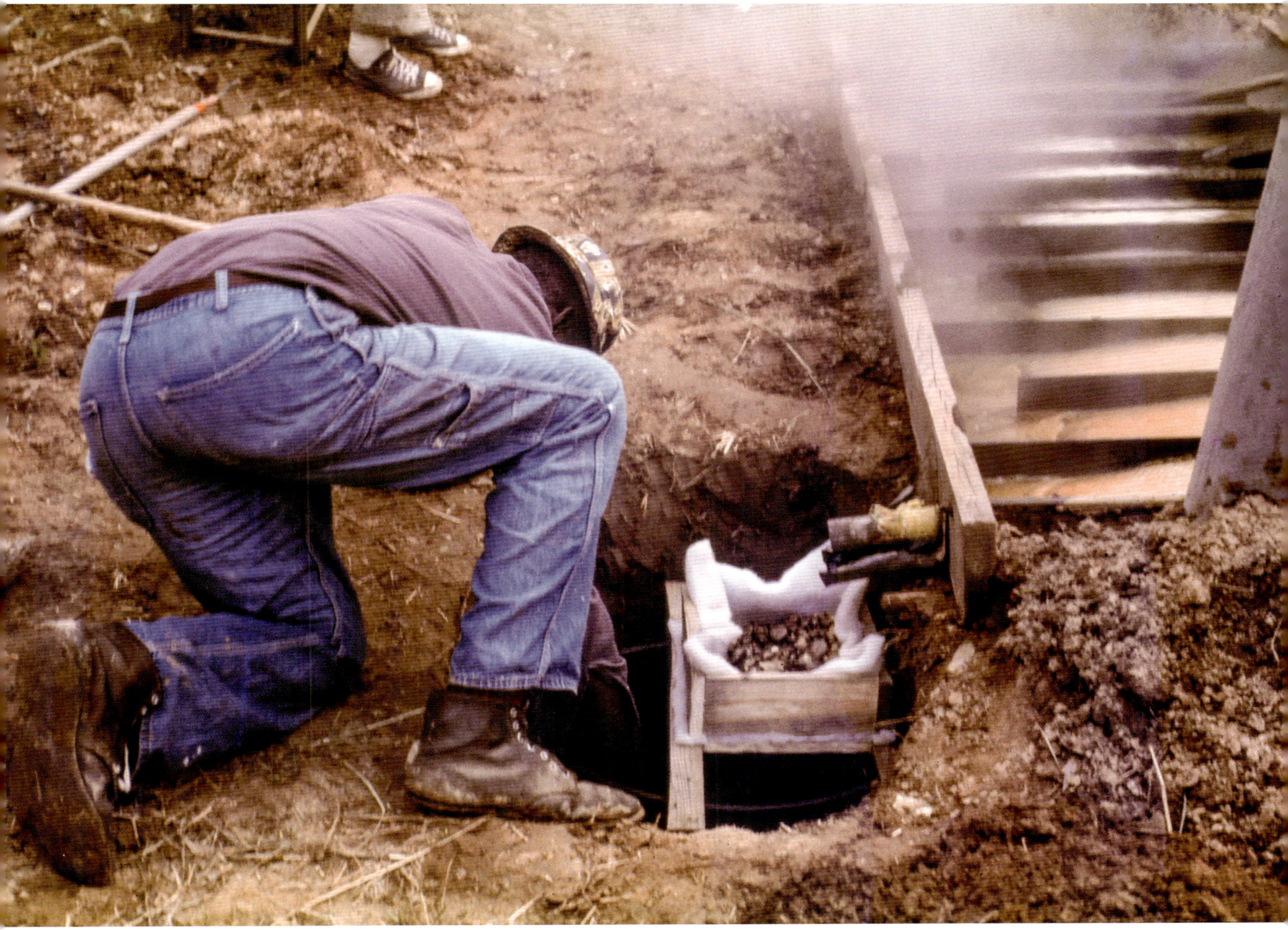

Drawing off the molasses, near Chulahoma, October 1972.

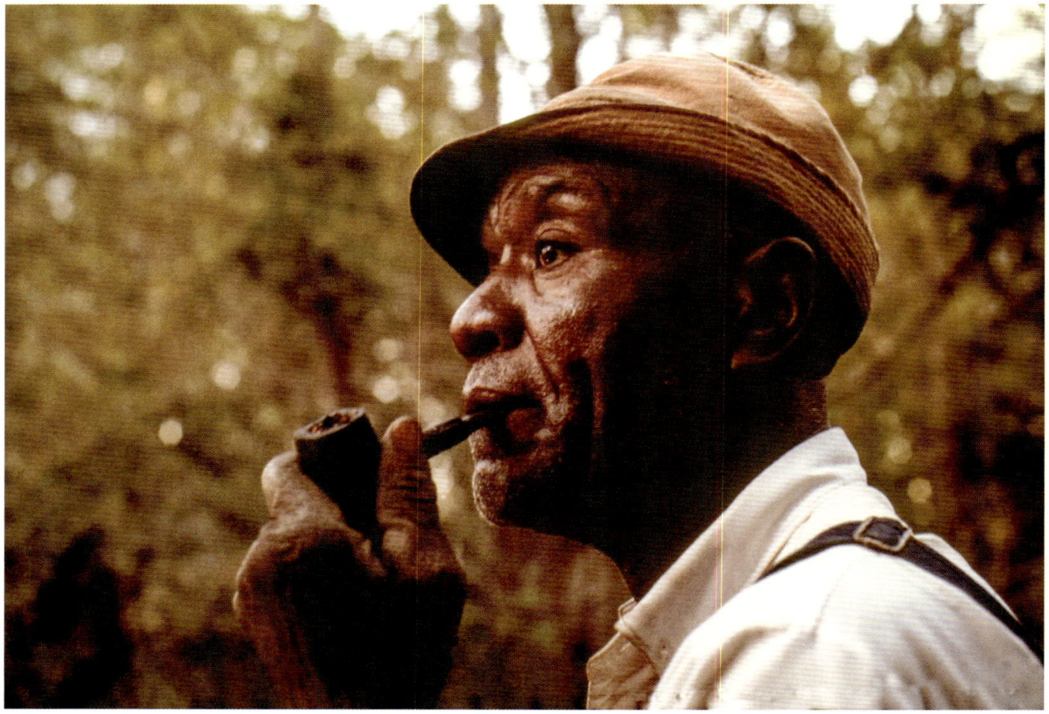

Judge Dean, near Chulahoma, October 1972. Judge fed the mill and took his breaks while tending the fire.

Sorghum mill, near Chulahoma, October 1972. Frank and Jake milling Doc James's molasses crop.

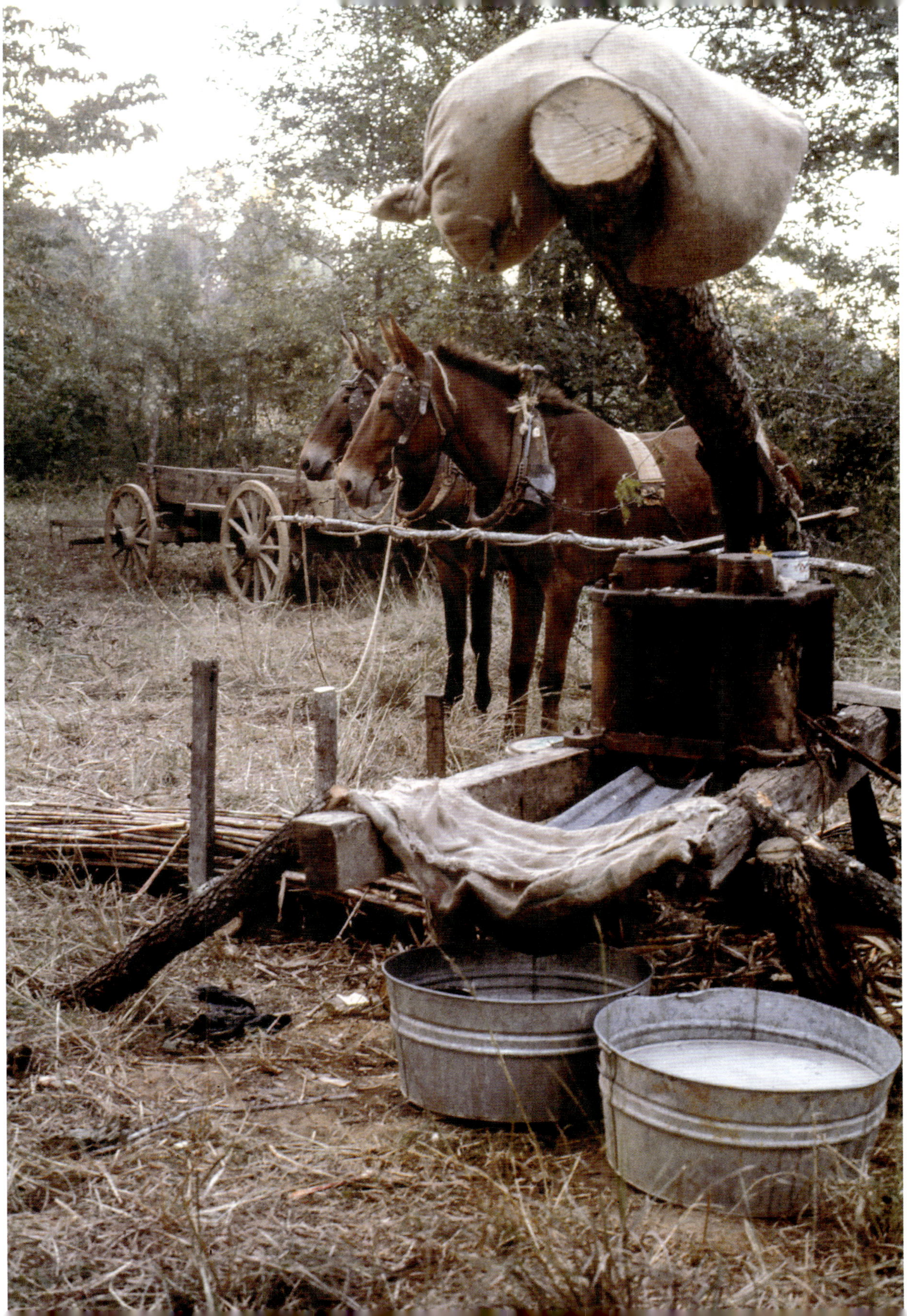

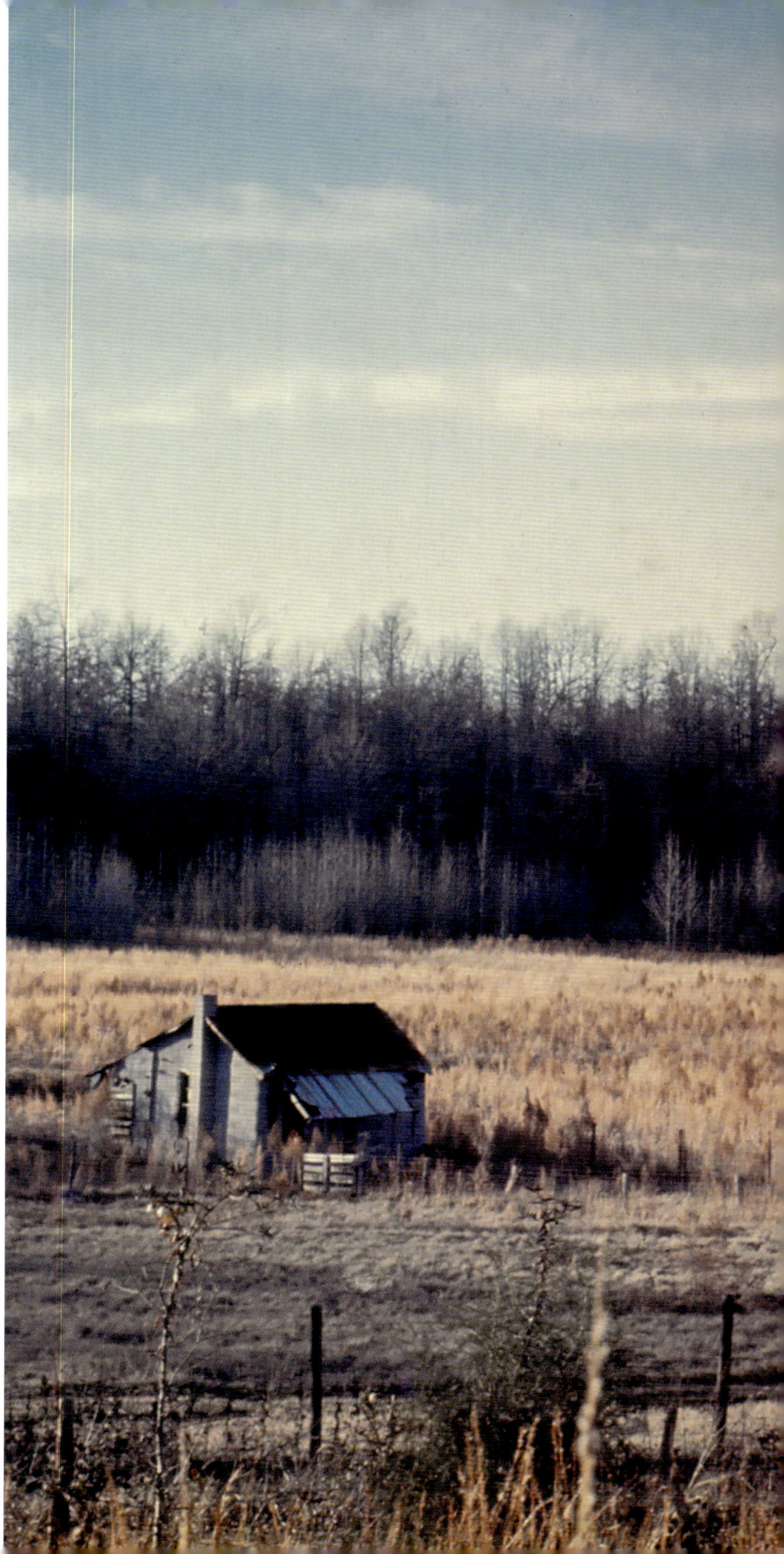

Winter colors, abandoned home,
Lafayette County, 1973.

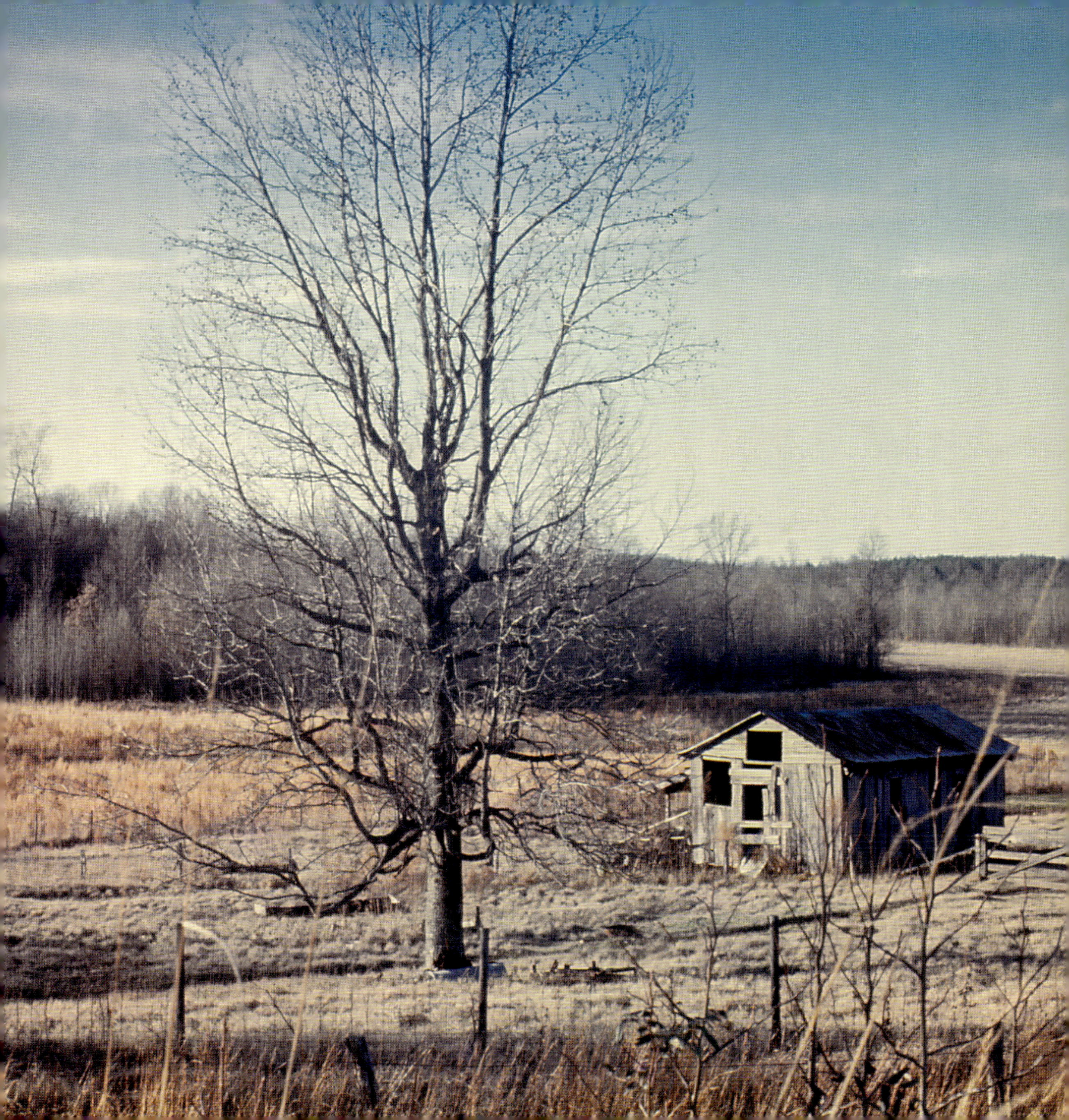

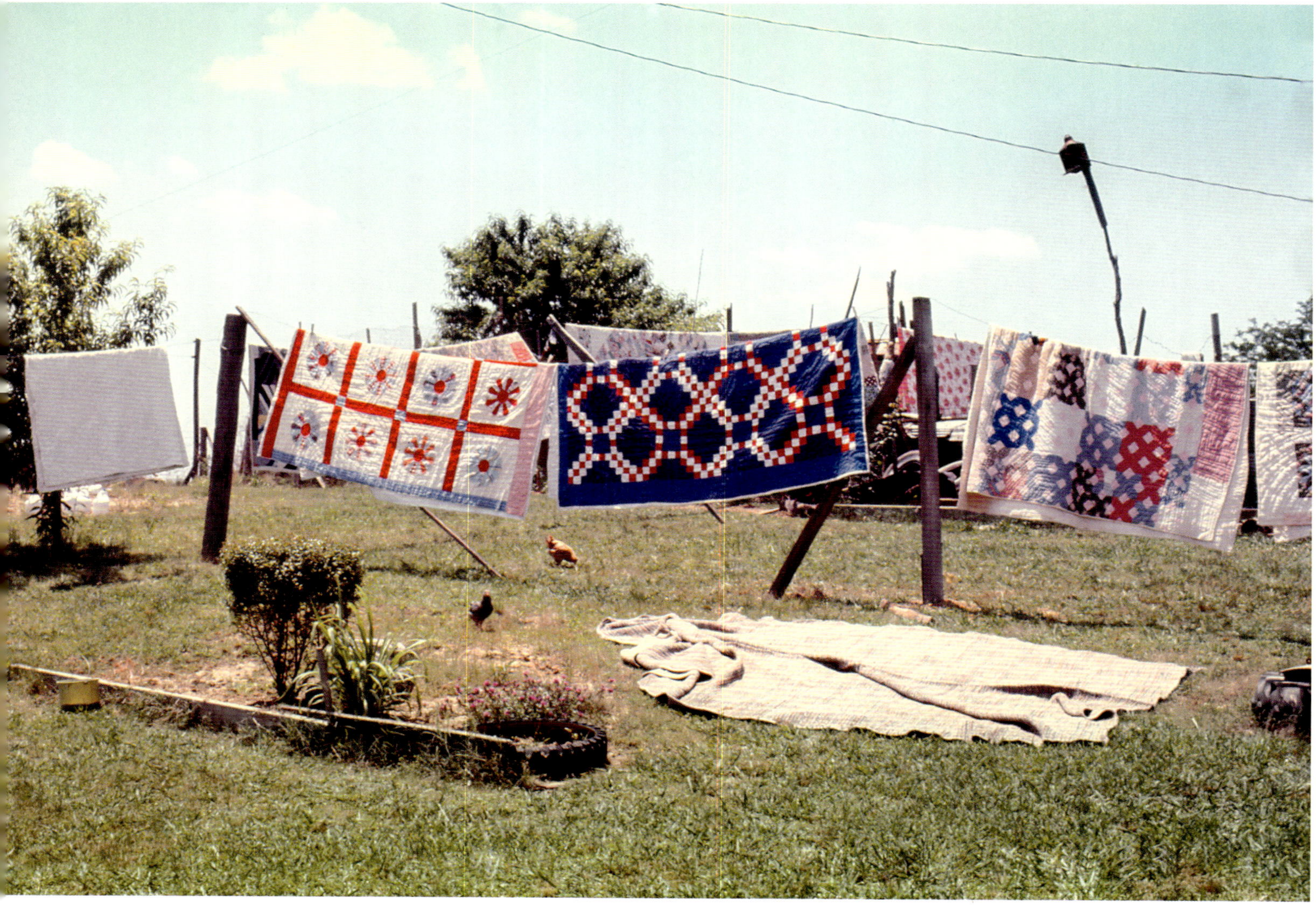

Riller Smith's quilts on the line, Highway 7 North near the Tallahatchie, Lafayette County, 1972–75.

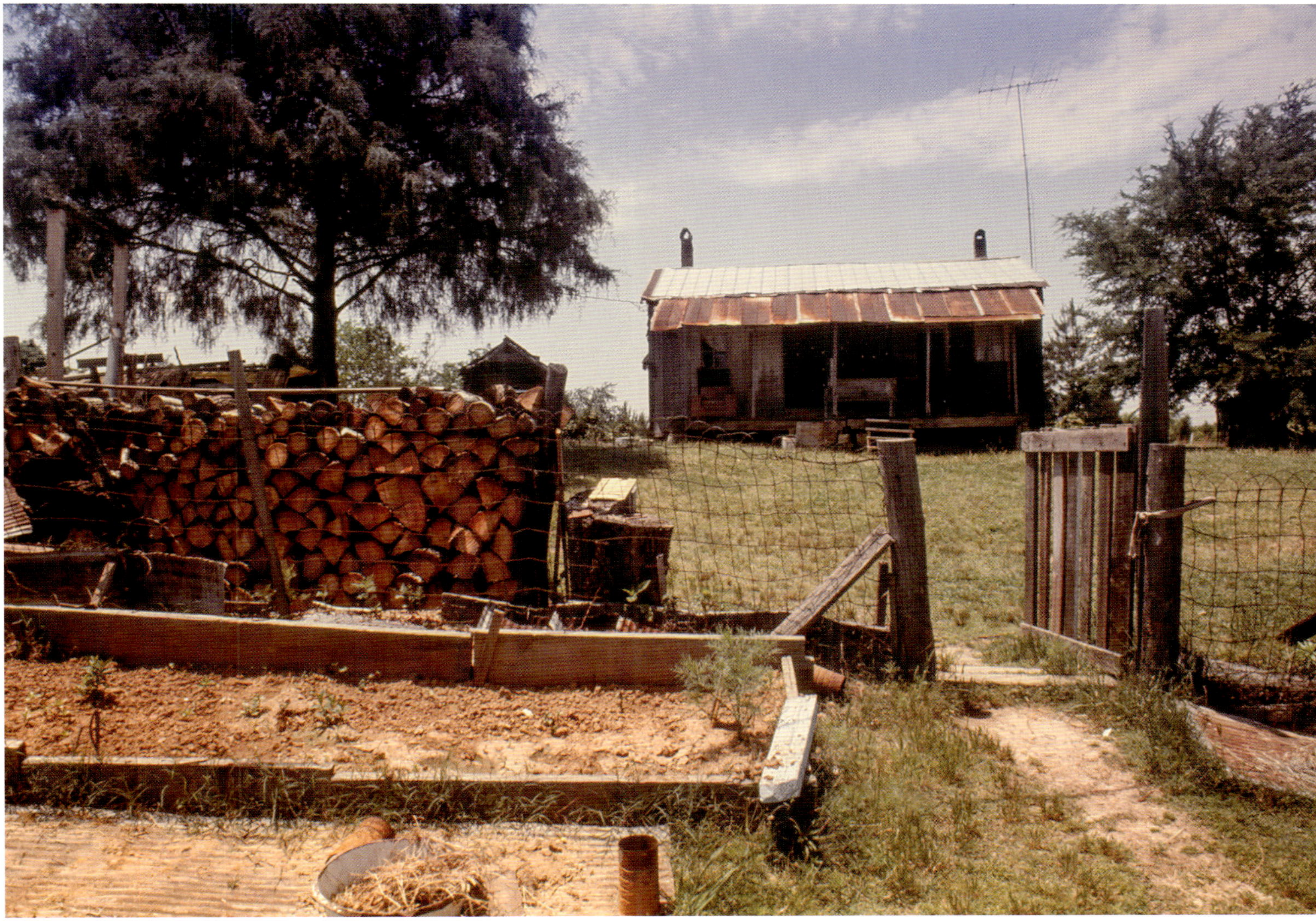

Riller Smith's homeplace, Highway 7 North, Lafayette County, 1972–75.

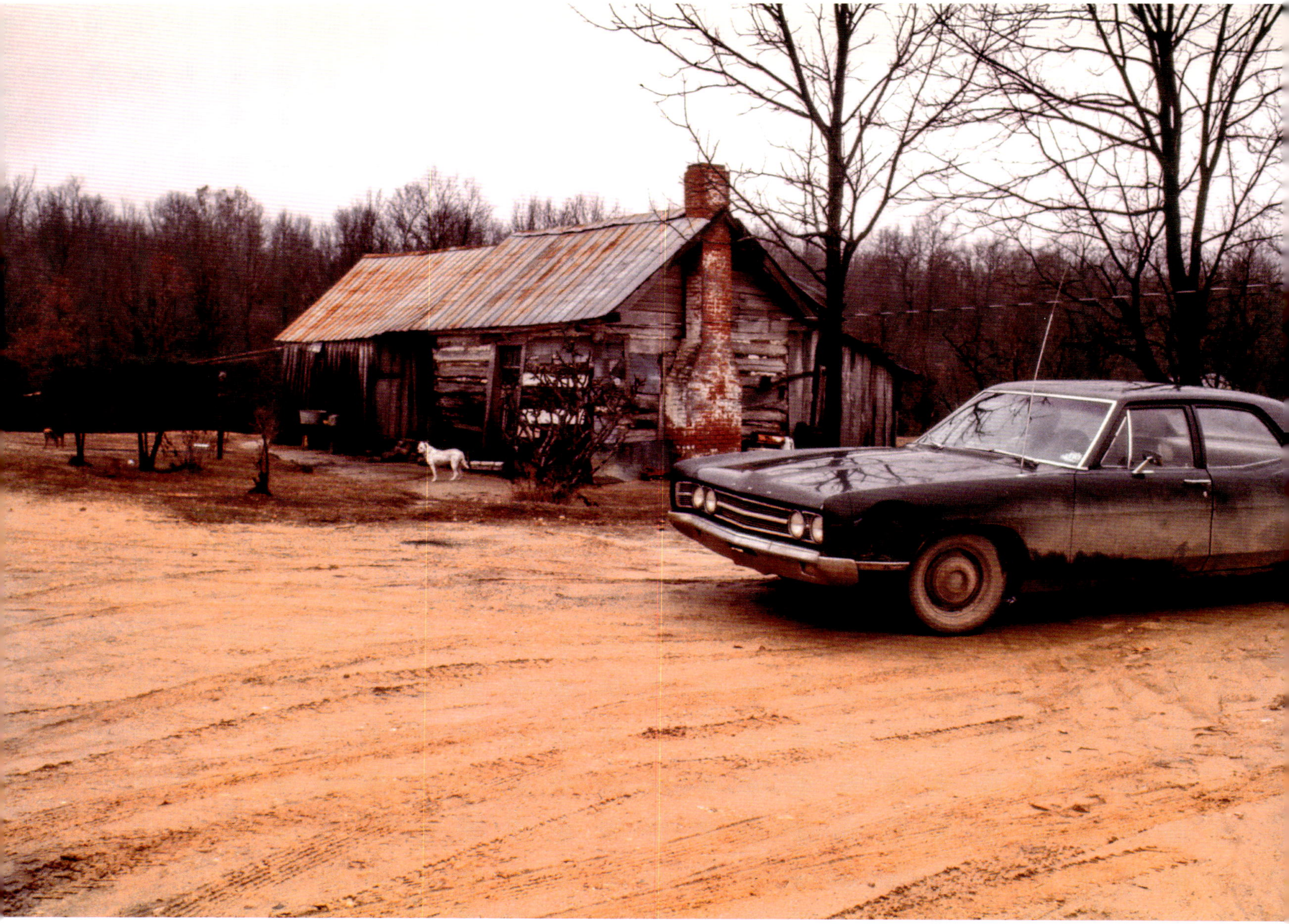

Winter colors with white dog,
near Waterford, 1972–75.

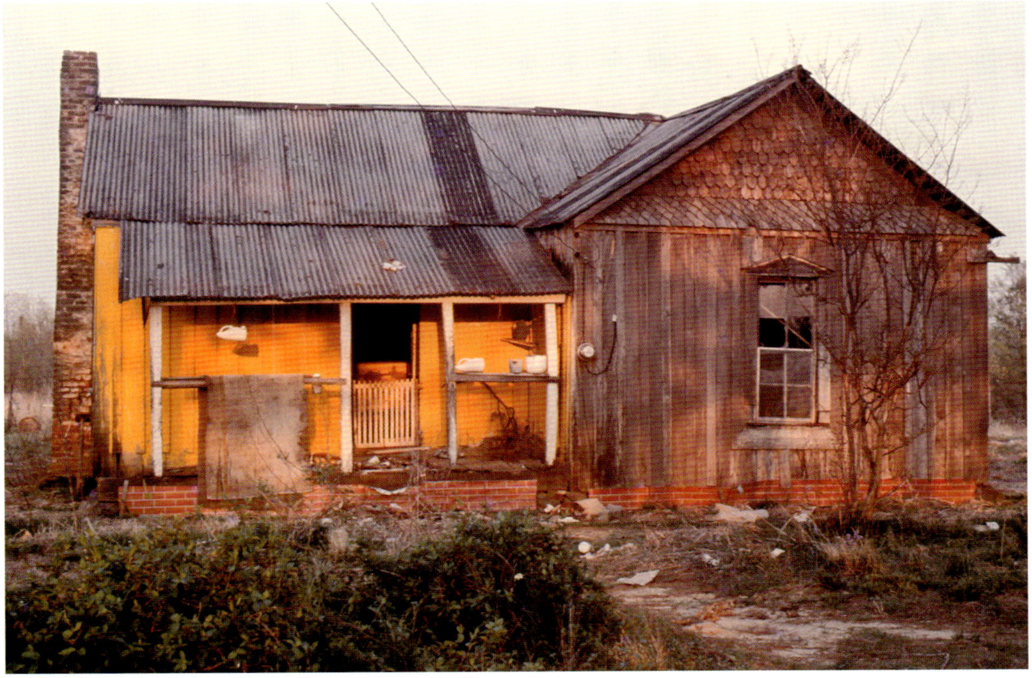

Yellow house, Marshall County, 1972–75.

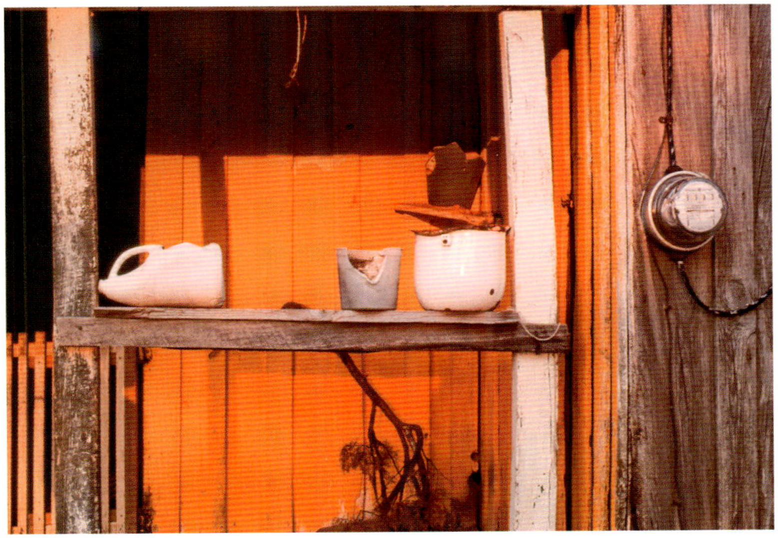

Yellow house, detail, Marshall County, 1972–75. This is where people washed after coming in from the fields. A basin, bar of soap, a bucket of water, and a clean towel were all that was needed.

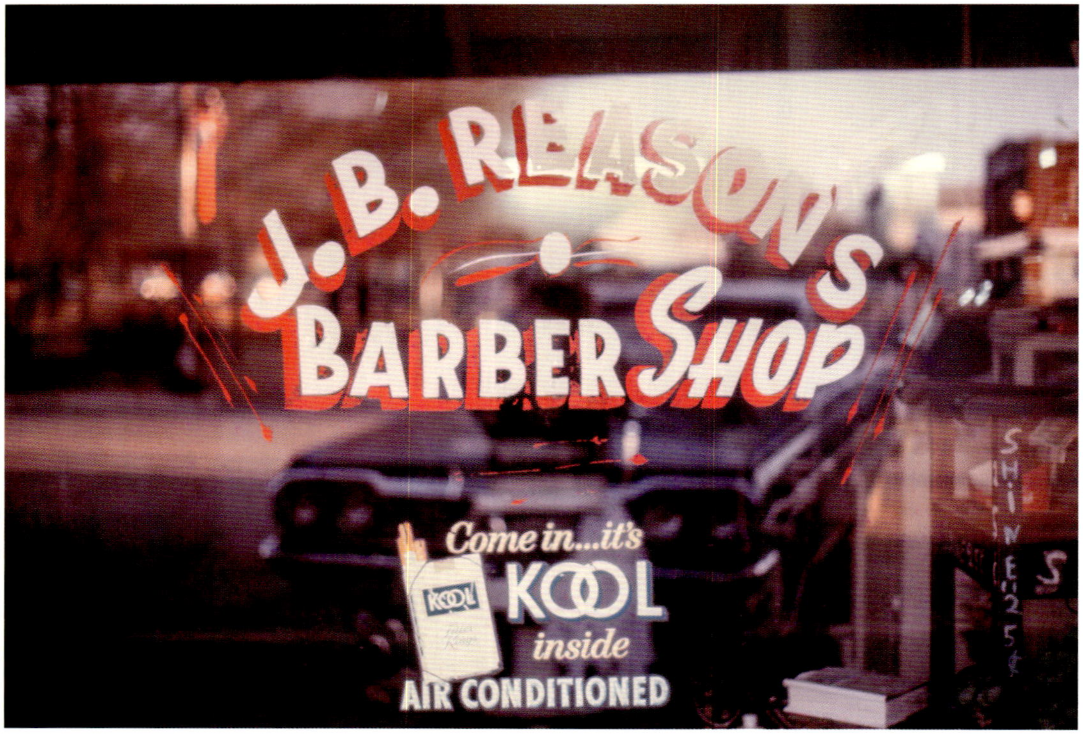

J. B. Reason's Barber Shop: it's kool inside,
Bruce, 1972–75.

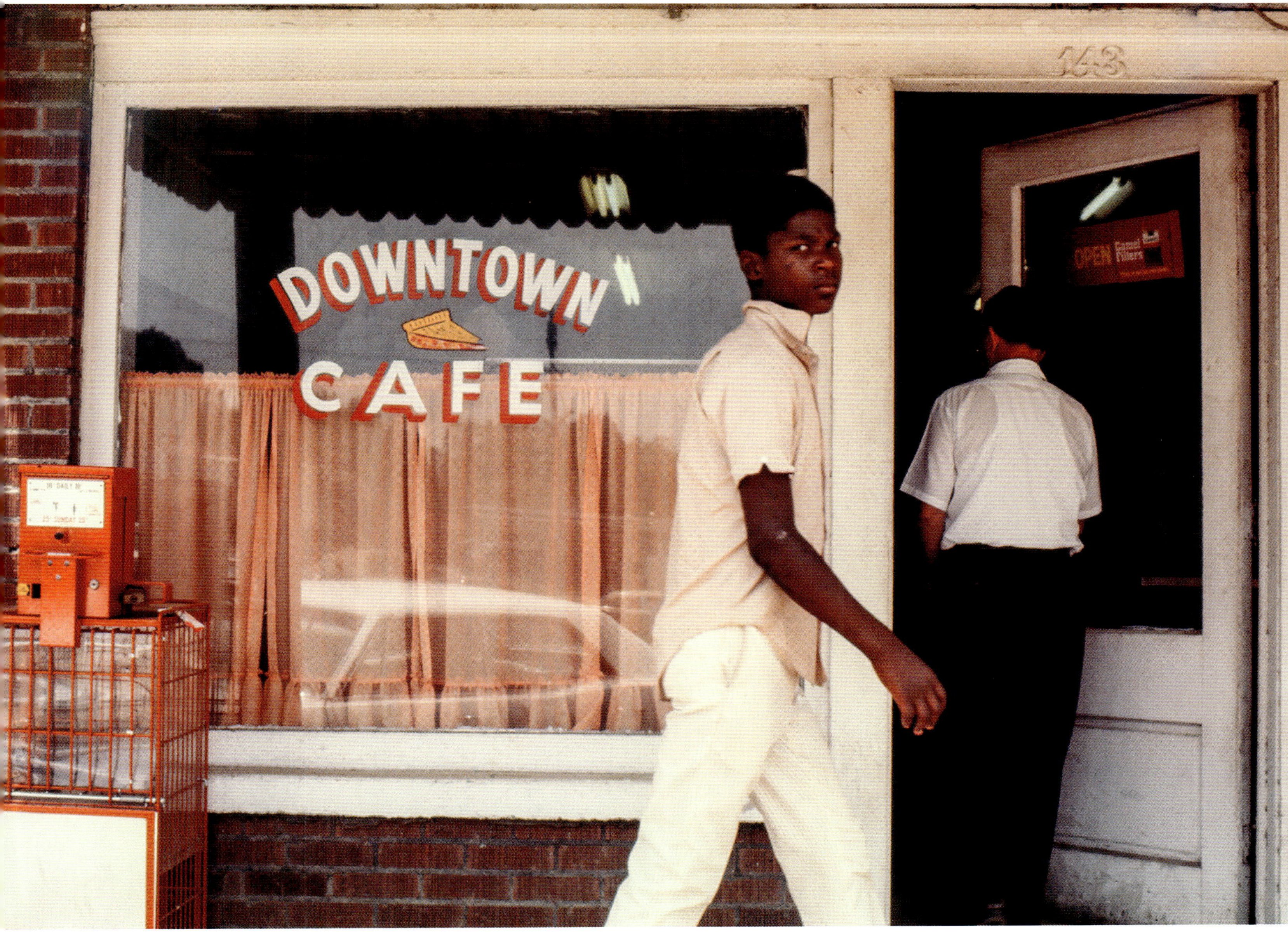

Downtown Café, Bruce, 1972–75.

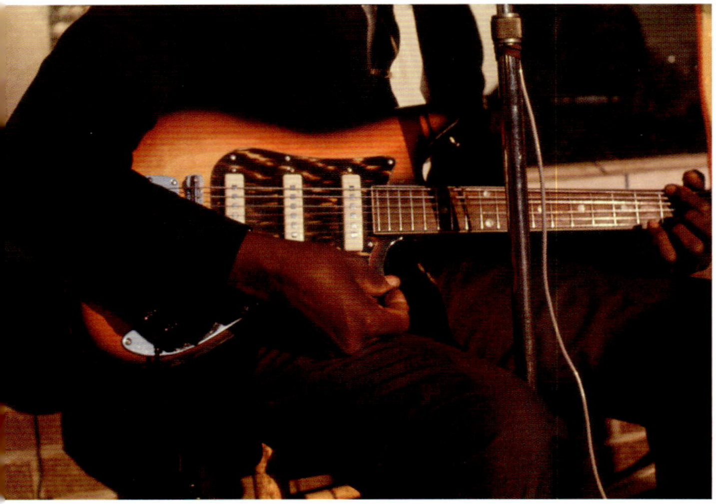

Rev. Leon Pinson,
Mound Bayou, 1972–75.

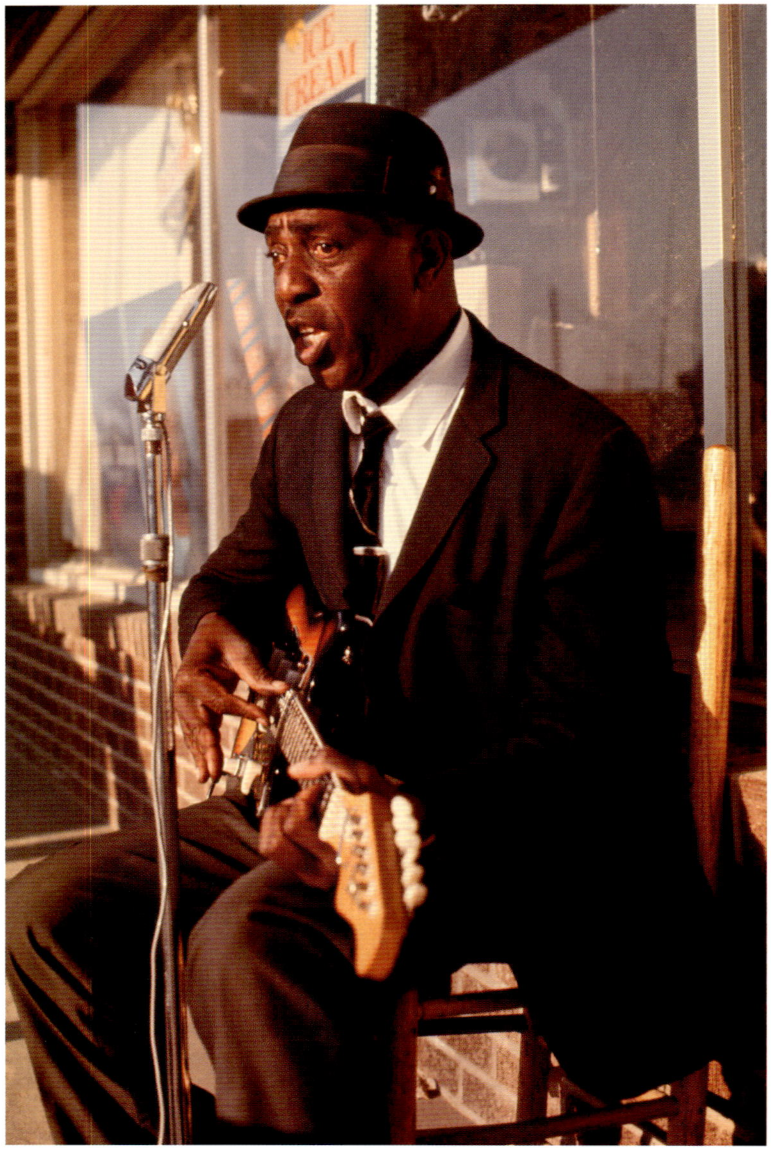

"Don't play no Rock 'n Roll," Mound Bayou, 1972–75. Rev. Leon Pinson was a blind gospel singer.

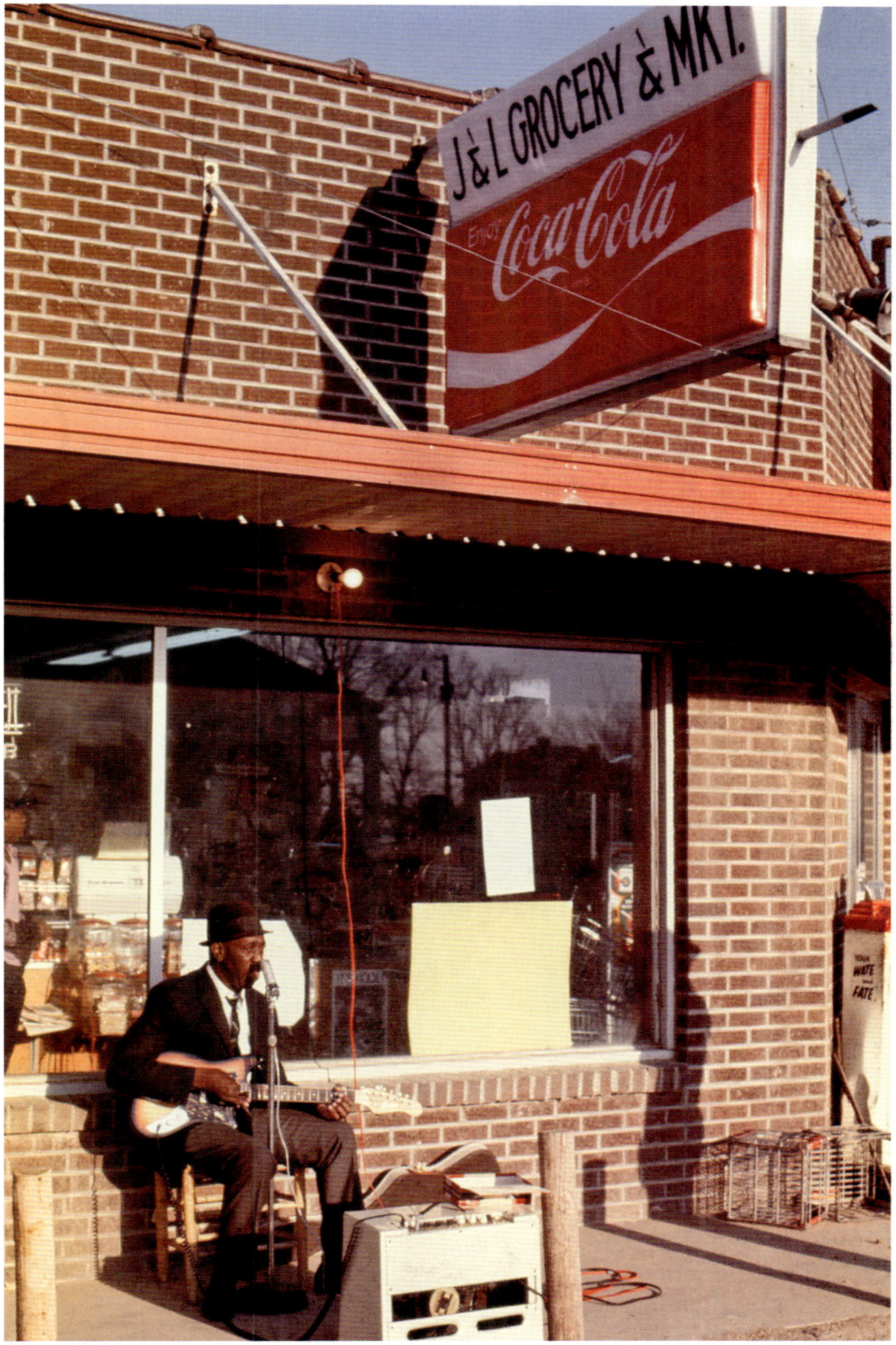

Rev. Leon Pinson,
Mount Bayou, 1972–75.

Rev. Leon Pinson, blind gospel singer, Mound Bayou, 1972–75. An Olevia Johnson campaign poster sits in the store window. The J&L was owned by Ms. Johnson, a civil rights' leader from Mound Bayou who worked with Fannie Lou Hamer in the 1970s. She was the first African American woman to run (unsuccessfully) for the Mississippi House of Representatives in 1972. Later she was elected to several county offices.

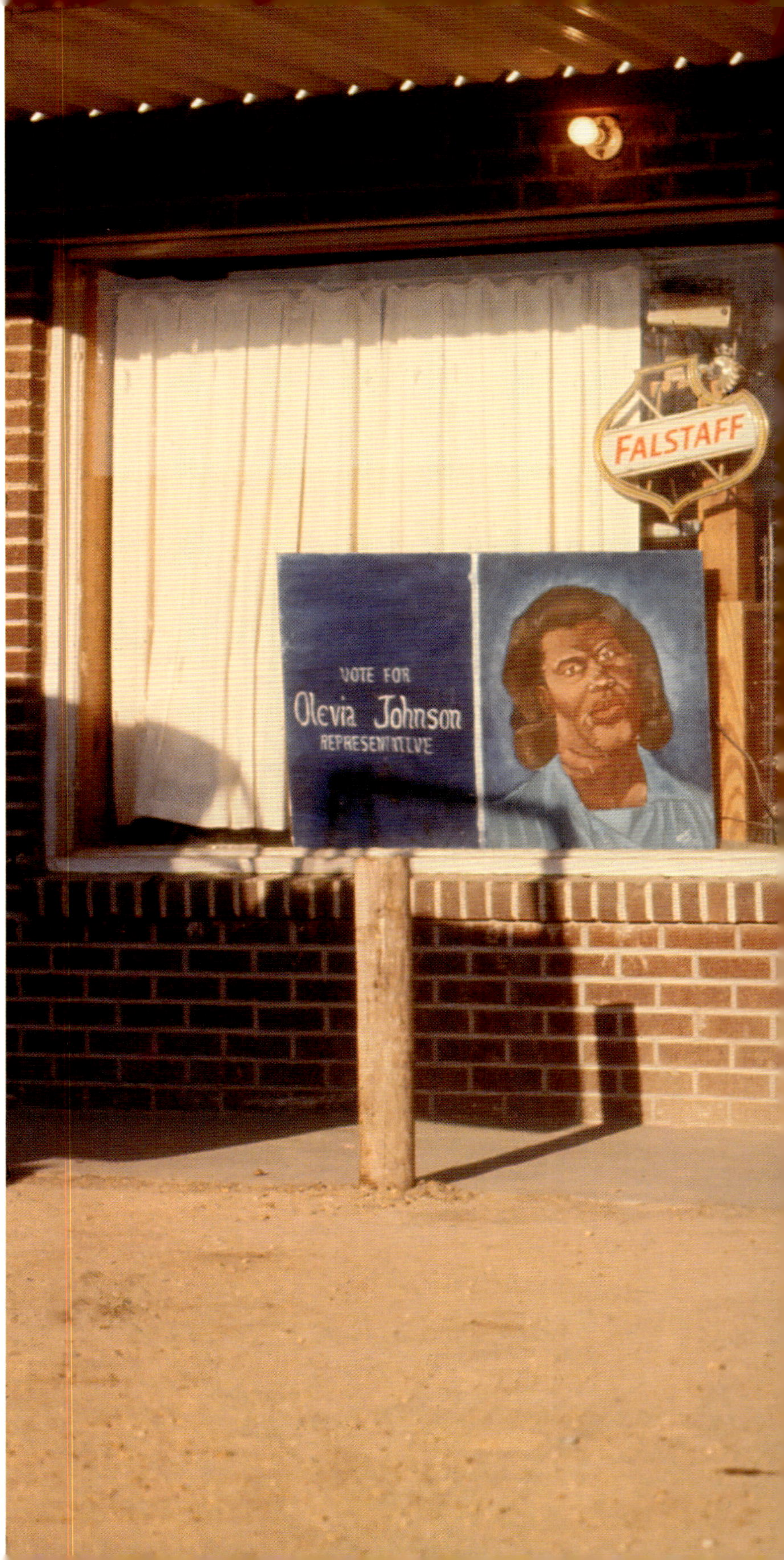

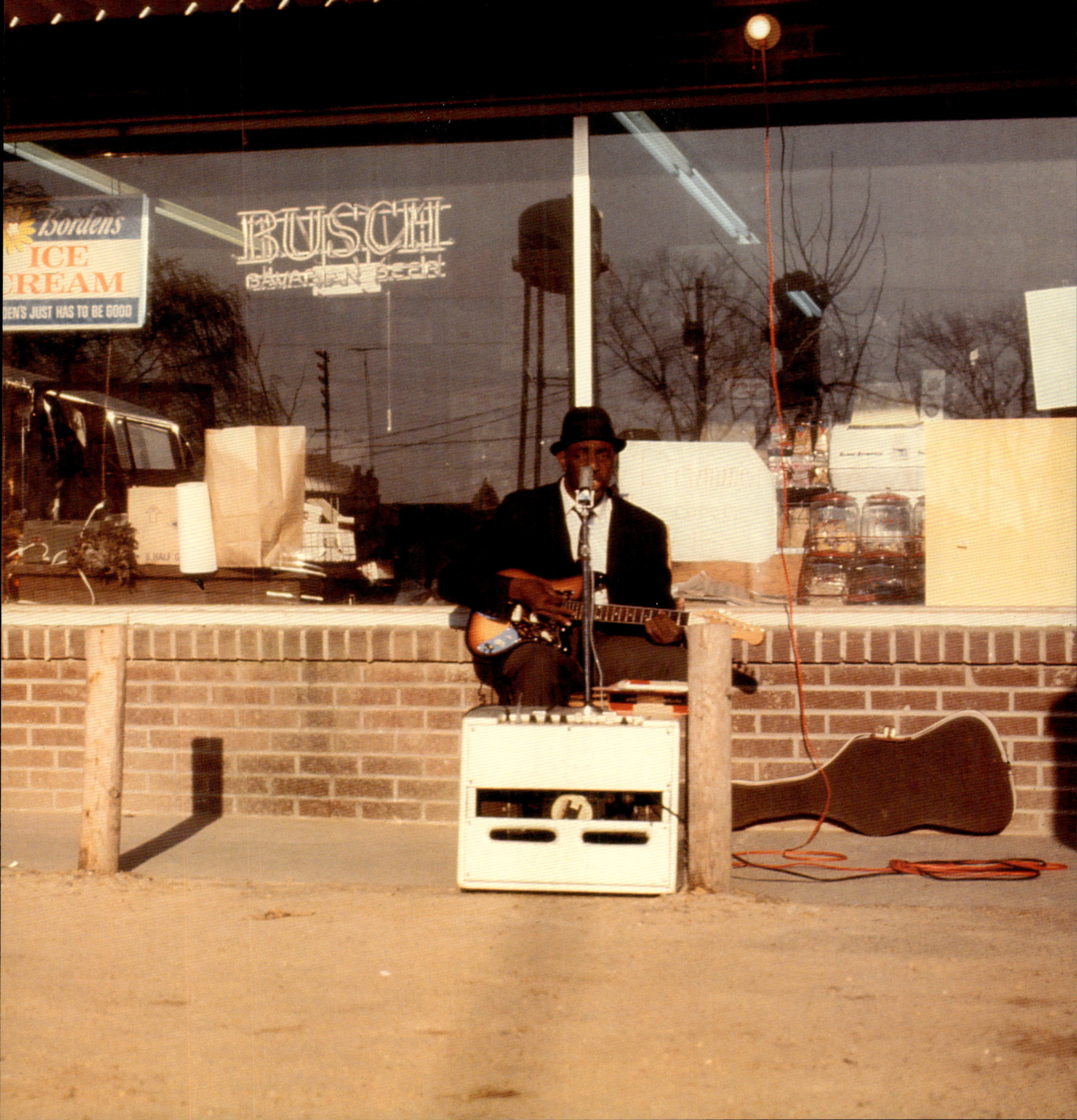
Bordens
ICE
BUSCH
BAVARIAN BEER

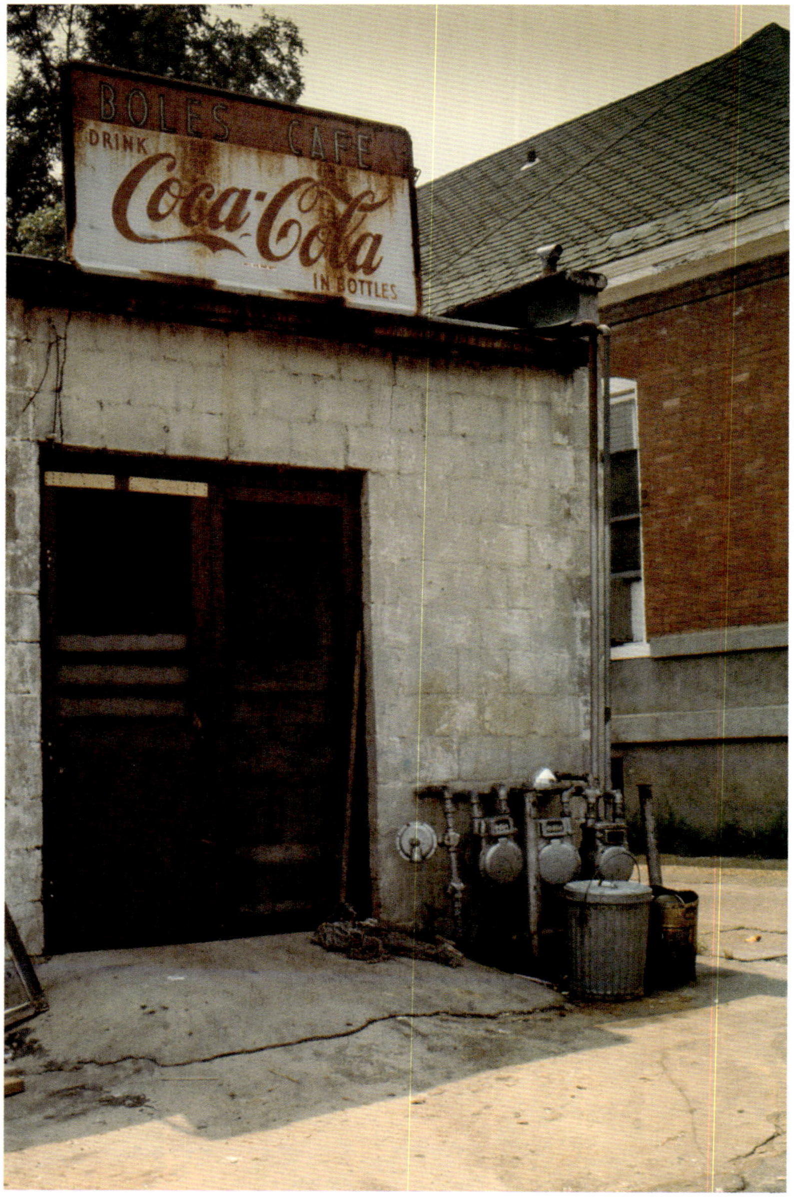

Boles' Café, Oxford, 1972–75. The Boles were the first African American business owners in Oxford. They opened their first shop in 1893.

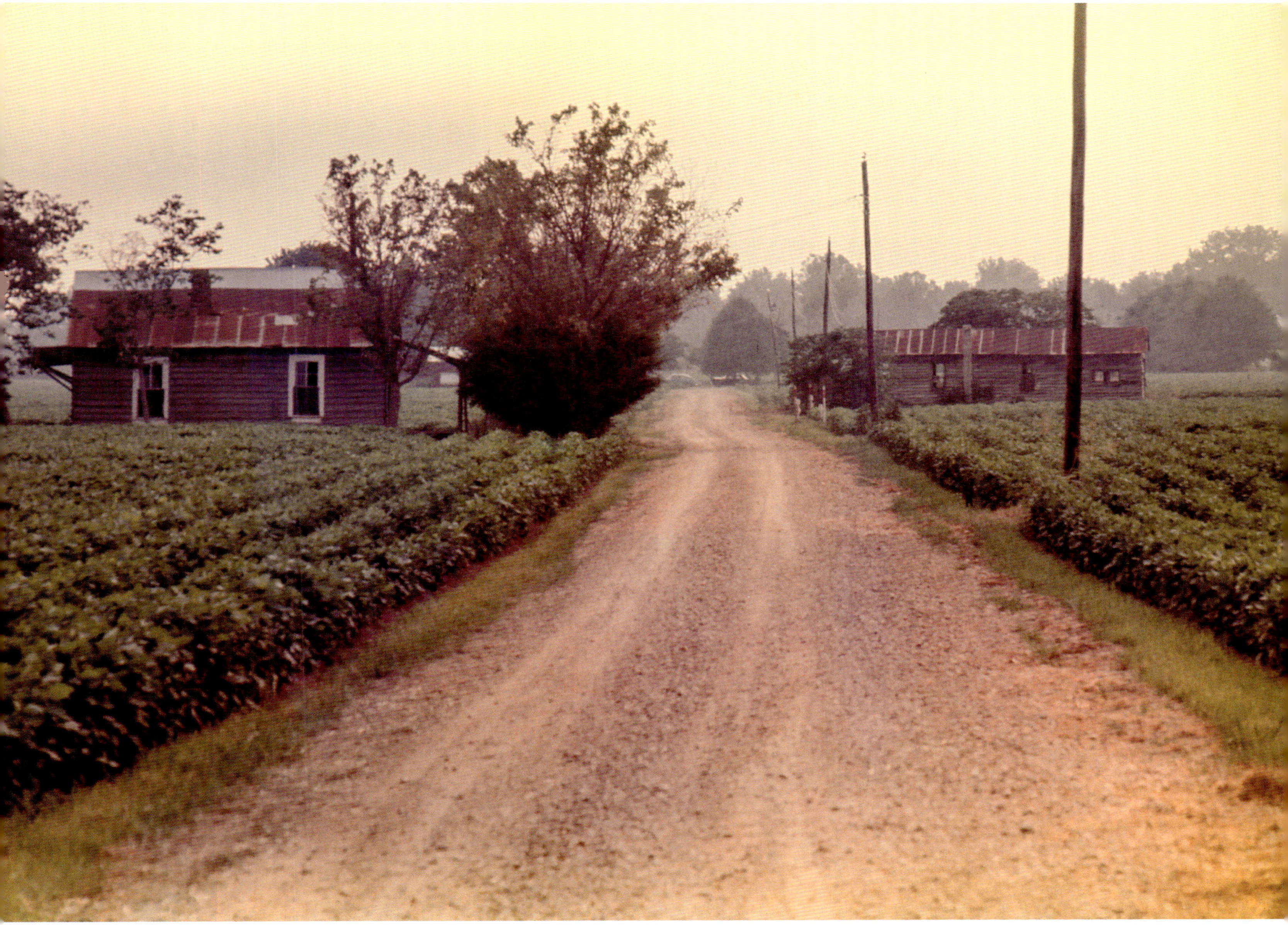

Delta, near Friar's Point, 1972–75.
Abandoned homes on a dirt road.

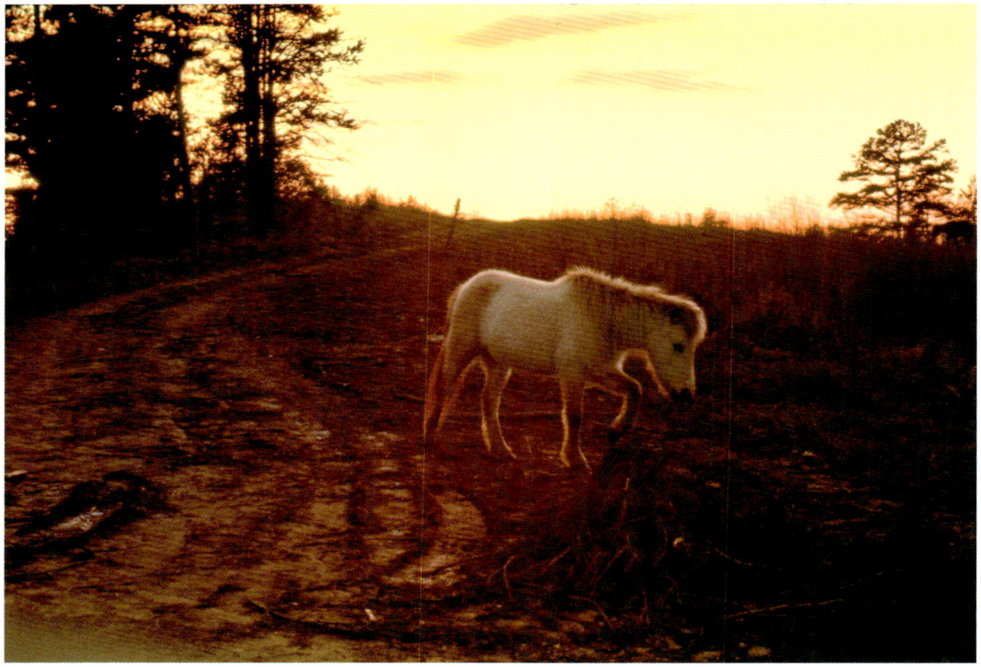

Winter sunset pony 2,
Lafayette County, 1972–75.

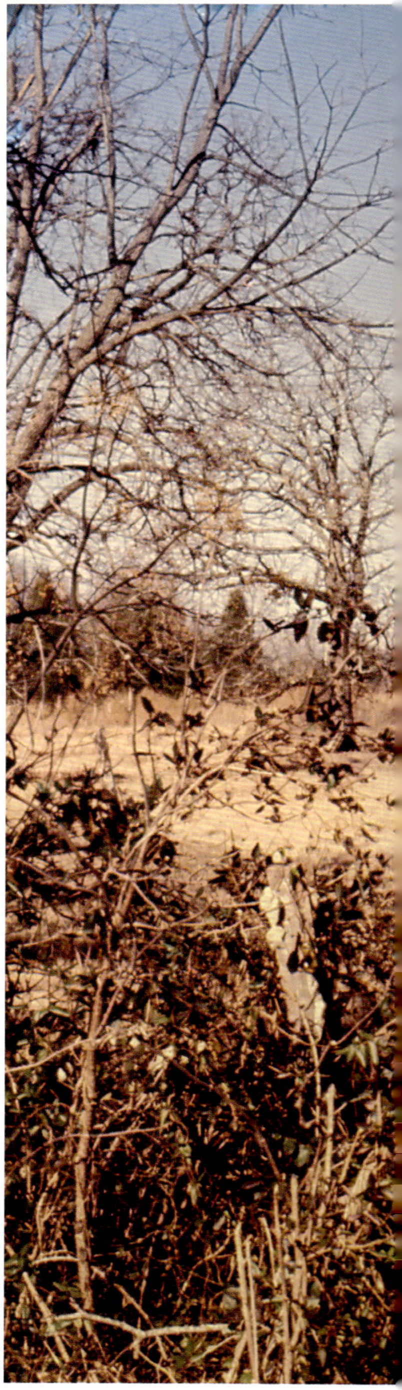

The "Big House" out near Taylor,
Lafayette County, 1972–75.

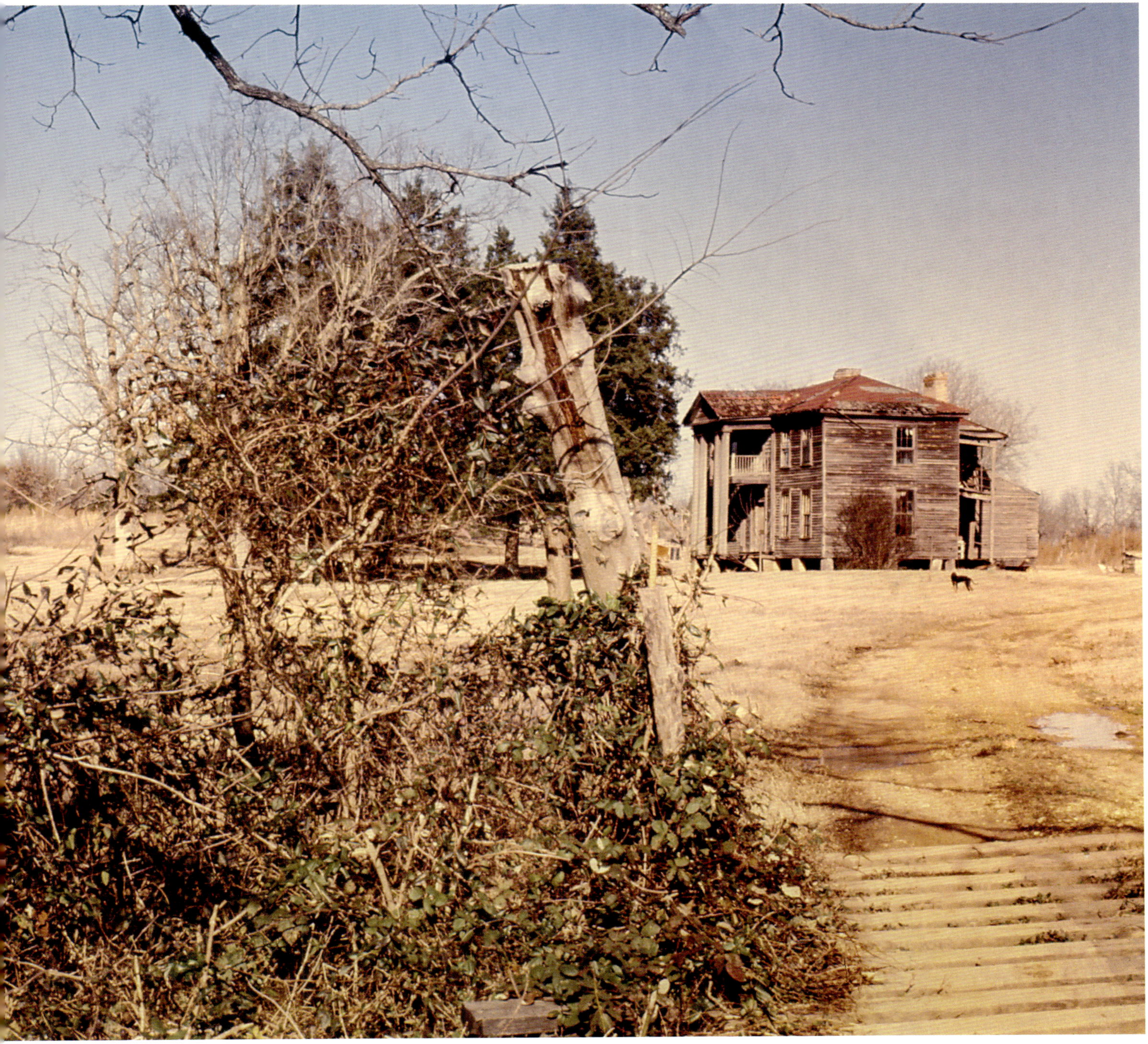

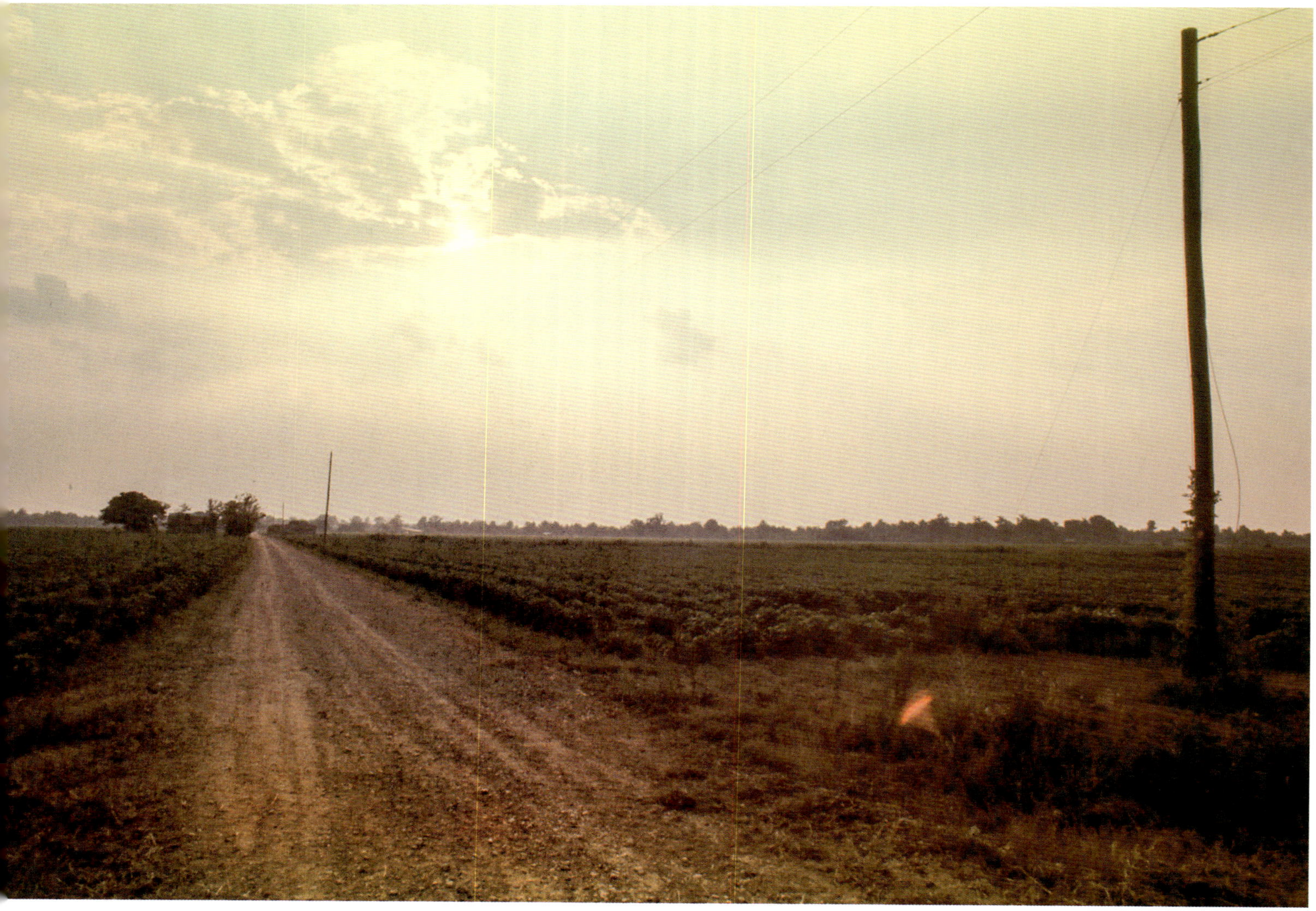

Pearl sky, Delta, near Friar's Point, 1972–75.

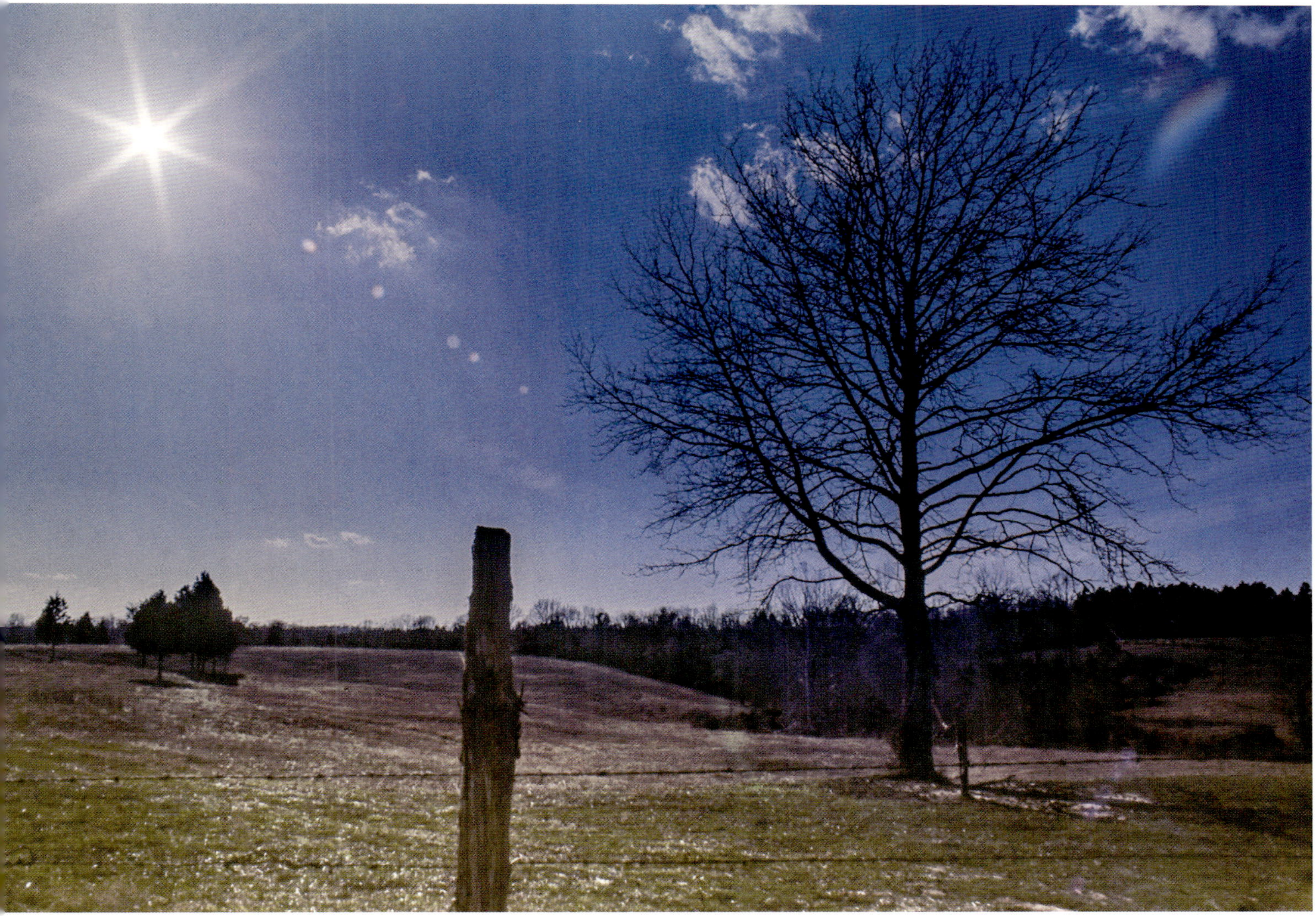

Winter, North Mississippi sky, Lafayette County, 1972–75.

Chapter 2 Returning to Mississippi

The photographs, film, and audiotape from my time in Mississippi sat in various closets over the next thirty-seven years, ignored but not forgotten. They made for a decent pile of film and boxes. There were several stacks of big round film cans: sixteen thousand feet of original film (about 7.5 hours), the work print, A-B rolls, internegatives, 16mm mag film audio tracks. Maybe thirty cans in all, plus a cardboard box of audiotape on five-inch reels (more than 10.5 hours of recordings). There were also more than one thousand 35mm Ektachrome transparencies. The stack drifted in and out of six homes over the ensuing decades.

As the old saying goes, when it comes time to railroad, you railroad. In November 2009 I started the long process of scanning images, transcribing audio, and digitizing film.

Two motivations arrived at about the same time. First, my daughter, Deirdre, became insistent that I do something with the Mississippi material before I croak, as she put it, and all the background information is lost. Second, excellent technological advances—computers, scanners, and software—now allowed someone like me to work independently at a professional level.

The scanned image files went into Lightroom, a digital photography program by Adobe. The files had to be tweaked, appraised, and cataloged, with key words and metadata added to each one. This work seemed to go on forever, but it was easy compared with what came next.

If you had told me I'd two-finger hunt and peck through some 155 pages, or 42,579 words, to transcribe all those hours of audiotape, I'd have said you were nuts. Some of the field recordings were rough, and there was always the Mississippi accent to be deciphered. But in nine short months I was done, and the voices had come alive again. There were complete logs and subcollections of sound. My typing had improved.

Soon came the time to face up to the film cans. In early fall 2011 a friend gave me the name of Pam Wintle, the film archivist at the Smithsonian Museum of Natural History. The museum had a 16mm flatbed editing machine that could be used for a small fee. My old friend Lou Linden and I loaded a cart with a small mountain of ancient tin cans and trundled off to the Smithy. Pam was there when we opened the first can. Our noses strained for the sharp vinegary smell of deteriorating film. It wasn't there. To our great surprise, the film was in almost perfect condition. Some fading. No weave or warping. No shrinkage. I was amazed it had survived so well. The next step was to transfer it to digital video.

Pam gave me a list of several labs the museum used that could handle the project. In no time we had wonderful transfers of old moving images in a new form.

In November 2012 my muse told me to cold-call the Library of Congress, just down the street from my home on Capitol Hill in Washington. It happened that Todd Harvey, a curator at the American Folklife Center, answered the phone. I asked whether he would be interested in the stuff I had. He thought he might. Somewhere along the line I started to wonder: What was there now? Was anyone left? What did the place look like?

Then one day I was listening to a recording of Mr. Hall talking to me, and I was swept by a feeling of nostalgia and curiosity. I went online and searched for "Mr. M R Hall, blacksmith," thinking perhaps I'd find an obituary. What I found was an article from the *Oxford Eagle* from years earlier. It was about a local smith named Andy Waller who had once been a striker for Mr. Hall. He started soon after I moved away. I hadn't known he had followed me. The article mentioned that Mr. Waller had bought out Mr. Hall when he retired and that Mr. Waller had Mr. Hall's anvil. Well hell, I had forty-year-old recordings of Mr. Hall talking about having that anvil for sixty years. That anvil was now at least a century old.

So I called him. I didn't say who I was.

"Hello?"

"Is this Andy Waller?"

"It is."

"I understand you have Mr. Hall's anvil."

"I do."

"Well, I stood over that anvil for many an hour."

"You must be Michael," he said. "I have tools from Mr. Hall for you."

I was stunned. That did it. I had to go get them. Andy had held them for forty years, and that was long enough.

I enlisted two friends and colleagues, Lou Linden and Albert Liesegang, to come with me. If I was going on another trip to Mississippi, it made sense to go with a crew and cameras just in case. Lou is a lawyer/sailor/musician by trade. He and I first met sailing tall-ships in 1985. Albert and I both spent time shooting in Africa, and we shared an understanding of the vagaries of searching for a story. Albert was from Cologne and had never been to the American South. Between the three of us could be found an interesting variety of viewpoints and observations.

At the very least I felt we needed to shoot my meeting with Andy Waller. That seemed like a unique one-time event that needed recording. We sketched a plan. Maps were studied and calls made. We'd meet up with Andy Waller and

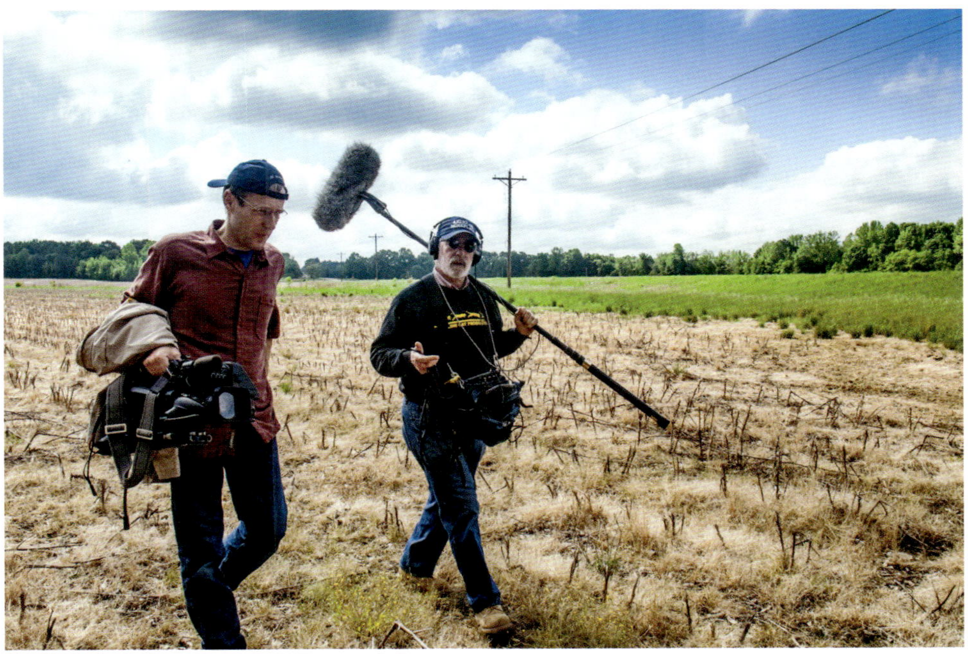

Albert and Lou, Lafayette County, 2013.

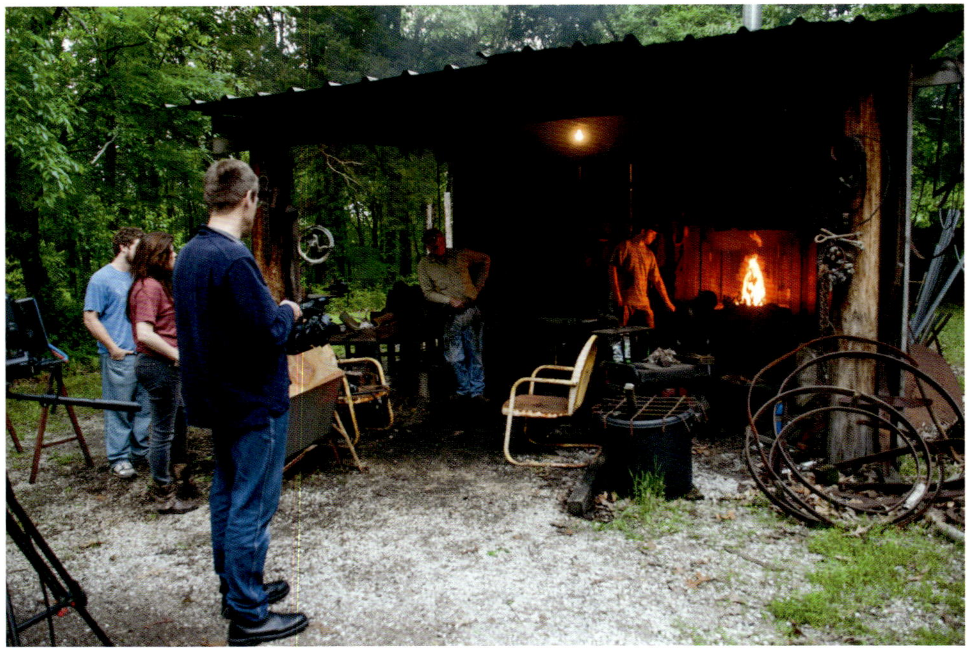

At Andy Waller's forge, Oxford, 2013.

seek out some people from forty years ago. I was sure most folks had died. We would go look at a few old haunts, drive by the house I'd lived in, see if the bait shop by the airport in Oxford still served breakfast and bait—satisfy some idle curiosity more than anything else. I didn't expect much. I was sure everything had changed. Still, it seemed worth doing.

We packed the minivan with a bunch of still and video cameras and shoved off for Mississippi in late April 2013. Once again I was heading to Mississippi with no concrete goal in mind. But this time I would look for remnants of the past and perhaps gain a new perspective on an old experience.

We left at dawn. Within an hour of leaving Washington, things began to feel more "South." We rolled down the Shenandoah Valley, up the Piedmont plateau, and into the mountains of eastern Tennessee. Although I'd not made the trip in forty years, it seemed as if every vista and landmark was deeply etched in memory. My mind flooded with snatches of previous trips at fifty-five miles per hour in that poor old VW bus.

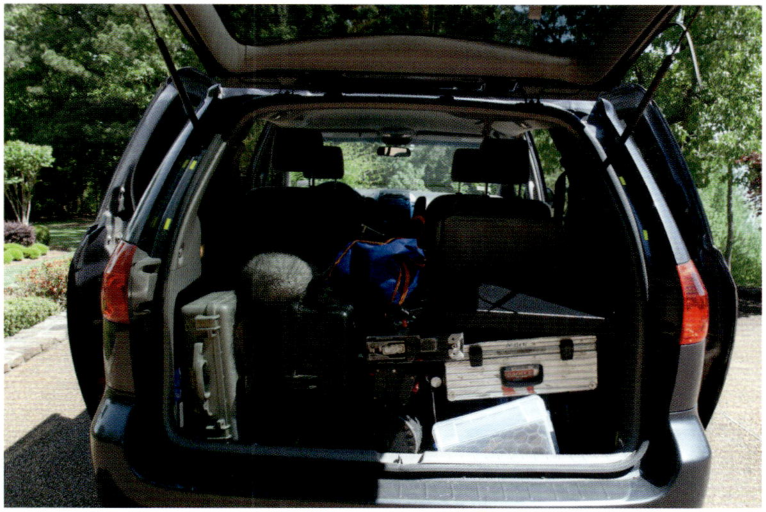

Our equipment in the minivan, April 2013.

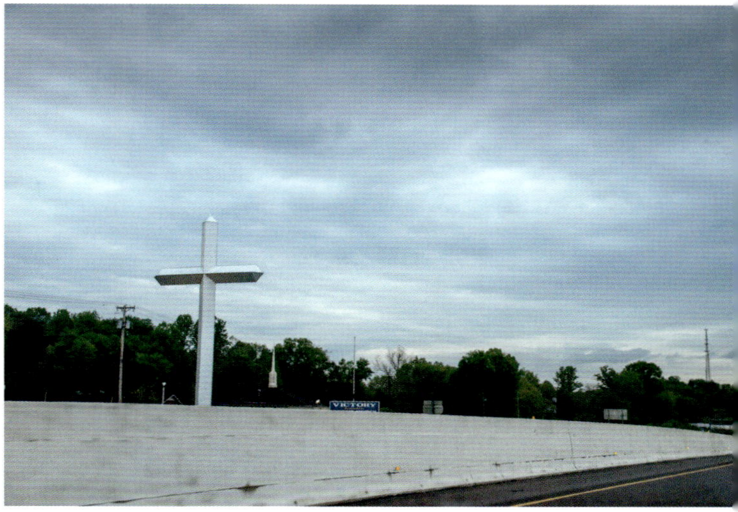

The road to Mississippi, Interstate 40, 2014.

The spring weather was perfect. Dogwoods and redbuds were blooming in the mountains. As we drove further southwest, the green haze enveloping the mountainsides grew denser, and the sun became hotter. After leaving the mountains, we turned due south from Interstate 40 at Jackson, Tennessee, and headed to Bolivar. We decided to spend the night there so that we could cross the border to Mississippi in the morning light.

The next day was stunning. We entered the state at Michigan City and headed toward Holly Springs on Highway 7 South. As I drove, the view opened into a vast expanse of brilliant yellow as far as the eye could see.

I pulled over and reached for a camera. A still camera and a video camera sat side by side—my hand closed on the still camera. "Interesting," I thought. That my first images of the revisit would be stills felt right.

I found things warmly familiar. Highway 4 West out of Holly Springs toward Chulahoma was one of my favorite motorcycle rides in the old days—a wonderful series of gentle hills and curves. The old dirt roads off Highway 4 were now paved, but the land was still recognizable. The old shacks, dogtrots, and shotgun houses were gone, replaced by brick ranch houses. But the people on their porches still waved as we drove by.

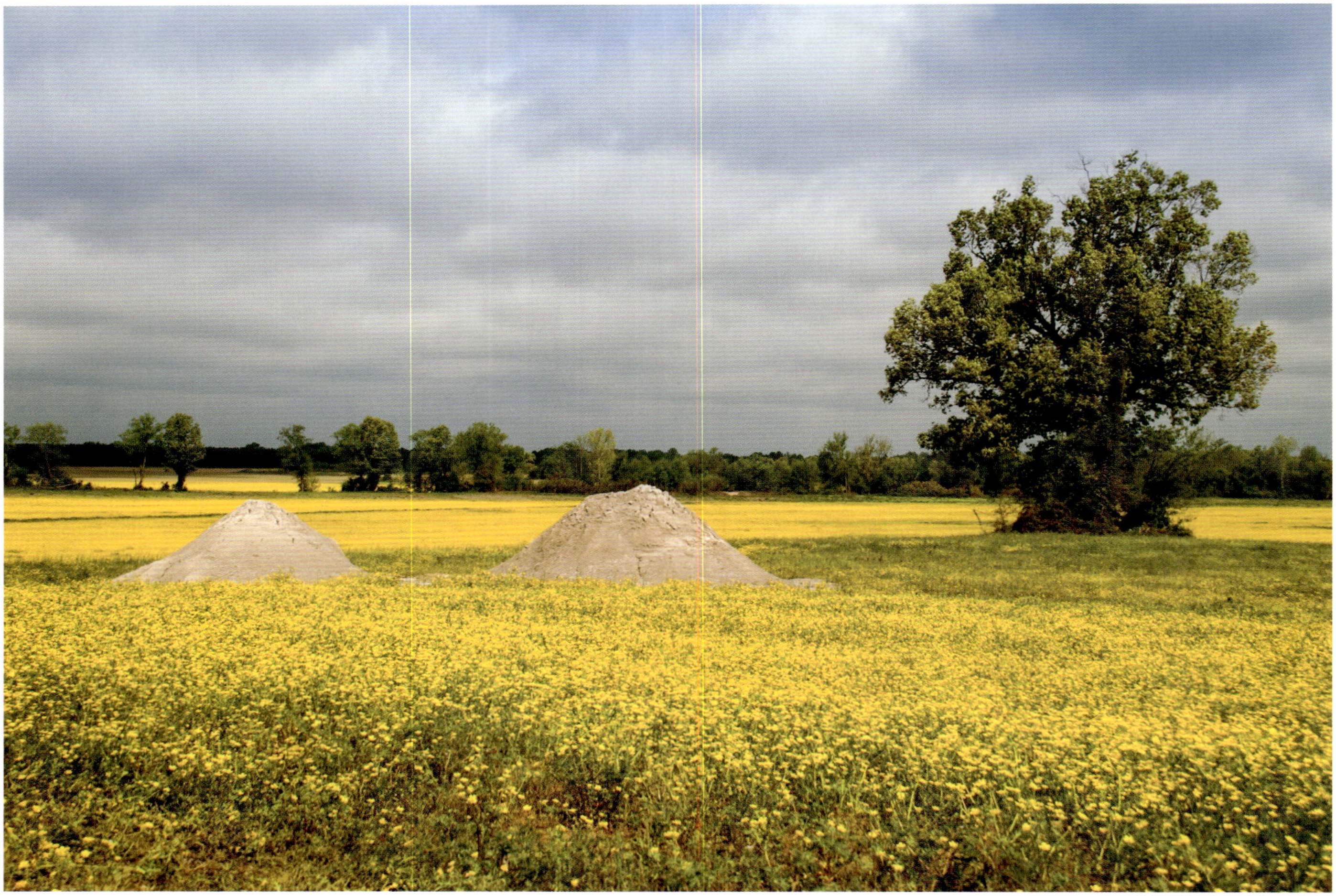

Mustard field, Highway 7, Marshall County, 2013.

We arrived at Chulahoma, a central location in my Mississippi story. Waldrip's General Store, like Mr. Hall's shop, was a place where the past was tangible. Now nothing was left but a grassy spot.

I was explaining the store to the crew when I noticed a middle-aged man watching us intently from the gas station up at the intersection of Chulahoma Road and Highway 4. I told the crew I wanted to go to the gas station to see if anybody remembered Hal Waldrip and to talk about what was here then.

The man at the station introduced himself as Gregory Shaw. I asked whether he remembered the old store. "Yeah, yeah, yeah," he said. "I saw the film . . .

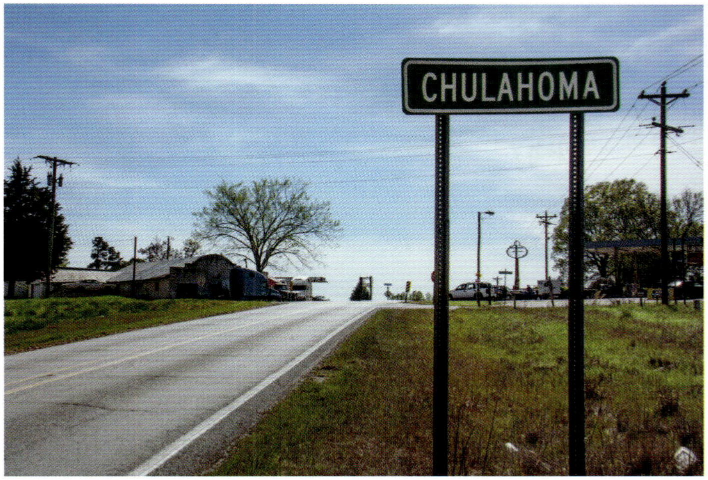

Entering Chulahoma, or what's left of it, 2016.

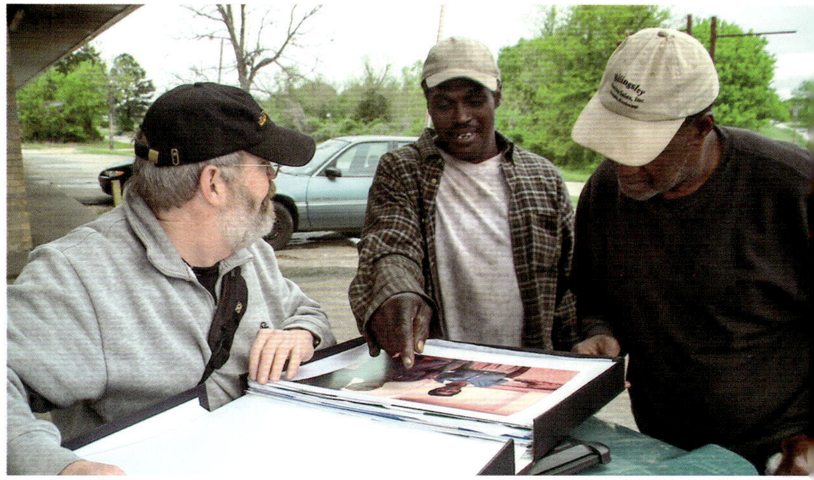

Talking with Greg Shaw and Willy Moore at the gas station in Chulahoma, 2013. Photo by Hillary Huston.

They made that . . . They made a film of that. I saw that over at the store. They showed up on the back wall where that old heater used to be. I remember that good as yesterday."

"That was me!" I said. "Christmas Eve."

SHAW: I sat there . . . I remember that. We sat right there, back of the store . . . The people hear that . . . They had it up on the wall there. I sat there and watched it.

FORD: So tell me about . . . You remember that night?

SHAW: Yeah, Christmas Eve. I was a young guy and y'all showed this film right there in the back of the old store there . . . That big old wood heater . . . They had a bench right and there. And they had the mill and the flour right there, and I saw this picture. I saw this movie that night. Y'all brought this movie and showed it there.

FORD: I came up here that afternoon, and I had the first print of that thing, and I came up and I . . . I guess the word went out. I got up here like two in the afternoon. Because I remember about six or seven that night . . .

SHAW: That's right.

FORD: You couldn't get in that store for love nor money . . .

SHAW: That's right. I was just a little guy then. So I always stayed by my daddy and Mr. Roman and all them. I always stayed with all of them. And I asked, and I pushed my way in . . . I had to push my way in so I could see. I saw that.

FORD: Everybody was there.

We looked at more photographs.

SHAW: Yeah. That picture. That's my mother!

Katie Mae Shaw at Waldrip's General Store, Chulahoma, 1972–75.

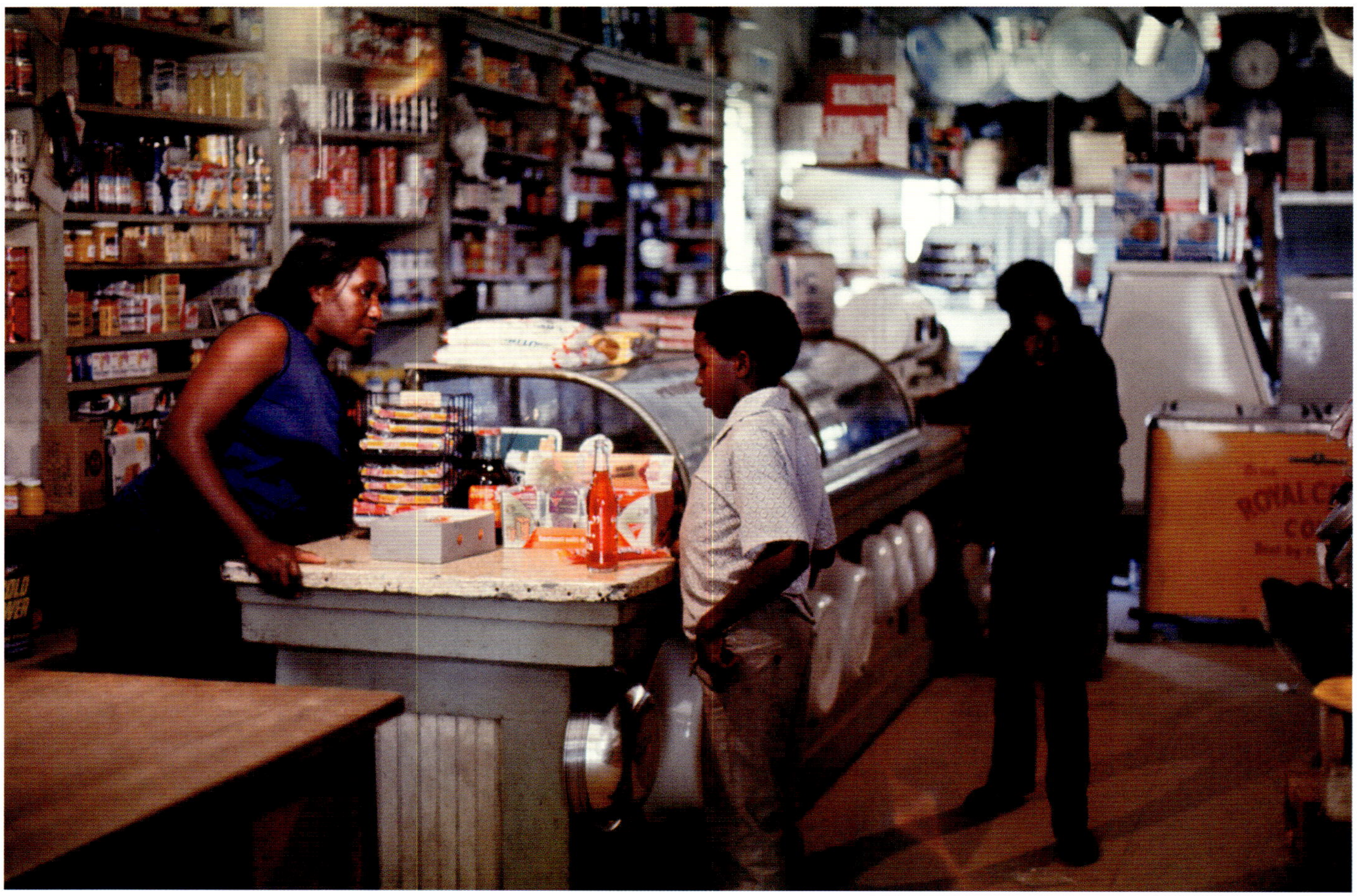

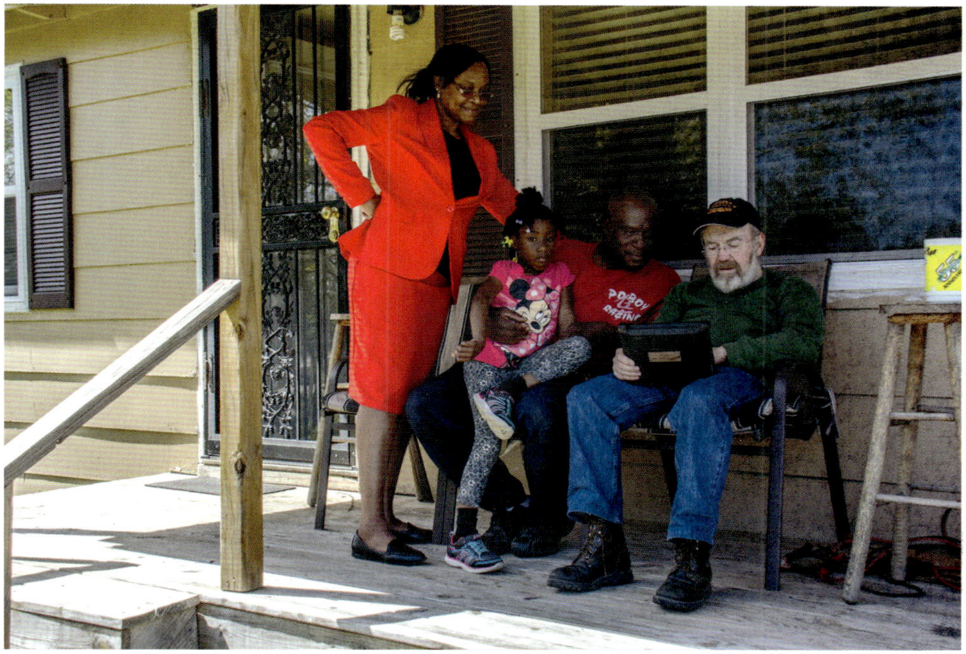

Talking about old times, Chulahoma, 2016. Photo by Albert Liesegang.

That was the first of many such conversations. Word got around; within several months the children and grandchildren of the major people in *Homeplace* had somehow found me. Soon I was showing people the old photographs and collecting new history. We met, talked, photographed, and recorded. Many forgotten names emerged from the past. I learned of fates. Time after time someone would tap on a photograph and say, "That's my mother," "That's Bernice," or "That's Calvin James as a boy!"

People were the same and different. The rural politesse, hospitality, and curiosity were still there. The lilt of the language, the open faces, and the friendliness were still there. But the people had traveled. They'd flown on airplanes and gone on cruises. Although still living in a rural world, people now had the Internet, smartphones, SUVs, satellite TV. The isolation was gone. The grandchildren of Doc James were getting PhDs.

A lot had changed. There were paved roads, trash collection, and air-conditioned homes. Big-box stores were everywhere, and the franchises had arrived, ushering Mississippians into mainstream consumer culture. A whole

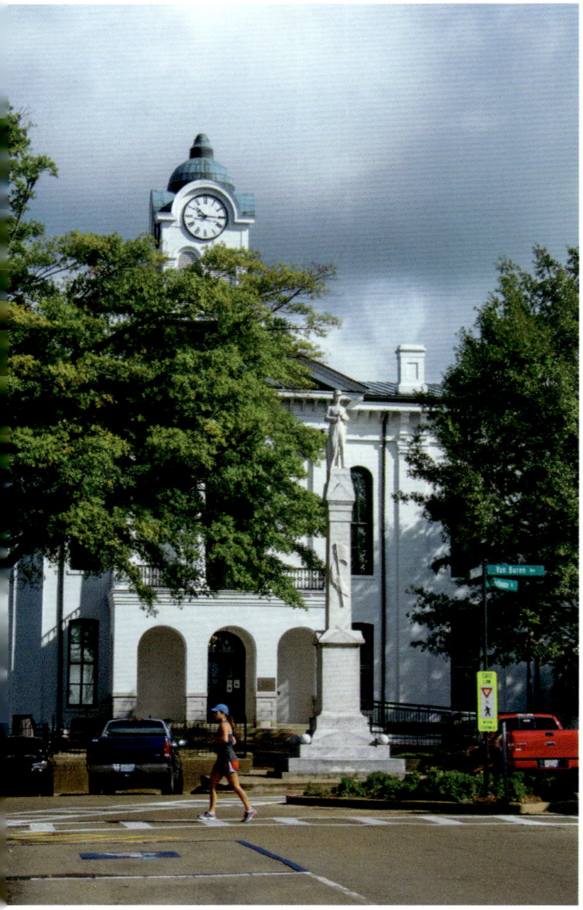

The courthouse in Oxford, 2014.

way of life had disappeared. The old-timey people were long gone. King Cotton had almost vanished from the hill country. The dogtrot and shotgun houses that covered the landscape had been torn down, or had fallen down, and were almost entirely gone. The new houses were the same brick ranch styles that you'd see in Kansas, Ohio, or California. Life had moved from the town squares to the shopping plazas. I found a couple of places that offered "an authentic sharecropper shack experience," but with AC, cable TV, thick mattresses, and flush toilets, they were nothing like what a sharecropper ever saw. The Mississippi I had known had become tourist material.

I went to visit the small towns I had known back then. Many of them had been way stations on my many Mississippi motorcycle jaunts. That area of Mississippi was, and still is, a collection of small, connected towns that vary in every way possible.

Oxford was far larger than I remembered, with bookstores, bakeries, all sorts of restaurants, and retail stores galore. The population had more than doubled since I'd been gone. For me, the Courthouse Square had lost the Yoknapatawpha County feel that Faulkner had described. The university itself was twice its old size.

In the nearby town of Bruce, the square was mostly empty. Tiny little Taylor, east of Oxford, still had great catfish at the old Taylor Grocery, but it also had acquired a serried rank of McMansions.

Water Valley seemed to be thriving. It has been adding residents slowly and restoring the downtown while maintaining its old charm. A new brewery that makes a fine IPA, gift shops, and art gallery were alive on Main Street. The town has instituted a series of festivals to build community harmony and cohesion, and it's the home of the "Be the Change" grocery—Gandhi down yonder. There was a quiet bustle about the place.

Holly Springs seemed to hang in the balance. I remembered it as a busy place. Now it seemed far quieter and a bit worn, but as Randy Hayes said, "I live a five-minute walk to the square and if I'm lucky it'll take me an hour and a half to get there."

The Delta starts just west of Como. The land around Como near Gravel Springs where Othar lived was still growing some cotton.

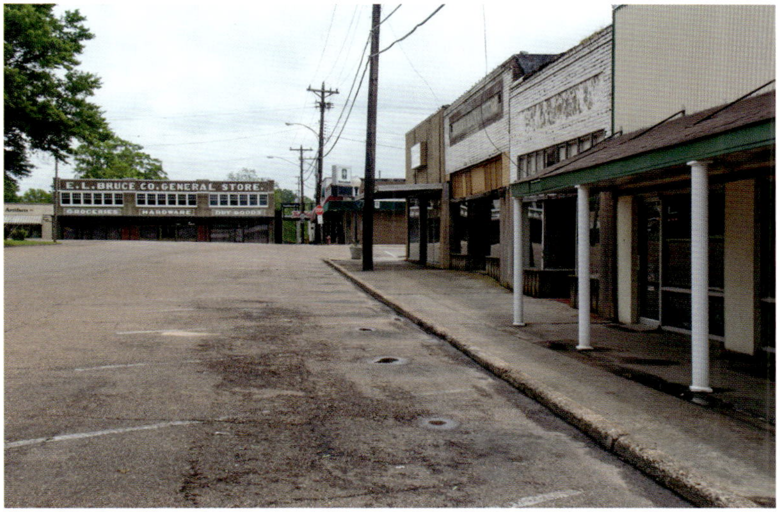

Bruce, 2013.

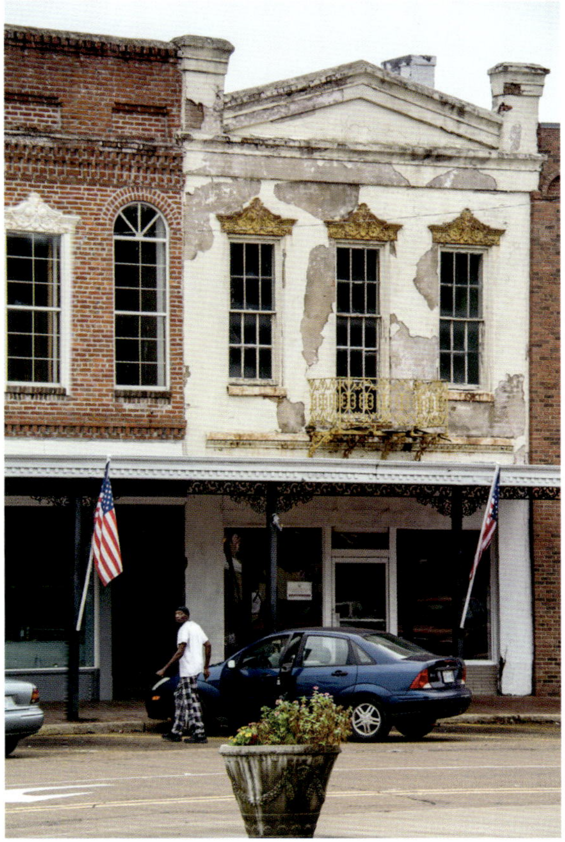

Holly Springs, 2014.

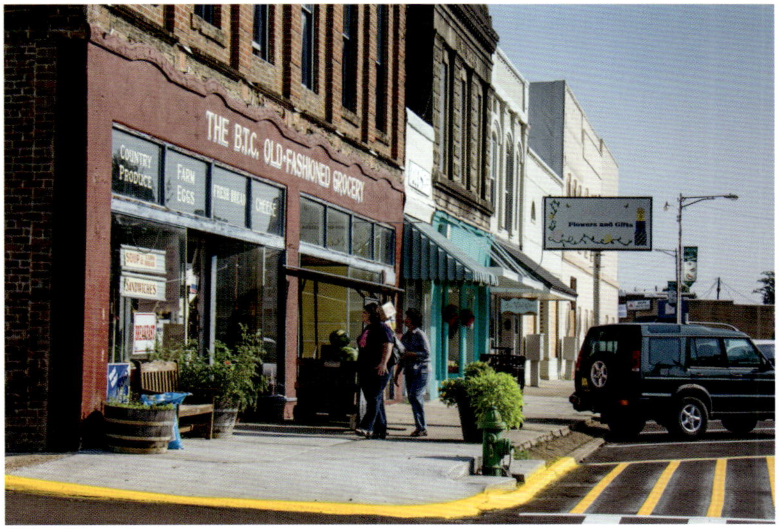

Water Valley, 2014.

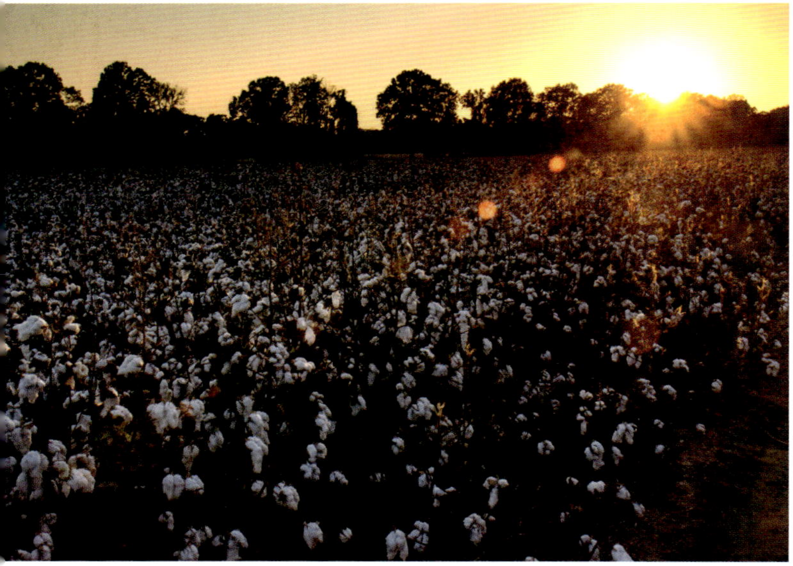

Cotton along Route 310 near Como, 2014.

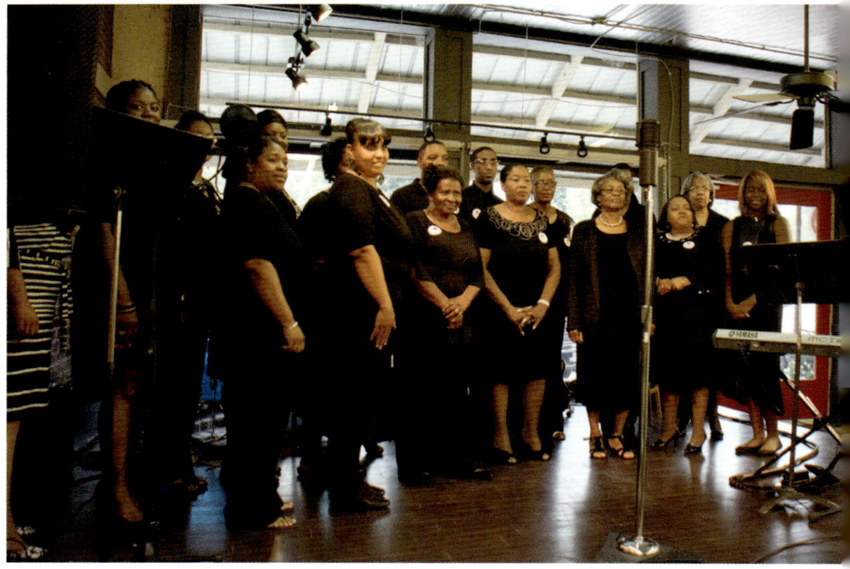

Hunter Chapel choir on stage in Como, 2014.

Como was still only about two or three blocks with a little more than twelve hundred people, yet the musical heritage has remained strong. The Reverend John Wilkins, RL Boyce, Cedric and Greg Burnside, Mark "Muleman" Massey, and the Como Mamas all call the area home. Frequent concerts featuring local talent, as well as festivals and fairs, are a testament to pride of place and the closeness of its community. I had many conversations with citizens who cared deeply about the town's quality of life and wanted a future there for the young people. During one of my visits, it felt like a "Como thing" to walk into the community library and see four young boys playing chess.

But Chulahoma—the second center of my Mississippi universe—was dead. It had survived for a time, until 2000, when Junior Kimbrough's juke joint burned down. The store and boarded-up buildings I knew had been torn down. All that was left was a crossroad with a small church, a gas station, and Sid Fore's boarded-up shop. The *Mississippi Gazetteer* now lists it as an extinct community.

My 2013 trip generated another, as has every trip since then. As of the fall of 2018 we've made seven trips back to Mississippi. And with any luck our trips are not over.

When I came to Mississippi in 1972, it was the people that drew me. They were agrarian Americans with a deeply ingrained way of life, making their way with a mule, or maybe an old tractor. Many had never been more than twenty-five miles from home. I came from an outside world and was privy to the last vestiges of an old-time rural America. I photographed the families and homeplaces, the fields, the livestock, the land. I made friends. Though homes were at times abandoned, they were still evocative of the lives they had contained—haunted. Most of the landscapes I shot contained relics of people's presence. Now little exists from that time except the land itself.

When I returned to Mississippi in 2013, the land reasserted itself and grabbed my attention. Coming back made me take another look at the land as the setting for back then. It's almost as if the images of 1972 were the gem and the new pictures are about the setting.

The mustard field in springtime on Highway 7 was the very start of my rediscovery of Mississippi. Next year, on another trip, I went by the spot in summer and shot again. Then fall. Two years later it was winter. It took four years to photograph that field in all four seasons. Each time I got the sky, the colors, the light I needed. I had the shape of the trees as a register, then found the frame and colors that dictated the particular view.

During the seven trips, I visited Sardis Lake often. Earlier, it had been the barrier that created my island of old Mississippi. Most people I met had lived north of the lake. It was where the photographs and film were made. Sardis had been an unseen presence in the earlier work.

Now I was looking directly at the sky and the water itself. It showed me many moods, and I worked with what it gave me. The familiar combinations of sky, water, light, and color provided an endless variety and a simplicity of form. I spent many hours watching the skies and water change while the light stood on its head. Periodically all the bits coalesced, and I'd press the shutter.

I also returned to the Delta. The first time around in Mississippi, I'd felt the Delta an alien place. The vastness of that huge open space made me feel like an ant on a serving platter. It was so flat that the rim of the horizon seemed to

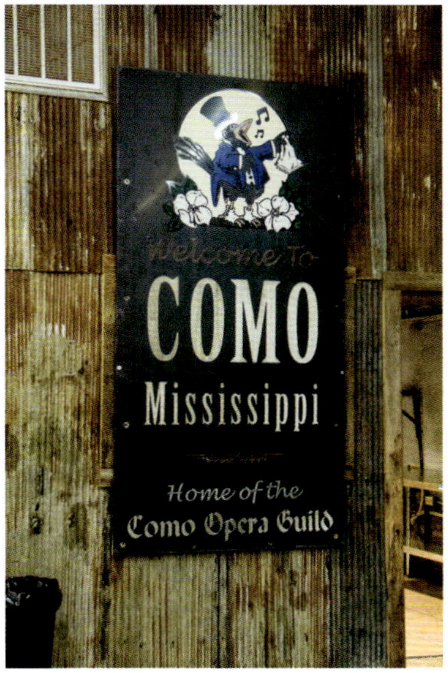

Welcome to Como sign, Como, 2014.

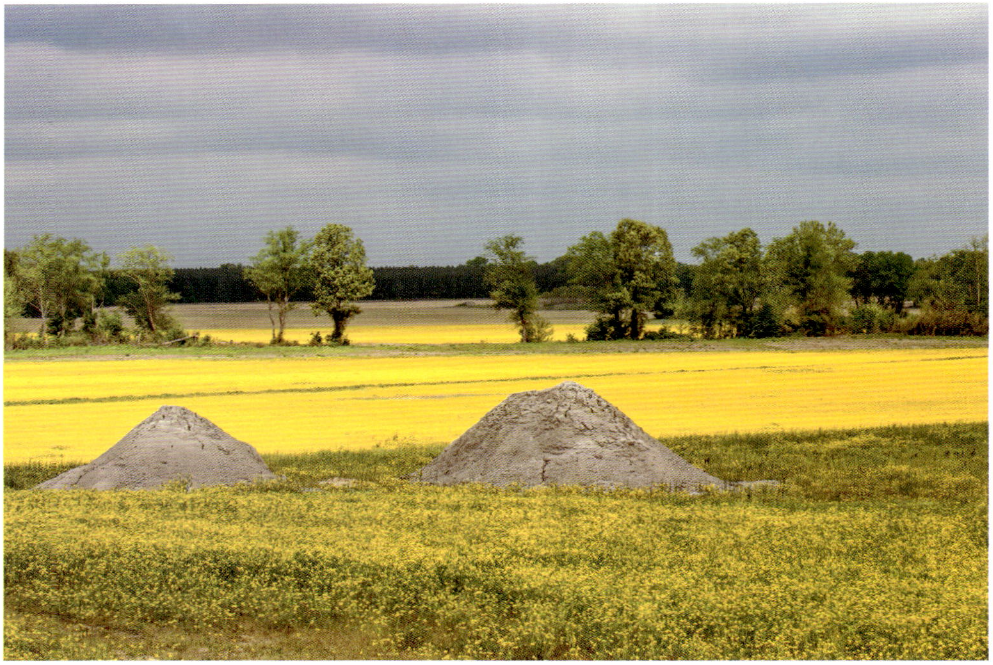

The spring field, Highway 7 North, Marshall County, 2013.

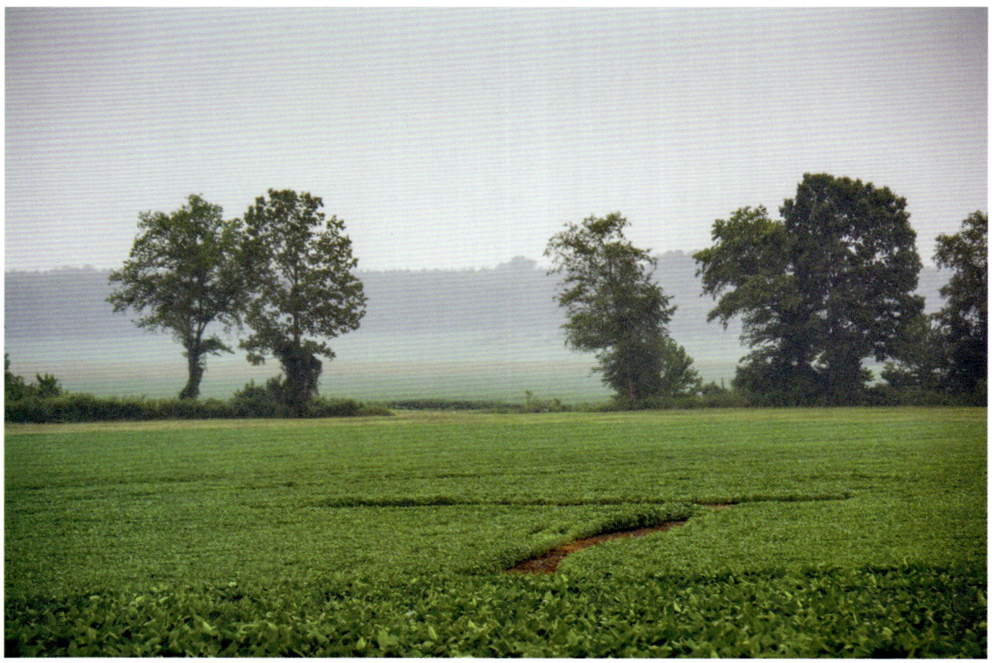

The summer field, Highway 7 North, Marshall County, 2014.

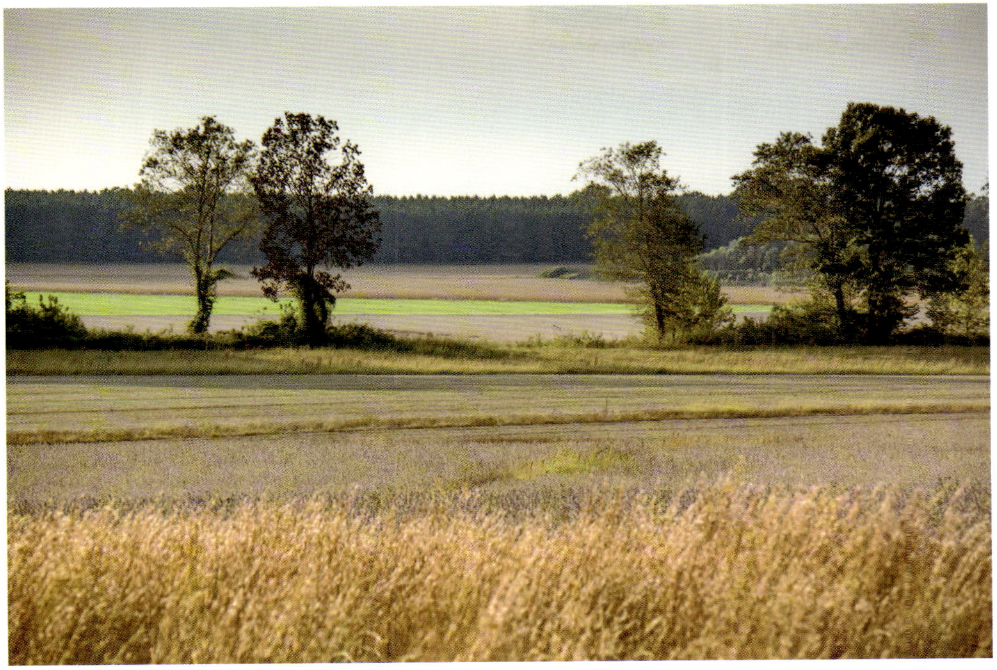

The fall field, Highway 7 North, Marshall County, 2014.

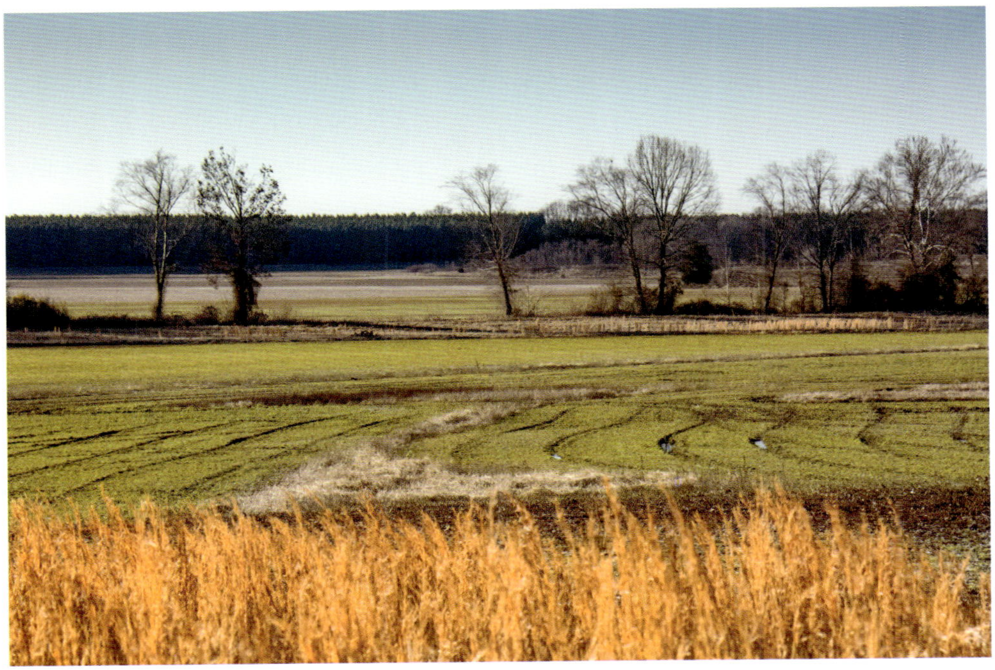

The winter field, Highway 7 North, Marshall County, 2015.

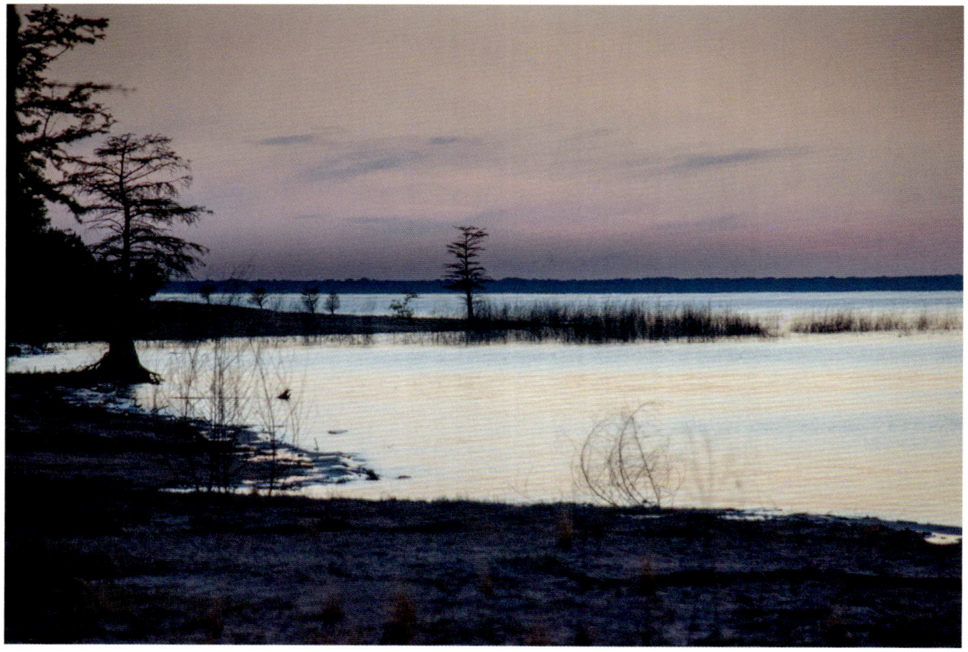

The cypress, Sardis sky at dusk, Lafayette County.

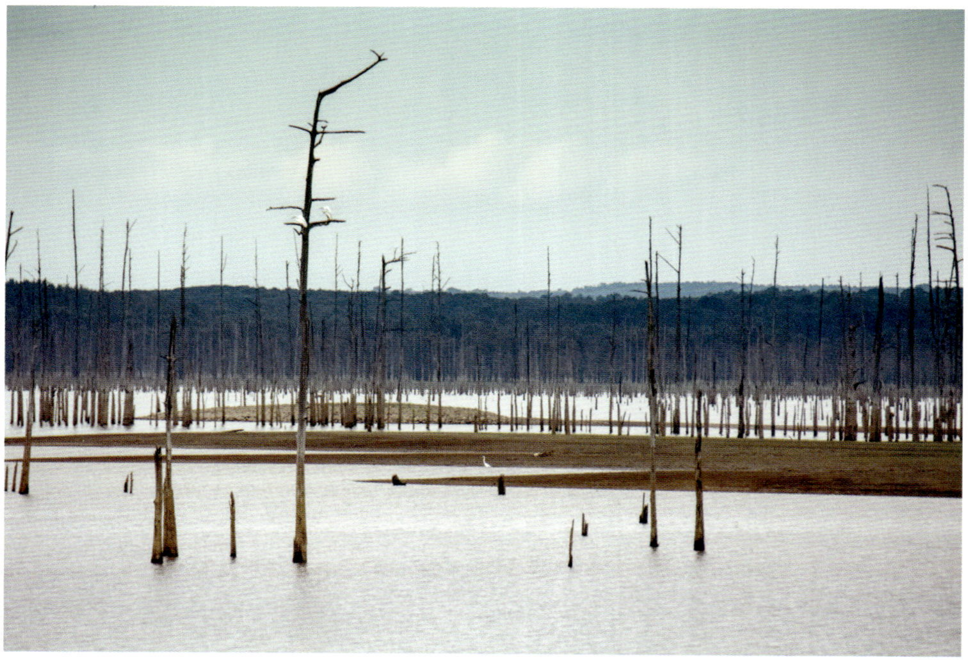

Sardis Lake with egrets, Lafayette County, October 2014.

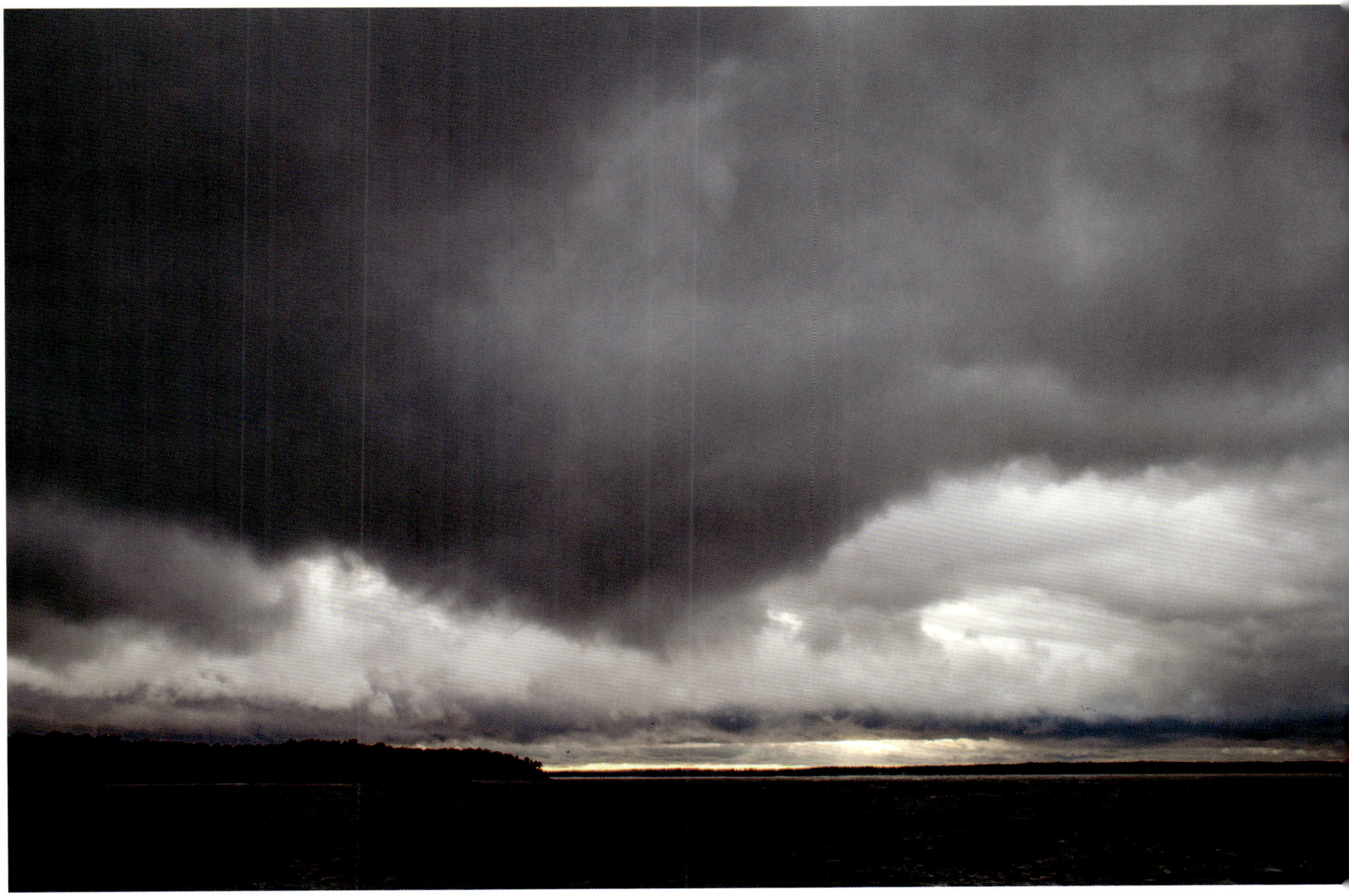

rise up around you no matter where you stood. I went there exploring and shot some, filmed some, but I didn't like the results all that much. I found it hard to relate to what I saw. Its size made people seem unimportant. And while the Delta did move me, I didn't feel at home there as I did in the gentle northern hills. This time, I wanted to see the dirt itself—the Delta—more clearly. As with Sardis, I went a number of times to look at it in different weather, seasons, and times of day. I wanted to see if I could express the feeling of space.

Fast storm over Sardis, Lafayette County, May 2013.

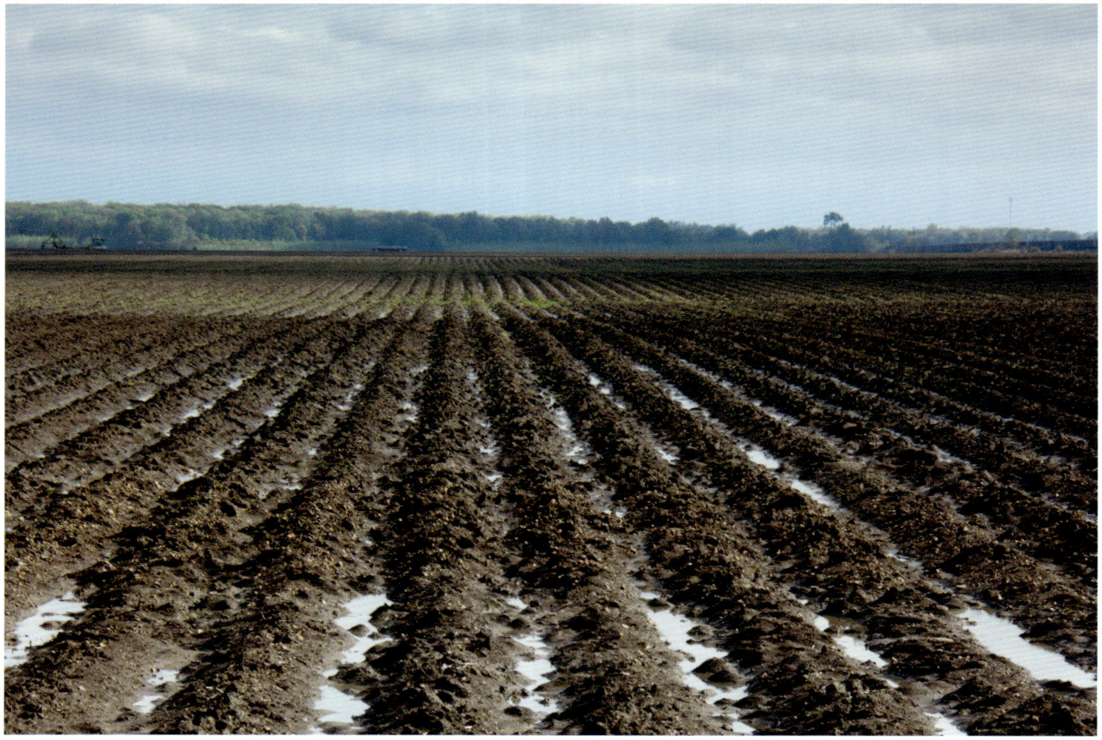

Delta dirt, off Highway 315 near Sledge, April 2016.

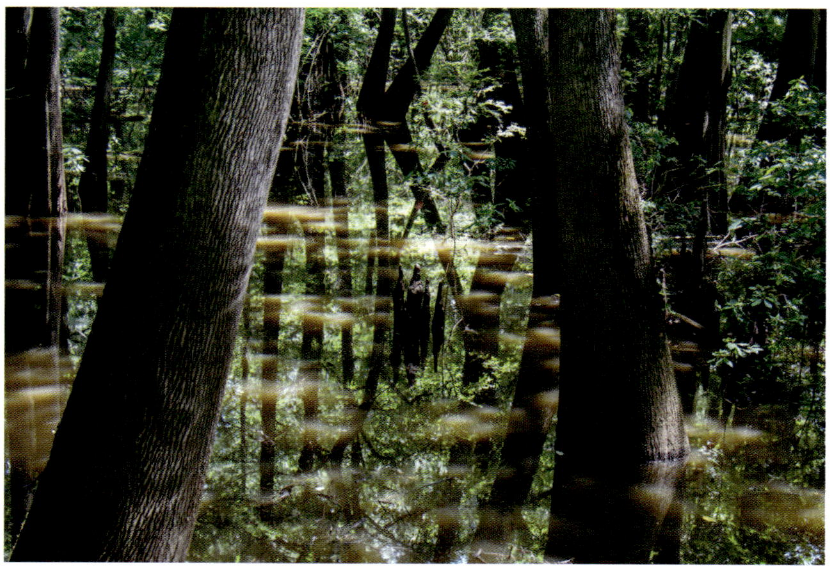

M. C. Escher in the Delta, Sky Lake, July 2014.

"Clearing the land" seems to be the way all histories of the Delta start. Before it was the flat black earth that exists now, it was swamp. Ninety percent of the Delta's almost 4.5 million acres were hardwood forest and tupelo and bald-cypress bottomland. The work to clear that morass for cotton had been a horrendous effort, decades long, beginning toward the end of the nineteenth century.

The 770 or so acres of Sky Lake are all that remains today of the natural Delta. Sky Lake lies eight miles north of Belzoni on Highway 7. It is an oxbow lake formed by a change in a tributary of the Mississippi some seven thousand years ago. Old-growth bald cypresses, some a thousand years old, live here in the last remaining bit of the primeval Delta. It is a quiet place, with slow movement and layer upon layer of detail. The quieter you get, the more layers pop out. Dappled light changes constantly. A half seen movement in the water becomes the swirling S of a moccasin. To see the Delta as it looked before it was cleared gave me a better understanding and feel for that land.

When I returned to Mississippi, I thought that I was seeking echoes of old times. Instead, I have discovered myself picking up not where I left off but further on down the line. Rather than finding answers or conclusions, I find a continuing love and sense of participation in the North Mississippi hill country. It seems this, in some ways, is still my homeplace.

Mississippi Then and Now

These new pictures of Mississippi seem to look for the past while perhaps not finding it. The sets of photos in this chapter are connected in one way or another. Sometimes the images are parallels, reflections, or equivalents, and sometimes they are contrasts. Or they can be just little visual stories about time. Others simply are places I knew long ago, and the new photographs mark the passage of time. Some images record the juxtaposition between old and new. They don't claim to be great art. I hope there's a bit of fun here. Almost always there's a thread of some sort, if only in my own mind, to the old photographs.

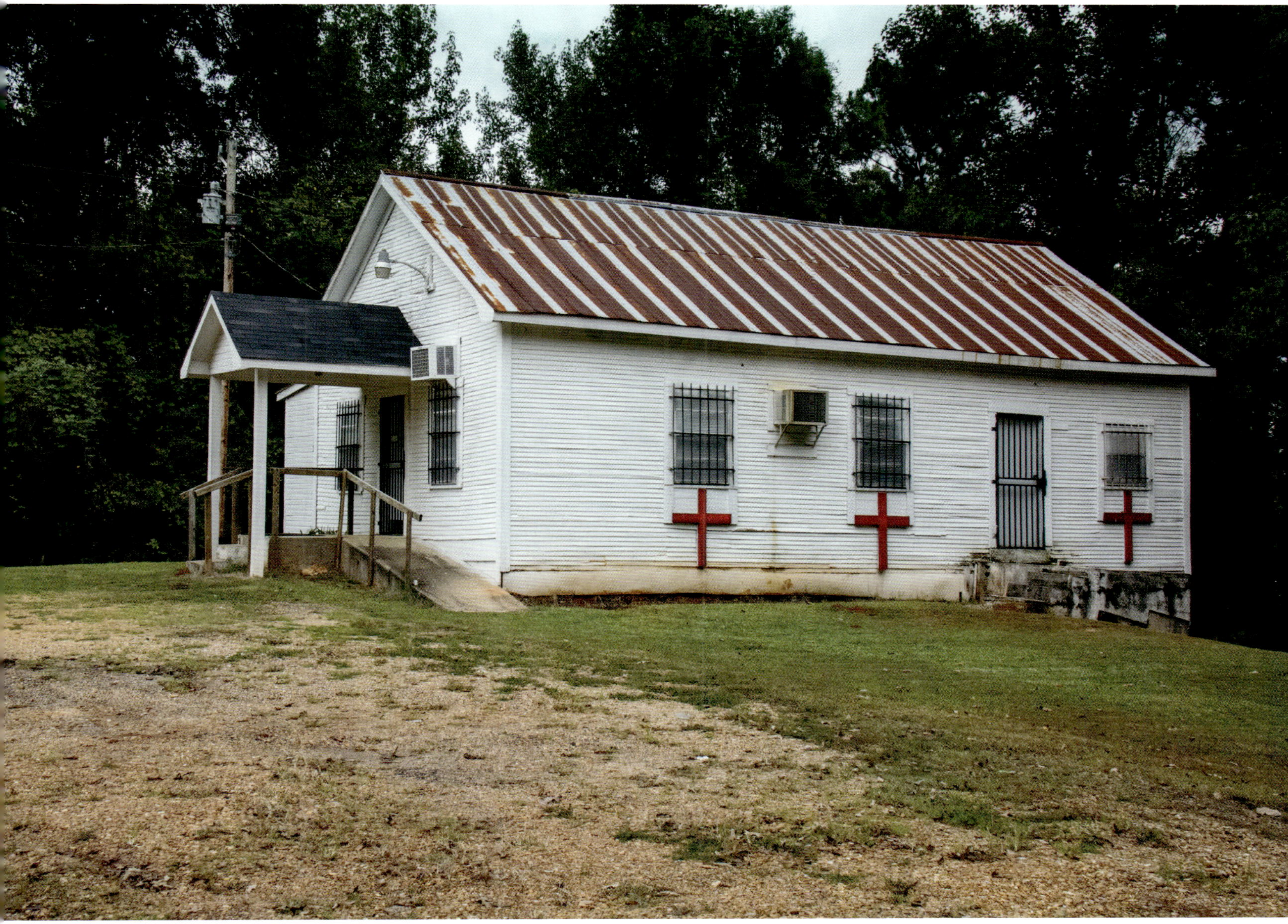

New Testament Holiness Church, Abbeville, Lafayette County, 2014.

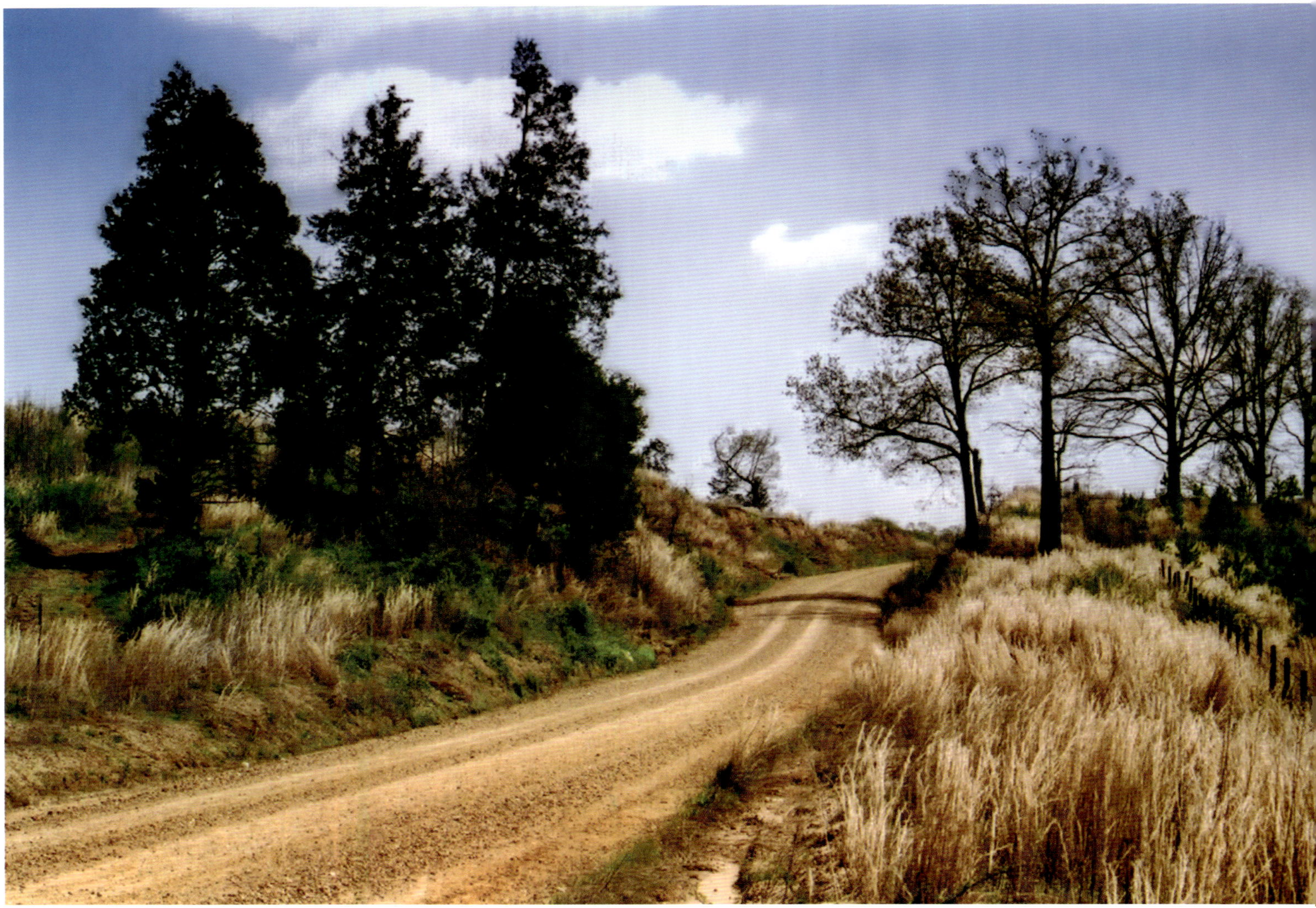

Tyro Road, Marshall County, 1974.

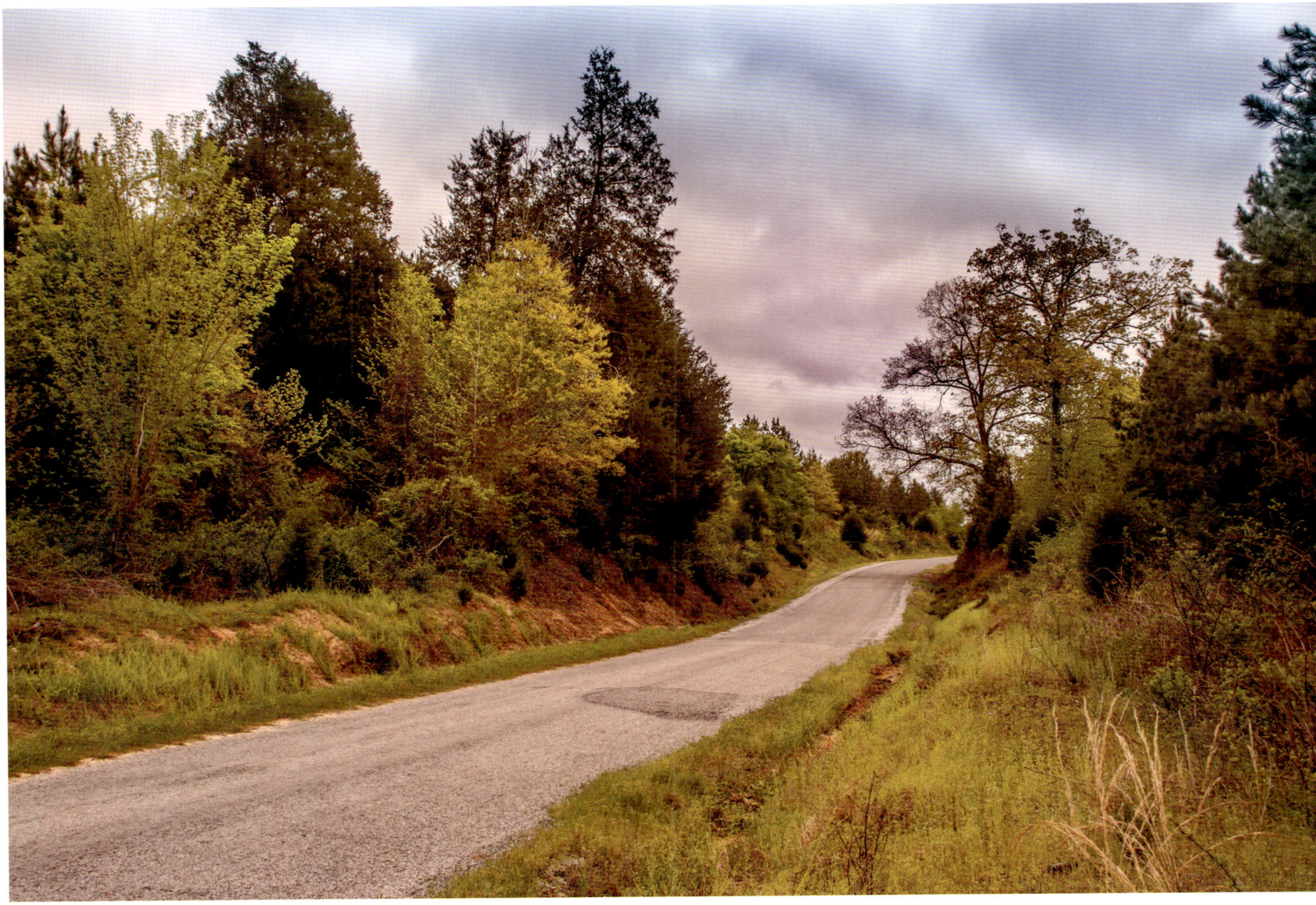

Tyro Road, 2013. The scene was instantly recognizable yet totally changed. One of the biggest changes I noticed was the disappearance of dirt roads. They were a rough ride; after a heavy rain they could be close to impassable until the road grader came through. But they could be beautiful, and they were the true color of the earth.

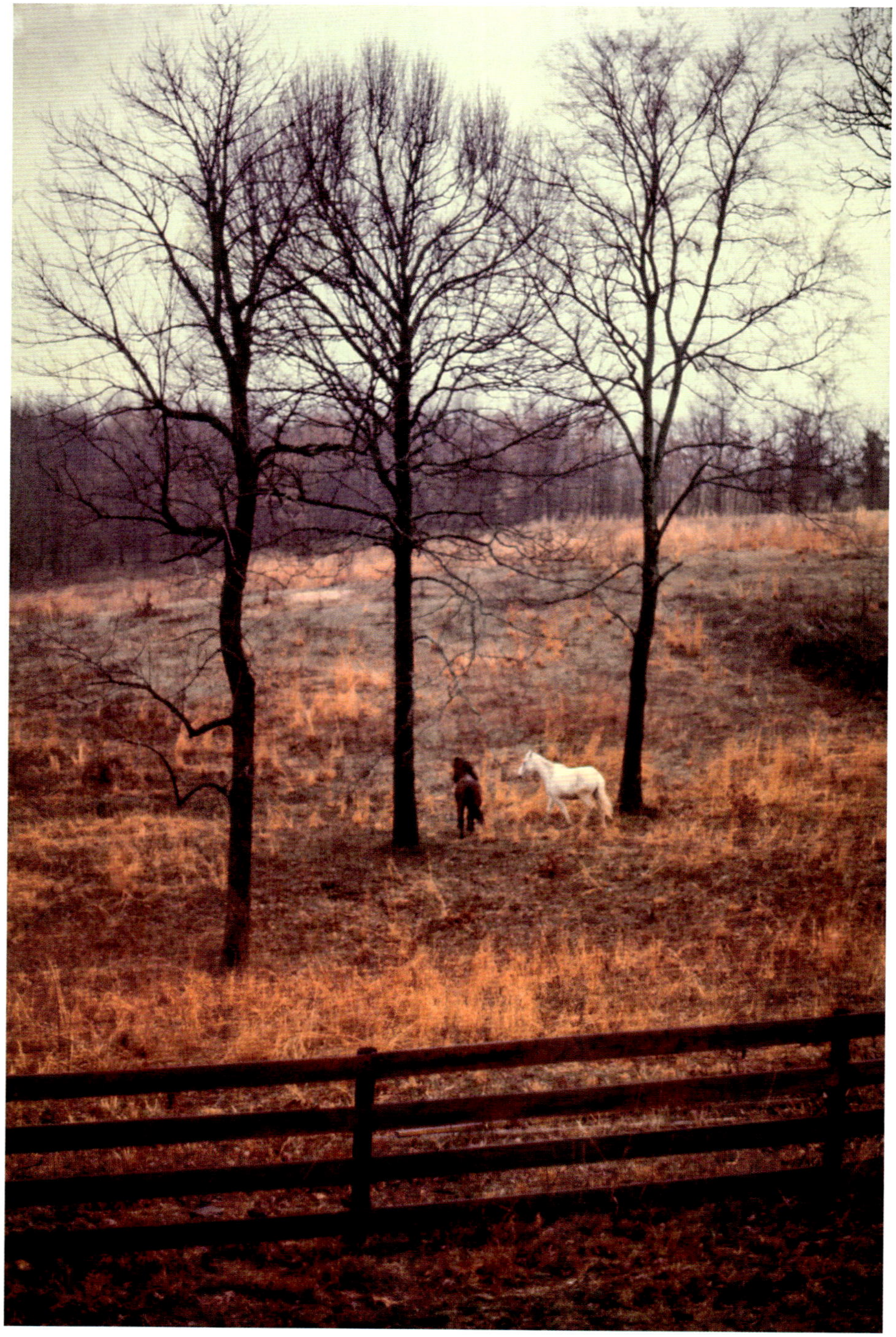

Winter colors 2, white horse, Lafayette County, 1973. Winter was earth tones—russets and tans, browns and blacks. The horses added their color and movement.

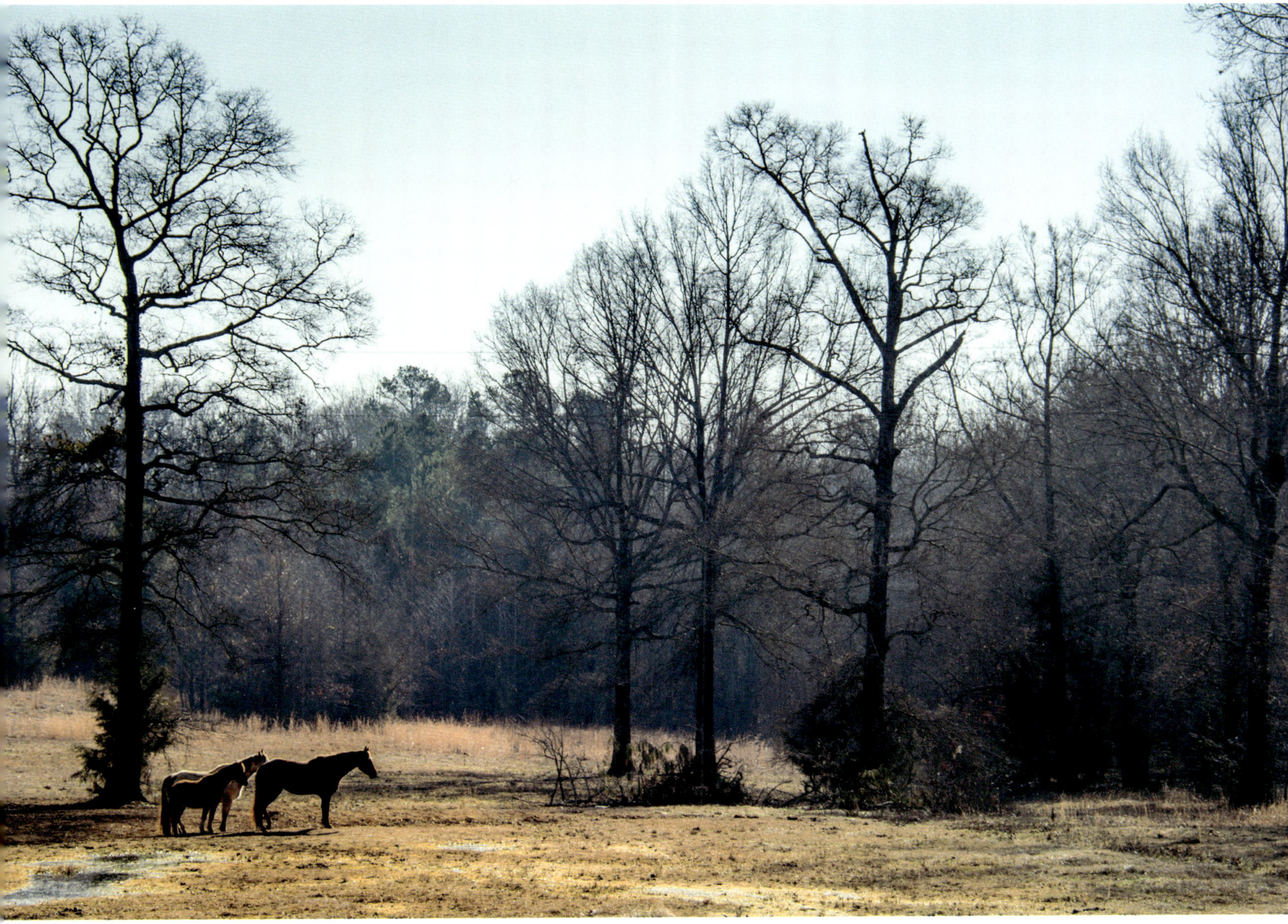

Holly Springs National Forest, 2013. Forty years later this is one place that is nearly the same.

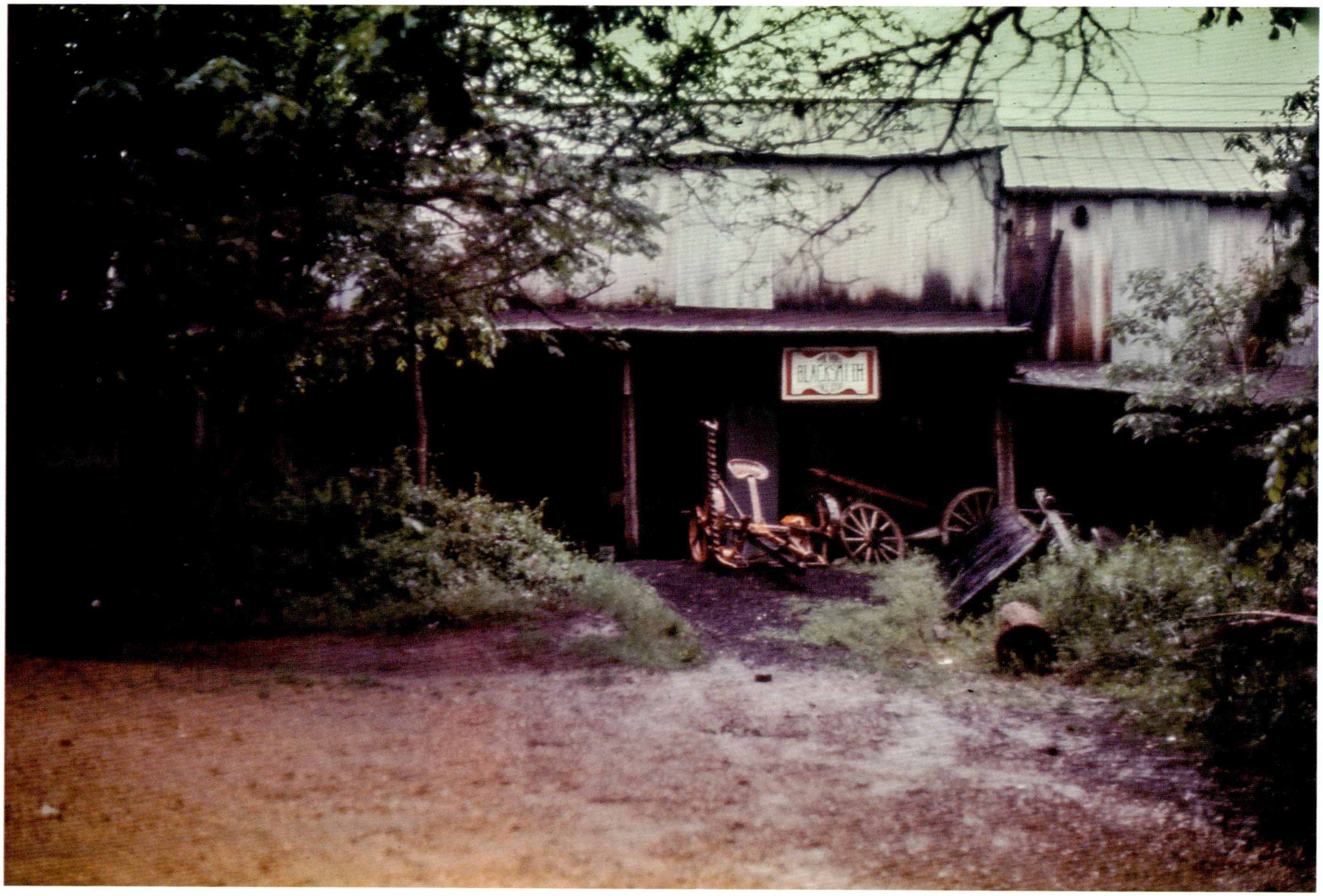

Mr. Hall's shop, Oxford, 1973. Mr. Hall's blacksmith shop was nestled in the back and underneath some buildings right off the square. It was a piece of 1910 stuck in time.

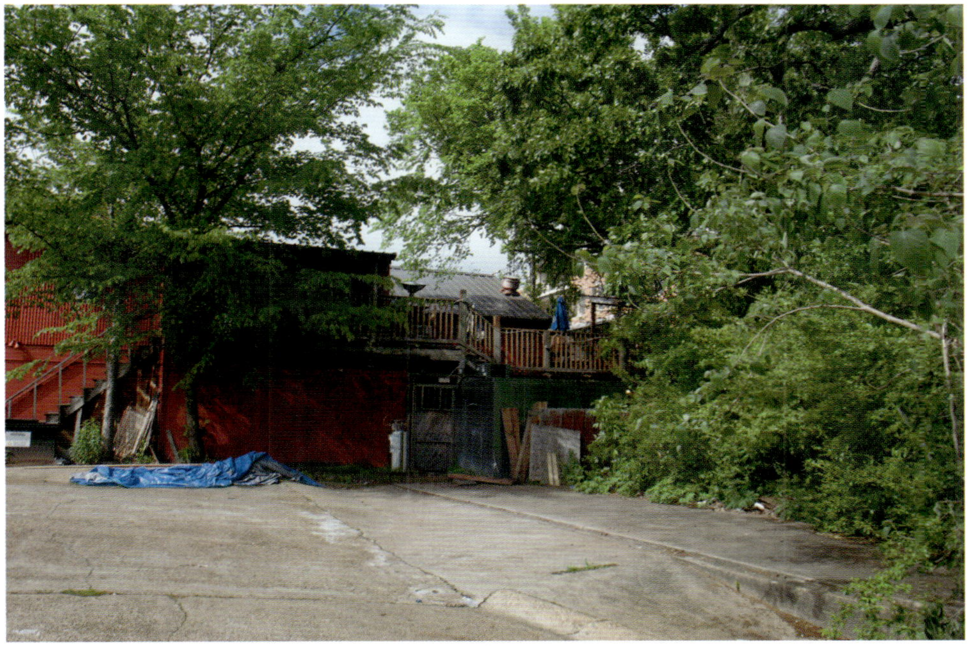

Site of Mr. Hall's shop, 2013. A restaurant patio can be seen up at street level, with storage below. There was no trace of the shop, but I could still recognize the place by the trees.

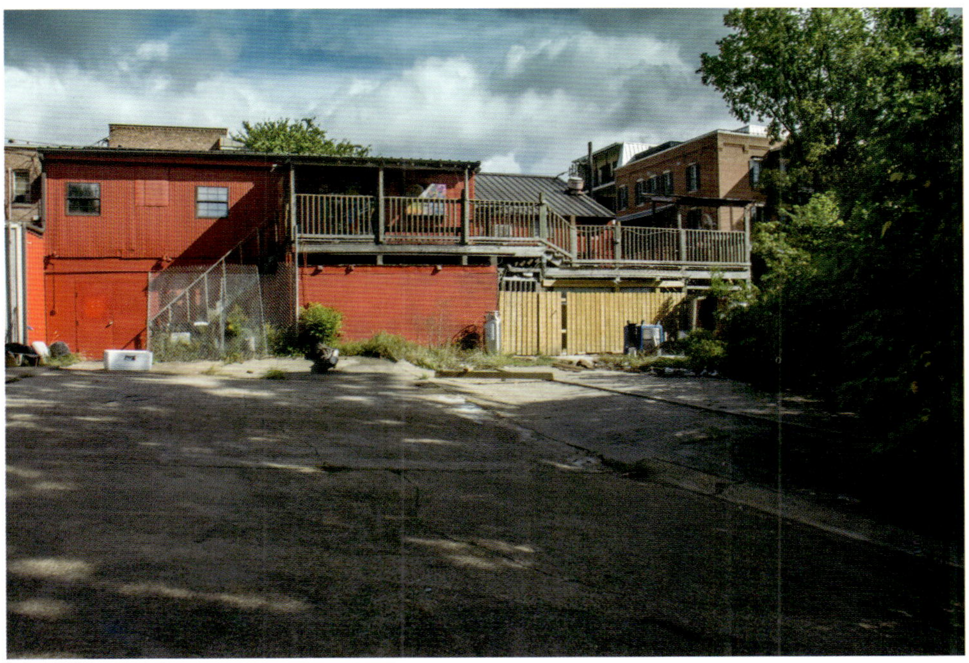

Site of Mr. Hall's shop, 2014. When I returned a year later, the trees had been cut down.

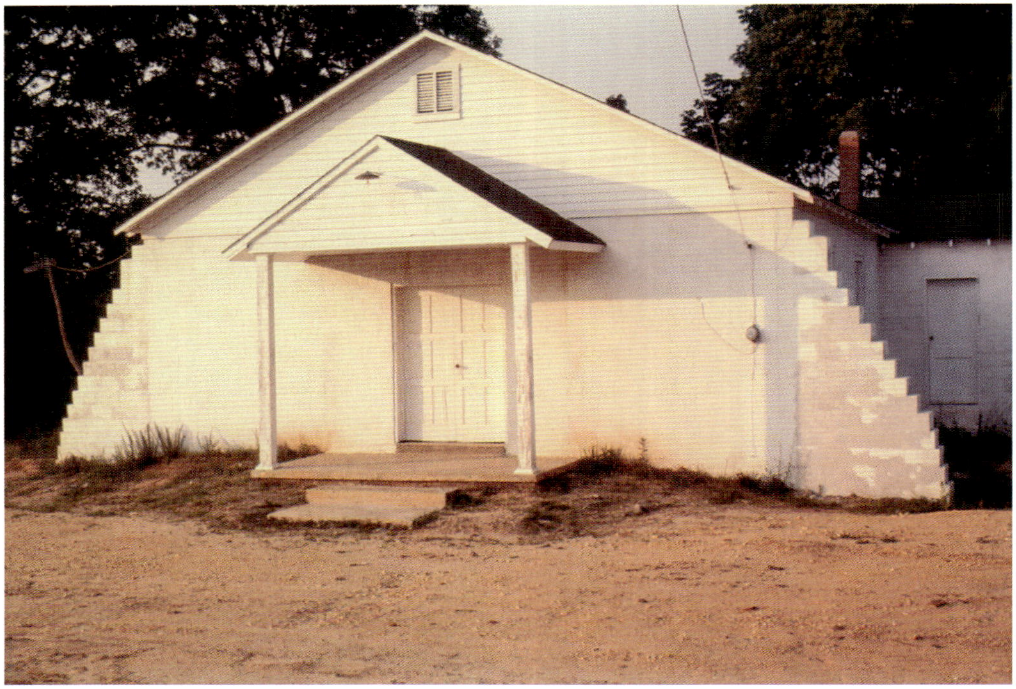

Bell Grove Missionary Baptist Church, Chulahoma, 1973.

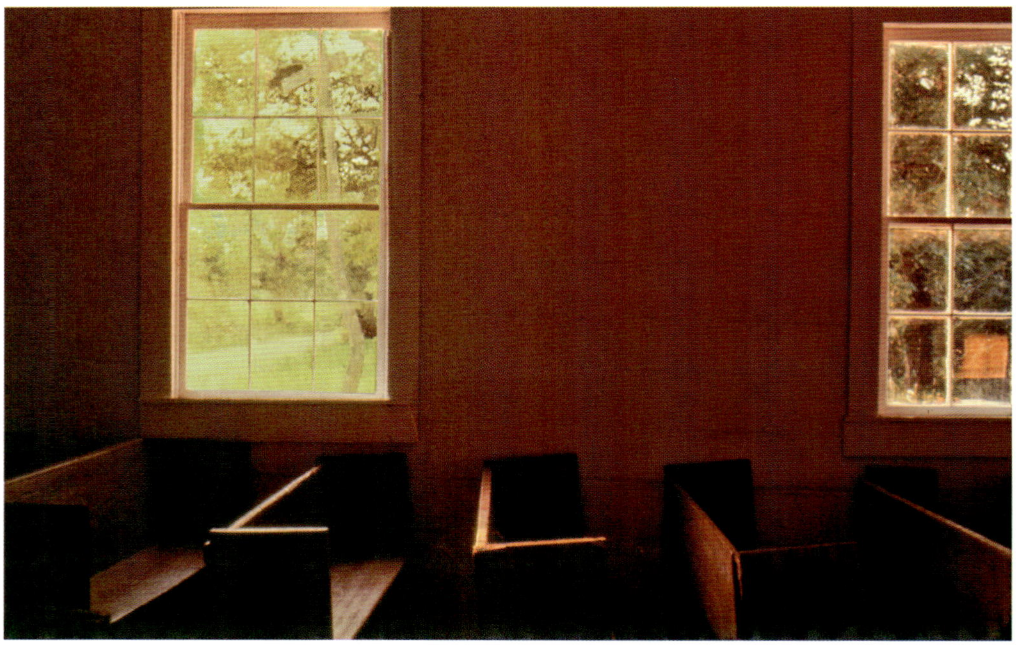

Inside Bell Grove, Chulahoma, 1973. Bell Grove was a simple country church that was loved and cared for by its congregation.

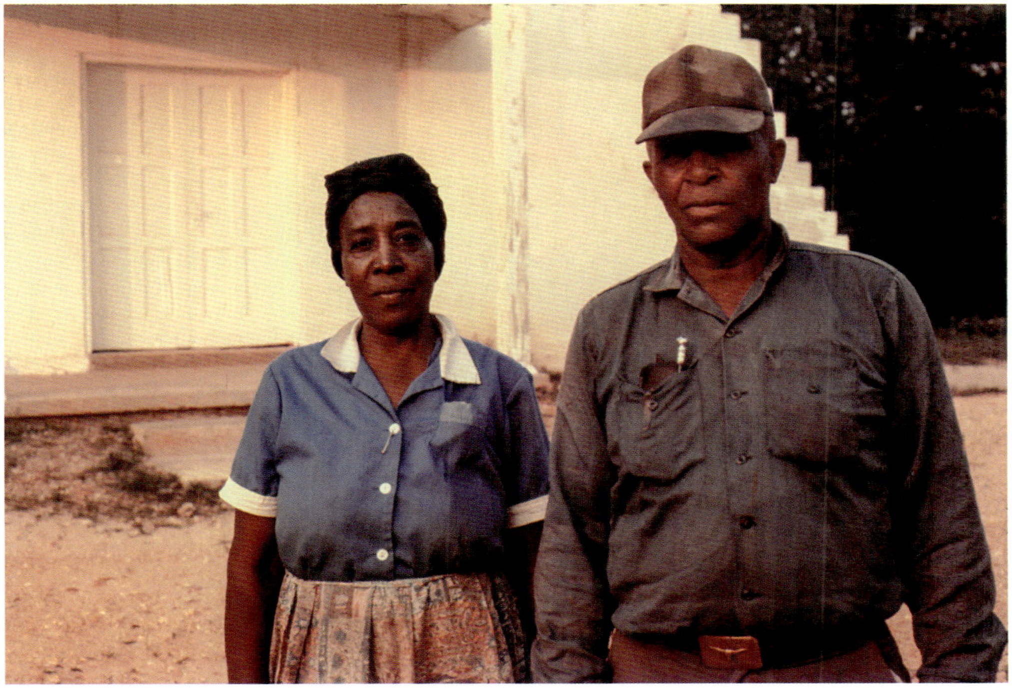

Mississippi Gothic,
Chulahoma, 1973. It was in front of the church that I made the portraits of Annie Mae and L. Q. Cole.

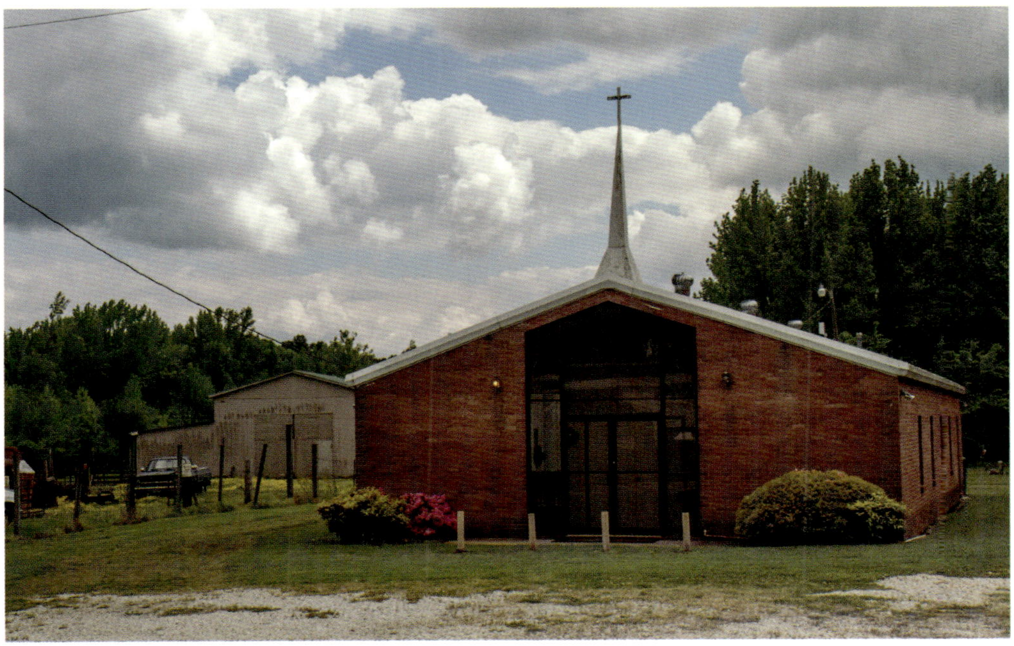

The new Bell Grove,
Bell Grove Missionary Baptist Church, Chulahoma Road, 2013. The old building is gone, but its successor is still a simple country church. The new church's address is in Holly Springs, since Chulahoma no longer exists.

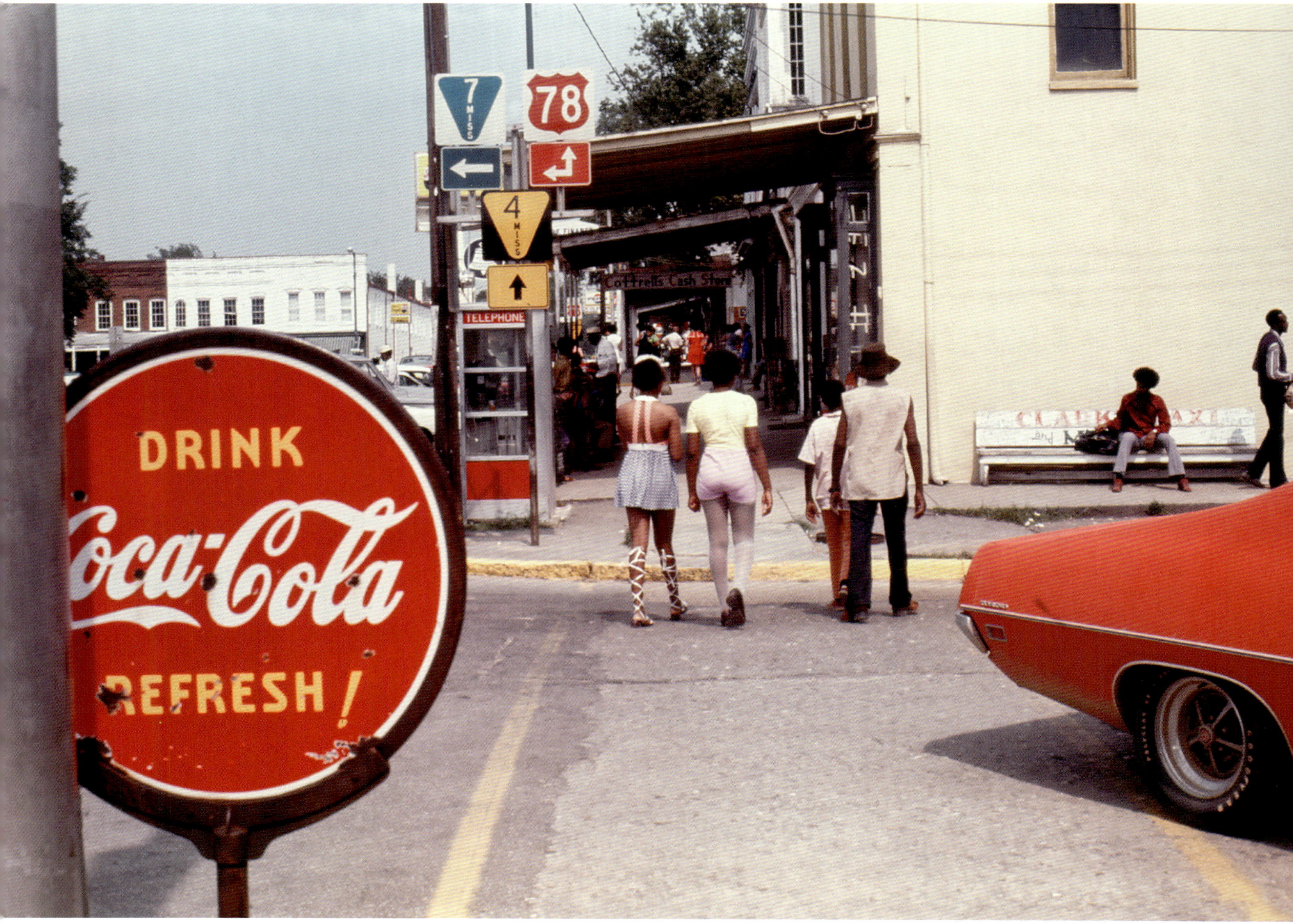

Saturday afternoon, Holly Springs, 1972.

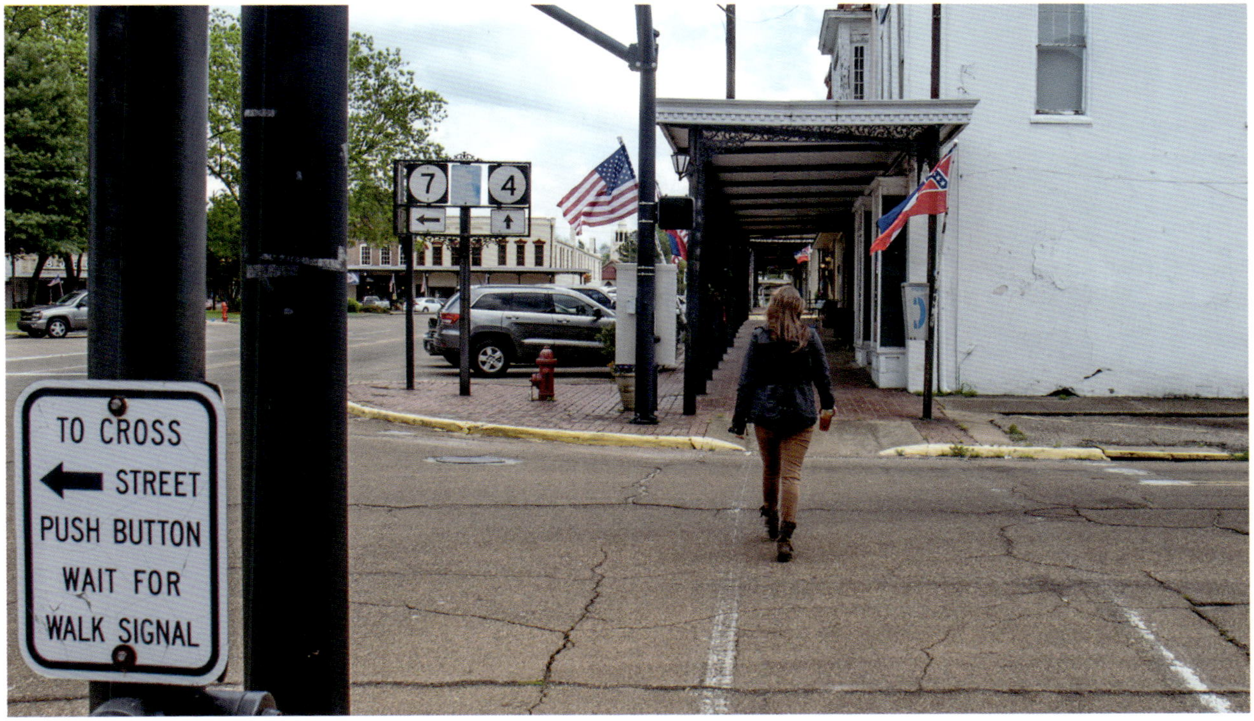

Here or gone? Holly Springs, 2013. You don't need a bench if there's no one to sit on it. The color and the people are gone. Holly Springs seems to hang in the balance. I have hope.

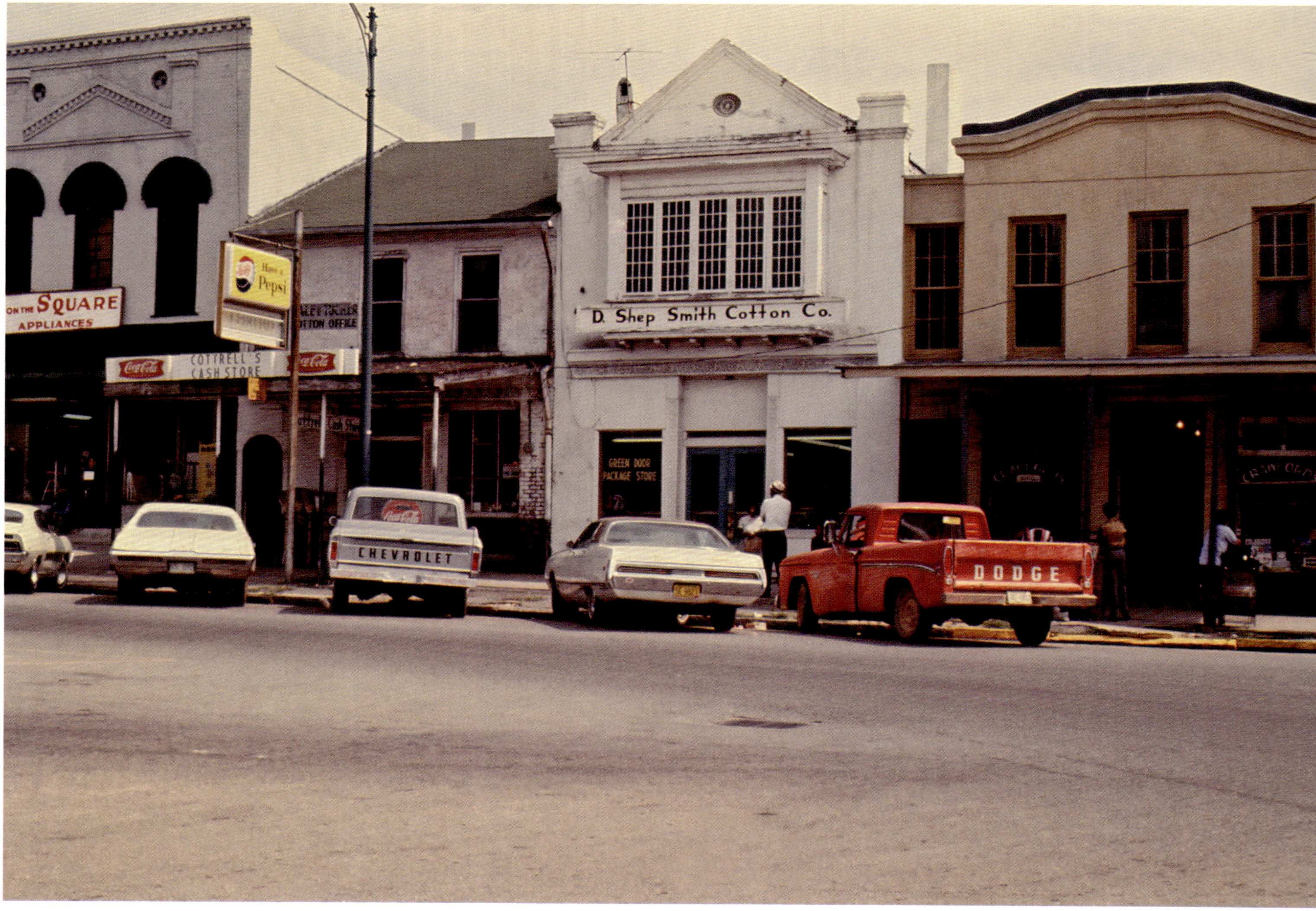

D Shep Smith Cotton Company, south side of the square, Holly Springs, 1972–75.

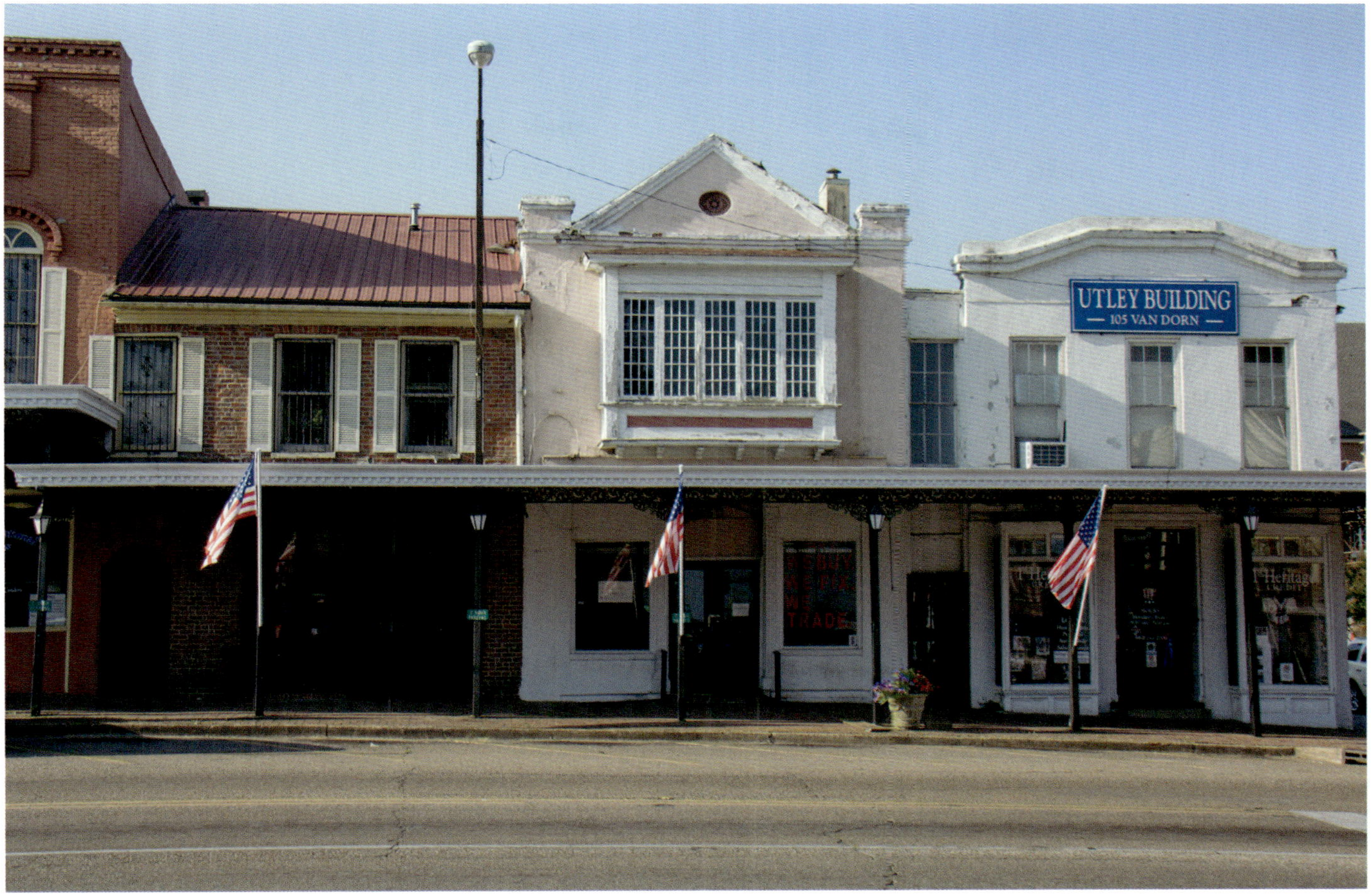

Van Dorn Street, south side of the square,
Holly Springs, 2013–15.

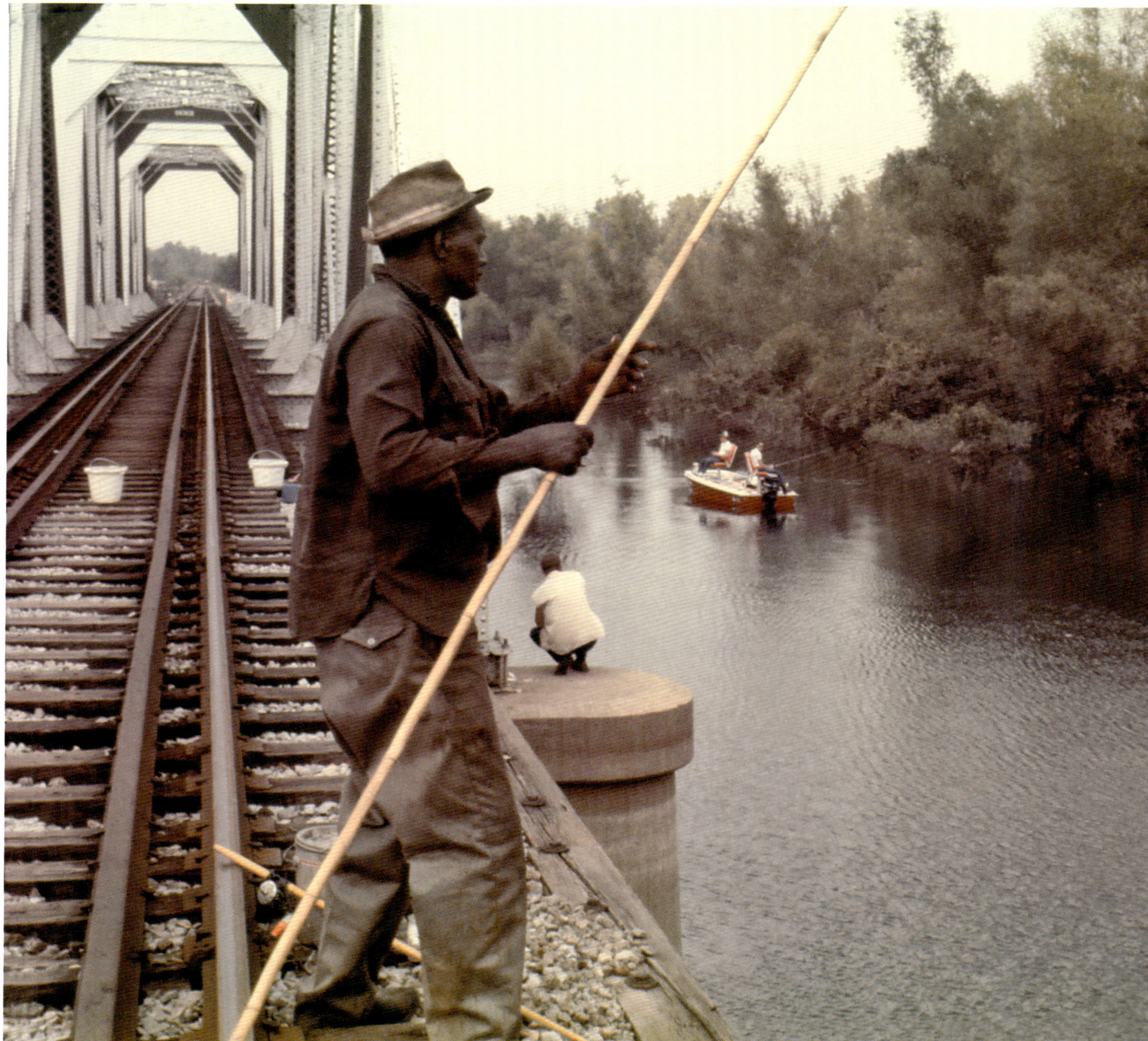

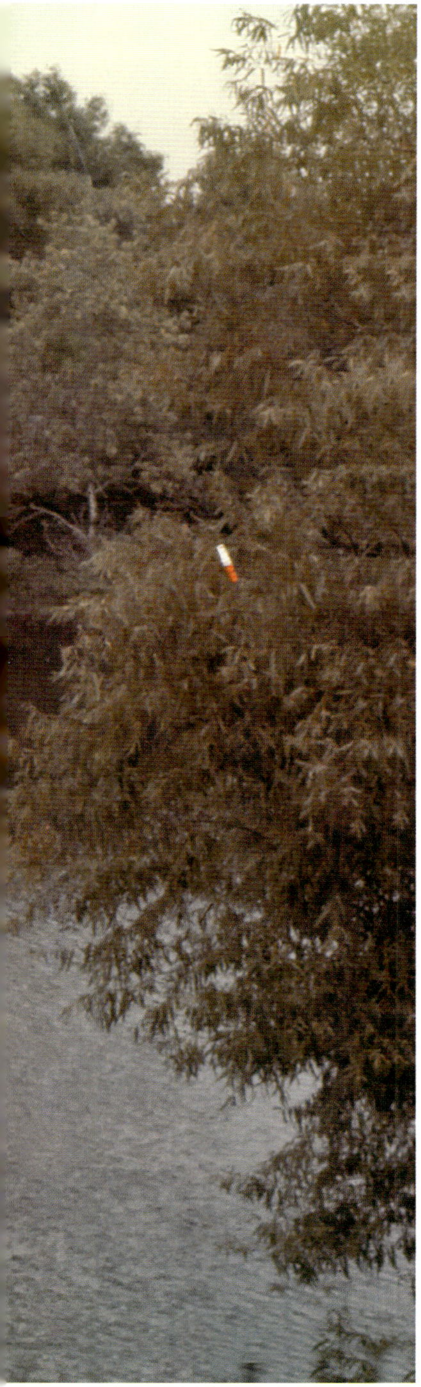

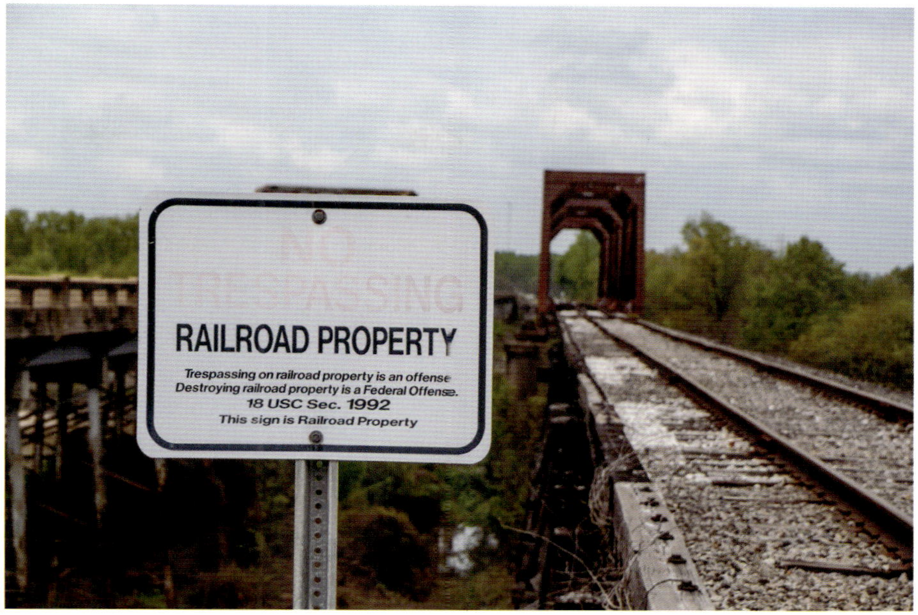

Keep off, Lafayette County, 2013.
The Tallahatchie Bridge, rusty and empty.

Fishing off the Tallahatchie River Bridge, Lafayette County, 1973. Built in 1908, the bridge was part of the Illinois Central Line. It always seemed to have fishermen, boaters, loafers, and lovers about. It was a cool spot on which to sit over the river after a beer run to the Marshall County line when Oxford was still dry.

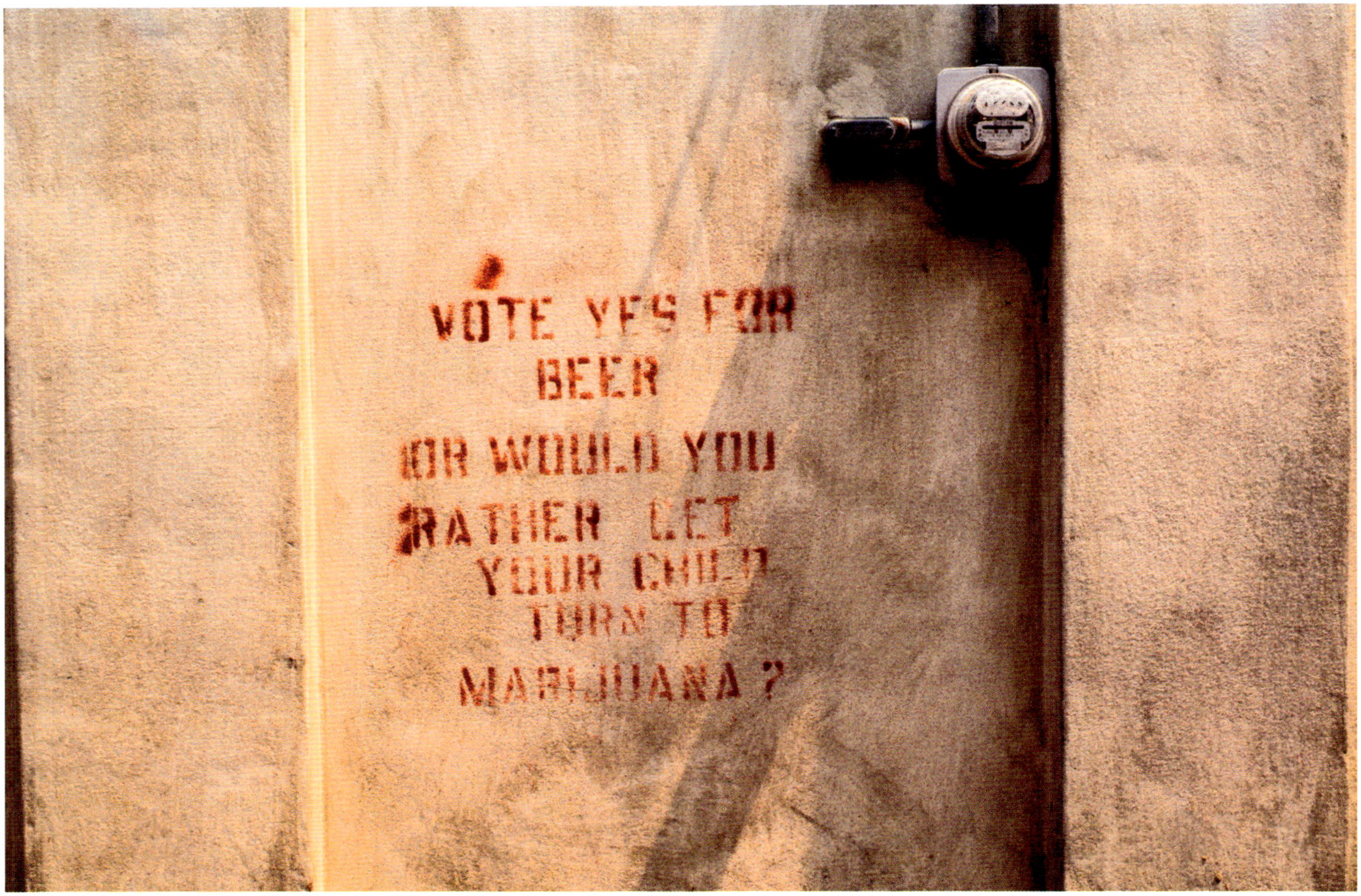

Vote for beer, on the wall of Boles Café, Oxford, 1972–75. Making beer legal was a tough battle. All "right-thinking" people were against it no matter how much they drank. The churches were against it. When it did pass in 1972, you still couldn't buy beer on a Sunday or a cold one in a store.

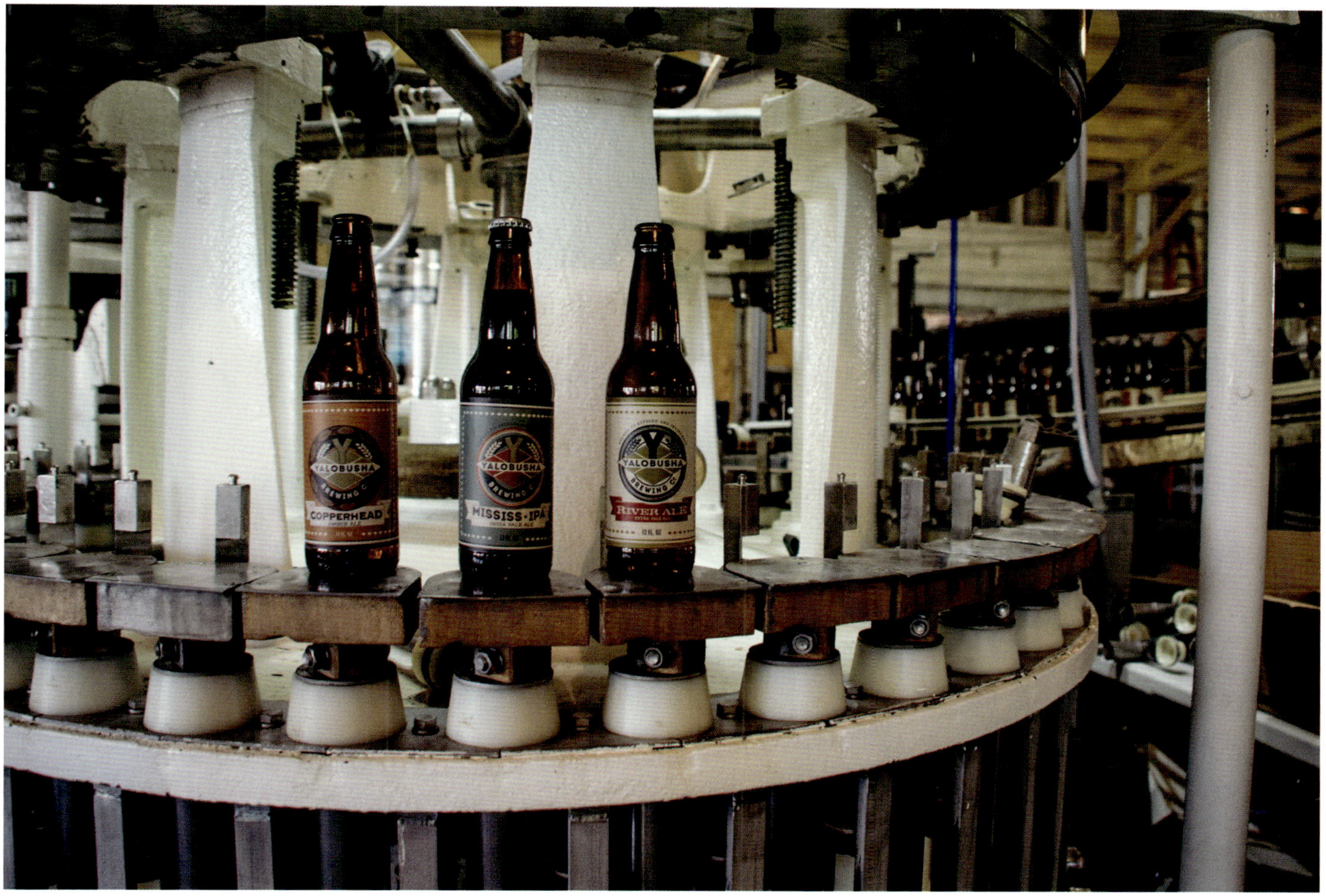

Yalobusha Brewery, Water Valley, 2013. A tasty IPA, made right in the hill country.

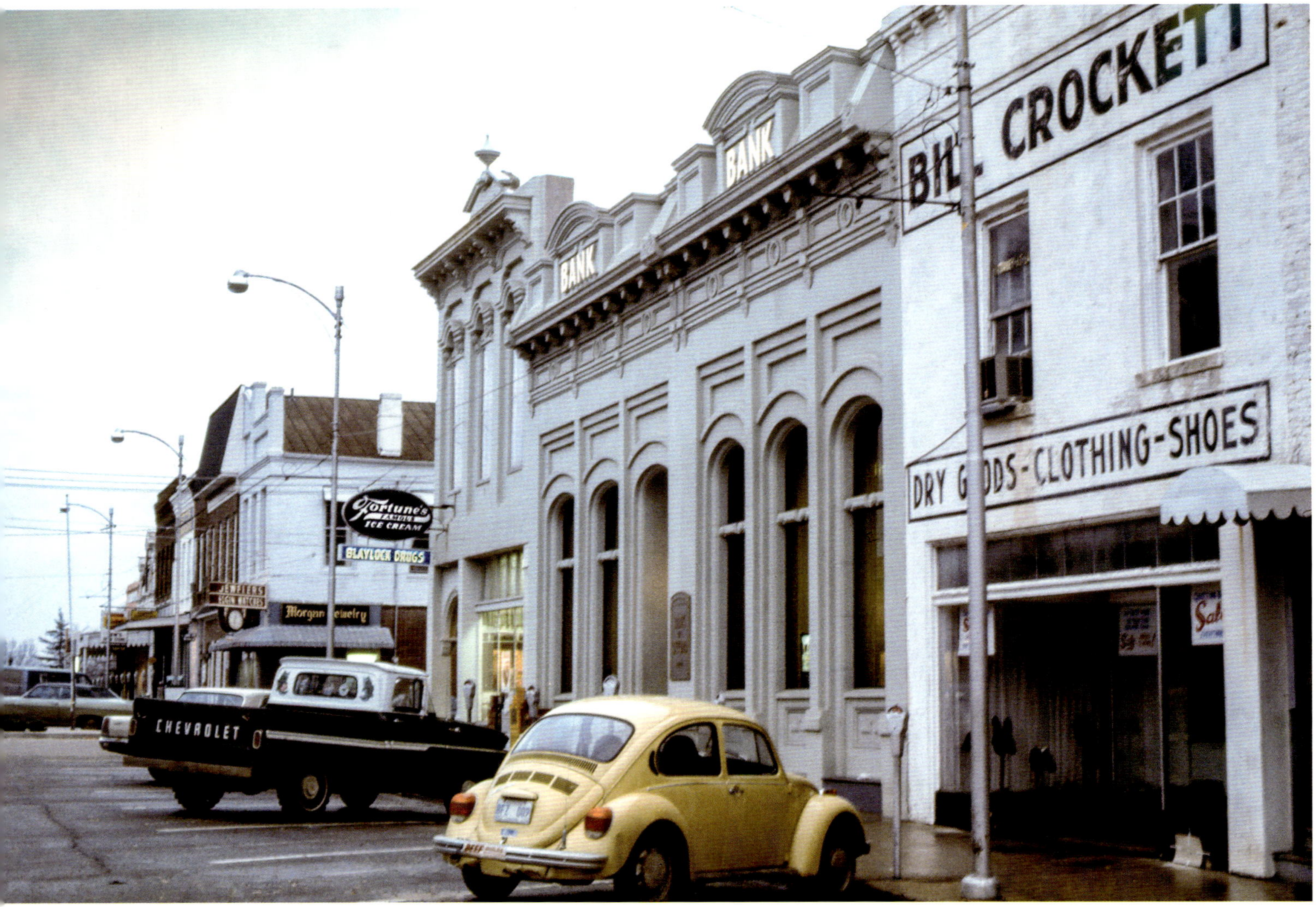

The Square, showing Blaylock Drugs, the bank, Crockett's Dry Goods, Oxford, 1973.

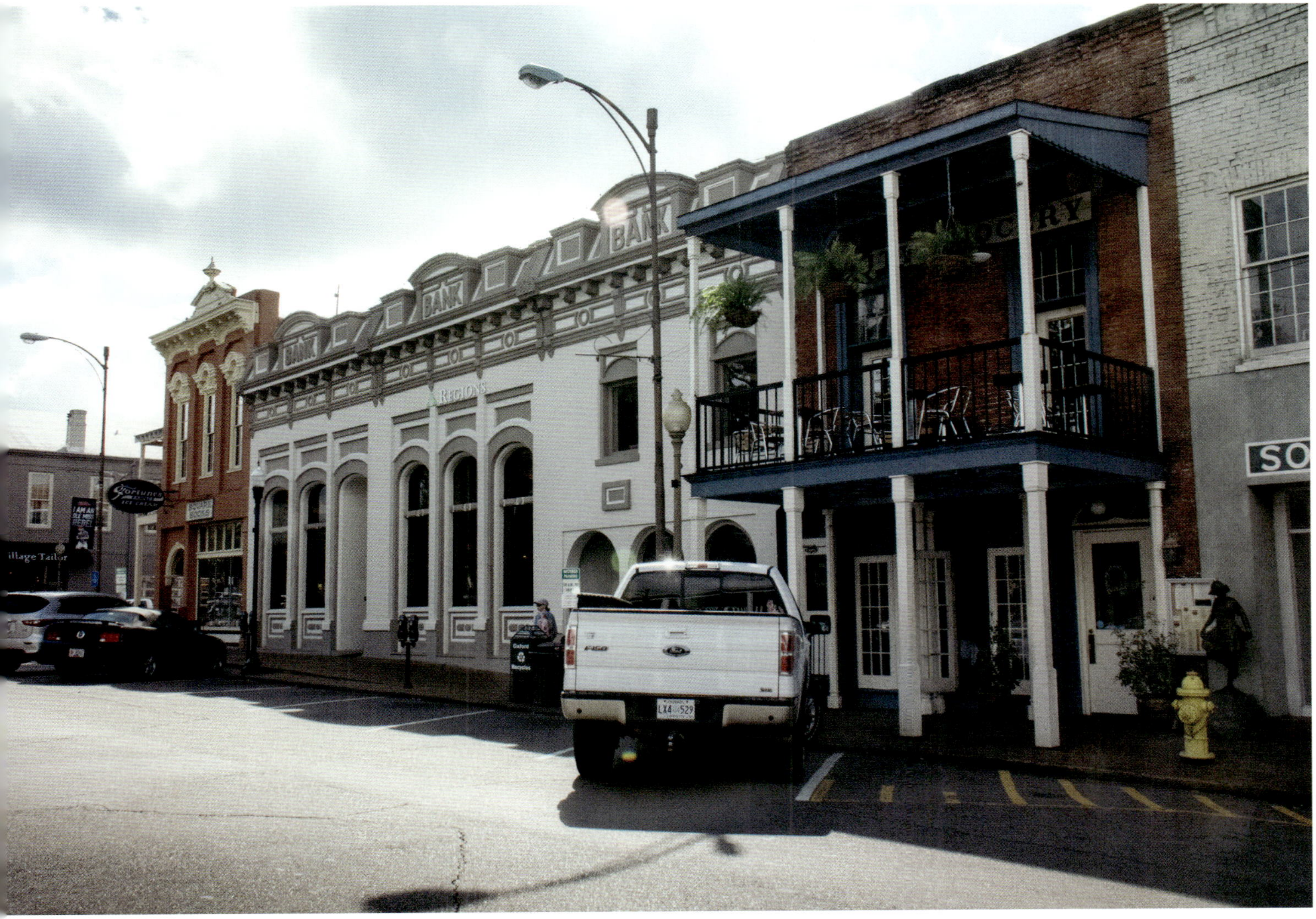

The Square, showing Square Books, the bigger bank, City Grocery, Oxford, 2014.

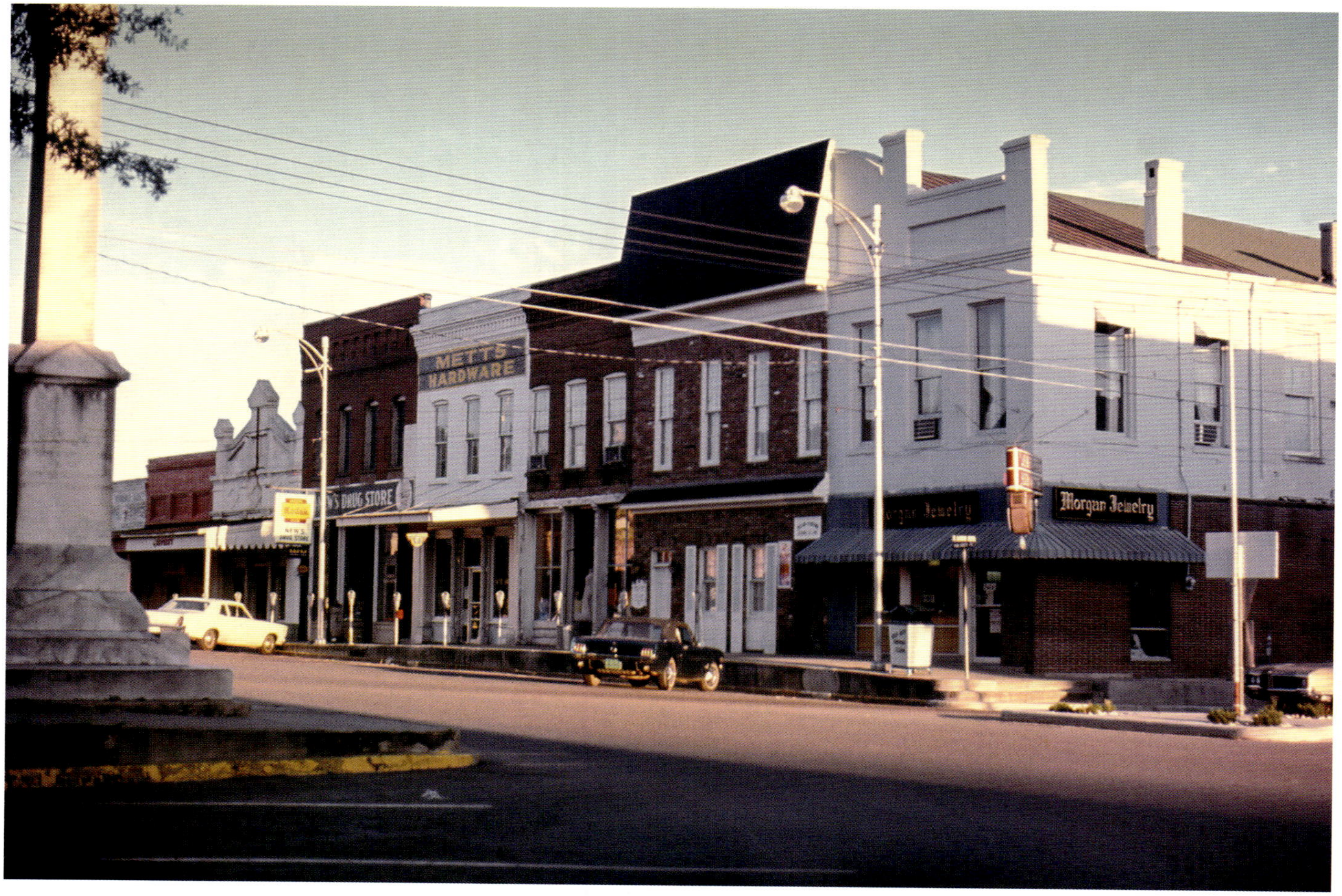

The Square, showing New's Drug, Metts Hardware, Oxford, 1973. A Mustang belonging to Chooky Falkner (the nephew of the novelist William Faulkner, although he spelled his surname without the "u") is parked in front of Morgan Jewelry. Chooky commanded the local National Guard unit during the Meredith riots. While his unit was guarding the university, Chooky's arm was broken by a thrown brick. Jimmy Faulkner, his brother, commandeered a bulldozer to use as cover for a group of armed rioters marching toward the university. Wearing an improvised sling, Chooky stepped into the middle of the road to stand down the bulldozer. People say that Chooky was the only man Jimmy wouldn't run down. At the last minute Jimmy swerved to avoid hitting his brother. The dozer hit an oak tree, the engine stalled, and the U.S. Marshalls seized it. Folks say the brothers were estranged until they died.

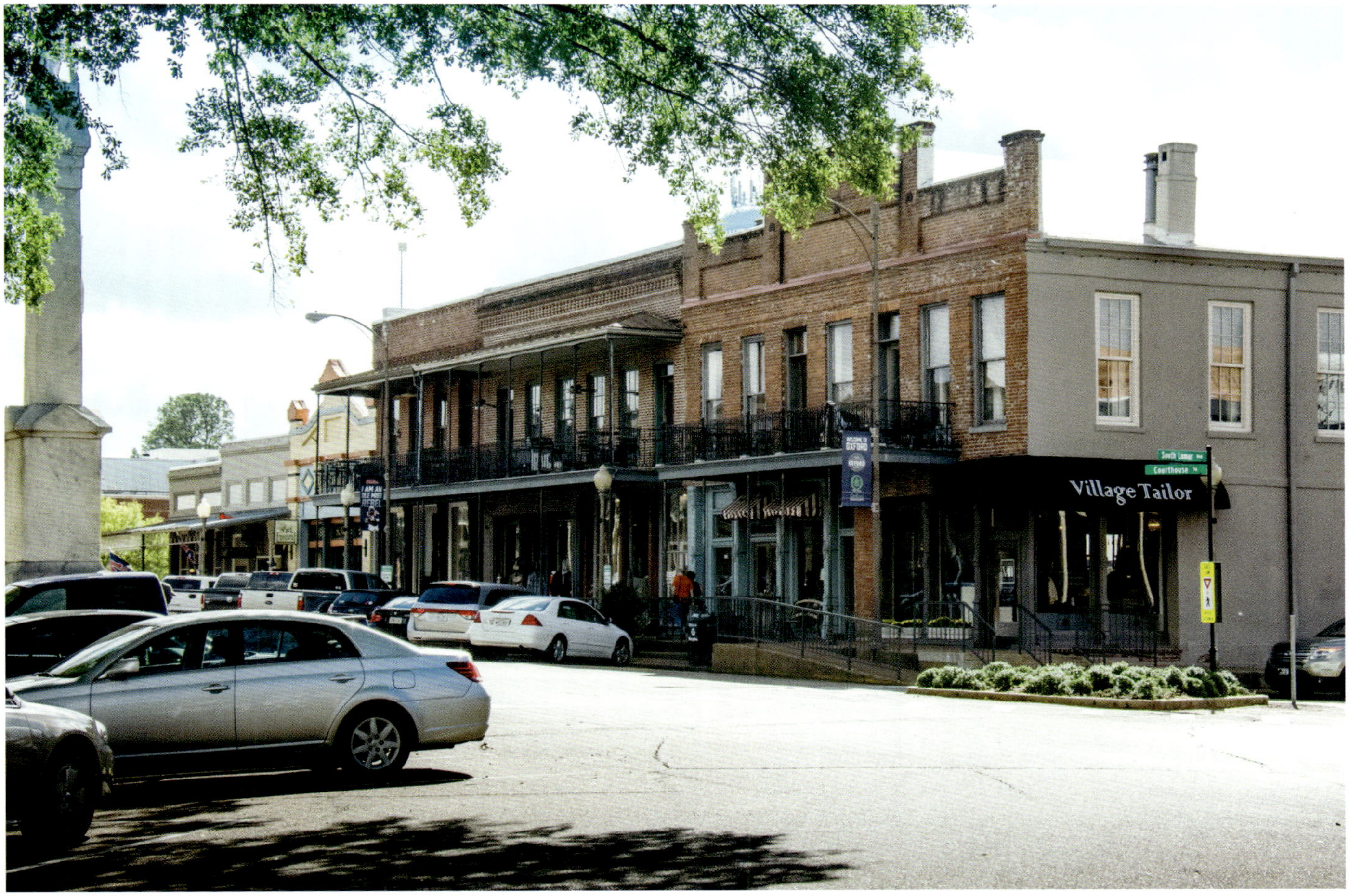

The Square, Oxford, 2014.

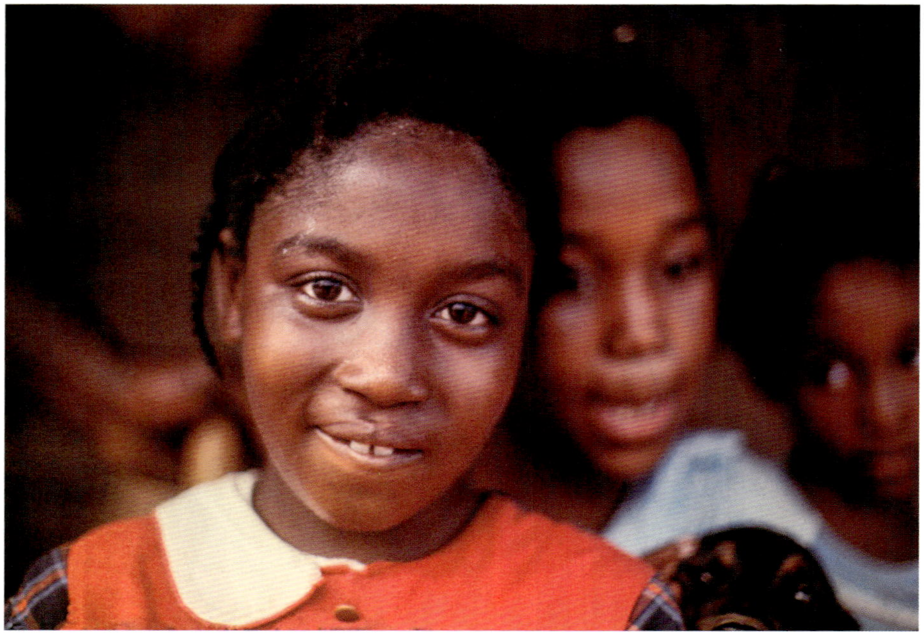

Nettie and Alameda Turner, Othar's daughters, Gravel Springs community, Como, 1973.

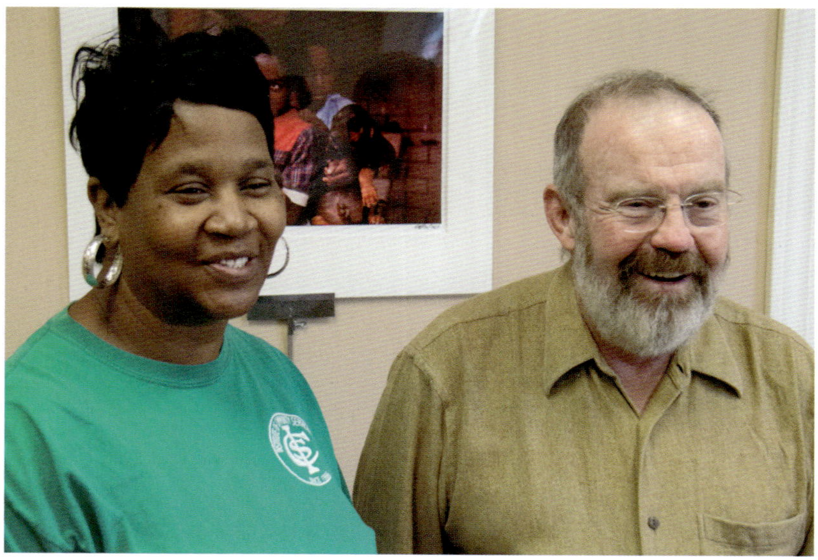

Nettie Turner, Como, October 2014. That's me beside Nettie. Another shot of the Turner sisters was on the wall at the Como Public Library during Como's yearly Tracks Festival. I gave a brown bag lecture and asked whether anyone had questions. A lady raised her hand, pointed to the photo, and asked, "Where did you get my picture?" At first I was dumbfounded, and then I was very pleased. Photo by Shaquille Conrad.

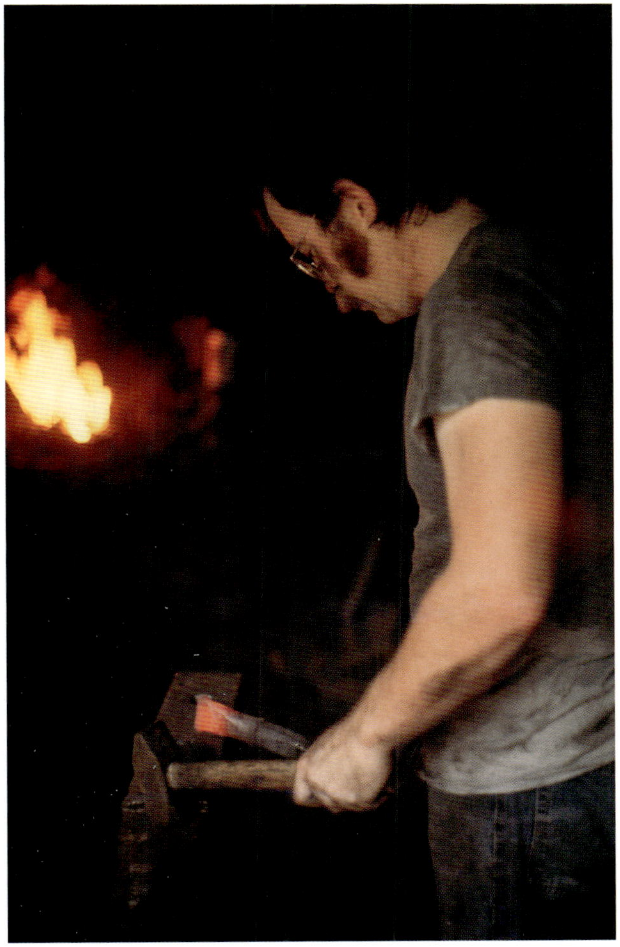

Mr. Hall's forge, Oxford, 1973. Mr. Hall shoed mules for the army in Texas during World War I. On the way home, in 1918, his anvil was stolen from the railroad baggage car. He replaced it with a used 175-pound Hay-Budden made in Brooklyn, New York. He knew it was a good anvil and was quite proud of it. I learned at that anvil. I know its ring. I've had my own anvil for over forty years, but Mr. Hall's is special. It never occurred to me that I would ever hammer on it again until I spoke to Andy Waller in 2013. Photo by Carol Parcher.

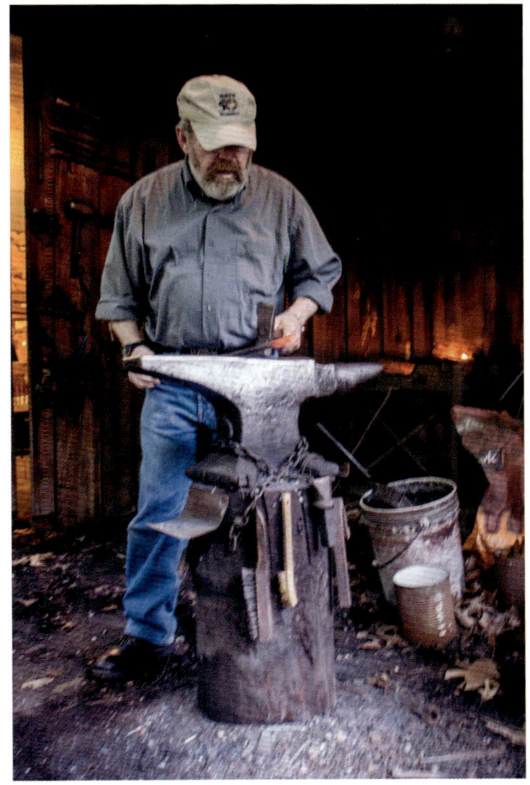

Mr. Hall's anvil at Andy Waller's forge, Oxford, 2013. As I stood at Mr. Hall's anvil, the memories came flooding back. There was some kind of water in my eyes that made it hard to see where to strike. The anvil still rang clear. Photo by Hillary Huston.

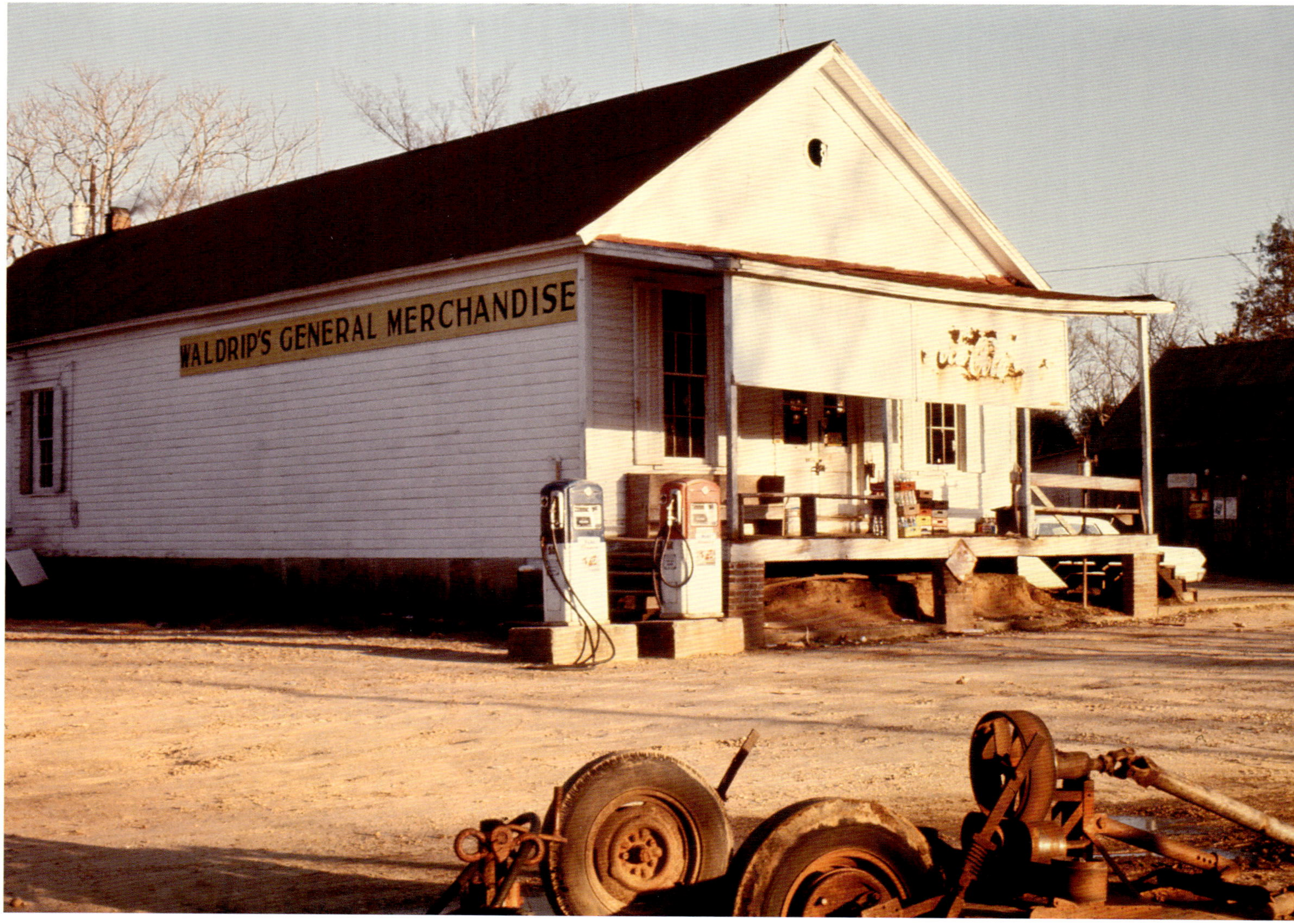

Waldrip's General Store, Chulahoma, 1972. While the store was there, the town was there. After Junior Kimbrough's juke joint burned down in 2000 not much was left of Chulahoma.

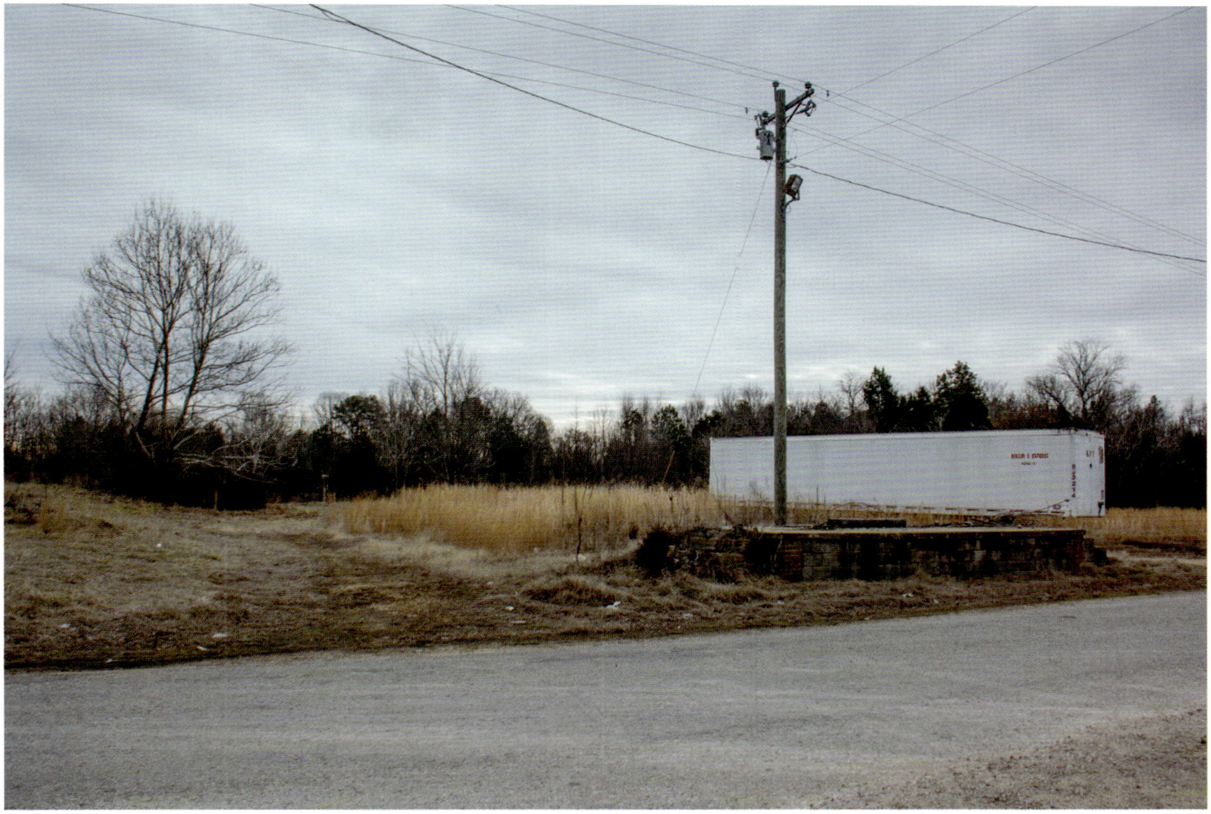

Site of Waldrip's General Store, 2015. There is no longer any sign of the richness that was once there.

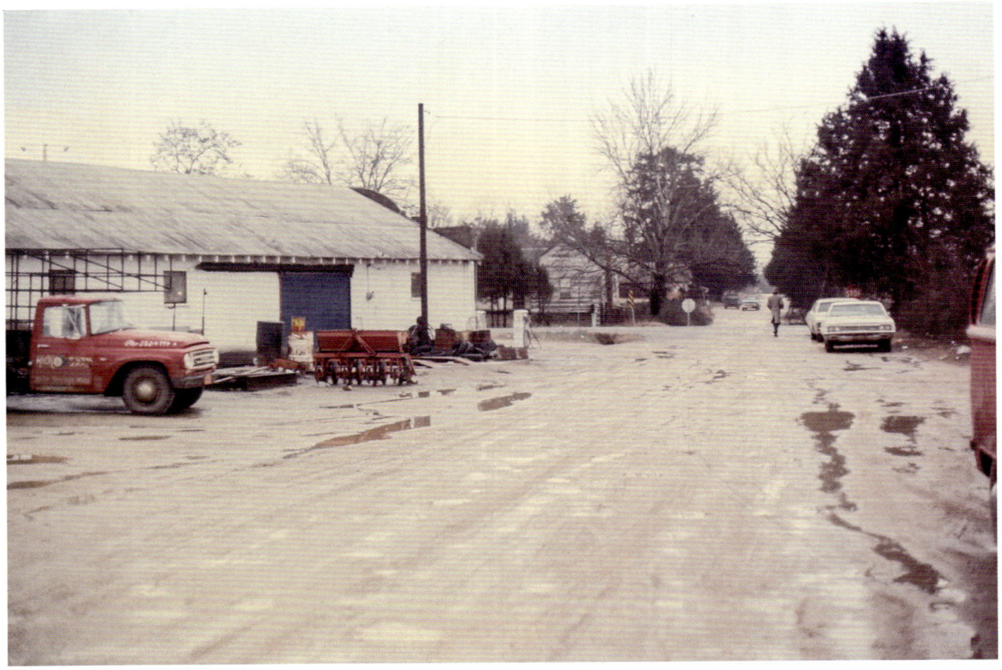

Sid Fore's shop, tractor repair, Chulahoma, 1973. Sid Fore's repair shop, across from the store, was the only other business left in the tiny town.

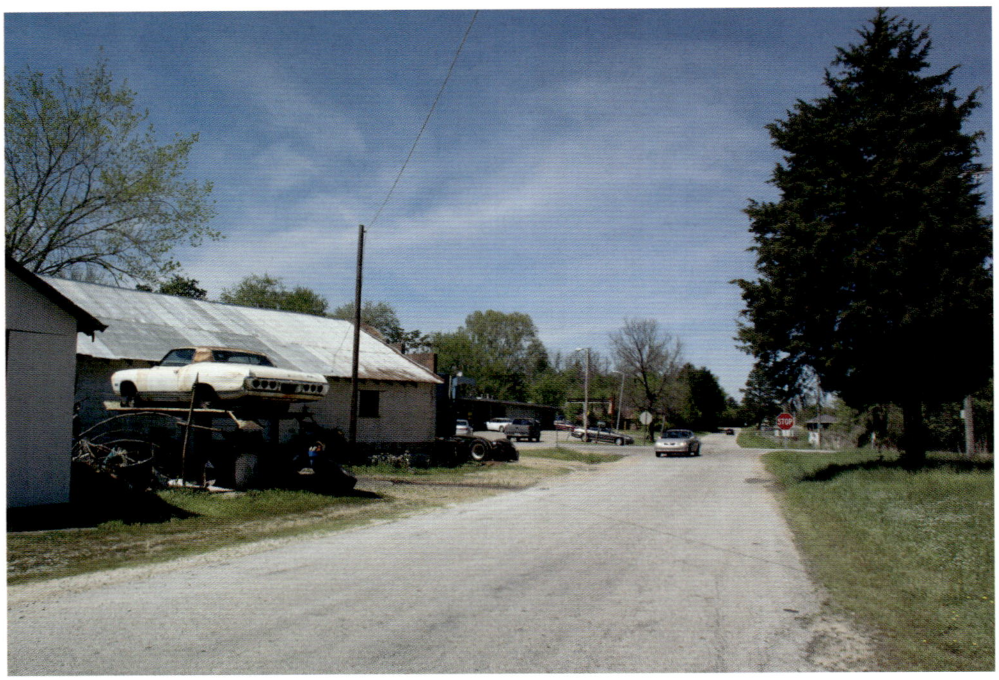

Site of Sid Fore's shop, Chulahoma, 2016.

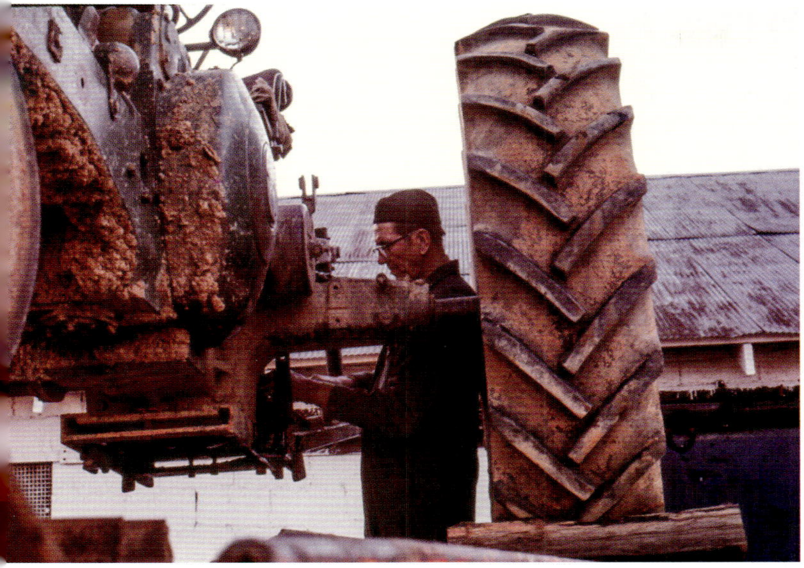

Sid Fore's shop, Chulahoma, 1972.

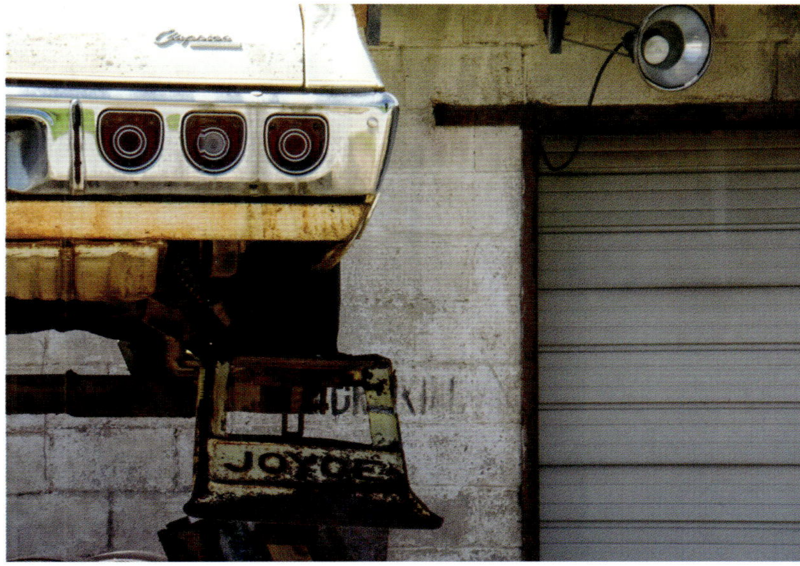

Left high in the air for decades, Sid Fore's shop, Chulahoma, 2016.

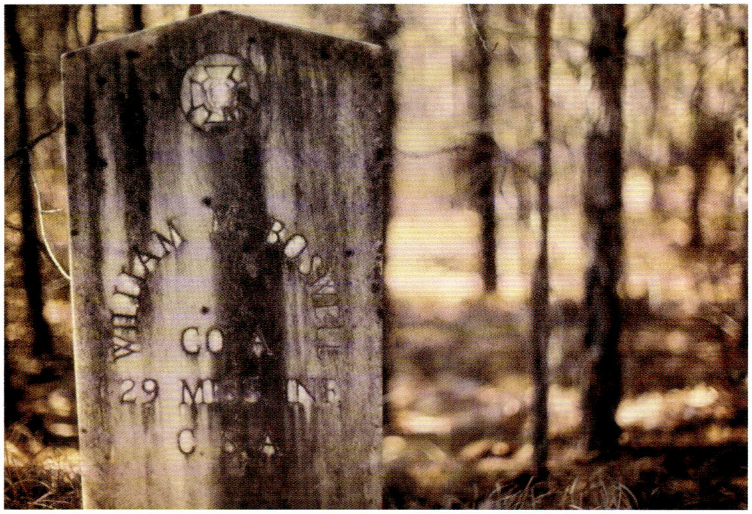

In the ground, Old Covered Wagon Cemetery, Lafayette County, 1974. William M. Boswell, Private, Company A, Twenty-Ninth Mississippi Infantry, fought at the Battles of Murfreesboro and Chickamauga. Born: September 17, 1823, Oxford. Enlisted: March 1, 1862. Discharged: April 26, 1865. Died: May 9, 1886, Lafayette Springs, Mississippi. Finding this grave in the forest made history real to me. This was the resting place of an “enemy” soldier in the soil of a short-lived “foreign” country.

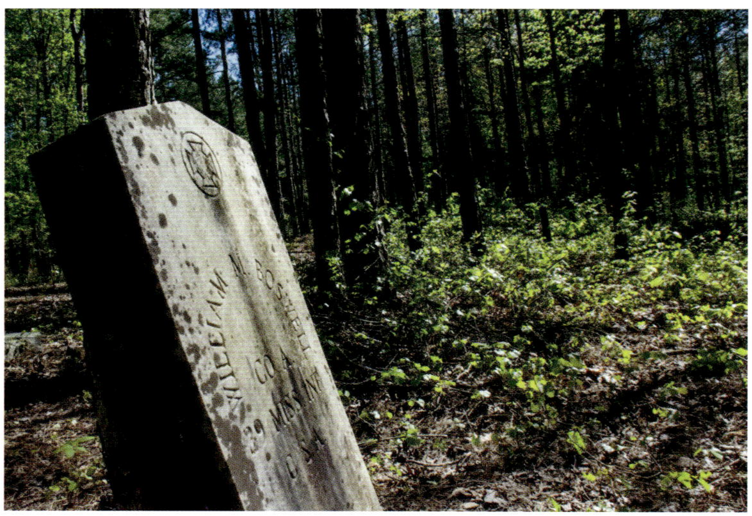

And out, Old Covered Wagon Cemetery, Lafayette County, 2016. After multiple searches over three years I finally found the stone leaning against a tree, I hope near the grave.

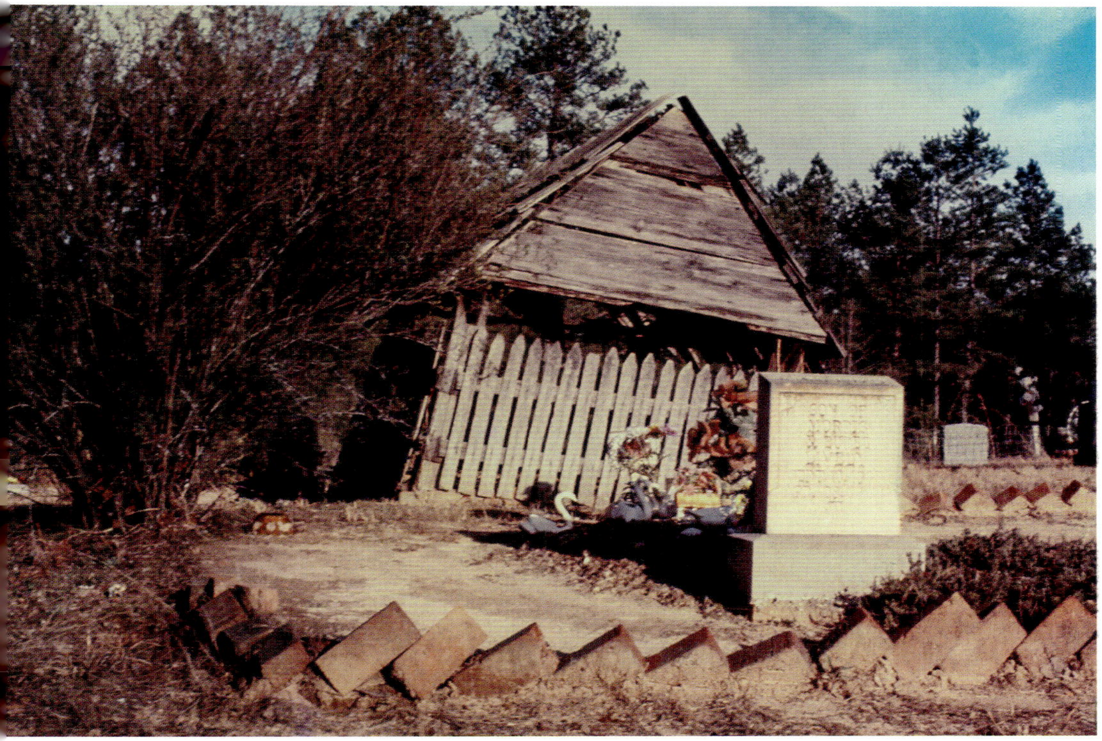

Grave shelter with swans, Christian Rest Cemetery, Holly Springs National Forest, Holly Springs, 1972. Grave shelters, or grave houses, were common in certain areas of the South from roughly the 1880s to the 1930s. This one has a gable roof, four corner posts, and palings. Some say grave shelters are of Scots-Irish origin; others claim Cajun. Only about two hundred are left in the South.

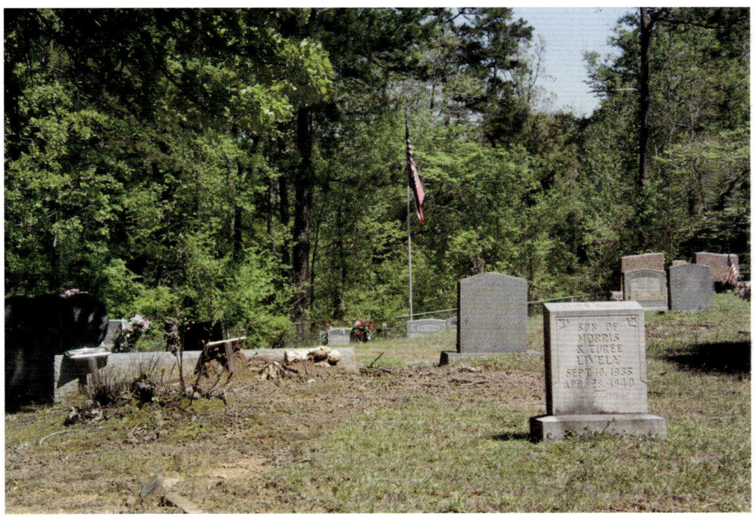

Site of grave shelter, 2016. The grave shelter is no longer there.

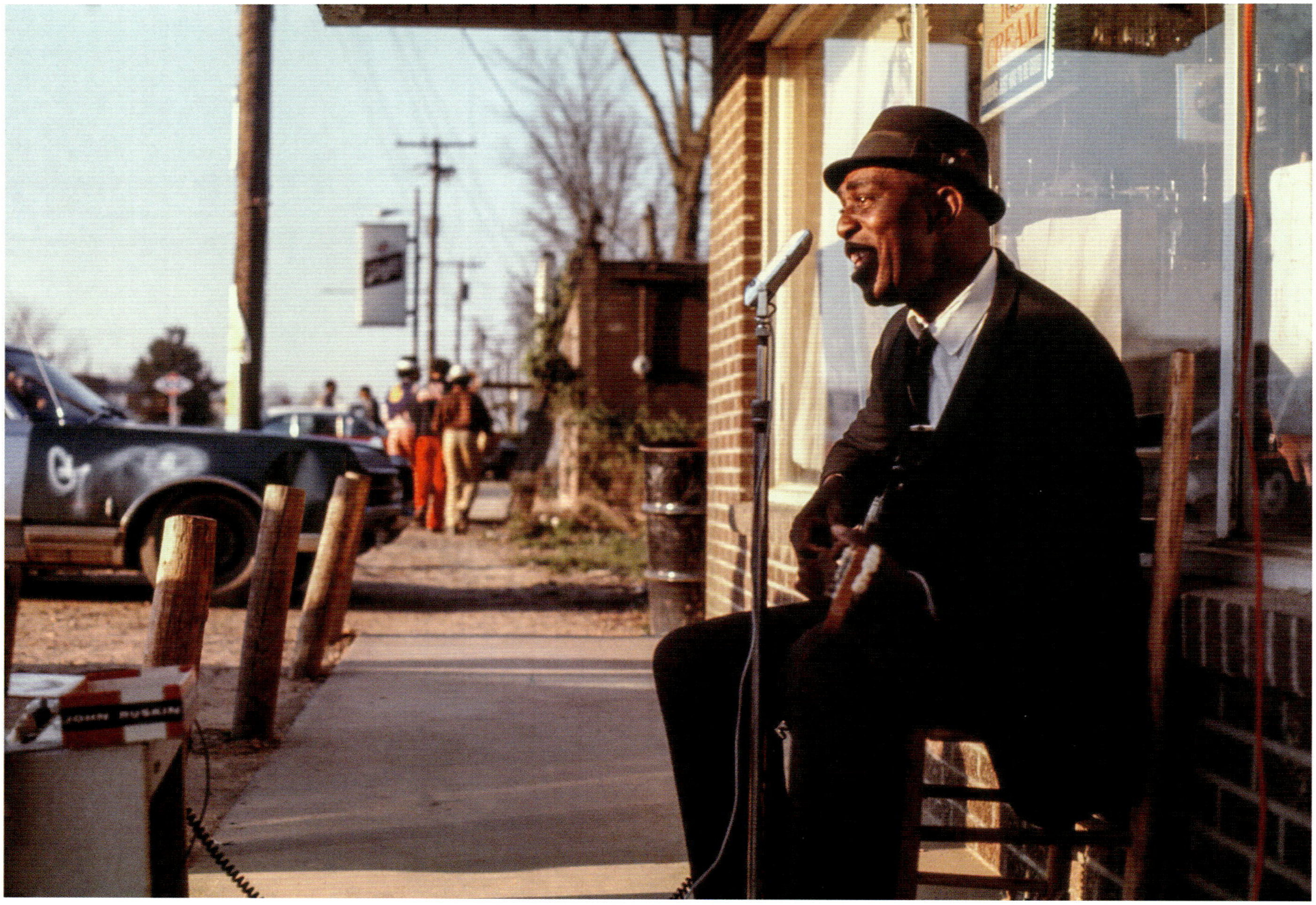

The start of Friday night, Mound Bayou, 1972. The Reverend Leon Pinson performs in front of the J&L Grocery.

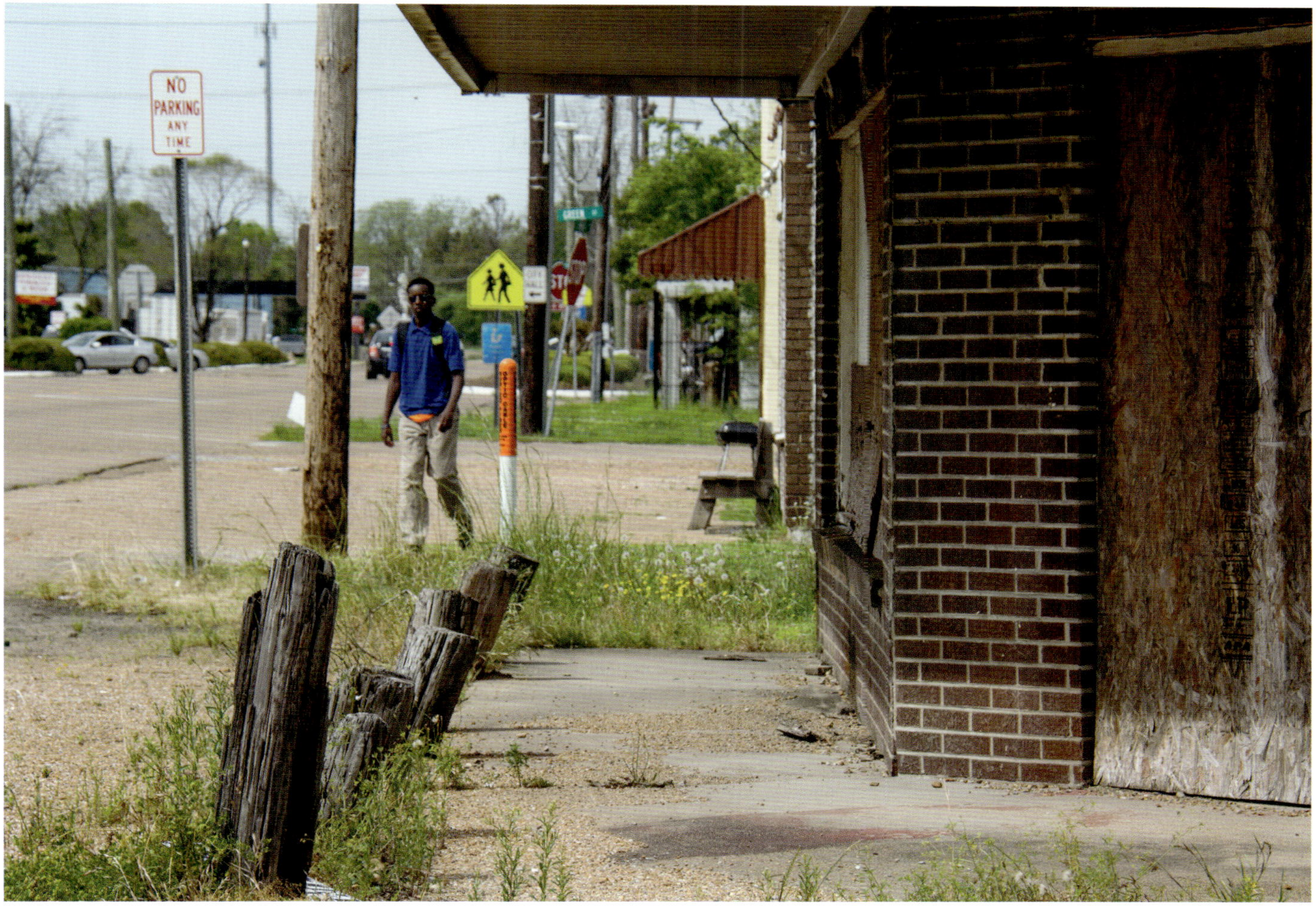

Where Rev. Pinson played, abandoned J&L Grocery,
Mound Bayou, 2016.

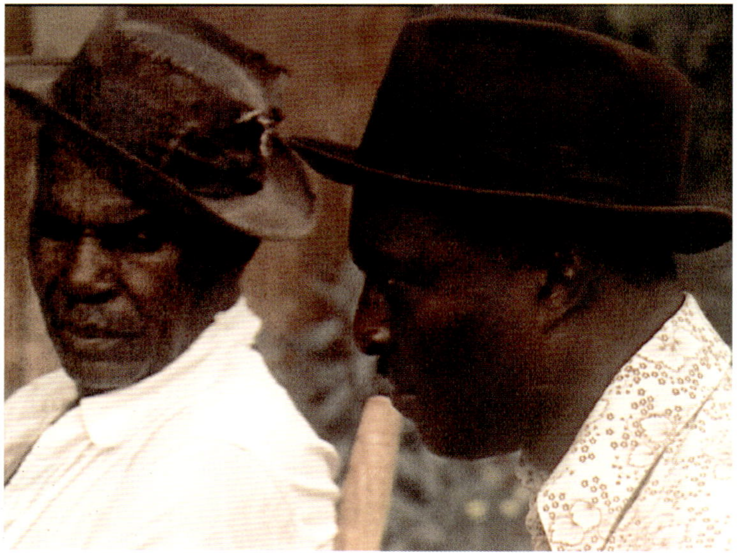

Othar Turner and Napoleon Strickland, Como, 1972–75. Como was home to the musicians Othar Turner and Napoleon Strickland. I had met them while traveling about the area, and whenever I got up there, I'd stop by. Their hospitality was great and truly appreciated.

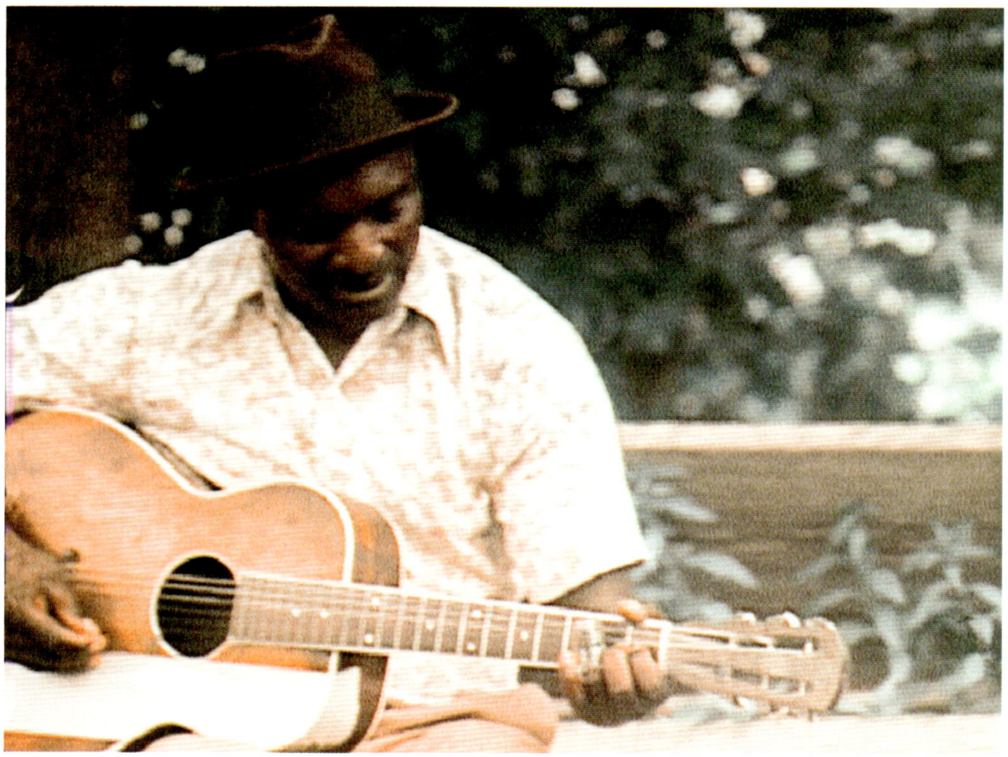

Napoleon Strickland, Como, 1972–75.

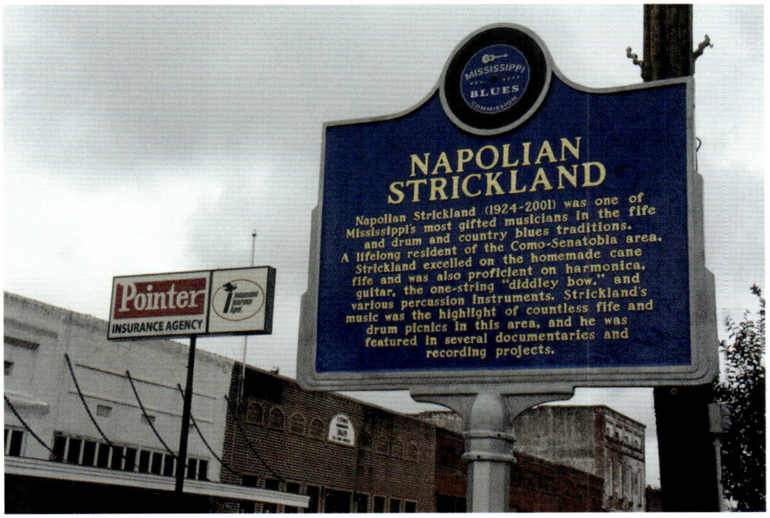

Mississippi honors homegrown music, Como, 2013–15. Turner's and Strickland's names are now emblazoned on Blues Trail markers in the center of their town.

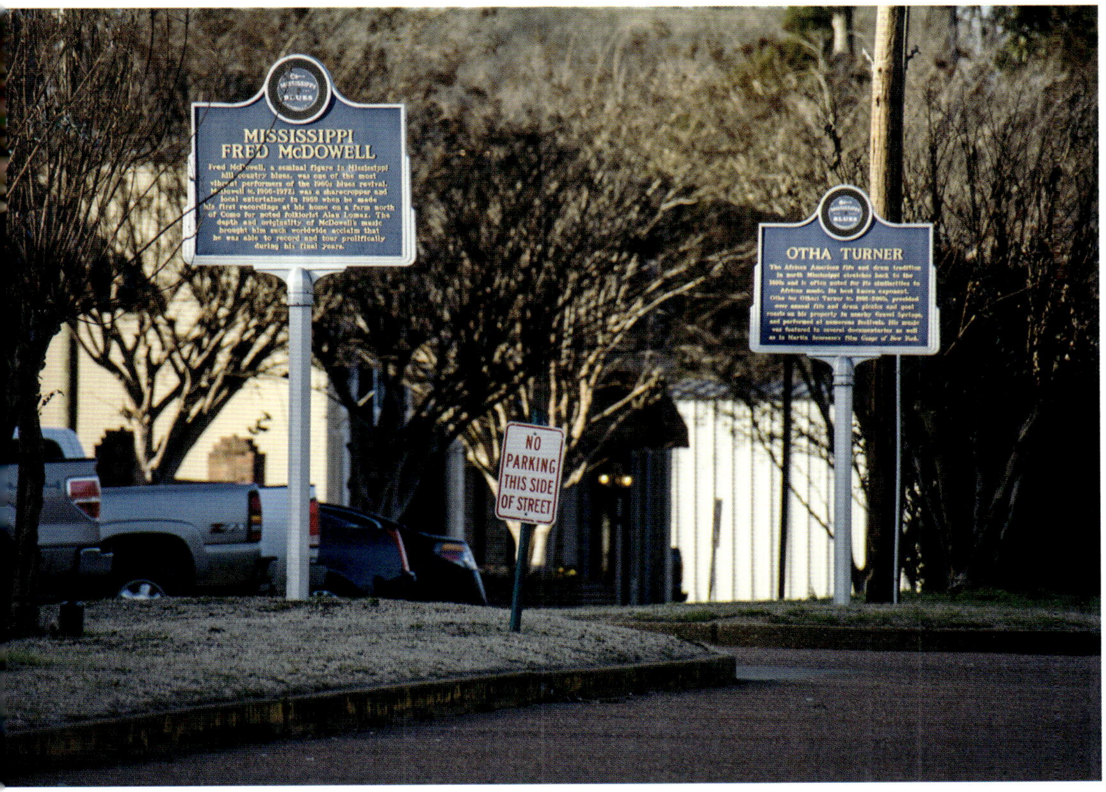

Como, 2013–15.

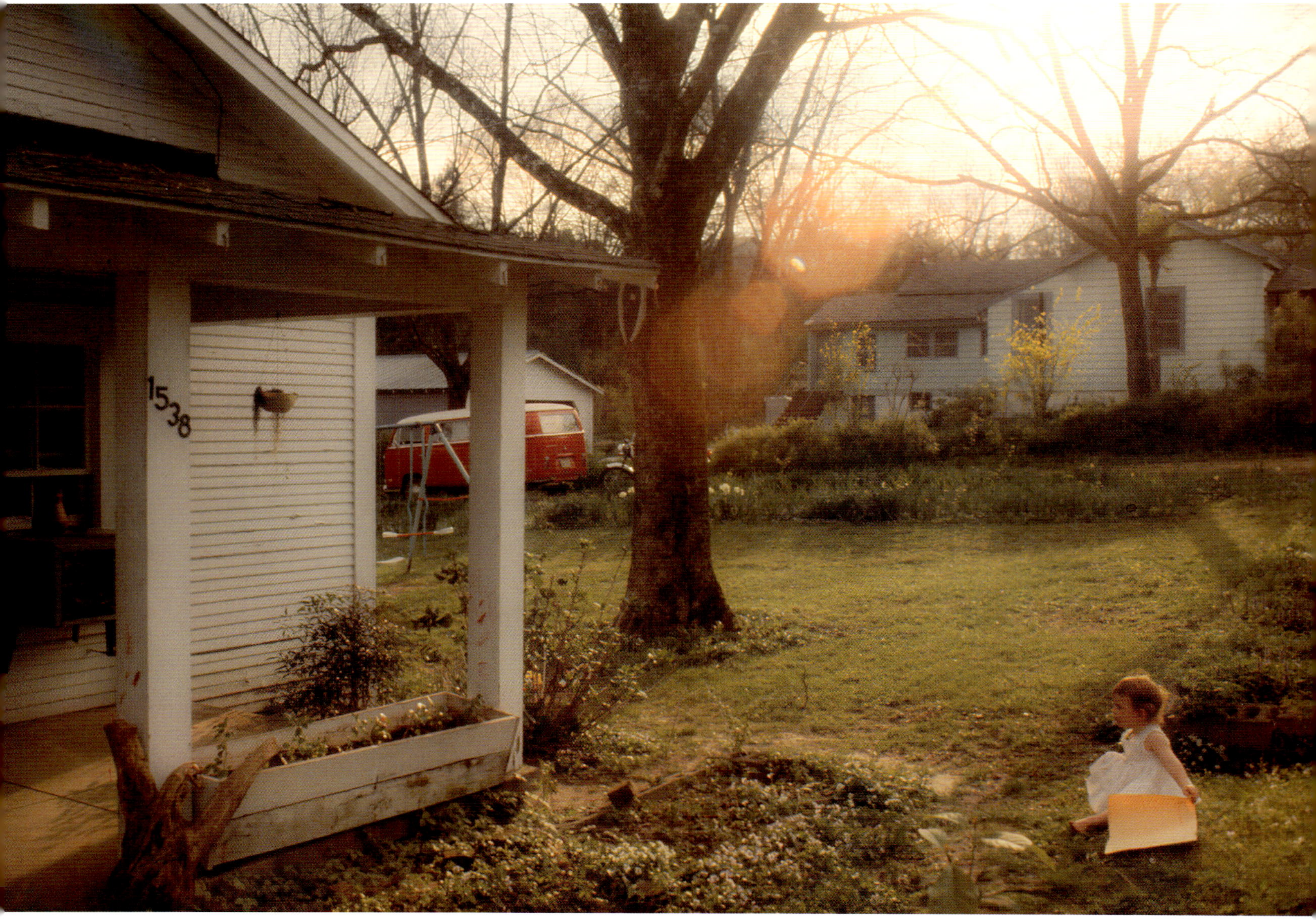

My daughter Deirdre at our home, 1538 Jackson Avenue,
Oxford, spring of 1973.

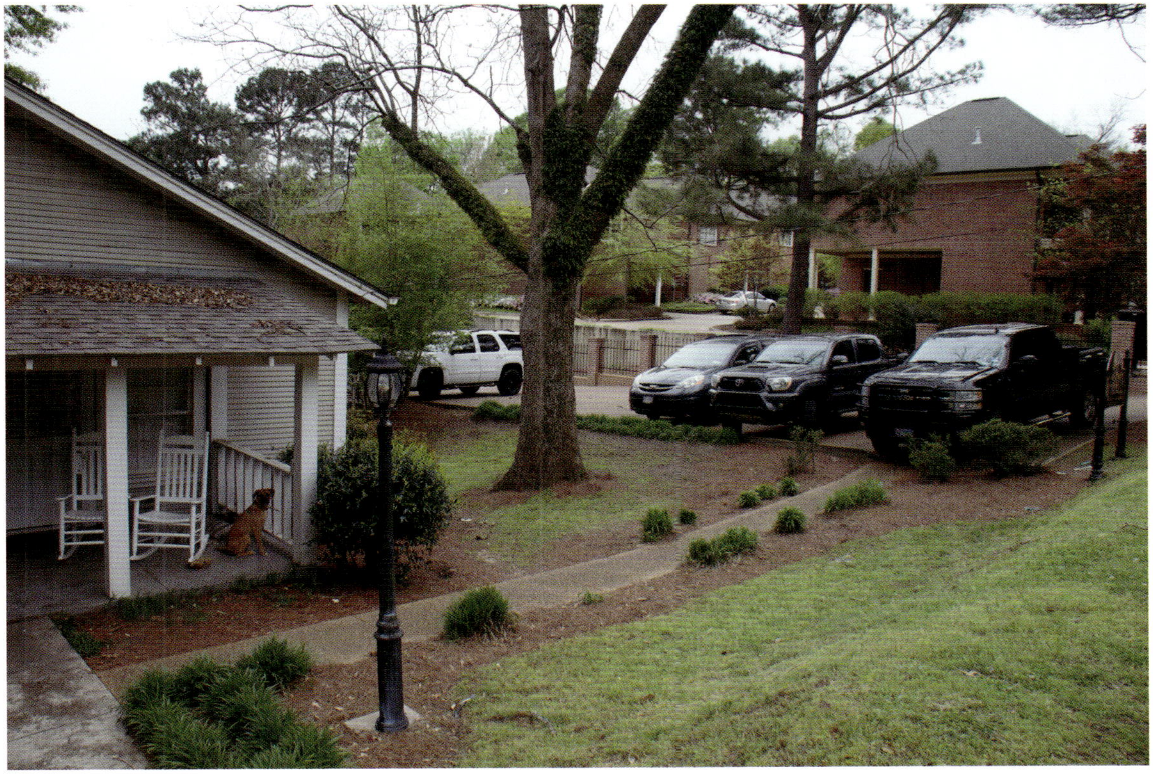

My old home, Oxford, 2016.

The Michael Ford Mississippi Collection

In 2014 the American Folklife Center at the Library of Congress acquired Michael Ford's collection of films and photographs documenting grassroots community life in northern Mississippi. The Michael Ford Mississippi Collection includes documentation of music, farming traditions, black-smithing, molasses making, and other aspects of community life in LaFayette, Marshall, Tate, and Panola Counties, Mississippi, during the early 1970s. Portions of this material have been published in the film *Homeplace* (1975), available online from the collection page, https://lccn.loc.gov/2013655469. The documentary tells the story of communities in vanishing agrarian America. Some of the places visited by the film crew, such as the town of Chulahoma, are now listed as extinct communities.

This important collection complements existing materials about 1940s musical traditions from the Mississippi Hill Country in the center's archive. Ford's material, made three decades later, includes music making but expands to occupational folklore, foodways, vernacular architecture, and other arenas of cultural expression.

Materials include thirty sound tape reels, approximately sixty sound cassettes, sixty-three film elements plus trims, seventy photographic prints and six hundred color slides, 0.5 linear feet of manuscripts, and 155 pages of audio transcipts.

To learn more about the Michael Ford Collection, as well as collections in the American Folklife Center and throughout other areas of the Library, please visit www.loc.gov.